REA

FRIENDS OF ACPL

Martha
Ellyn Kaschak, PhD
Editors

Women with Visible and Invisible Disabilities: Multiple Intersections, Multiple Issues, Multiple Therapies

Women with Visible and Invisible Disabilities: Multiple Intersections, Multiple Issues, Multiple Therapies has been co-published simultaneously as *Women & Therapy*, Volume 26, Numbers 1/2 and 3/4 2003.

Pre-publication
REVIEWS,
COMMENTARIES,
EVALUATIONS . . .

"**B**RAVO . . . PROVIDES POWERFUL AND DIRECT ANSWERS to the questions, concerns, and challenges all women with disability experience. The voices in this book are speaking loud and clear to a wide range of readers and audiences. . . . Centered on the core principle that quality of life revolves around one's mental health, a sense of strength, and resiliency."

Theresa M. Rankin, BA, NCE
National Community Educator,
Brain Injury Services, Inc.;
MidAtlantic Traumatic Brain Injury
Consortium;
Fairhaven Institute for Brain Injury/
University of Wisconsin-Scott

The Haworth Press, Inc.

Women with Visible
and Invisible Disabilities:
Multiple Intersections,
Multiple Issues,
Multiple Therapies

Women with Visible and Invisible Disabilities: Multiple Intersections, Multiple Issues, Multiple Therapies has been co-published simultaneously as *Women & Therapy*, Volume 26, Numbers 1/2 and 3/4 2003.

The *Women & Therapy* Monographic "Separates"

Below is a list of "separates," which in serials librarianship means a special issue simultaneously published as a special journal issue or double-issue *and* as a "separate" hardbound monograph. (This is a format which we also call a "DocuSerial.")

"Separates" are published because specialized libraries or professionals may wish to purchase a specific thematic issue by itself in a format which can be separately cataloged and shelved, as opposed to purchasing the journal on an on-going basis. Faculty members may also more easily consider a "separate" for classroom adoption.

"Separates" are carefully classified separately with the major book jobbers so that the journal tie-in can be noted on new book order slips to avoid duplicate purchasing.

You may wish to visit Haworth's website at . . .

http://www.HaworthPress.com

. . . to search our online catalog for complete tables of contents of these separates and related publications.

You may also call 1-800-HAWORTH (outside US/Canada: 607-722-5857), or Fax 1-800-895-0582 (outside US/Canada: 607-771-0012), or e-mail at:

getinfo@haworthpressinc.com

Women with Visible and Invisible Disabilities: Multiple Intersections, Multiple Issues, Multiple Therapies, edited by Martha E. Banks, PhD, and Ellyn Kaschak, PhD (Vol. 26, No. 1/2/3/4, 2003). *"BRAVO . . . PROVIDES POWERFUL AND DIRECT ANSWERS to the questions, concerns, and challenges all women with disability experience. The voices in this book are speaking loud and clear to a wide range of readers and audiences. . . . Centered on the core principle that quality of life revolves around one's mental health, a sense of strength, and resiliency." (Theresa M. Rankin, BA, NCE, National Community Educator, Brain Injury Services, Inc.; MidAtlantic Traumatic Brain Injury Consortium; Fairhaven Institute for Brain Injury/University of Wisconsin-Scott)*

Violence in the Lives of Black Women: Battered, Black, and Blue, edited by Carolyn M. West, PhD (Vol. 25, No. 3/4, 2002). *Helps break the silence surrounding Black women's experiences of violence.*

Exercise and Sport in Feminist Therapy: Constructing Modalities and Assessing Outcomes, edited by Ruth L. Hall, PhD, and Carole A. Oglesby, PhD (Vol. 25, No. 2, 2002). *Explores the healing use of exercise and sport as a helpful adjunct to feminist therapy.*

The Invisible Alliance: Psyche and Spirit in Feminist Therapy, edited by Ellyn Kaschak, PhD (Vol. 24, No. 3/4, 2001). *"The richness of this volume is reflected in the diversity of the collected viewpoints, perspectives, and practices. Each chapter challenges us to move out of the confines of our traditional training and reflect on the importance of spirituality. This book also brings us back to the original meaning of psychology–the study and knowledge of the soul." (Stephanie S. Covington, PhD, LCSW, Co-Director, Institute for Relational Development, La Jolla, California; Author, A Woman's Way Through the Twelve Steps)*

A New View of Women's Sexual Problems, edited by Ellyn Kaschak, PhD, and Leonore Tiefer, PhD (Vol. 24, No. 1/2, 2001). *"This useful, complex, and valid critique of simplistic notions of women's sexuality will be especially valuable for women's studies and public health courses. An important compilation representing many diverse individuals and groups of women." (Judy Norsigian and Jane Pincus, Co-Founders, Boston Women's Health Collective; Co-Authors, Our Bodies, Ourselves for the New Century)*

Intimate Betrayal: Domestic Violence in Lesbian Relationships, edited by Ellyn Kaschak, PhD (Vol. 23, No. 3, 2001). *"A groundbreaking examination of a taboo and complex subject. Both scholarly and down to earth, this superbly edited volume is an indispensable resource for clinicians, researchers, and lesbians caught up in the cycle of domestic violence." (Dr. Marny Hall, Psychotherapist; Author of The Lesbian Love Companion, Co-Author of Queer Blues)*

The Next Generation: Third Wave Feminist Psychotherapy, edited by Ellyn Kaschak, PhD (Vol. 23, No. 2, 2001). *Discusses the issues young feminists face, focusing on the implications for psychotherapists of the false sense that feminism is no longer necessary.*

Minding the Body: Psychotherapy in Cases of Chronic and Life-Threatening Illness, edited by Ellyn Kaschak, PhD (Vol. 23, No. 1, 2001). *Being diagnosed with cancer, lupus, or fibromyalgia is a traumatic event. All too often, women are told their disease is 'all in their heads' and therefore both 'unreal and insignificant' by a medical profession that dismisses emotions and scorns mental illness. Combining personal narratives and theoretical views of illness,* Minding the Body *offers an alternative approach to the mind-body connection. This book shows the reader how to deal with the painful and difficult emotions that exacerbate illness, while learning the emotional and spiritual lessons illness can teach.*

For Love or Money: The Fee in Feminist Therapy, edited by Marcia Hill, EdD, and Ellyn Kaschak, PhD (Vol. 22, No. 3, 1999). *"Recommended reading for both new and seasoned professionals. . . . An exciting and timely book about 'the last taboo.' . . ." (Carolyn C. Larsen, PhD, Senior Counsellor Emeritus, University of Calgary; Partner, Alberta Psychological Resources Ltd., Calgary, and Co-Editor,* Ethical Decision Making in Therapy: Feminist Perspectives*)*

Beyond the Rule Book: Moral Issues and Dilemmas in the Practice of Psychotherapy, edited by Ellyn Kaschak, PhD, and Marcia Hill, EdD (Vol. 22, No. 2, 1999). *"The authors in this important and timely book tackle the difficult task of working through . . . conflicts, sharing their moral struggles and real life solutions in working with diverse populations and in a variety of clinical settings. . . . Will provide psychotherapists with a thought-provoking source for the stimulating and essential discussion of our own and our profession's moral bases " (Carolyn C. Larsen, PhD, Senior Counsellor Emeritus, University of Calgary, Partner, Alberta Psychological Resources Ltd., Calgary, and Co-Editor,* Ethical Decision Making in Therapy: Feminist Perspectives*)*

Assault on the Soul: Women in the Former Yugoslavia, edited by Sara Sharratt, PhD, and Ellyn Kaschak, PhD (Vol. 22, No. 1, 1999). *Explores the applications and intersections of feminist therapy, activism and jurisprudence with women and children in the former Yugoslavia.*

Learning from Our Mistakes: Difficulties and Failures in Feminist Therapy, edited by Marcia Hill, EdD, and Esther D. Rothblum, PhD (Vol. 21, No. 3, 1998). *"A courageous and fundamental step in evolving a well-grounded body of theory and of investigating the assumptions that, unexamined, lead us to error." (Teresa Bernardez, MD, Training and Supervising Analyst, The Michigan Psychoanalytic Council)*

Feminist Therapy as a Political Act, edited by Marcia Hill, EdD (Vol. 21, No. 2, 1998). *"A real contribution to the field. . . . A valuable tool for feminist therapists and those who want to learn about feminist therapy." (Florence L. Denmark, PhD, Robert S. Pace Distinguished Professor of Psychology and Chair, Psychology Department, Pace University, New York, New York)*

Breaking the Rules: Women in Prison and Feminist Therapy, edited by Judy Harden, PhD, and Marcia Hill, EdD (Vol. 20, No. 4 & Vol. 21, No. 1, 1998). *"Fills a long-recognized gap in the psychology of women curricula, demonstrating that feminist theory can be made relevant to the practice of feminism, even in prison." (Suzanne J. Kessler, PhD, Professor of Psychology and Women's Studies, State University of New York at Purchase)*

Children's Rights, Therapists' Responsibilities: Feminist Commentaries, edited by Gail Anderson, MA, and Marcia Hill, EdD (Vol. 20, No. 2, 1997). *"Addresses specific practice dimensions that will help therapists organize and resolve conflicts about working with children, adolescents, and their families in therapy." (Feminist Bookstore News)*

More than a Mirror: How Clients Influence Therapists' Lives, edited by Marcia Hill, EdD (Vol. 20, No. 1, 1997). *"Courageous, insightful, and deeply moving. These pages reveal the scrupulous self-examination and self-reflection of conscientious therapists at their best. An important contribution to feminist therapy literature and a book worth reading by therapists and clients alike." (Rachel Josefowitz Siegel, MSW, retired feminist therapy practitioner; Co-Editor,* Women Changing Therapy; Jewish Women in Therapy; *and* Celebrating the Lives of Jewish Women: Patterns in a Feminist Sampler*)*

Sexualities, edited by Marny Hall, PhD, LCSW (Vol. 19, No. 4, 1997). *"Explores the diverse and multifaceted nature of female sexuality, covering topics including sadomasochism in the therapy room, sexual exploitation in cults, and genderbending in cyberspace." (Feminist Bookstore News)*

Couples Therapy: Feminist Perspectives, edited by Marcia Hill, EdD, and Esther D. Rothblum, PhD (Vol. 19, No. 3, 1996). *Addresses some of the inadequacies, omissions, and assumptions in* traditional couples' therapy to help you face the issues of race, ethnicity, and sexual orientation in helping couples today.

A Feminist Clinician's Guide to the Memory Debate, edited by Susan Contratto, PhD, and M. Janice Gutfreund, PhD (Vol. 19, No. 1, 1996). *"Unites diverse scholars, clinicians, and activists in an insightful and useful examination of the issues related to recovered memories." (Feminist Bookstore News)*

Classism and Feminist Therapy: Counting Costs, edited by Marcia Hill, EdD, and Esther D. Rothblum, PhD (Vol. 18, No. 3/4, 1996). *"Educates, challenges, and questions the influence of classism on the clinical practice of psychotherapy with women." (Kathleen P. Gates, MA, Certified Professional Counselor, Center for Psychological Health, Superior, Wisconsin)*

Lesbian Therapists and Their Therapy: From Both Sides of the Couch, edited by Nancy D. Davis, MD, Ellen Cole, PhD, and Esther D. Rothblum, PhD (Vol. 18, No. 2, 1996). *"Highlights the power and boundary issues of psychotherapy from perspectives that many readers may have neither considered nor experienced in their own professional lives." (Psychiatric Services)*

Feminist Foremothers in Women's Studies, Psychology, and Mental Health, edited by Phyllis Chesler, PhD, Esther D. Rothblum, PhD, and Ellen Cole, PhD (Vol. 17, No. 1/2/3/4, 1995). *"A must for feminist scholars and teachers . . . These women's personal experiences are poignant and powerful." (Women's Studies International Forum)*

Women's Spirituality, Women's Lives, edited by Judith Ochshorn, PhD, and Ellen Cole, PhD (Vol. 16, No. 2/3, 1995). *"A delightful and complex book on spirituality and sacredness in women's lives." (Joan Clingan, MA, Spiritual Psychology, Graduate Advisor, Prescott College Master of Arts Program)*

Psychopharmacology from a Feminist Perspective, edited by Jean A. Hamilton, MD, Margaret Jensvold, MD, Esther D. Rothblum, PhD, and Ellen Cole, PhD (Vol. 16, No. 1, 1995). *"Challenges readers to increase their sensitivity and awareness of the role of sex and gender in response to and acceptance of pharmacologic therapy." (American Journal of Pharmaceutical Education)*

Wilderness Therapy for Women: The Power of Adventure, edited by Ellen Cole, PhD, Esther D. Rothblum, PhD, and Eve Erdman, MEd, MLS (Vol. 15, No. 3/4, 1994). *"There's an undeniable excitement in these pages about the thrilling satisfaction of meeting challenges in the physical world, the world outside our cities that is unfamiliar, uneasy territory for many women. If you're interested at all in the subject, this book is well worth your time." (Psychology of Women Quarterly)*

Bringing Ethics Alive: Feminist Ethics in Psychotherapy Practice, edited by Nanette K. Gartrell, MD (Vol. 15, No. 1, 1994). *"Examines the theoretical and practical issues of ethics in feminist therapies. From the responsibilities of training programs to include social issues ranging from racism to sexism to practice ethics, this outlines real questions and concerns." (Midwest Book Review)*

Women with Disabilities: Found Voices, edited by Mary Willmuth, PhD, and Lillian Holcomb, PhD (Vol. 14, No. 3/4, 1994). *"These powerful chapters often jolt the anti-disability consciousness and force readers to contend with the ways in which disability has been constructed, disguised, and rendered disgusting by much of society." (Academic Library Book Review)*

Faces of Women and Aging, edited by Nancy D. Davis, MD, Ellen Cole, PhD, and Esther D. Rothblum, PhD (Vol. 14, No. 1/2, 1993). *"This uplifting, helpful book is of great value not only for aging women, but also for women of all ages who are interested in taking active control of their own lives." (New Mature Woman)*

Refugee Women and Their Mental Health: Shattered Societies, Shattered Lives, edited by Ellen Cole, PhD, Oliva M. Espin, PhD, and Esther D. Rothblum, PhD (Vol. 13, No. 1/2/3, 1992). *"The ideas presented are rich and the perspectives varied, and the book is an important contribution to understanding refugee women in a global context." (Contemporary Psychology)*

Women, Girls and Psychotherapy: Reframing Resistance, edited by Carol Gilligan, PhD, Annie Rogers, PhD, and Deborah Tolman, EdD (Vol. 11, No. 3/4, 1991). *"Of use to educators, psychotherapists, and parents–in short, to any person who is directly involved with girls at adolescence." (Harvard Educational Review)*

Monographs "Separates" list continued at the back

Women with Visible and Invisible Disabilities: Multiple Intersections, Multiple Issues, Multiple Therapies

Martha E. Banks, PhD
Ellyn Kaschak, PhD
Editors

Women with Visible and Invisible Disabilities: Multiple Intersections, Multiple Issues, Multiple Therapies has been co-published simultaneously as *Women & Therapy*, Volume 26, Numbers 1/2 and 3/4 2003.

The Haworth Press, Inc.
New York • London • Oxford

Women with Visible and Invisible Disabilities: Multiple Intersections, Multiple Issues, Multiple Therapies has been co-published simultaneously as *Women & Therapy*™, Volume 26, Numbers 1/2 and 3/4 2003.

The development, preparation, and publication of this work has been undertaken with great care. However, the publisher, employees, editors, and agents of The Haworth Press and all imprints of The Haworth Press, Inc., including The Haworth Medical Press® and Pharmaceutical Products Press®, are not responsible for any errors contained herein or for consequences that may ensue from use of materials or information contained in this work. Opinions expressed by the author(s) are not necessarily those of The Haworth Press, Inc. With regard to case studies, identities and circumstances of individuals discussed herein have been changed to protect confidentiality. Any resemblance to actual persons, living or dead, is entirely coincidental.

Cover design by Marylouise Doyle

Library of Congress Cataloging-in-Publication Data

Women with visible and invisible disabilities : multiple intersections, multiple issues, multiple therapies / Martha E. Banks, Ellyn Kaschak, editors.
    p. cm.
    Includes bibliographical references and index.
    "Co-published simultaneously as Women & therapy, volume 26, numbers 1/2/3/4 2002."
    ISBN 0-7890-1936-1 (hard : alk. paper) – ISBN 0-7890-1937-X (soft : alk. paper)
    I.Women with disabilities. I. Banks, Martha E. II. Kaschak, Ellyn, 1943- III. Women & therapy.
HV1569.3.W65W666 2003
362.4'082–dc21

2003001533

Indexing, Abstracting & Website/Internet Coverage

This section provides you with a list of major indexing & abstracting services. That is to say, each service began covering this periodical during the year noted in the right column. Most Websites which are listed below have indicated that they will either post, disseminate, compile, archive, cite or alert their own Website users with research-based content from this work. (This list is as current as the copyright date of this publication.)

Abstracting, Website/Indexing Coverage . . . . Year When Coverage Began

- *Academic Abstracts/CD-ROM* **1995**
- *Academic ASAP <www.galegroup.com>* **1992**
- *Academic Index (on-line)* **1992**
- *Academic Search Elite (EBSCO)* **1994**
- *Alternative Press Index (print, online & CD-ROM from NISC)*
    <www.altpress.org> **1982**
- *Behavioral Medicine Abstracts* . . . . , , , ... **1996**
- *Child Development Abstracts & Bibliography (in print & online)*
    <www.ukans.edu> **1994**
- *CINAHL (Cumulative Index to Nursing & Allied Health*
    Literature) <www.cinahl.com> **2000**
- *CNPIEC Reference Guide: Chinese National Directory*
    of Foreign Periodicals **1996**
- *Contemporary Women's Issues* **1998**
- *Current Contents/Social & Behavioral Sciences*
    <www.isinet.com> **1995**
- *e-psyche, LLC <www.e-psyche.net>* **2001**
- *Expanded Academic ASAP <www.galegroup.com>* **1992**
- *Expanded Academic Index* **1993**

(continued)

- *Family Index Database <www.familyscholar.com>* 2001
- *Family & Society Studies Worldwide <www.nisc.com>* 1996
- *Family Violence & Sexual Assault Bulletin* 1992
- *Feminist Periodicals: A Current Listing of Contents* 1982
- *FINDEX <www.publist.com>* 1999
- *GenderWatch <www.slinfo.com>* 1998
- *Health Source: Indexing & Abstracting of 160 selected health related journals, updated monthly: EBSCO Publishing* 1996
- *Health Source Plus: expanded version of "Health Source": EBSCO Publishing* 1996
- *Higher Education Abstracts* 1991
- *HOMODOK/"Relevant" Bibliographic Database, Documentation Centre for Gay & Lesbian Studies, University of Amsterdam* 2002
- *IBZ International Bibliography of Periodical Literature <www.saur.de>* 1996
- *Index Guide to College Journals (core list compiled by integrating 48 indexes frequently used to support undergraduate programs in small to medium-sized libraries)* 1999
- *Index to Periodical Articles Related to Law* 1990
- *InfoTrac Custom <www.galegroup.com>* 1996
- *ONS Nursing Scan in Oncology–NAACOG's Women's Health Nursing Scan* 1996
- *Periodical Abstracts, Research I (general & basic reference indexing & abstracting data-base from University Microfilms International (UMI))* 1993
- *Periodical Abstracts, Research II (broad coverage indexing & abstracting data-base from University Microfilms International (UMI))* 1993
- *Psychological Abstracts (PsycINFO) <www.apa.org>* 1992
- *Published International Literature on Traumatic Stress (The PILOTS Database) <www.ncptsd.org>* 1996
- *RESEARCH ALERT/ISI Alerting Services <www.isinet.com>* 1995
- *Sage Family Studies Abstracts (SFSA)* 1985
- *Social Sciences Citation Index <www.isinet.com>* 1995
- *Social Scisearch <www.isinet.com>* 1995
- *Social Services Abstracts <www.csa.com>* 1997
- *Social Work Abstracts <www.silverplatter.com/catalog/swab.htm>* 1990

(continued)

- *Sociological Abstracts (SA) <www.csa.com>* 1997
- *Studies on Women Abstracts <www.tandf.co.uk>* 1982
- *SwetsNet <www.swetsnet.com>* 2001
- *Violence and Abuse Abstracts: A Review of Current Literature on Interpersonal Violence (VAA)* 1995
- *Women Studies Abstracts* 1991
- *Women's Studies Index (indexed comprehensively)* 1992

Special Bibliographic Notes related to special journal issues (separates) and indexing/abstracting:

- indexing/abstracting services in this list will also cover material in any "separate" that is co-published simultaneously with Haworth's special thematic journal issue or DocuSerial. Indexing/abstracting usually covers material at the article/chapter level.
- monographic co-editions are intended for either non-subscribers or libraries which intend to purchase a second copy for their circulating collections.
- monographic co-editions are reported to all jobbers/wholesalers/approval plans. The source journal is listed as the "series" to assist the prevention of duplicate purchasing in the same manner utilized for books-in-series.
- to facilitate user/access services all indexing/abstracting services are encouraged to utilize the co-indexing entry note indicated at the bottom of the first page of each article/chapter/contribution.
- this is intended to assist a library user of any reference tool (whether print, electronic, online, or CD-ROM) to locate the monographic version if the library has purchased this version but not a subscription to the source journal.
- individual articles/chapters in any Haworth publication are also available through the Haworth Document Delivery Service (HDDS).

Women with Visible and Invisible Disabilities: Multiple Intersections, Multiple Issues, Multiple Therapies

CONTENTS

Foreword   xix
Jean Lau Chin

Preface   xxi
Martha E. Banks

VISIBLE AND INVISIBLE IMPAIRMENTS EXPERIENCED
BY WOMEN

"MEN'S" ILLNESS OVERLOOKED IN WOMEN
AND "WOMEN'S" ILLNESS MISDIAGNOSED OR DISMISSED

Women Living with Traumatic Brain Injury: Social Isolation,
Emotional Functioning and Implications for Psychotherapy   3
Debjani Mukherjee
Judy Panko Reis
Wendy Heller

African American Women Living with HIV/AIDS:
Mental Health Issues   27
Sonja Feist-Price
Lynda Brown Wright

Chronic Pain Syndromes and Violence Against Women   45
 Kathleen Kendall-Tackett
 Roberta Marshall
 Kenneth Ness

Eating Disorders Among Urban and Rural African American
 and European American Women   57
 Cherie A. Bagley
 Colleen D. Character
 Lisamarie Shelton

DORMANT AND PART-TIME DISABILITIES

The Influence of Silent Learning Disorders on the Lives
 of Women   81
 Sara J. Hoffschmidt
 Cheryl S. Weinstein

Part-Time Disabled Lesbian Passing on Roller Blades,
 or PMS, Prozac, and Essentializing Women's Ailments   95
 Carmen Poulin
 Lynne Gouliquer

PERSONAL AND INTERPERSONAL CONCERNS FOR WOMEN
 WITH DISABILITIES

SOCIAL CONSTRUCTION OF DISABILITY:
 IMPACT ON IDENTITY

Chronic Disease Health Beliefs and Lifestyle Practices
 Among Vietnamese Adults: Influence of Gender and Age 111
 Barbara W. K. Yee
 Ha T. Nguyen
 Martin Ha

Keep Moving: Conceptions of Illness and Disability
 of Middle-Aged African-American Women with Arthritis 127
 Scott I. Feldman
 Georgina Tegart

To Be or Not to Be Disabled   145
   Monique Williams
   Wendy Schutt Upadhyay

ACCOMMODATION IN EDUCATION AND EMPLOYMENT:
APPLICATION OF THE AMERICANS
WITH DISABILITIES ACT

ADA Accommodation of Therapists with Disabilities
   in Clinical Training   155
   Hendrika Vande Kemp
   Jennifer Shiomi Chen
   Gail Nagel Erickson
   Nancy L. Friesen

Obsessive Compulsive Disorder in the Workplace:
   An Invisible Disability   169
   Angela Neal-Barnett
   Lorre Leon Mendelson

SEXUALITY ISSUES: "WHO?!," "NO!" AND "HOW?"

Representations of Disability and the Interpersonal
   Relationships of Women with Disabilities   179
   Danette Crawford
   Joan M. Ostrove

"People Tell Me I Can't Have Sex": Women with Disabilities
   Share Their Personal Perspectives on Health Care,
   Sexuality, and Reproductive Rights   195
   Lori Ann Dotson
   Jennifer Stinson
   LeeAnn Christian

Sexual Options for People with Disabilities: Using Personal
   Assistance Services for Sexual Expression   211
   Linda R. Mona

WORST CASE SCENARIOS: INTERSECTIONS OF GENDER,
DISABILITY, ETHNICITY, CLASS AND SOCIAL DISAPPROVAL

Substance Abuse, Disabilities, and Black Women:
   An Issue Worth Exploring   223
    Lula A. Beatty

Women with Physical Disabilities Who Want to Leave
   Their Partners: A Feminist and Disability-Affirmative
   Perspective   237
    Rhoda Olkin

Prostitution and the Invisibility of Harm   247
    Melissa Farley

EMPOWERMENT: USING CULTURE AND CONTEXT
TO ENHANCE AND FACILITATE FEMINIST THERAPY

INTEGRATING SPIRITUALITY, HISTORY, AND WOMEN'S
WAYS OF KNOWING INTO THERAPY

Prayer as Interpersonal Coping in the Lives of Mothers with HIV   283
    E. James Baesler
    Valerian J. Derlega
    Barbara A. Winstead
    Anita Barbee

The Call of the Wild Woman: Models of Healing   297
    Marie A. DiCowden

ONE SIZE DOES NOT FIT ALL: INTEGRATING MULTIPLE
ISSUES INTO FEMINIST THERAPY FOR WOMEN
WITH DISABILITIES

Special Issues in Psychotherapy with Minority Deaf Women   311
    Carolyn A. Corbett

Womanist Therapy with African American Women
   with Disabilities   331
    Nina A. Nabors
    Melanie F. Pettee

Assessment, Treatment, and Rehabilitation for Interpersonal
   Violence Victims: Women Sustaining Head Injuries   343
     Rosalie J. Ackerman
     Martha E. Banks

Index   367

ABOUT THE EDITORS

Martha E. Banks, PhD, is a research neuropsychologist in the Research & Development Division of ABackans Diversified Computer Processing, Inc., in Akron, Ohio. She has been instrumental in the development of neuropsychological assessment and rehabilitation tests, including the Ackerman-Banks Neuropsychological Rehabilitation Battery© and the Post-Assault Traumatic Brain Injury Interview & Checklist©. Dr. Banks has also served as a clinical psychologist with the Brecksville Department of Veterans Affairs Medical Center and as Associate Professor of Psychology at The College of Wooster. She has published widely in books and professional journals, including *The Clinical Neuropsychologist, Archives of Clinical Neuropsychology, Women & Therapy, Social Science Computer Review,* the *Association for Women in Psychology Newsletter: A Feminist Voice, Silver Pathways,* and *Topics in Geriatric Rehabilitation.*

Dr. Banks is a member of numerous professional organizations, and has been a member of the American Psychological Association since 1982, serving on its Committee on Ethnic Minority Affairs (CEMA), Committee on Women in Psychology (CWP), and Committee on Social Justice. She has also been President of the Society of the Psychology of Women's Collaboration. Since 1977, Dr. Banks has presented at over 150 conferences and symposia on topics involving women, trauma, and health care.

Ellyn Kaschak, PhD, is Professor of Psychology at San Jose State University in San Jose, California. She is the author of *Engendered Lives: A New Psychology of Women's Experience,* as well as numerous articles and chapters on feminist psychology and psychotherapy. Dr. Kaschak is also editor of *Intimate Betrayal: Domestic Violence in Lesbian Relationships* (2001), *Minding the Body: Psychotherapy in Cases of Chronic and Life-Threatening Illness* (2001), *The Next Generation: Third Wave Feminist Psychotherapy* (2001), and *The Invisible Alliance: Psyche and Spirit in Feminist Therapy* (2001), and co-editor of *Beyond the Rule Book: Moral Issues and Dilemmas in the Practice of Psychotherapy*

(1999), *Assault on the Soul: Women in the Former Yugoslavia* (1999), *For Love or Money: The Fee in Feminist Therapy* (2000), and *A New View of Women's Sexual Problems* (2002), all published by The Haworth Press, Inc.

Dr. Kaschak has had 30 years of experience practicing psychotherapy and is past Chair of the Feminist Therapy Institute and the APA Committee on Women in Psychology. In addition, Dr. Kaschak is a Fellow of Division 35 (Psychology of Women), Division 12 (Clinical Psychology), Division 45 (Ethnic Minority Issues), and Division 52 (International Psychology) of the American Psychological Association.

Foreword

Jean Lau Chin

SUMMARY. Technology increasingly dominates our lives; advances in medicine enable us to live longer, reduce pain and suffering, and improve our quality of life from its consequences. Yet, persons with disabilities continue to experience bias and neglect as a result of our social constructions of disability. A re-construction to address the intersections of voices of women, ethnic minorities, lesbians, and invisible disabilities is now heard in this volume through a feminist perspective of disabilities. *[Article copies available for a fee from The Haworth Document Delivery Service: 1-800-HAWORTH. E-mail address: <getinfo@haworthpressinc.com> Website: <http://www.HaworthPress.com> © 2003 by The Haworth Press, Inc. All rights reserved.]*

KEYWORDS. Disabilities, gender, ethnicity, women

Technology increasingly dominates our lives; advances in medicine enable us to live longer, reduce pain and suffering associated with disease and illness, and improve quality of life from its consequences. Per-

Jean Lau Chin, EdD, ABPP is President, CEO Services, providing organizational development and clinical services to families and businesses with a focus on cultural competence. She is currently core faculty at the Center for Multicultural Training in Psychology at Boston University School of Medicine, and Series Co-Editor of *Race and Ethnicity in Psychology* by Praeger Publishers.

Address correspondence to: Jean Lau Chin, EdD, ABPP, CEO Services, Clinical-Educational-Organizational Services, 614 Dedham Street, Newton, MA 02459 (E-mail: CEOServices@yahoo.com, Website: www.culturalcompetence2.com).

[Haworth co-indexing entry note]: "Foreword." Chin, Jean Lau. Co-published simultaneously in *Women & Therapy* (The Haworth Press, Inc.) Vol. 26, No. 1/2, 2003, pp. xxi-xxii; and: *Women with Visible and Invisible Disabilities: Multiple Intersections, Multiple Issues, Multiple Therapies* (ed: Martha E. Banks, and Ellyn Kaschak) The Haworth Press, Inc., 2003, pp. xix-xx. Single or multiple copies of this article are available for a fee from The Haworth Document Delivery Service [1-800-HAWORTH, 9:00 a.m. - 5:00 p.m. (EST). E-mail address: getinfo@haworthpressinc.com].

sons with physical disabilities can now participate more fully in society. Yet, persons with disabilities, and in particular, women with disabilities continue to experience bias and neglect from the social construction of disability.

This volume takes a broad step in addressing visible and invisible disabilities. It expands disabilities beyond the more obvious physical disabilities to include cognitive, emotional, and those that we may not typically describe as disabilities, e.g., substance abuse, irritable bowel syndrome, eating disorders; women with these invisible, part-time, or dormant disabilities face many of the similar challenges of those with physical disabilities. It includes the concerns of women, ethnic minorities, lesbians, and social situations that complicate and compound the issues faced by persons with disabilities. It looks at the neglect and bias faced by women with disabilities in accessing services developed for White men. It addresses real and unique needs faced by women with disabilities, e.g., personal assistance services, and situations that increase their vulnerability, risk, and safety.

These are the voices often omitted from the literature, research, and service programs operating from a mindset that is male dominated. The treatment of disabilities has been limited to those more often experienced by men, i.e., results of violence, war, motor vehicle and sports accidents. The accommodation of disabilities has been limited to and compared with the needs of those with physical and visible disabilities. Women's concerns and symptoms have been defined as hysterical, treated as mental dysfunction, trivialized, and viewed as self-inflicted, i.e., chronic fatigue syndrome, fibromyalgia, and multiple chemical sensitivities. Sexuality and the needs of women with disabilities have been all but ignored.

This special collection has a role in calling for a new and feminist perspective of disabilities that avoids victim blaming, dehumanizing labels of persons with disabilities, and patronizing treatment. A reversal and shift in perspectives is needed from the current social construction of disability as inability and deficit, stigma and neglect; a re-construction is needed to expand the focus on impairment of persons with disabilities toward resiliency and strength based models that focus on how society does or does not accommodate persons with disabilities. A re-construction is also needed to address the multiple intersections of gender, ethnicity, class, and disability. Technology provides opportunities to empower women with disabilities so that they might achieve their potential and participate more fully in society; as the authors have suggested, we have yet to make full use of its potential.

Preface

Martha E. Banks

SUMMARY. Women who have disabilities represent a very broad spectrum in terms of ability to manage their personal and social affairs. This collection reflects many of the issues faced by Women with Disabilities, the social construction of disability, and suggests development and modifications of culturally-relevant therapy to meet the needs of those women.

Martha E. Banks, PhD, is a research neuropsychologist in the Research and Development Division of ABackans DCP, Inc.

Address correspondence to: Dr. Martha E. Banks, Research & Development Division, ABackans Diversified Computer Processing, Inc., 1700 West Market Street, Department RD301, Akron, OH 44313-7002 (E-mail: Banks@abackans.com, Website: http://www.abackans.com).

The editor would like to thank all of the authors who proposed and contributed submissions for this special collection. For some of the authors, disabilities impaired their progress toward completion of articles. Others experienced exacerbation of chronic health problems due to the added stress of research, writing, and deadlines. Two authors with disabilities wrote with coauthors who did not have the same disabilities. Some of the topics addressed in this preface reflect concerns raised by authors whose work is not included in this special volume. She would also like to thank Dr. Rosalie J. Ackerman who provided a second set of eyes in the editing of this article. A special thanks goes to Drs. Ellyn Kaschak and Beverly Greene who provided encouragement and support to bring this volume to fruition.

Portions of this article were presented at the National Multicultural Conference and Summit in Santa Barbara, CA in January, 2001 and the 2002 annual convention of the American Psychological Association.

This volume is dedicated to the memories of Women with Disabilities who have been the victims of terrorists, with the hope that increased understanding will lead to the decrease of institutionalized and personalized violence. It is my prayer that the terror will be replaced with acceptance and a focus on increased safety.

[Haworth co-indexing entry note]: "Preface." Banks, Martha E. Co published simultaneously in *Women & Therapy* (The Haworth Press, Inc.) Vol. 26, No. 1/2, 2003, pp. xxiii-xli; and: *Women with Visible and Invisible Disabilities: Multiple Intersections, Multiple Issues, Multiple Therapies* (ed: Martha E. Banks, and Ellyn Kaschak) The Haworth Press, Inc., 2003, pp. xxi-xxxix. Single or multiple copies of this article are available for a fee from The Haworth Document Delivery Service [1-800-HAWORTH, 9:00 a.m. - 5:00 p.m. (EST). E-mail address: getinfo@haworthpressinc.com].

Many of the selections address the concerns of age, ethnicity, sexual orientation, size, relationships, and other social situations that complicate the lives of Women with Disabilities. Several authors address safety concerns and the vulnerability of Women with Disabilities, while others focus on successful coping strategies. Many include the voices of Women with Disabilities. Those voices reveal to therapists the need to increase sensitivity and conduct the research that provides the foundation for developing appropriate therapies. Feminist therapists describe the extensions they have made to traditional psychotherapy in order to directly address a wide range of issues faced by Women with Disabilities. *[Article copies available for a fee from The Haworth Document Delivery Service: 1-800-HAWORTH. E-mail address: <getinfo@haworthpressinc.com> Website: <http://www.HaworthPress.com> © 2003 by The Haworth Press, Inc. All rights reserved.]*

KEYWORDS. Women, disability, rehabilitation, ethnic, sexual orientation, lesbian, relationships, violence, health, disease, identity, psychotherapy, feminist therapy, education, employment

SOCIAL CONSTRUCTION OF DISABILITY

As therapists, it is our business to gain as complete an understanding of disability as possible and to determine where we can best provide assistance, advocacy, support, and service. Thirty years ago, *Webster's Seventh New Collegiate Dictionary* (1971) provided one definition of disability as the "inability to pursue an occupation because of physical or mental impairment" (p. 236). That definition currently appears on the website for *Webster's New Collegiate Dictionary* (http://www.m-w.com/home.htm). Unfortunately, some people focus only on that definition, ignoring the difference between an *impairment* (the actual physical and/or mental limitation) and the *social situations* which interfere with the ability of *people with impairments* to be gainfully employed at all levels (Kendall-Tackett, 2000; Neath, 1997). Now, it is recognized that people with impairments, usually referred to as People with Disabilities, represent a broad spectrum in terms of ability to manage gainful employment and reliance on others for assistance. The reality is that, in a healthy, supportive society, barriers are removed and opportunities for *all* people are provided, without question. Power in the United States has been shared or distributed somewhat through a seldom acknowledged caste system which assigns social status on the basis of physical ability, sex, ethnicity, color, age, sexual orientation, religion, etc. Often referred to as "class," that caste system is the basis for dehumanizing those with less power in order to enhance the privilege of those with more power. It is the continuance of the caste system that has resulted in a society that maintains barriers that prevent many people with disabilities from fulfilling their true potential.

The focus of this special collection is on the breadth of issues facing Women with Disabilities (Farber, 2000) and women as providers (DiCowden, this volume; Mukherjee, Reis, & Heller, 2003) and personal care assistants[1] to other People with Disabilities (Ackerman & Banks, 1992; Banks, Ackerman, & Clark, 1986; Feldman & Tegart, 2003; Joslin & Harrison, 1998; Pruchno, Patrick, & Burant, 1996, 1997), relying on the social construction of disability as a combination of impairments and social environments which incapacitate people with impairments. Most of the literature on disability addresses the concerns of young European American men, yet there are many issues facing Women with Disabilities.

An overview of the prevalence of disability among women in the United States is available online in the *Chartbook on Women and Disability in the United States,* a project supported by the National Institute on Disability and Rehabilitation Research (NIDRR). Approximately one fifth of U.S. citizens have disabilities. The percentage is slightly higher among women and girls (21.3%) than among men and boys (19.8%). Among women, Native American women and African American women have the highest percentages of disabilities. The severity of the disabilities for women is demonstrated through the average number of days lost annually per person due to disability and the percentages of women in different age groups who require personal assistance. Despite the greater severity of disability for women, on average, men have more access to Social Security Disability Income. When women *do* receive Social Security Disability, they, on average, receive less than men. In 1960, women received approximately 83% of what men did, but in 1995 women received only 73%. As a result of limited access to funds, more than one third of women with work disabilities and more than 40% of those with severe work disabilities are living in poverty (Jans & Stoddard, 1999; see also Browne, Salomon, & Bassuk, 1999; Kington & Smith, 1997; Liao, McGee, Cao, & Cooper, 1999; McDonough, 1997). Olkin addresses the negative impact of limited finances on Women with Disabilities as they make decisions about relationships, pay for adaptive equipment, consider purchase of personal assistance, and seek medical care.

VISIBLE AND INVISIBLE IMPAIRMENTS EXPERIENCED BY WOMEN

"Men's" Illness Overlooked in Women and "Women's" Illness Misdiagnosed or Dismissed

Women are at risk for misdiagnosis in a society that gives them limited voice. Medical conditions that are stereotypically experienced by men, such as brain trauma and cardiac disorders, are underdiagnosed in women. However, women tend to be overdiagnosed with psychiatric disorders, and older women are at risk for being misdiagnosed with irreversible dementia rather than being examined for relatively transient and treatable medical conditions. Invisible disabilities are a serious problem for women.

In a society that encourages stoic suffering, there is a tendency to ignore or minimize women's symptoms. Research on "women's ailments" is very limited. Words have even been invented for invisible disabilities, referring to parts of women's bodies. For example, "Creeping paralysis" as multiple sclerosis (MS) was formerly called, was considered a mental condition caused by "female hysteria." It was not until 1996 that MS was recognized as an autoimmune reaction linked to viruses (Krupp & Elkins, 2000). Today, women with disorders such as chronic fatigue syndrome, fibromyalgia, and multiple chemical sensitivities are often referred to as "hysterical" before they are given serious medical evaluations. In some arenas, the diagnoses are still not taken seriously enough for the development of appropriate treatments (Caplan, 2001).

While most considerations of disability focus on physical mobility problems, there are other, less visible, disabilities faced by women. Visible physical problems include arthritis (Feldman & Tegart, 2003, limited vision (Tobacman et al., 1998), and deafness (Corbett, 2003). Among the invisible physical disorders are cardiac disease (Guyll, Matthews, & Bromberger, 2001; McNeilly et al., 1995), chronic fatigue syndrome (Caplan, 2001; Jason, Taylor, & Kennedy, 2000), diabetes (Feldman & Tegart, 2003), fibromyalgia (Vande Kemp, Chen, Erickson, & Friesen, 2003), gastrointestinal problems (Ackerman & Banks, 2003; Drossman et al., 2000), HIV/AIDS (Baesler, Derlega, Winstead, & Barbee, 2003;

Feist-Price & Wright, 2003), interstitial cystitis (Ackerman & Banks, 2003; Ritter, 1994), weight (Bagley, Character & Shelton, 2003; Feldman & Tegart, 2003), and pain (Ackerman & Banks, 2003; Kendall-Tackett, Marshall, & Ness, 2003; Kolotylo & Broome, 2000; Vande Kemp et al., 2003).

Women suffering the disabilities related to cancers struggle with issues of potential loss of life and devastating side effects of treatments predominantly developed for men. Cancers involving the breast, ovaries, and uterus, or other disorders of the reproductive system, also involve confrontation with feminine identity (Chang & Spruill, 2000). It is important to consider the impact of the broad spectrum of cancers on women (E. Kaschak, personal communication, March 19, 2001). As members of health treatment teams, it is critical that therapists attend to the complexities of medical conditions specific to women.

Most rehabilitation professionals are not prepared to work with Women with HIV/AIDS. Such women are apt to be discouraged from seeking rehabilitation as they are considered "poor" prospects. Most of the medical research on HIV/AIDS has focused on men. It is known that women, especially Women of Color, tend to die sooner after diagnosis than men and that they have poorer response to medications than men (Beatty, 2003). Mortality from progressively disabling AIDS is addressed by Feist-Price and Wright (2003) and Baesler et al. (2003).

Cognitive problems, such as traumatic brain injury (Ackerman & Banks, 2003; Ackerman, Banks, & Corbett, 1998; Banks & Ackerman, 2002; Banks, Ackerman, & Corbett, 1995; Gordon et al., 1998; Jenny, Hymel, Ritzen, Reinert, & Hay, 1999; Monahan & O'Leary, 1999; Mukherjee et al., 2003; Raskin, 1997; Vande Kemp et al., 2003); learning disabilities (Hoffschmidt & Weinstein, 2003; Williams & Upadhyay, 2003), and attention disorders are particularly of concern as they involve both visible and invisible features and, especially for women, are not taken seriously, fully diagnosed, and/or treated. Women who have sustained head injuries with resulting brain dysfunction are seldom evaluated for neurological problems and they are not referred for rehabilitation. Repeated head injuries sustained during interpersonal violence lead to symptoms which are recognized in athletes; athletes, however, are closely observed and provided with immediate treatment (see, e.g., Collins et al., 1999). Some of the symptoms observed in women with traumatic brain injuries include communication breakdown (Friedland & Miller, 1998); startle reactions (Metzger et al., 1999); thyroid dysfunction (Yoshida, 1996), and loss of ability to express and understand emotional communication (Zeitlin, McNally, & Cassiday, 1993).

Several types of disabilities are temporary, recurrent, and/or inconsistent. Psychiatric disabilities include anxiety disorders (Neal-Barnett & Mendelson, 2003), eating disorders (Bagley et al., 2003; Nagata, Kiriike, Iketani, Kawarada, & Tanaka, 1999), and substance abuse (Beatty, 2003; Li, 1998). Frustration, depression, posttraumatic stress disorder, and anxiety are consequences of disability and can become additional disabilities (Cascardi, O'Leary, & Schlee, 1999; Feldman & Tegart, 2003; Levi, Drotar, Yeates, & Taylor, 1999; Turner & Beiser, 1990). For women without adequate supports, resources, and coping skills, substance abuse is a risk (Li, 1998). Beatty (2003) explores the difficulty for Women with Disabilities who have substance abuse problems. Much current treatment is provided either for disabilities or for substance abuse, but, in many cases, people dealing with both issues are excluded. In addition, for some disabilities, the role of depression as a causative factor or a response is unclear (see, e.g., Bagley et al., 2003).

Dormant and Part-Time Disabilities

Situational disabilities, which can be either physical or psychiatric, include migraines (Ackerman & Banks, 2003), premenstrual syndrome (Poulin & Gouliquer, 2003), motion sickness, morning sickness in pregnancy, social anxiety, and prostitution (Farley, 2003). Women who do not work outside of their homes until they reach middle age are sometimes found to have silent cognitive disorders which become symptomatic due to the stresses of new and unfamiliar tasks (Hoffschmidt & Weinstein, 2003).

Fatness[2] is a problem in that a society which bases its standards of beauty on thinness, penalizes people who are not thin. Fat women with disabilities are sometimes blamed for causing their disabilities. They are perceived as poor candidates for rehabilitation due strictly to their size, despite the availability of effective programs for weight loss and health improvement which could be provided as an integral part of treatment.

As People with Disabilities age, they tend to accumulate chronic health conditions. Older women, on average, are more likely than men to have more than one chronic condition (Jans & Stoddard, 1999). Therapists must be prepared to focus on the issues that Women with Disabilities face across the lifespan (Feldman & Tegart, 2003; Nabors & Pettee, 2003; Thierry, 1998).

PERSONAL AND INTERPERSONAL CONCERNS FOR WOMEN WITH DISABILITIES

Social Construction of Disability: Impact on Identity

There are multiple stigma and discrimination issues faced by Women with Disabilities. Girls and elderly women are often denied the privilege of making decisions about their treatment or participating in goal-setting on their own behalf (Daltroy, Larson, Eaton, Phillips, & Liang, 1999). Symptoms are often ignored or not taken seriously (Macintyre, Ford, & Hunt, 1999).

Women of Color with Disabilities are at least triply jeopardized due to discrimination on the basis of gender, ethnicity, and disability (Beatty, 2003; Feldman & Tegart, 2003; Yee, Nguyen, & Ha, this volume). In preparing this article, I was unable to locate resources which directly addressed the levels of disability, financial support, education, or employment of Women of Color with Disabilities. While some of the research is disaggregated by gender *or* by ethnicity, we need to further disaggregate the data so that we understand differences by gender within ethnic and cultural groups. Much more disability research is needed to address the multiple concerns of these women.

Lesbian and bisexual[3] Women with Disabilities are also multiple victims of discrimination (Poulin & Gouliquer, 2003). Their relationship and sexuality needs are often ignored or ridiculed. In some cases, lesbians and bisexual women with acquired disabilities have their support systems disrupted as "punishment" for their sexual orientation (Thompson & Andrzejewski, 1989).

Another issue related to stigma is the public image, or perhaps, more accurately, the lack of public images of Women with Disabilities. There is a still dearth of images in the training materials for health (particularly mental health) professionals. For example, although Women with Disabilities are pursuing careers in psychology and although women psychologists acquire disabilities, it is almost impossible to find pictures in textbooks of women psychologists with visible disabilities or discussions of the issues that women with either visible or invisible disabilities face when pursuing and maintaining careers in psychology (Vande Kemp et al., 2003).

Some Women with Disabilities embrace their disabled status with pride as they demonstrate what they are able to do, whereas others experience disability as a state of vulnerability which they would prefer to hide or keep private (Feldman & Tegart, 2003; Williams & Upadhyay, 2003). In some communities, People with Disabilities develop a culture which they perceive as reflecting a minority status. This has been noted, for example, in some Deaf communities where members consider themselves to be part of a linguistic minority using American Sign language rather than oral English (Corbett, 2003). While some people outside of the Deaf community work toward eliminating the deafness through technology or surgical procedures or by forcing Deaf[4] people to speak despite the lack of aural feedback, some Deaf people prefer to maintain their language and utilize other coping strategies that they themselves have developed. Similarly, there is considerable research on electrical stimulation of nerves of people with quadriplegia or paralysis (e.g., Phillips & Hendershot, 1991). Some people with severely limited mobility would prefer that buildings and walkways be ramped and made accessible to anyone whether walking erectly or using a wheelchair.

Accommodation in Education and Employment: Application of the Americans with Disabilities Act

Accommodation in education and employment has been one of the primary concerns for Women with Disabilities. In order to break out of poverty, those who are not totally disabled seek careers for which they are qualified (Neal-Barnett & Mendelson, 2003) and the educational preparation for those careers (Vande Kemp et al., 2003). Rehabilitation therapists, and particularly those actively involved in vocational rehabilitation, assist People with Disabilities in career preparation. As one reads the literature, however, it is difficult to find material pertinent to Women with Disabilities. Most of the focus has been on men, and specifically, on young European American men with disabilities acquired through interpersonal violence and motor vehicle accidents. This is due, in part, to the initial rehabilitation programs developed in the Veterans Administration for men injured in wars. Those programs were later offered to civilians, but maintained a focus on treatment of men. As a result, several issues specific to women have been overlooked, even though women are now being treated in most rehabilitation settings (Mukherjee et al., 2003), including veterans' medical facilities. DiCowden (2003) addresses some of the problems that arise when the wisdom of women is ignored in the treatment process.

Sexuality Issues: "Who?!," "No!" and "How?"

Sexuality and reproduction have been very difficult issues for Women with Disabilities. In a society which uses very high and usually unattainable standards of beauty and physical attractiveness, Women with Disabilities are often discouraged about being able to enter meaningful and satisfying romantic relationships with others (Chandler & Brown, 1998; Crawford & Ostrove, 2003; Dotson, Stinson, & Christian, 2003; Olkin, 2003).

Until recently, Women with Disabilities were presumed to be unable to function as adults *regardless of the nature of their disabilities* (Crawford & Ostrove, 2003). In addition, it was equally erroneously assumed that women's disabilities were genetic. As a result of those assumptions, many Women with Disabilities were sterilized against their will. Although it is difficult to find data to indicate that the rate of such sterilization has decreased with increased awareness, one remnant of this practice is the continuing difficulty faced by Women with Disabilities who want to address their reproduction and sexuality in treatment (Crawford & Ostrove, 2003). We live in an era in which some women are struggling to maintain reproductive choice, with a focus on being able to choose when and when *not* to have children. It is sometimes difficult for people *without* disabilities to understand that some People *with* Disabilities have had the choice to *have* children forcibly and irrevocably removed. These are issues about which therapists should be concerned, in order to provide appropriate support, advocacy, and education (Mona, 2001, 2003).

Nearly one-third of Women with Disabilities are actively parenting children under the age of 18 years (Jans & Stoddard, 1999; see Baesler et al., 2003; Beatty, 2003; Dotson et al., 2003; Feist- Price & Wright, 2003; Mukherjee et al., 2003; Olkin, 2003; Uysal, Hibbard, Robillard, Pappadopulos, & Jaffe, 1998 for descriptions of conflicts and discrimination faced by those mothers). Parents with Disabilities are more likely than parents without disabilities to be People of Color, older than parents without disabilities, have less than 12 years of education, be married to another Person with a Disability, and to have children with disabilities. It should be noted that some of those Women with Disabilities are grandmothers raising their grandchildren (Caputo, 1999; Feldman & Tegart, 2003). Women with Disabilities who are mothers struggle to parent in a society that questions their competence (Olkin, 2003) and provides minimal supports to assist them in the raising of their children; Mukherjee et al. (2003) provide a poignant example of the multiple issues faced by mothers who have disabilities.

Worst Case Scenarios: Intersections of Gender, Disability, Ethnicity, Class, and Social Disapproval

There are many safety concerns for Women with Disabilities. They are more likely to be targets of physical and emotional abuse than women without disabilities, especially if they need to rely on others for assistance (Díaz-Olavarrieta, Campbell, Garcia de la Cadena, Paz, & Villa, 1999; Kyriacou et al., 1999; Mitchell & Buchele-Ash, 2000; Nosek, Howland, & Young, 1997; Olkin, 2003). Nearly two-thirds of the People with Disabilities who need personal assistance are women (Jans & Stoddard, 1999); yet, as Coble (2001) noted, many People with Disabilities, due to inexperience with interviewing and other evaluation, are not skilled in selection of the most effective or trustworthy personal assistants. Because personal assistants often deal with Women with Disabilities in private, there is little protection in the event of violence. Women with Disabilities are particularly at risk because, if they are in need of personal assistance, they are unlikely to be strong enough to defend themselves.

Domestic violence is a serious problem in multiple ways for Women with Disabilities. First, because until recently domestic violence was treated as a private matter between family members, there is little epidemiological information available. It is clear, however, that family members, and particularly intimate partners, are more apt than strangers to inflict violence on girls and women to the extent that they acquire disabilities (Thompson, Simon, Saltzman, & Mercy, 1999). In addition, as mentioned earlier, Women with Disabilities are at high risk for domestic violence and mistreatment at the hands of others. In 1979, Stark, Flitcraft, and Frazier documented that physicians, *in the absence of formal diagnosis*, treated victims of intimate partner violence differently from other patients by, for example, prescribing "pain medication and/or minor tranquilizers *in spite* of the fact that such medication may be contraindicated by the head and abdominal injuries prevalent among these patients" (p. 474). Such maltreatment constitutes revictimization of women seeking medical support, and is a violation of the ethical principle of doing no harm. This is an ongoing problem for Women with Disabilities, especially if their disabilities were caused and/or exacerbated by domestic and other interpersonal violence (Acierno, Resnick, & Kilpatrick, 1997; Ackerman & Banks, 2003; Arata, 1999; Banks & Ackerman, 1999, 2002; Beatty, 2003; Campbell et al., 1999; Dotson et al., 2003; Felitti, 1991; Harrison-Felix et al., 1998; Kendall-Tackett et al., 2003; Kilpatrick, Resnick, & Acierno, 1997; Love et al., 2001;

Mona, 2003; Mukherjee et al., 2003; Olkin, 2003; Skolnick, 1996; Thompson et al., 1999).

One group of women on whom there is virtually no literature is prostituted Women with Disabilities. This group is at extremely high risk due to abuse from their employers and their customers. Prostituted women of all ethnicities remain at the lowest level in the caste system and have the least access to resources. A few psychologists are starting to recognize and address the complex issues facing these women who, when injured, are apt to lose whatever minimal support they had when they were able-bodied (Farley, 2003).

In preparing this article, one of the most frightening articles I read addressed the issue of pornography with Women with Disabilities as the focus (Elman, 1997). Such pornographic materials underscore the vulnerability of women with disabilities and portray them as desperate for sexual attention and/or easy targets for rape, having no credibility, and/or unable to complain. It was particularly disheartening to read that consumers of such pornography expressed wishes that adaptive technology be withheld from Women with Disabilities in order to enforce their vulnerability.

EMPOWERMENT:
USING CULTURE AND CONTEXT
TO ENHANCE AND FACILITATE FEMINIST THERAPY

Integrating Spirituality, History, and Women's Ways of Knowing into Therapy

Many Women with Disabilities exhibit excellent coping strategies. Two such strategies are the inclusion of spirituality in their lives (Baesler et al., 2003) and the active use of technology (Scherer, 1993). There is minimal literature on spirituality; this is a cross-disciplinary area which has been largely avoided by mental health professionals, yet it is critical for the survival of many people. Kaschak (2002) addresses feminist perspectives on the inclusion of spirituality in treatment. More research has been devoted to technology, although use by Women with Disabilities has been minimally covered. Today, when we consider technology, most of us immediately conjure up images of computers and the Internet, yet mechanical technology, in the form of framed magnifying glasses, is making it possible for me to write this article. What we *do* know about Women with Disabilities and technology is that there has to be a good fit between the user and the technology. Specifically, women need to perceive the technology as something they have chosen (not that someone else has foisted on them), as something that will help them to accomplish at least part of their goals, and that the technology is something that they can readily manipulate in order to use it. Too often, there is a poor fit and Women with Disabilities find themselves unnecessarily limited (Scherer, 1993).

One critical psychological issue is the impact of people without disabilities making decisions for Women with Disabilities without seeking input from the women themselves. For this reason, several articles in this special collection include the voices of the women (Crawford & Ostrove, 2003; Dotson et al., 2003; Farley, 2003; Poulin & Gouliquer, 2003). Poulin and Gouliquer (2003) describe frustration with a health care industry that promotes panaceaic pharmaceutical treatment at the expense of accurate diagnosis of women's illness and the lack of attention to the impact of illness on personal function. Mukherjee et al. (2003) provide not only the voices of Women with Disabilities, but also the voices of psychotherapists. Similarly, Williams and Upadhyay (2003) provide the voices of a woman with a disability and her coach; together, they describe the negative impact of ignoring the personal needs of Women with Disabilities and inappropriate attempts to make change where none was requested.

One Size Does Not Fit All: Integrating Multiple Issues into Feminist Therapy for Women with Disabilities

Yee et al. (2003), Dotson et al. (2003), and Corbett (2003) underscore the importance of making health care materials accessible to all people. Therapists *must* pay attention to the voices of Women with Disabilities in order to provide relevant treatment.

Several articles in this collection provide psychotherapeutic models for Women with Disabilities. Corbett (2003) and Nabors and Pettee (2003) emphasize the importance of culturally relevant psychotherapy for Women of Color who have disabilities. DiCowden (2003) demonstrates the integration of intuitive and the rationale into a holistic approach that includes the community and moves far from the medical pathologizing of the individual that is characteristic of many rehabilitation programs. Ackerman and Banks (2003) and Kendall-Tackett et al. (2003) describe the benefits of using biofeedback as an adjunct to traditional psychotherapy. All of the approaches involve extensions of traditional feminist psychotherapy to meet the needs of a diverse group of Women with Disabilities.

CONCLUSION

This has been a brief overview of some of the issues facing Women with Disabilities. The intersection between gender and disability is very complex. Much more work is needed to ensure that Women with Disabilities receive the opportunities due to them. Therapists and other health professionals need to give Women with Disabilities greater priority in both clinical work and research.

The research is started and we can anticipate a new literature in the next few years. The American Psychological Association's (APA) Committee on Disabilities in Psychology (CDIP) has been contributing quarterly articles on issues faced by People with Disabilities to the Division of Rehabilitation (APA Division 22) newsletter, *Rehabilitation Psychology News*; those are available on the APA Division 22 website (http://www.apa.org/divs/div22/). There is clearly a need for more information and I am encouraged that feminist therapists will soon be well-equipped to provide appropriate assistance, advocacy, support, and service to Women with Disabilities.

NOTES

1. Personal care assistance refers to assistance provided to People with Disabilities (see Mona, 2003 for a detailed definition). In the past, "caregiving," a term which connotes passive reception of care by a Person with a Disability, was used. Personal care assistance, however, portrays more accurately the cooperative effort between the Person with the Disability and the assistant. Feldman and Tegart (2003) provide considerations from the perspective of Women with Disabilities who are simultaneously providing "care" and trying to avoid the need to receive it.

2. The term "fat" is preferred over "obesity" by women whose weight exceeds societal expectations (L. Mona, personal communications, January 2001). For alternative perspectives, see Bagley, Character, and Shelton (2003) and Feldman and Tegart (2003).

3. I was unable to locate literature on transgendered People with Disabilities.

4. The term "Deaf" is capitalized to reflect the culture or linguistic minority as opposed to a disability (Corbett, 2003). See Crawford and Ostrove (2003) for a clinical example of a woman who is considered "deaf" rather than "Deaf."

REFERENCES

Acierno, R., Resnick, H. S., & Kilpatrick, D. G. (1997). Health impact of interpersonal violence 1: Prevalence rates, case identification, and risk factors for sexual assault, physical assault, and domestic violence in men and women. *Behavioral Medicine, 23*, 53-64.

Ackerman, R. J., & Banks, M. E. (1992). Family therapy for caregivers of brain-injured patients. In J. C. Chrisler & D. Howard (Eds.) *New Directions in Feminist Psychology: Practice, Theory, and Research* (pp. 66-84), New York: Springer Publishing Company.

Ackerman, R. J., & Banks, M. E. (2003). Assessment, Treatment, and Rehabilitation for Interpersonal Violence Victims: Women Sustaining Head Injuries. *Women & Therapy, 26*(3/4), 343-363.

Ackerman, R. J., Banks, M. E., & Corbett, C. A. (1998). When women deal with head injuries. *Women in Africa and the African Diaspora: Building Bridges of Knowledge and Power. Volume II: Health, Human Rights, and the Environment* (pp. 5-22). Indianapolis: Association of African Women Scholars.

Arata, C. M. (1999). Repeated sexual victimization and mental disorders in women. *Journal of Child Sexual Abuse, 7*, 1-17.

Baesler, E. J., Derlega, V. J., Winstead, B. A., & Barbee, A. (2003). Prayer as interpersonal coping in the lives of mothers with HIV. *Women & Therapy, 26*(3/4), 283-295.

Bagley, C., Character, C. D., & Shelton, L. (2003). Eating disorders among urban and Rural African American and European American women. *Women & Therapy, 26*(1/2), 57-80.

Banks, M. E., & Ackerman, R. J. (1999). *Intimate/Domestic Violence Resources: Breaking the Cycle.* Available: <http://abackans.com/dvresour.html>.

Banks, M. E., & Ackerman, R. J. (2002). Head and brain injuries experienced by African American women victims of intimate partner violence. *Women & Therapy, 25* (3/4), 133-143.

Banks, M. E., Ackerman, R. J., & Clark, E. O. (1986). Elderly women in family therapy. *Women & Therapy, 5*, 107-116.

Banks, M. E., Ackerman, R. J., & Corbett, C. A. (1995). Feminist neuropsychology: Issues for physically challenged women. In J. Chrisler & A. Hemstreet (Eds.), *Variations on a theme: Diversity and the psychology of women.* Albany: State University of New York Press.

Beatty, L. (2003). Substance abuse, disabilities, and Black women: An issue worth exploring. *Women & Therapy, 26*(3/4), 223-236.

Browne, A., Salomon, A., & Bassuk, S. S. (1999). The impact of recent partner violence on poor women's capacity to maintain work. *Violence Against Women, 5*, 393-462.

Campbell, J., Torres, S., Ryan, J., King, C., Campbell, D. W., Stallings, R. Y., & Fuchs, S. C. (1999). Physical and nonphysical partner abuse and other risk factors for low birth weight among full term and preterm babies: A multiethnic case-controlled study. *American Journal of Epidemiology, 150*, 714-726.

Caplan, P. J. (2001). Chronic fatigue syndrome: A first-person story. *Women & Therapy, 23* (1), 23-43.

Caputo, R. K. (1999). Grandmothers and coresident grandchildren. *Families in Society: The Journal of Contemporary Human Services, 80*, 120-126.

Cascardi, M., O'Leary, K. D., & Schlee, K. A. (1999). Co-occurrence and correlates of posttraumatic stress disorder and major depression in physically abused women. *Journal of Family Violence, 14*, 227-249.

Chandler, B. J., & Brown, S. (1998). Sex and relationship dysfunction in neurological disability. *Journal of Neurology, Neurosurgery, & Psychiatry, 65*, 877-880.

Chang, A. F., & Spruill, K. M. (2000). *A survivor's guide to breast cancer*. Oakland, CA: New Harbinger Publications.

Coble, A. C. (2001, Winter). When the challenge of maintaining personal care attendants becomes the focus of treatment. *Rehabilitation Psychology News, 28* (2), 6-7. Available: http://www.apa.org/divisions/div22/Winter2001news.html.

Collins, M. W., Grindel, S. H., Lovell, M. R., Dede, D. E., Moser, D. J., Phalin, B. R., Nogle, S., Waist, M., Cordry, D., Daugherty, M. K., Sears, S. F., Nicolette, G., Indelicato, P., & McKeag, D. B. (1999). Relationship between concussion and neuropsychological performance in college football players. *Journal of American Medical Association, 282*, 964-970.

Corbett, C. A. (2003). Special issues in psychotherapy for minority deaf women. *Women & Therapy, 26*(3/4), 311-329.

Crawford, D., & Ostrove, J. M. (2003). Representations of disability and the interpersonal relationships of women with disabilities. *Women & Therapy, 26*(3/4), 179-194.

Daltroy, L. H., Larson, M. G., Eaton, H. M., Phillips, C. B., & Liang, M. H. (1999). Discrepancies between self-reported and observed physical function in the elderly: The influence of response shift and other factors. *Social Science & Medicine, 48*, 1549-1561.

Díaz-Olavarrieta, C., Campbell, J., Garcia de la Cadena, C., Paz, F., & Villa, A. R. (1999). Domestic violence against patients with chronic neurologic disorders. *Archives of Neurology, 56*, 681-685.

DiCowden, M. (2003). The call of the wild woman: Models of healing. *Women & Therapy, 26*,(3/4), 297-301.

Dotson, L. A., Stinson, J., & Christian, L. (2003). "People tell me I can't have sex": Women with disabilities share their personal perspectives on health care, sexuality, and reproductive rights. *Women & Therapy, 26*(3/4), 195-209.

Drossman, D. A., Leserman, J., Li, Z., Keefe, F., Hu, Y. J. B., & Toomey, T. C. (2000). Effects of coping on health outcome among women with gastrointestinal disorders. *Psychosomatic Medicine, 62*, 309-317.

Elman, R. A. (1997). Disability pornography: The fetishization of women's vulnerabilities. *Violence Against Women, 3*, 257-270.

Farber, R. S. (2000). Mothers with disabilities: In their own voice. *The American Journal of Occupational Therapy, 54*, 260-268.

Farley, M. (2003). Prostitution and the Invisibility of Harm. *Women & Therapy, 26*(3/4), 247-280.

Feist-Price, S., & Wright, L. B. (2003). African American Women Living with HIV/AIDS: Mental Health Issues. *Women & Therapy, 26*(1/2), 27-44.

Feldman, S. I., & Tegart, G. (2003). Keep moving: Conceptions of illness and disability of middle-aged African-American women with arthritis. *Women & Therapy, 26*(1/2), 127-143.

Felitti, V. J. (1991). Long-term medical consequences of incest, rape, and molestation. *Southern Medical Journal, 84,* 328-331.

Friedland, D., & Miller, N. (1998). Conversation analysis of communication breakdown after closed head injury. *Brain Injury, 12,* 1-14.

Gordon, W. A., Brown, M., Sliwinski, M., Hibbard, M. R., Patti, N., Weiss, M. J., Kalinsky, R., & Sheerer, M. (1998). The enigma of "hidden" traumatic brain injury. *Journal of Head Trauma Rehabilitation, 13,* 39-56.

Guyll, M., Matthews, K. A., & Bromberger, J. T. (2001). Discrimination and unfair treatment: Relationship to cardiovascular reactivity among African American and European American women. *Health Psychology, 20,* 315-325.

Harrison-Felix, C., Zafonte, R., Mann, N., Dijkers, M., Englander, J., & Kreutzer, J. (1998). Brain injury as a result of violence: Preliminary findings from the Traumatic Brain Injury Model Systems. *Archives of Physical Medicine and Rehabilitation, 79,* 730-737.

Hoffschmidt, S. J., & Weinstein, C. S. (2003). The influence of silent learning disorders on the lives of women. *Women & Therapy, 26*(1/2), 81-94.

Jans, L., & Stoddard, S. (1999). *Chartbook on women and disability in the United States. An InfoUse report.* Washington, DC: U.S. Department of Education, National Institute on Disability and Rehabilitation Research. Available: http://www.infouse.com/disabilitydata/.

Jason, L. A., Taylor, R. R., & Kennedy, C. L. (2000). Chronic fatigue syndrome, fibromyalgia, and multiple chemical sensitivities in a community-based sample of persons with chronic fatigue syndrome-like symptoms. *Psychosomatic Medicine, 62,* 655-663.

Jenny, C., Hymel, K. P., Ritzen, A., Reinert, S. E., & Hay, T. C. (1999). Analysis of missed cases of abusive head trauma. *Journal of American Medical Association, 281,* 621-626.

Joslin, D., & Harrison, R. (1998). The "hidden patient": Older relatives raising children orphaned by AIDS. *Journal of the American Medical Women's Association, 53,* 65-71, 76.

Kaschak, E. (Ed.). (2002). *Spirit in feminist therapy.* New York: The Haworth Press, Inc.

Kendall-Tackett, K. (2000, Fall). Time as an issue of accessibility in the workplace. *Rehabilitation Psychology News, 28* (4), 4-5. Available: http://www.apa.org/divisions/div22/Fall2000news.html

Kendall-Tackett, K., Marshall, R., & Ness, K. (2003). Chronic pain syndromes and violence against women. *Women & Therapy, 26*(1/2), 45-56.

Kilpatrick, D. G., Resnick, H. S., & Acierno, R. (1997). Health impact of interpersonal violence 3: Implications for clinical practice and public policy. *Behavioral Medicine, 23,* 79-85.

Kington, R. S., & Smith, J. P. (1997). Socioeconomic status and racial and ethnic difference in functional status associated with chronic diseases. *American Journal of Public Health, 87,* 805-810.

Kolotylo, C. J., & Broome, M. E. (2000). Exploration of migraine pain, disability, depressive symptomatology, and coping: A pilot study. *Health Care for Women International, 21*, 203-218.

Krupp, L. B., & Elkins, L. E. (2000). Fatigue and declines in cognitive functioning in multiple sclerosis. *Neurology, 55*, 934-939.

Kyriacou, D. N., Angelin, D., Taliaferro, E., Stone, S., Tubb, T., Linden, J. A., Muelleman, R., Barton, E., & Kraus, J. F. (1999). Risk factors for injury to women from domestic violence. *New England Journal of Medicine, 341*, 1892-1898.

Levi, R. B., Drotar, D., Yeates, K. O., & Taylor, H. G. (1999). Posttraumatic stress symptoms in children following orthopedic or traumatic brain injury. *Journal of Clinical Child Psychology, 28*, 232-243.

Li, L. (1998). Illicit drug use by women with disabilities. *American Journal of Drug and Alcohol Abuse, 24*, 405-418.

Liao, Y., McGee, D. L., Cao, G., & Cooper, R. S. (1999). Black-White differences in disability and morbidity in the last years of life. *American Journal of Epidemiology, 149*, 1097-1103.

Love, C., Gerbert, B., Caspers, N., Bronstone, A., Perry, D., & Bird, W. (2001, January). Dentists' attitudes and behaviors regarding domestic violence: The need for an effective response. *Journal of the American Dental Association.* Available: http://www.ada.org/prof/pubs/jada/0101/ab-6.html.

Macintyre, S., Ford, G., & Hunt, K. (1999). Do women "over-report" morbidity? Men's and women's responses to structured prompting on a standard question on long standing illness *Social Science & Medicine, 48*, 89-98.

McDonough, P. A. (1997). The social patterns of work disability among women in Canada. *Journal of Disability Policy Studies, 8*, 75-98.

McNeilly, M. D., Robinson, E. L., Anderson, N. B., Pieper, C. F., Shah, A., Toth, P. S., Martin, P., Jackson, D., Saulter, T. D., White, C., Kuchibatla, M., Collado, S. M., & Gerin, W. (1995). Effects of racist provocation and social support on cardiovascular reactivity in African American women. *International Journal of Behavioral Medicine, 2*, 321-338.

Metzger, L. J., Orr, S. P., Berry, N. J., Ahern, C. E., Lasko, N. B., & Pitman, R. K. (1999). Physiologic reactivity to startling tones in women with posttraumatic stress disorder. *Journal of Abnormal Psychology, 108*, 347-352.

Mitchell, L. M., & Buchele-Ash, A. (2000). Abuse and neglect of individuals with disabilities: Building protective supports through public policy. *Journal of Disability Policy Studies, 10*, 225-243.

Mona, L. R. (2001). Sexuality and disability: Comprehensive treatment considerations. *Rehabilitation Psychology News, 29* (1), 10-11. Available: http://www.apa.org/divisions/div22/Fall2001news.html.

Mona, L. R. (2003). Sexual options for people with disabilities: Using personal assistance services for sexual expression. *Women & Therapy, 26*(3/4), 211-221.

Monahan, K., & O'Leary, K. D. (1999). Head injury and battered women: An initial inquiry. *Health & Social Work, 24*, 269-278.

Mukherjee, D., Reis, J. P., & Heller, W. (2003). Women living with traumatic brain injury: Social isolation, emotional functioning and implications for psychotherapy. *Women & Therapy, 26*(1/2), 3-25.

Nabors, N. A., & Pettee, M. F. (2003). Womanist therapy with African American women with disabilities. *Women & Therapy, 26*(3/4), 331-341.

Nagata, T., Kiriike, N., Iketani, T., Kawarada, Y., & Tanaka, H. (1999). History of childhood sexual or physical abuse in Japanese patients with eating disorders: Relationship with dissociation and impulsive behaviours. *Psychological Medicine, 29*, 935-942.

Neal-Barnett, A. M., & Mendelson, L. L. (2003). Obsessive compulsive disorder in the workplace: An invisible disability. *Women & Therapy, 26*(1/2), 169-178.

Neath, J. (1997). Social causes of impairment, disability, and abuse: A feminist perspective. *Journal of Disability Policy Studies, 8*, 195-230.

Nosek, M. A., Howland, C. A., & Young, M. E. (1997). Abuse of women with disabilities: Policy implications. *Journal of Disability Policy Studies, 8*, 157-175.

Olkin, R. (2003). Women with physical disabilities who want to leave their partners: A feminist and disability-affirmative perspective. *Women & Therapy, 26*(3/4), 237-246.

Phillips, C. A., & Hendershot, D. M. (1991). A systems approach to medically prescribed functional electrical stimulation: Ambulation after spinal cord injury. *Paraplegia, 29*, 505-513.

Poulin, C., & Gouliquer, L. (2003). Part-time disabled lesbian passing on roller blades, or PMS, Prozac, and essentializing women's ailments. *Women & Therapy, 26*(1/2), 95-108.

Pruchno, R., Patrick, J. H., & Burant, C. J. (1996). Aging women and their children with chronic disabilities: Perceptions of sibling involvement and effects on well-being. *Family Relations, 45*, 318-326.

Pruchno, R., Patrick, J. H., & Burant, C. J. (1997). African American and white mothers of adults with chronic disabilities: Caregiving burden and satisfaction. *Family Relations, 46*, 335-346.

Raskin, S. A. (1997). The relationship between sexual abuse and mild traumatic brain injury. *Brain Injury, 11*, 587-603.

Ritter, J. C. (1994). A self-regulatory treatment of interstitial cystitis using biofeedback and therapies. *Dissertation Abstracts International: Section B: The Sciences and Engineering, 54*(9-B), 4932.

Scherer, M. J. (1993). What we know about women's technology use, avoidance, and abandonment. *Women & Therapy, 14*, 117-132.

Skolnick, A. A. (1996, January 24/31). Images gleaned at radiologists' annual meeting. *Medical News & Perspectives, 275*. Available: http://www.ama-assn.org/sci.pubs/journals/archive/jama/vol_275/no_4/mednews.htm#mn6008.

Stark, E., Flitcraft, A., & Frazier, W. (1979). Medicine and patriarchal violence: The social construction of a "private event." *International Journal of Health Services, 9*, 461-493.

Thierry, J. M. (1998). Promoting the health and wellness of women with disabilities. *Journal of Women's Health, 7*, 505-507.

Thompson, K., & Andrzejewski, J. (1989). *Why can't Sharon Kowalski come home?* Denver: Spinsters Ink.

Thompson, M. P., Simon, T. R., Saltzman, L. E., & Mery, J. A. (1999). Epidemiology of injuries among women after physical assaults: The role of self-protective behaviors. *American Journal of Epidemiology, 150*, 235-244.

Tobacman, J. K., Zimmerman, B., Lee, P., Hilborne, L., Kolder, H., & Brook, R. H. (1998). Visual function impairments in relation to gender, age, and visual acuity in patients who undergo cataract surgery. *Ophthalmology, 105*, 1745-1750.

Turner, R. J., & Beiser, M. (1990). Major depression and depressive symptomatology among the physically disabled: Assessing the role of chronic stress. *The Journal of Nervous and Mental Disease, 178*, 343-350.

Uysal, S., Hibbard, M. R., Robillard, D., Pappadopulos, E., & Jaffe, M. (1998). The effect of parental traumatic brain injury on parenting and child behavior. *Journal of Head Trauma Rehabilitation, 13*, 57-71.

Vande Kemp, H., Chen, J. S., Erickson, G. N., & Friesen, N. L. (2003). ADA accommodation of therapists with disabilities in clinical training. *Women & Therapy, 26*(1/2), 155-168.

Webster's Seventh New Collegiate Dictionary (1971). Springfield, MA: G. & C. Merriam Company.

Williams, M., & Upadhyay, W. S. (2003). To be or not be disabled. *Women & Therapy, 26*(1/2), 145-154.

Yee, B. W. K., Nguyen, H. T., & Ha, M. (2003). Chronic disease health beliefs and lifestyle practices among Vietnamese adults: Influences of gender and age. *Women & Therapy, 26*(1/2), 111-125.

Yoshida, D. (1996). Thyroid storm precipitated by trauma. *The Journal of Emergency Medicine, 14*, 697-701.

Zeitlin, S. B., McNally, R. J., & Cassiday, K. L. (1993). Alexithymia in victims of sexual assault: An effect of repeated traumatization? *American Journal of Psychiatry, 150*, 661-663.

VISIBLE AND INVISIBLE IMPAIRMENTS EXPERIENCED BY WOMEN

"MEN'S" ILLNESS OVERLOOKED IN WOMEN AND "WOMEN'S" ILLNESS MISDIAGNOSED OR DISMISSED

Women Living with Traumatic Brain Injury: Social Isolation, Emotional Functioning and Implications for Psychotherapy

Debjani Mukherjee
Judy Panko Reis
Wendy Heller

Debjani Mukherjee is affiliated with the MacLean Center for Clinical Medical Ethics, The University of Chicago. Judy Panko Reis is affiliated with the Health Resource Center for Women with Disabilities, Rehabilitation Institute of Chicago. Wendy Heller is affiliated with the Psychology Department and The Beckman Institute, University of Illinois at Urbana-Champaign.

Address correspondence to: Debjani Mukherjee, PhD, MacLean Center for Clinical Medical Ethics, The University of Chicago, AMB W732 MC6098, 5841 South Maryland Avenue, Chicago, IL 60637 (E-mail: dmukherj@medicine.bsd.uchicago.edu).

The authors would like to thank Kristi Kirschner, MD, and the members of the Hastings Center/Rehabilitation Institute of Chicago working group on "Families and Traumatic Brain Injury: The Moral Landscape" for their encouragement and support.

[Haworth co-indexing entry note]: "Women Living with Traumatic Brain Injury: Social Isolation, Emotional Functioning and Implications for Psychotherapy." Mukherjee, Debjani, Judy Panko Reis, and Wendy Heller. Co-published simultaneously in *Women & Therapy* (The Haworth Press, Inc.) Vol. 26, No. 1/2, 2003, pp. 3-26; and: *Women with Visible and Invisible Disabilities: Multiple Intersections, Multiple Issues, Multiple Therapies* (ed: Martha E. Banks, and Ellyn Kaschak) The Haworth Press, Inc., 2003, pp. 3-26. Single or multiple copies of this article are available for a fee from The Haworth Document Delivery Service [1-800-HAWORTH, 9:00 a.m. - 5:00 p.m. (EST). E-mail address: getinfo@haworthpressinc.com].

SUMMARY. Women living with Traumatic Brain Injury (TBI) typically experience social and emotional sequelae that can be effectively
addressed in the context of a psychotherapeutic relationship. Traumatic
Brain Injuries can affect the full range of human functioning, from activities of daily living to experiencing a coherent sense of self. In this article, we focus on two issues, social isolation and emotional functioning,
that encompass a number of key challenges facing women with TBI and
are common and fruitful foci of psychotherapy. Social isolation includes
marginalization in multiple communities, the invisibility of cognitive
disabilities, difficulties in interpersonal relationships, and difficulties in
employment and access to transportation. Emotional functioning includes posttraumatic stress symptoms, loss of self-esteem, anxiety, depression, anger, and shame. Two exemplary cases are used to illustrate the
themes and underscore the complexities and realities of adjusting to TBI.
Recommendations for therapists and consumers are woven throughout the
paper. *[Article copies available for a fee from The Haworth Document Delivery
Service: 1-800-HAWORTH. E-mail address: <getinfo@haworthpressinc.com>
Website: <http://www.HaworthPress.com> © 2003 by The Haworth Press, Inc. All
rights reserved.]*

KEYWORDS. Women, psychotherapy, traumatic brain injury, social
functioning, emotional functioning

Traumatic Brain Injury (TBI) has become a major public health
problem in the United States. It is estimated that a little more than 2% of
the U.S. population currently lives with disabilities resulting from TBI,
and recent legislation (Traumatic Brain Injury Act), as well as governmental reports, have acknowledged the magnitude of the problem (e.g.,
U.S. General Accounting Office, 1998; National Institutes of Health
(NIH) Consensus Statement, 1998). The value, complexity, and various
theoretical frameworks for conducting psychotherapy with individuals
with TBI have been discussed elsewhere (e.g., Cicerone, 1989; Langer,
1992; Pollack, 1994; Prigatano, 1994, 1999), although issues particular
to women have not, to our knowledge, been published in the literature.
In this article, we will be focusing on the experiences of the three authors as contextualized exemplars of the process of conducting psychotherapy with women with brain injury.

The goals of this paper are not to represent the enormous range of issues faced by women with TBI, but to focus on the particulars of three

perspectives in order to illustrate broader themes. Judy Panko Reis (JPR), the Director of the Health Resource Center for Women with Disabilities at the Rehabilitation Institute of Chicago, sustained a TBI in 1980. She will discuss her experiences as a woman living with TBI. Wendy Heller (WH), a Full Professor, the Director of Clinical Training, and a licensed Clinical Psychologist at the University of Illinois at Urbana-Champaign, has been JPR's therapist since 1984 and has trained graduate students in neuropsychological assessment and intervention. Debjani Mukherjee (DM), a postdoctoral Ethics Fellow at the University of Chicago and a graduate of the Clinical/Community Psychology program at the University of Illinois, will focus on her psychotherapy with an Asian American university student whose needs were not being met by traditional models of rehabilitation.

In the United States, more men than women sustain TBIs (NIH Consensus Statement, 1998). Because of this fact, because rehabilitation medicine was conceptualized primarily to treat male war victims, and because medicine has more generally ignored gender-specific health concerns, the physical and psychosocial concerns of women with TBI have been neglected by service providers (e.g., Gill, Kirschner, & Reis, 1994). Furthermore, the nature of TBI and the "invisibility" of cognitive disabilities has typically led to marginalization within both the women's and disability communities.

Although traumatic brain injuries can affect various brain structures and the insults are not uniform, common areas of difficulty have been identified by clinicians and researchers. The areas include:

1. activities of daily living, such as problems with grooming, eating, using public transportation or managing finances;
2. cognitive functioning, such as memory, language, and communication problems, and limited compensatory strategies;
3. emotional functioning, such as anger, anxiety, apathy, depression or disinhibition;
4. physical health issues, such as pain or fatigue;
5. preinjury factors, such as cultural and class barriers, substance abuse, or family dysfunction;
6. impaired sense of self, such as unawareness of deficits or inappropriate expectations for self and others; and
7. social functioning, such as lack of social support, loss of power and control, lack of access to services or funding, or social devaluation of persons with brain injury.

(e.g., Bergquist et al., 1994; Corrigan, Smith-Knapp & Granger, 1998; Heller, 1997; Lezak, 1995; Malec & Basford, 1996; Mukherjee, Heller, & Alper, 2001; Ponsford, Sloan & Snow, 1995; Prigatano, 1994; Rosenthal & Ricker, 2000). These areas of functioning overlap and are sometimes artificially separated for clinical and research purposes but generally, after a TBI, multiple areas of functioning are affected. Moreover, the adjustment and accommodation process is complex and dynamic and women can experience difficulties in various areas as they adjust to the TBI.

Typically, a woman who sustains a brain injury receives acute hospital services (possibly including time in a critical care or intensive care unit), post acute services, inpatient rehabilitation, and outpatient rehabilitation. The extent of services received depends on many factors such as the severity of the injury, services available at the hospital where the woman is being served, and in today's health care climate, the ability to pay for services. In the hierarchy of "required" services, psychotherapy might fall lower than other forms of therapy such as physical, speech and language, and occupational therapies, but at some point during the adjustment process, usually while experiencing extreme emotional distress, women might enter into psychotherapeutic relationships. It should also be noted that given the high estimates of brain injury, including undiagnosed cases or mild brain injuries, it is likely that a therapist practicing in the United States will encounter clients who have sustained brain injuries. To the degree that psychotherapists become more cognizant of the impact brain injuries can have on cognitive, emotional, and adaptive function, the more they will be able to identify the role a TBI might play in a particular client's life. Then, the primary task for the psychotherapist becomes one of determining how best to intervene given the woman's relative cognitive and emotional strengths and weaknesses, and understanding that the social and cultural context of the injury affects the way that it is experienced, talked about and (de)valued.

According to a National Institutes of Health (NIH) Consensus Statement on Rehabilitation of Persons with Traumatic Brain Injury (1998),

> Psychotherapy, an important component of a comprehensive rehabilitation program, is used to treat depression and loss of self-esteem associated with cognitive dysfunction. Specific goals for this therapy emphasize emotional support, providing explanations of the injury and its effects, helping to achieve self-esteem in the context of realistic self-assessment, reducing denial, and increasing ability to relate to family and society.

For women with TBI, therapeutic goals have to acknowledge societal and cultural expectations of women, individual differences in negotiating role changes and disability status, and longstanding patterns of interacting in families and society. Teasing apart the organic and non-organic sequelae of a TBI often becomes a complicated and lengthy process. For example, the denial which is mentioned in the NIH report can be on many levels. Damage to specific areas of the brain can result in anosognosia (literally not knowing that you do not know) or unawareness of deficits (Prigatano & Schacter, 1991). Psychological denial, of the type with which therapists are familiar can look behaviorally similar to the denial due to brain damage (Lewis, 1991). There are some differences, however. The time course is different in that psychological denial is more persistent. Furthermore, denial that reflects neural damage does not occur in isolation but is part of a pattern of functional deficits. Clinically, the individual who is employing psychological denial is more likely to become distressed when confronted with reality than the person with denial caused by TBI. This example underscores the ways in which traditional views of psychological mechanisms, such as denial, are complicated by damage to the brain.

Prigatano (1994, p. 175) reported that, in working with individuals with brain injury, "one repeatedly encounters them [sic] asking three questions: 1. Why did this happen to me?, 2. Will I be normal again?, and 3. Is life worth living after brain injury?" We would like to expand upon this conceptualization. Many women who enter into a psychotherapeutic relationship are struggling with issues of how to negotiate and incorporate new identities (e.g., woman with disability, person who has "survived" traumatic experience, mother with disability), how to overcome institutional obstacles (e.g., applying for and receiving governmental benefits, using the public transportation system), adjustment to brain injury, and dealing with the emotional sequelae (e.g., depression due to site of injury, loss, social isolation) associated with TBI. In this article, we focus on two issues, social isolation and emotional functioning, that encompass a number of key challenges facing women with TBI and are common and fruitful foci of psychotherapy. We will also use JPR's narrative of becoming a mother as an exemplar of the new roles and developmental life-experiences that are affected by the social and emotional sequelae of TBI.

Social isolation is a broad area including marginalization in multiple communities, the invisibility of cognitive disabilities, difficulties in interpersonal relationships, and challenges in employment and transportation. After a TBI, specific brain structures might be affected that influence the social repertoire of individuals. For example, damage to the right hemisphere can affect the ability to understand nonverbal communication that involves processing facial expression, voice intonation, and gestures. Right hemisphere damage can also affect the ability to take another's perspective, respond appropriately in an emotional situation, and show appropriate affect. Damage to the left hemisphere can cause expressive speech problems, which lead to difficulties in communication, and damage to anterior brain regions can cause problems with social judgment and behavior (for review, see Heller, 1997; Lezak, 1995). TBI-related problems in social functioning can be further compounded by the social and institutional factors that impede adjustment, such as difficulty receiving appropriate services without an effective advocate and cultural assumptions about disability and dependence (Mukherjee et al., 2001).

Emotional functioning is another broad area and would include post-traumatic stress symptoms, loss of self-esteem, anxiety, depression, anger, and shame. Langer (1992) discussed postmorbid emotional themes that arise after brain injury regardless of age, gender, or cultural background. She viewed them as universal themes that are expressed to a different extent depending on the individual's circumstances. The themes she outlined include: humiliation, fear of failure, helplessness, powerlessness, loss of dignity, love, competence, identity and control, issues of manhood/womanhood, sexual feelings, fear of the future, sense of mortality and financial concerns. Obviously a unique configuration of some or all of these themes can be present in any individual. A systematic exploration of at least some of these themes might have great therapeutic value and may not be formally addressed in rehabilitation. For example, an exploration of the sense of loss is typically an important part of the therapy process. The possibilities of loss are myriad and can include loss of physical abilities, loss of cognitive abilities such as processing of information or memory, loss of time from valued activities, loss of memory for events surrounding the injury, loss of previous relationships, and perhaps especially, a loss of the previously-defined self.

In sum, TBIs can affect the full range of human functioning from activities of daily living to experiencing a coherent sense of self. We begin with brief case histories of two women who experienced brain injury and describe some initial reactions. Throughout the rest of the paper, we will be using their experiences to illustrate the kinds of issues that are commonly faced by women with TBI. JPR has written her own narrative and Jessica's (pseudonym) narrative has been (re)created by her therapist (DM).

CLIENT EXAMPLES

(JPR) The winter I was twenty-eight, life was lush with promise and I loved it. I lived independently, traveled frequently for business and pleasure and when I became torn between lucrative job offers from competitors on both coasts, I rejoiced in the knowledge that I had exceeded my career goals as a research manager for a top actuarial firm in Chicago. Blessed with good health and a loving family, I looked forward to taking a leave from my job to join my fiancé in Hawaii where he was finishing his medical residency. Shortly before our planned marriage, while tent camping in a Hawaiian state park, assailants bludgeoned the right hemisphere of my brain into raw meat and left me for dead in an assault that murdered my fiancé. Days after authorities slipped his corpse into a rubber bag and sent him home to his family in New York, a flight nurse transferred me onto a stretcher that occupied two rows of seating, and my parents accompanied me home to Chicago. My parents told me that once back home, living with them, I would need to learn how to live life anew. Like a limp marionette I went along with the program.

Three years after my brain injury, laurels of victory were lavished upon me by family, friends, and physicians. Enduring an Everest of intensive rehabilitation therapies, I conquered the wheelchair, and learned scores of compensatory strategies for so-called irrecoverable losses. Most critically, I managed to resume a physical and emotional quality of life that again held the promise of marriage and graduate school. But problems prevailed. Although I had achieved more in three years than countless numbers of individuals with TBI would accomplish through a lifetime of therapies, the victory was hollow. I felt isolated and mutilated. The assault claimed function of my left leg, resulting in the use of a leg brace and cane and decimated use of my left hand and arm. With impairments in the left visual field of both eyes, I was unable to resume driving. Less apparent but equally humiliating was the devastation wreaked by a host of cognitive and perceptual deficits that were yet to reveal their full ravages.

I figured that my malaise would vanish once I left my parents' home to marry my husband. After all, I had worked diligently to set myself up for success by taking things slowly. My husband and I knew one another before the injury and he had vigilantly remained by my side throughout the three years of rehab.

Heeding my vocational counselor I started grad school sensibly, carrying only two classes; surely the worst was behind me. Things were bound to improve!

(WH) I met JPR for the first time after she was married and had become a graduate student at the University of Chicago. Before I started working with her as a therapist, my graduate advisor in the Biopsychology program, Dr. Jerre Levy, had suggested I interview her as a potential case study of a person with a right hemisphere injury. In the course of that interview process, JPR shared with me some of her journals and I had an opportunity to evaluate her psychological status pre-injury. This assessment made it clear that JPR had some enormous strengths that would prove to contribute in important ways to her unique adjustment to brain injury. JPR is an exceptionally intelligent and motivated person who has personality characteristics that are typical of people who approach challenges head-on, as opposed to avoiding them. She combines this trait with a contemplative side and is able to reflect upon her self and her behavior in a non-defensive way. She is also capable of engagement, trust, and attachment to others, a characteristic that helped her to cope with the remarkable post-traumatic sequelae of having been the victim of a murderous attack.

Despite her intellectual and emotional strengths, JPR had quite a few issues that needed attention. She experienced changes in her cognitive and physical abilities that interfered with her ability to function in the same ways and with the same efficiency and ease that she had in the past. She was finding herself forced to deal with losses in status and sense of self on many levels, including changes in her appearance that she viewed as negative and inability to drive an automobile. The impact of these losses became more, not less, obvious as she progressed in her adjustment to the brain injury and as the most pressing demands of survival diminished. This is a common pattern among people with brain injuries and their families, who often face, at some point, the painful reality that recovery is not a simple, straightforward process. (Mukherjee, 2000)

(DM) Jessica emigrated from Taiwan to the United States when she was in her early twenties. She had spent the first few years working in her family's business and then saved up enough money to attend university. Jessica was about to start her second year when she sustained a traumatic brain injury. She was crossing the street to go to the grocery store in her neighborhood and was standing on the median of the busy road when a truck jumped over the median and hit her. The next moment she recalled was waking up in the hospital with a really bad headache. No one would answer her questions about why she was there. She knew her parents were very worried and that her "face had been smashed in." She had no idea that the accident might have affected the way that she was thinking, remembering, concentrating or experiencing emotion.

After the accident, she was in the hospital for about 10 days, received some outpatient rehabilitation and then left to start her sophomore year of college. Within a month, she was back at home. She was unable to stay awake, had unbearable headaches, and could not concentrate or focus on her schoolwork. She tried to go back to college the next semester and ended up dropping to below half-time status. It was at this point that she first found out about the office for students with disabilities and decided to learn more about receiving services.

Approximately 16 months after her accident, Jessica was referred to me for psychotherapy by the Counseling Center at the University. I had over seven years of experience working with women (and men) with brain injury in the context of neuropsychological assessment, but was relatively new to the enterprise of doing therapy with individuals with cognitive disabilities. Like many women with a brain injury, Jessica's difficulties were not visibly apparent. If you looked closely, you could see some scars on her face (which she later reported were from her face "being smashed by the truck driven by a drunk driver"), but she did not have any other physical signs of her brain injury. Jessica cried during most of the intake interview. She had been from office to office on campus seeking services that were appropriate for her problems. She told me that I was her "last hope." She kept referring to me as a neuropsychologist who would be able to help her figure out what was going on.

Jessica had many strengths when she entered the psychotherapeutic relationship but because she sought therapy when she was in acute distress, she felt as if she had lost all control over her life and felt helpless and hopeless. Before the accident, she had been the sort of person who worked consistently towards long-term goals, such as immigrating to the United States or completing a university degree. She had overcome personal losses and disappointments, always with the hope of a better future. The brain injury (temporarily) undermined her sense of hope and her spiritual belief that if she worked hard and lived a "good life," then she would be at peace. And although she was from a tight-knit family and identified with the Asian American community, she preferred to keep to herself and only open up to those that she knew very well. Her need for services and support subsequent to the accident was counter to the way in which she had coped and succeeded before. The brain injury not only affected her attention, concentration and language skills, but also forced Jessica to alter deeply ingrained ways of interacting with her environment and question her fundamental beliefs and worldview.

PSYCHOTHERAPY ISSUES

Social Isolation

Often unemployed, living alone, and having few if any friends, women with TBI are isolated from mainstream women's support networks and social activities as well as from dating opportunities. Social stigma and the common problem of transportation, if the TBI results in a visual or mobility impairment, are significant isolating factors. Women who are married at the time of injury commonly express concerns about marriage problems. Many women report that their slow cognitive processing, memory and communication deficits add to their frustrations and can cause them to feel sad or depressed. Frequently living with invisible disabilities, women with TBI can be shunned by other individuals with disabilities, leaving them on the sidelines within the disability and disabled women's communities, denied the supports these groups can offer. Getting the right emotional and psychological support is critical to dismantling the barriers of social alienation that accompanies TBI.

(JPR) Soon after I entered therapy it became clear that I was struggling with deep remorse over the loss of my identity as a successful able-bodied businesswoman. No longer employed or able to drive, I lost access to pre-injury friends and was too self-conscious about my TBI to make new friends. My life was so different . . . strangers in parks and students on campus stopping to ask if I needed help or "whether I was born this way?" I spent countless moments filling empty days desperately yearning for the professional respect, collegiality, and socializing that had once come to me so easily. It horrified me that the reactions of my one-time colleagues and new acquaintances seemed to rob me of the social cachet of "being one of the crowd." How would I ever recover a sense of belonging to the world, any world?

The answer came very unexpectedly when I found myself randomly deemed ineligible for the accessible public transportation service that had been transporting me to therapy. Outraged that neither transportation bureaucrats or my state senators were willing to help me counter this grave injustice, I reluctantly allowed myself to connect with the local independent living center for people with disabilities that advocated to increase transit options. In order to make this contact I was forced to swallow my pride and acknowledge that I was a disenfranchised person with a disability, sorely in need of help. In therapy we addressed my initial discomfort in making the contact and how frightening it was for me to identify with the people working at the center. For a long time I kept saying that these people were not like me because I was a businesswoman.

But with support in therapy I permitted myself to work with other professional women with disabilities from the suburbs and watched my consciousness slowly begin to shift. Then when we confronted board members of the transit agency who angrily referred to us as "you people, making unreasonable demands," I realized that my business persona was quickly yielding to the truth that I was more like the women with disabilities at my side standing up for what we believed to be just than the suited businessmen from the transit agency taking great pleasure in denouncing our entitlements as taxpayers.

It was at that moment that a new community and sense of pride emerged for me. For years to come, in therapy we used that experience as a platform to launch an empowering range of breakthroughs in my consciousness that included lifetime firsts such as publishing a magazine, participating in school parenting activities and becoming gainfully employed as the director of a women's health center.

(WH) JPR's story illustrates the difficulties women face in coping with real and perceived losses in status and identity, and the challenges inherent in re-authoring their life stories in a positive way (Stewart, 2000). JPR's first challenge was to regain her self-esteem after losing the identity she had worked so hard to foster and in which she had taken so much pride. Accepting a new identity depended a great deal upon her ability to see that such a change was not a compromise, although at first it was impossible to see it any other way. As a therapist, it was necessary for me to resist being drawn into the despair she felt and to tolerate my own horror as she relived and re-experienced the initial trauma as well as a series of subsequent blows to her prior sense of self (e.g., the development of rheumatoid arthritis). Then, it was important to reframe her experience of her current condition in terms that allowed her to perceive possibilities for herself and her future that she found difficult to envision. Note that reframing does not mean denying the magnitude of distress, injustice, or pain: The feelings must be acknowledged and honored. Reframing means introducing or fostering narratives or perspectives that provide an alternative to the limiting, self-defeating, or self-denigrating ones within which the woman with TBI may find herself locked. To the degree that such reframing can be accompanied by concrete opportunities to experience mastery, social connectedness, and self-fulfillment, it will contribute to the (re)construction of a transformed, but rewarding, identity.

(DM) Jessica's isolation was on many levels. Her friends and family did not understand what it was like for her to have had a brain injury. Even before her accident, she had experienced some feelings of being an "outsider" because English was not her first language and she was a "mature" student. She had coped by immersing herself in her academic work and focusing on the fact that her tenure at the university was temporary. After the injury, she was unable to concentrate, focus, and work "as hard" as she used to. She had "lost" time and had to drop numerous courses. She reported that she felt ashamed and angry at herself. While one of my supervisors wanted me to focus on the issues of shame that are stereotypically associated with Asian American women, I knew that the feelings of hopelessness, self-blame and regret were intertwined with Jessica's brain injury. Her cultural upbringing and pride were being shaken by having to access services and "fail" at tasks at which she had easily excelled before the accident. But the injury itself had resulted in more concrete and literal thinking about her situation as well as perseveration; she perseverated on being unable to accomplish her goals and therefore felt more ashamed than she would have had she not been perseverating on her difficulties.

Jessica's religious beliefs had always been a source of comfort for her. But now, after her injury, she felt distant from God. She also did not want to "waste time" going to church, an activity she had engaged in regularly since her childhood, because her schoolwork was taking exponentially longer to complete than it did before her injury. She felt very alone.

Jessica's acceptance of her cognitive disability was the key to alleviation of some of her difficulties. Like JPR, Jessica did not initially feel comfortable identifying as someone with a disability. She reported that the only reason she used the office of rehabilitative services was because she had no other choice. She worried that someone would see her enter the office or ask her why she was able to receive extended time on her exams. She reported that she did not want others to think that she was trying to get away with doing less work or having it easier. She did not identify with the students in wheelchairs or with more obvious disabilities who were typically in the office of rehabilitative services.

Jessica did not enter psychotherapy until she "couldn't take it on her own." She was seen by the counseling center on campus after her Resident Advisor expressed concern about suicidality and only agreed to see me for therapy because she had heard that I was a "specialist in Neuropsychology" and could help her with her "brain problems." The fact that I was a South Asian American woman also helped the process. Jessica agreed that Taiwanese and Indians in Asia might not have a lot in common, but in the Midwestern American context, she felt that I understood her cultural, family, social and interpersonal issues more than a non-Asian woman would have understood. Jessica's multiple identities (Asian American, Woman, Person with Cognitive Disability, University Student, Therapy Client) played out in various ways to simultaneously isolate her and offer opportunities for making connection with a variety of support services. In therapy, we explored the diverse communities with which she identified and brainstormed about how best to connect with various parts of herself and her experiences to help her cope with the difficulties that she was experiencing. I underscored that identifying with one community did not mean disowning another community and that the process was dynamic and continuously open to reconfiguration.

Emotional Functioning

Women with TBI often enter a psychotherapeutic relationship when they are in emotional distress. The distress can take the form of a range of clinical and subsyndromal mood and anxiety disorders including depression, anxiety, and post-traumatic stress reactions such as emotional numbness. Some of the symptoms are directly related to the brain injury itself (e.g., specific sites of damage are associated with depression), while others are related to the cultural experience of living life after brain injury (e.g., adjusting to living in the United States as a woman with a disability) and still others to an individual's reactions to acquiring a brain injury and the associated losses mentioned above. Often through the therapeutic process the conceptualizations of loss turn into conceptualizations of new opportunities or new challenges, but working through and alleviating emotional distress is typically a major focus of therapy.

> (JPR) Two months after marriage and into grad school, my successes withered into a thicket of miseries. Increasingly, my husband was coming home from work to find me crumpled on the floor weeping uncontrollably. Nights offered little respite and were punctured by torrents of terrors and nightmares that hijacked me underneath a shield of blankets that I clutched tightly over my head until I felt safe enough to fall asleep. That I was "coming undone" came as a big disappointment and shock to my parents, who urged me to shape up before my husband got fed up and left. The injury had been trying for them too; always hoping for the best as they watched and cheered me to inch my way back to sit up, walk in the parallel bars, dress one-handedly, toilet, bathe and feed myself independently. To my parents, my rehabilitation was short of miraculous. When I walked down the aisle with my husband they were convinced that their "old vibrant" daughter was back. And so was I until my emotional state began to disintegrate. With my husband's support I soon sought help.
>
> While I was always privy to therapists and counselors, locking into the right fit would prove arduous. At the rehab hospital I was assigned a competent male psychologist who worked effectively with me in the bubble world of an in-patient. But upon discharge my discomfort in discussing matters of sexuality with a man and his disconnection from my pre-injured life drove me to re-connect with my female pre-injury counselor. Resuming ther-

apy with her was comforting and familiar but short-lived. By the fourth session it was clear that something was missing. For the first time in our five-year relationship, she was coming up short on guidance–ending every session suggesting that perhaps I ought to consult with my neurologist on this fear or that anxiety. I welcomed her honesty but found her frequent urgings to consult with my neurologist untenable. Living on a fixed income I was strapped financially, in no position to pay for ongoing sessions with both my counselor and my neurologist simply to save my marriage. Relentless in my quest I tried another venue, investigating support groups for TBI and those for violence, only to reaffirm my need for individual therapy.

Alone, once again I found myself isolated and terrified. That I had lost most of my close business friends post-injury and the fact that my former employer was unwilling to re-hire me at a wage comparable to my pre-injury salary just added to my terror. On the verge of losing my new husband and quitting grad school, my life was quickly spiraling downward when something extraordinary happened. Studying at the University of Chicago, I immersed myself in the philosophy of science focusing on the mind/brain relationship and soon stumbled upon Professor Jerre Levy, a woman brain researcher on campus. I absorbed her comments about my "smart" brain putting me in good stead for additional recovery like a wilted rose bush soaks up drops of rain after a drought. But when it came to my request for help in finding a therapist, she was hard-pressed. Upon further reflection, she referred me to WH.

When WH and I began our relationship in 1984, I was struggling with meaning. I told her that I had lost touch with what it "meant" to engage in everyday activities like ordering meat from a butcher, going to hear a concert, or reading a book. Everything, I complained, "felt like cardboard." Like someone who had forgotten the knack of riding a bicycle, I had lost the feel for life, didn't know how to get it back. What was worse was the fear. . . . Everything terrified me; the terror itself petrified me. I became obsessed with the idea that bugs were breeding and living all over my body.

Within the first year of therapy I devoted much of my therapy time to describing y fears and anxieties and to the hallucinogenic-like quality of my new reality. We uncovered problems with first time phobias and perseveration, and then created our own strategies for managing them. Meeting steadily two to three times a week, and paying for my sessions with Medicare, I gradually began to trust WH's understanding of the complexities of the damage to the right hemisphere of my brain. As we sleuthed back and forth through issues of my childhood and current day dilemmas that included an array of issues ranging from my risk for and terror of seizures to my frustrations trying to get into the physically inaccessible campus library, developmental questions concerning my biological clock pressed forward.

(WH) My work with JPR illustrates that psychotherapy with women who have experienced brain injuries is best viewed as an ongoing process. Short-term interventions may be helpful, but the complexity of the problems generally benefits from a lengthier intervention. In JPR's case it was necessary to unravel the threads that originated in her family of origin from those that stemmed from her traumatic experience. In turn, these had to be differentiated from the cognitive and physical sequelae of damage to the particular parts of her brain that had been injured.

Furthermore, the intensity of the trauma had far-reaching psychological consequences. Issues from JPR's childhood re-emerged and anything not fully resolved in the past was re-cycled with a vengeance. Her defense mechanisms and psychological buffers were eroded by the intensity of her pain and loss. Like anyone in the throes of extreme grief, her emotional resources were stretched to the limit. However, the circumstances made it difficult for her support network to perceive and respond to that grief.

Typically, parents, friends, and rehabilitation therapists (physical, speech and language, etc.) are focused on encouraging the person with a brain injury to "buck up," to tackle the task, to have a "stiff upper lip," to tough it out. This type of coaching is very positive with regard to getting a person to the point where they can experience a success in a particular domain (e.g., walking a certain distance). However, that domain is generally limited to a specific activity or behavior. Few individuals in the grieving person's world have the opportunity or time to acknowledge and explore the pain that she is experiencing. The data, however, are incontrovertible in showing that the degree to which a person is able to express and process the emotions surrounding a traumatic event is directly related to the degree to which that event has an impact on one's subsequent physical and mental health (e.g., Pennebaker, 1995). Psychotherapy has a unique contribution to make in this process and hence in the emotional, physical, and social adjustment to trauma.

Frequently compounding the grieving process in cases of brain injury, as exemplified in JPR's case, are the sequelae of post-traumatic stress symptoms. These can interfere with the emotional process of confronting the feelings and experiences in the context of a safe and supportive environment. Emotional numbing is a core characteristic of post-traumatic stress, as is a tendency to over-react to a variety of stimuli with catastrophic fear and anxiety. JPR struggled with this sense of numbness, experienced as a lack of "meaning" and emotional connection. She was also overcome by a host of fears that interfered with her daily activities and well-being in a variety of ways.

JPR's sense of numbness and her catastrophic anxiety were resolved in therapy through a patient but persistent process of acknowledging her feelings in all of their intensity and by providing a "holding environment" in which JPR could experience them. These experiences were bounded by feedback and discussion that put things gradually in perspective by reflecting upon and understanding the causes of the feelings, which diminished the tendency to generalize them to other situations.

(DM) Like JPR, Jessica also had to search for the appropriate therapeutic service provider. She wanted someone who understood the ways in which her brain injury could have affected her functioning. A male counselor at the University counseling center had worked with her for a few sessions and "it wasn't working out." He simultaneously referred her to the neuropsychological assessment practicum (a course which provides clinical training by combining didactic instruction with hands-on experience) and to me for psychotherapy. She was in the process of undergoing a neuropsychological assessment when she was referred to me and searching for answers to questions that she felt would clear up her problems. The neuropsychological test results did not prove to be as helpful as she and I had hoped they would be. For example, on tests of cognitive functioning, Jessica consistently scored in the average to low-average range with relative weaknesses in language and concentration. *The evaluator was unsure whether Jessica's difficulties were due to English being her second language or to changes due to her brain injury. There was no baseline information for comparison and furthermore, neuropsychological assessment measures are typically not normed on Asian American populations.* Experientially, Jessica felt "like a different person" after the injury and she expected to hear clear-cut findings that documented her difficulties and justified a biological basis for her problems. In therapy we examined what it meant for her to have a brain injury and how best to work with her strengths. We focused on alleviating her symptoms independent of the etiology of the difficulties.

Jessica was depressed and anxious. Sometimes she could not get out of bed. She had trouble concentrating, had lost interest in friends, and did not enjoy anything. My supervisor felt strongly that she should be on antidepressants but Jessica refused. Jessica was also anxious, especially around academic issues. She reported at least one panic attack during an exam, and often "went blank" when she was under pressure. She cried through sessions and cancelled others because she was too stressed. She reported that her symptomatology was new to her. She had been sad before and had experienced and overcome difficulties, but the TBI and her subsequent problems were of a magnitude that she had no measure for nor words to express. How would she earn her living, who would accept her and love her with her new difficulties, how would she pass her exams and graduate with the degree for which she had been working for so many years? She was overwhelmed with worries and could not sleep, further exacerbating her inability to concentrate and overwhelming feeling of fatigue.

In therapy, cognitive-behavioral techniques were used to help Jessica reduce her levels of anxiety and manage the stress she was experiencing. Relaxation techniques such as guided relaxation and breathing were also used. I encouraged her to meditate and go to church (sources of relaxation for her before her injury). We sat on the floor during therapy sessions and turned off the lights because the chairs made it difficult for her to relax and the fluorescent lights exacerbated her headaches. In addition, we explored her emotional reactions in the context of her current abilities and experiences and supportive psychotherapy was provided to encourage her to re-frame her distress in a more positive way, while at the same time acknowledging the losses and difficulties she was facing. She reported that the therapy session was the one hour a week that she could focus on herself and "be free to be herself."

Parenting

For JPR, the decision to become pregnant was a pivotal point in the therapeutic process. We end our discussion of social and emotional functioning in women with brain injury with JPR's narrative about deciding to and becoming a mother.

(JPR) Two years into therapy I felt more secure in my marriage and expressed an interest in becoming pregnant. The subject was a loaded one for me because it seemed as though I was still struggling to learn how to dress, transport and bathe myself. How could I accept responsibility for mothering a helpless infant when I hadn't yet fully learned to manage my own personal care? The issue became even more daunting when my search for resources and supports for mothers with disabilities came up empty. Once again WH and I negotiated new ground by discovering methods and frameworks for me to embrace that could help me shift the activity of mothering with the effects of TBI from the pathological realm, as something I shouldn't or couldn't do, to a framework of wholeness and normality; something at which I could thrive and succeed.

When I did get pregnant with my son, my neurologist assured me that carrying the baby during pregnancy and delivering safely would be no problem. In therapy we confronted the delicate issue of what it meant to be a mother when one was physically incapable of independently performing most parenting tasks such as bathing, dressing and diapering. This discussion of parenting competence, given my limitations due to the brain injury, was to be an ongoing one, starting with addressing how to meet the basic needs of the infant and evolving into a focus on my physical constraints at keeping up with a robust toddler and my anxieties as my son moved into school life. Irritating inconveniences like inaccessible preschools, disability unfriendly pediatricians and my loneliness as a mom with unique concerns were topics addressed and usually resolved positively in therapy. However, there never seemed to be enough time to adequately quell the lack of confidence I felt in my new role as mom when it came to my perceived reactions of his teachers, his friends and their mothers to my disabilities. My sense of entitlement as a mother was yet a long time to come.

As my son grew, so did I. Like any other parent I faced uncertainties in his development, but as time progressed it was becoming abundantly clear that underlying the secret fears I shared in therapy as a woman with a brain injury, there were two recurring themes in particular that like shifting tectonic plates, reconfiguring seaboard communities, these forces had the power to create new worlds as well as shatter current ones. For me were the nagging problems of "transportation/my mobility" and the residue of emotions I carried inside me regarding the "violence/my former fiancé's murder/my survival."

Living with serious mobility impairments due to paralysis on the left side of my body, coupled with my inability to resume driving, I experienced a wave of insecurities that often seemed to swamp the healing potential of therapy. It wasn't uncommon for me to be without reliable transportation to get to and from my home and the university. Unable to take the inaccessible public transit I relied on a form of special transit for the disabled that was limited in its scope of service and its reliability. Sometimes it seemed that all I was addressing in therapy was my frustration in attempting to get my baby around town or my ability to even get to and from therapy.

Shortly after my son was born we discovered in therapy that I was struggling to disassociate him from my dead former fiancé. For example, I kept calling my son by my late fiancé's name. Slowly, after some years in therapy, WH began to guide me back to Hawaii, occasionally referring to the night in the tent. But another few years would pass before we were able to relocate me back inside the tent. The process would be long, tender, and confusing, but in the end enormously rewarding—once we were able to clearly identify and understand the tenuous connections between the normal emotional baggage I carried pre-injury together with the fears I had resulting from the organic nature of the brain injury itself and those triggered by the post-traumatic stress from my assault and my fiancé's murder.

CONCLUSION AND RECOMMENDATIONS

We have used two exemplary cases of women who sustained a brain injury to illustrate the social and emotional sequelae of TBI and the issues that may be addressed in the context of psychotherapy. While JPR and Jessica had different histories and experiences, common themes emerged in their adjustment process. Social isolation included relating differently to friends and family, struggling with gaining access to services such as transportation or academic supports, and having difficulty finding appropriate therapeutic services. Emotional functioning included fear, anxiety, shame, hopelessness, helplessness, and posttraumatic stress symptoms. In working with both JPR and Jessica, their therapists had to try various strategies, be flexible in their approach and be open to novel ways of relating in a therapeutic relationship. We end with some suggestions that may help practitioners and women living with TBI facilitate the adjustment process.

Understanding the individual as belonging to multiple communities (e.g., based on class, gender, ethnicity, religion, sexual orientation, disability status) is one helpful way to increase access to support and services. The TBI might have changed the level of comfort and feelings of belonging within the various communities of which a woman is a member. Therefore, new alliances might need to be formed and explored. For some women, the disability community can be a source of empowerment. We recommend that therapists make themselves aware of the disability advocates and support groups in their geographic areas. The Brain Injury Association (www.biausa.org), a non-profit agency started by a woman with a child with TBI, has regional and state offices which can provide information on resources. The Health Resource Center for Women with Disabilities at the Rehabilitation Institute of Chicago can also be a good starting place. They regularly publish an educational newsletter, *Resourceful Woman*, which is free of charge and available by contacting hrcwd@rehabchicago.org. For women who do not identify as someone with a disability or who do not feel accepted by the disability community, alliance with other communities of support can be explored.

It is helpful for the therapist to have information from a neuro-psychological evaluation. While it is best to have current data, historical information might also be helpful in understanding the dynamics of various areas of functioning. A neuropsychological examination will typically address motor, sensory-perceptual, visuo-spatial, intellectual, cognitive flexibility, memory, language, and academic functioning. For example, standardized information about verbal, nonverbal, short-term and long-term memory would be helpful in tailoring psychotherapeutic goals realistically. While performance on time-constrained, standardized measures can serve as guidelines for designing appropriate interventions, *the ecological validity of neuropsychological assessment measures is not as strong as the reliability and content and construct validity.* For example, a woman who shows impairment on a test of facial recognition may or may not have difficulties recognizing "real world" faces in which other contextual cues are present. But a neuropsychological evaluation will give the therapist a reasonable idea about which areas are relative strengths and weaknesses for the woman with TBI. The neuropsychologist may also have creative ideas for intervention or have found out key social and historical information which will facilitate the psychotherapeutic process.

Exploring loss is often a fundamental task of psychotherapy with women with TBI and it is important to remember that there are individual differences in response to loss (e.g., Wortman & Silver, 1989). The therapist should be careful not to perpetuate assumptions about healthy or "normal" reactions to loss and to understand that the range of reactions may be much wider than is commonly assumed.

The specific context of the brain injury is also very important. For example, if the TBI is a result of violence, there might be posttraumatic stress responses such as emotional numbing. If the injury occurred in the context of interpersonal or domestic violence, then the woman might have had to deal with the police and medical professionals who do not investigate the context of the injury, and who are relatively insensitive to cultural norms about privacy and denial of violence. This can be particularly challenging if the individual is experiencing cognitive deficits and symptoms of post-traumatic stress.

The meaning of the injury to the individual is another issue that can affect responses. Awareness of compromised cognitive abilities that were fundamental to their previous lives (e.g., a teacher who has problems organizing verbal information) might not only pose obvious problems in returning to work, but can undermine the sense of self that the woman has created. Again, if these issues are not dealt with in a therapeutic setting, they can have a potent influence on an individual's ability to function effectively.

The cultural context of the injury should also be addressed. If the person has an observable disability (e.g., one that leads to the use of a wheelchair) issues (both positive and negative) about acceptance and societal attitudes might need to be addressed. Cultural beliefs may be internalized and affect the individual's self-concept. In addition, individuals from minority groups may have beliefs about health and competence that are not shared by the majority culture. In fact, given the diversity of experiences and worldviews regardless of ethnicity, systematically addressing beliefs about health, well-being, and competence will give the therapist a broader context for understanding the impact of the TBI.

In summary, the value of psychotherapy for women living with TBI is inestimable. This article has highlighted two of the most intractable problems women face, social isolation and emotional distress, that can be meaningfully addressed in psychotherapy, with important consequences for adjustment and well-being.

REFERENCES

Bergquist, T. F., Boll, T. J., Corrigan, J. D., Harley, J. P., Malec, J. F., Millis, S. R., & Schmidt, M. F. (1994). Neuropsychological rehabilitation: Proceedings of a consensus conference. *Journal of Head Trauma Rehabilitation, 9* (4), 50-61.

Cicerone, K. D. (1989). Psychotherapeutic interventions with traumatically brain-injured patients. *Rehabilitation Psychology, 34,* 105-114.

Corrigan, J. D., Smith-Knapp, K., & Granger, C.V. (1998). Outcomes in the first 5 years after traumatic brain injury. *Archives of Physical Medicine and Rehabilitation, 79,* 298-305.

Gill, C., Kirschner, K., & Reis, J. P. (1994). Health services for women with disabilities: Barriers and portals. In A. J. Dan (Ed.) *Reframing women's health: Multidisciplinary research and practice.* (pp. 357-366). Thousand Oaks, CA: Sage.

Heller, W. (1997). Emotion. In Banich, M. T., *Neuropsychology: The neural bases of mental function.* Boston: Houghton & Mifflin. 398-429.

Langer, K. G. (1992). Psychotherapy with the neuropsychologically impaired adult. *American Journal of Psychotherapy, 46* (4), 620-639.

Lewis, L. (1991). Role of psychological factors in disordered awareness. In Prigatano, G. P. & Schacter, D. L. (Eds.). *Awareness of deficit after brain injury: Clinical and theoretical issues.* (pp. 223-239). New York: Oxford University Press.

Lezak, M. D. (1995). *Neuropsychological assessment,* 3rd ed. New York: Oxford University Press.

Malec, J. F., & Basford, J. S. (1996). Postacute brain injury rehabilitation. *Archives of Physical Medicine and Rehabilitation, 77,* 198-207.

Mukherjee, D. (2000). *Multiple perspectives, one decision: An ethnographic study of life support withdrawal after severe traumatic brain injury.* Unpublished dissertation thesis, University of Illinois, Urbana-Champaign.

Mukherjee, D., Heller, W. & Alper, J. S. (2001). Social and institutional factors in adjustment to traumatic brain injury. *Rehabilitation Psychology, 46,* 82-99.

Pennebaker, James W. (Ed). (1995). *Emotion, disclosure, & health.* (pp. 671-702). Washington, DC: American Psychological Association.

Pollack, I. W. (1994). Individual psychotherapy. In Silver, J. M., Yudofsky, S. C., & Hales, R. E. (Eds.). *Neuropsychiatry of traumatic brain injury.* (pp. 671-702). Washington, D.C.: American Psychiatric Press, Inc.

Ponsford, J. with Sloan, S. & Snow, P. (1995). *Traumatic brain injury: Rehabilitation for everyday adaptive living.* Hove, East Sussex, UK: Lawrence Erlbaum Associates, Ltd.

Prigatano, G. P. (1994). Individuality, lesion location, and psychotherapy after brain injury. In Christensen, A. & Uzzell, B. P. (Eds). *Brain injury and neuropsychological rehabilitation: International perspectives.* (pp. 173-186). Hillsdale, NJ: Lawrence Erlbaum Associates.

Prigatano, G. P. (1999). Motivation and awareness in cognitive rehabilitation. In Stuss, D. T., Winocur, G., & Robertson, I. H. (Eds.) *Cognitive neurorehabilitation.* New York: Cambridge University Press.

Prigatano, G. P. & Schacter, D. L. (1991). *Awareness of deficit after brain injury: Clinical and theoretical issues*. New York: Oxford University Press.

Rehabilitation of persons with traumatic brain injury. NIH consensus statement. Online 1998 Oct 26-28; 16(1): (pp. 1-41). http://www.nichd.nih.gov/publications/pubs/traumatic/NIH_Consensus_Statement.htm.

Rosenthal, M. & Ricker, J. (2000). Traumatic brain injury. In Frank, R. G. & Elliott, T. R. (Eds). *Handbook of rehabilitation psychology*. (pp. 49-74). Washington, DC: American Psychological Association.

Stewart, J. E. (2000). *Ascribed and acquired identities: Women's collective renegotiation of social and personal identity following brain injury*. Unpublished dissertation, University of Illinois, Urbana-Champaign.

U.S. General Accounting Office. (1998). *Traumatic brain injury: Programs supporting long-term services in selected states*. (Report, GAO/HEHS-98-55). Washington, D.C.: Author.

Wortman, C. B. & Silver, R. C. (1989). The myths of coping with loss. *Journal of Consulting and Clinical Psychology*, *57*, 349-357.

African American Women Living with HIV/AIDS: Mental Health Issues

Sonja Feist-Price
Lynda Brown Wright

SUMMARY. The number of African American women infected with the human immunodeficiency virus (HIV) and the acquired immunodeficiency syndrome (AIDS) is alarming. As with any other reaction to catastrophe or life threatening diseases, from the time African American women first learn of their HIV-positive serostatus they navigate various levels of acceptance and a multitude of mental health issues. This manuscript explores these issues related to African American women with HIV/AIDS. Careful consideration is given to the stages of adjustment and related mental health challenges that women might experience. Also explored are the reciprocal impact of children, other family members and significant others on the mental health status of African American women living with HIV/AIDS. Implications for clinical practice are also identified. *[Article copies available for a fee from The Haworth Document Delivery Service: 1-800-HAWORTH. E-mail address: <getinfo@haworthpressinc.*

Sonja Feist-Price is affiliated with the Department of Special Education and Rehabilitation Counseling, University of Kentucky. Lynda Brown Wright is affiliated with the Department of Educational and Counseling Psychology, University of Kentucky.

Address correspondence to: Sonja Feist-Price, Department of Special Education and Rehabilitation Counseling, University of Kentucky, 224 Taylor Education Building, Lexington, KY 40506-0001 (E-mail: smfeis@pop.uky.edu).

[Haworth co-indexing entry note]: "African American Women Living with HIV/AIDS: Mental Health Issues." Feist-Price, Sonja, and Lynda Brown Wright. Co-published simultaneously in *Women & Therapy* (The Haworth Press, Inc.) Vol. 26, No. 1/2, 2003, pp. 27-44; and: *Women with Visible and Invisible Disabilities: Multiple Intersections, Multiple Issues, Multiple Therapies* (ed: Martha E. Banks, and Ellyn Kaschak) The Haworth Press, Inc., 2003, pp. 27-44. Single or multiple copies of this article are available for a fee from The Haworth Document Delivery Service [1-800-HAWORTH, 9:00 a.m. - 5:00 p.m. (EST). E-mail address: getinfo@haworthpressinc.com].

27

KEYWORDS. Mental health, HIV/AIDS, African American women, adjustment

The impact of HIV and AIDS among African American women has been devastating. Since the beginning of the epidemic, over 100,000 cases of AIDS have been reported among women, and 57% of these cases were among African American women (Centers for Disease Control and Prevention [CDC], 2000). Presently, 1 in 160 African American women are infected with HIV, and in 1999 alone, almost two-thirds (63%) of all women reported with AIDS were African American (CDC, 2000). Among all AIDS cases reported for African American women since the epidemic began, 42% were as a result of injection drug use and 38% resulted from heterosexual contact (CDC, 2001). Among these women, 43% were in their 30s, 22% were in their 40s, and 21% were in their 20s. A large number of women infected heterosexually were infected through sex with an injection drug user (IDU), and most women were unaware of their partners' risk factors.

Nearly 90% of African American women infected are in the prime of their lives, and in their childbearing years. The diagnosis of HIV is perceived as a death sentence and results in a multitude of mental health issues. Not only are these women impacted by their HIV-positive diagnosis, families are deeply affected as well. According to Havens and Mellins (1996), HIV/AIDS commonly occur in families already struggling with substance abuse, psychiatric disorder, and multi-generational histories of victimization and trauma. Therefore, the added burden of HIV on a struggling family system is overwhelming to say the very least.

Scant literature exist regarding African American women living with HIV/AIDS, most of which is focused on medication and the multiple barriers to health care that confront these women. Literature has just begun to explore psychosocial issues associated with women living with HIV/AIDS. Ethnic and cultural differences among women infected with HIV mean different psychological reactions and require specific kinds of family support. Because the mental health of women can exacerbate symptoms of the disease (McCain & Zeller, 1994), psychosocial adaptation and coping strategies are extremely important for African American women living with HIV/AIDS. In what follows we will discuss mental health issues related to African American women with HIV and AIDS. In so doing, we will explore the stages of adjustment and related mental health issues that occur during each stage. We will also address the impact of family and significant others on the mental health status of African American women living with HIV and AIDS, and explore implications for clinical practice.

OVERVIEW

A diagnosis of HIV-positive has social and psychological implications that are far reaching for women. In comparison to their HIV-positive male counterparts, women with HIV must deal with more stigma (Angell, 1991), a significant decline in quality of life (Atkins & Hancock, 1993; Sowell & Seals, 1997), and a greater incidence of psychopathology and psychiatric morbidity (Mellers et al., 1994; Vedhara, Schifitto, & McDermott, 1999). These issues are even more conspicuous for African American women living with HIV/AIDS. Researchers have noted that African American women living with HIV/AIDS reported more emotional distress and psychiatric symptoms as well as greater difficulty in coping with the disease (Bedimo, Bennett, Kissinger, & Clark, 1998; Kalichman, Williams, Cherry, Belcher, & Nachumson, 1998; Orr, Celentano, Santelli, & Burwell, 1994) than their HIV-positive male counterparts. For example, Van Servellen et al. (1998) studied HIV-positive women, many of whom where African American, and observed major levels of distress, anxiety, depression, limits on normal functioning, and disturbances to physical well-being. Linn, Poku, Cain, Holzapfel, and Crawford (1995) conducted a study on psychosocial outcomes of HIV illness in African American male and female clients. Results indicated that African American women living with HIV were more depressed than African American men regardless of the stage of their disease, had less support than men, and had low morale. In a study on perceived health, HIV illness, and mental distress in African American women attending AIDS counseling centers (Bright, Arnett, Blair, & Bayona, 1996), respondents indicated involvement in high-risk activities, depression, a lack of social support, stress, and under-recognition of their disease. They also requested assistance in building and maintaining social support networks. African American women who contract HIV from IDU, which is the primary mode of transmission among this population, experience even higher levels of psychiatric distress than women who contracted HIV from heterosexual contact and male HIV-positive injection drug users (Rabkin et al., 1997).

Fatigue is a common symptom of HIV that has been associated with psychological problems. While fatigue is consistent among all persons infected with HIV, research has shown that women living with HIV were significantly more likely to report fatigue than men (Breitbart, McDonald, Rosenfeld, Monkman, & Passik, 1998). In a study by Van Servellen et al. (1998), fatigue was the most frequently reported symptom and the worst symptom for 98% of women living with HIV. While fatigue is thought to be consistent among women across ethnic groups, differences between African American and White women have been reported on emotional distress and psychiatric symptoms.

African American women living with HIV/AIDS are overwhelmed with severe and multiple illnesses, decreased cognitive functioning, devastating weaknesses and limitations, weight loss, fevers, cancers, opportunistic infections, disfigurement, blindness, pain, and psychiatric disorders. They must also face the concomitant losses of health, fitness, attractiveness, strength, independence, family, and friends. The overwhelming issues of HIV/AIDS cause these women to review their life experiences and examine their values, beliefs, sexual behaviors, views of death and dying, relationship development, fears, hopes, dreams, religion, and more (Atkins & Hancock, 1993).

Some of the issues associated with the mental health status of African American women are consistent with the stages of psychosocial adjustment and acceptance. Nichols (1985) recognized a four-stage psychosocial process specific to persons with HIV/AIDS: initial crisis-catastrophic effect, transitional state, deficiency state, and preparation for death. Havens and Mellins (1996) developed a model that they use for HIV-infected women and affected children and families, which organizes HIV illness into specific predictable stages, taking into account the dynamic course of HIV illness. Among these stages are the diagnosis of HIV infection, illness progression, late stage illness, death, and family reconfiguration. Dunbar and Mueller (1995) developed a model for women living with HIV/AIDS known as *The Process of Transcendence.* Included are reckoning with death, life affirmation, creation of meaning, self-affirmation, and redefining relationships. Individually, none of these models appear to adequately address the myriad of mental health issues that are confronted by African American women living with HIV/AIDS and their families. The process proposed by Nicholas (1985) identifies the psychosocial stages of adjustment of all persons with HIV/AIDS. However, recognition is not given to the issues specific to women, particularly African American women, who experience innumerable mental health issues associated with their HIV-positive status. The model by Havens and Mellins (1996) provides an excellent overview of issues that are confronted by children and other family members that are affected by HIV/AIDS, but provides limited information on how persons overcome the mental health issues associated with their diagnosis. The Dunbar and Mueller (1995, 1998) model of tran scendence, implicitly and explicitly communicated that within each woman exists the ultimate ability to *transcend* having HIV/AIDS, and all the negativity that accompanies this diagnosis. Additionally, this model provides a sound theoretical framework with which to understand mental health issues among women. However, scant information exists on the impact of HIV/AIDS on family and significant others. It is the belief of these authors that children, family and significant others must be included in order to have a holistic conceptual understanding of the mental health issues of African American women with HIV/AIDS. Collectively, these models provide detailed information in which to better understand African American women with HIV and their families. Using Dunbar and Mueller's model as the primary theoretical framework, and adding supplemental information from the models of Havens and Mellins, and Nichols, we will explore mental health issues associated with African American women with HIV/AIDS.

MENTAL HEALTH ISSUES AND STAGES OF ADJUSTMENT

Prior to one's HIV-positive diagnosis, most African American women communicated thinking, "It could not happen to me," even though they were aware of the modes of HIV transmission and they were involved in a number of high-risk behaviors (e.g., injection drug users, sex exchange, unprotected sex) (Russell & Smith, 1999). Deering (1993) believed that these women might have been in denial as well as underestimated their personal vulnerability. Siegal, Ravels, and Gorey (1998) reported that the major obstacles to women recognizing their at-risk status is due to a lack of understanding of risk behavior patterns, ignorance of their sexual partner's risk practices, a lack of information on HIV-related symptoms, and perceived invulnerability to infection. Therefore, shock and denial are the most common responses experienced by most African American women when initially diagnosed as having HIV. Table 1 presents a description of the relevant characteristics of stages of adjustment for African American women.

In the Dunbar and Mueller (1995) model titled *The Process of Transcendence,* women are thought to experience emotions that vary from despair to fulfillment on a path that is conceptualized as spiraling rather than linear. The evolutionary process of transcendence is individualized and unique to each woman, with past experiences, perceived sense of control, role integration, social support, and spirituality as core factors influencing the transcendent process. While African American women living with HIV/AIDS experience horrendous challenges related to their physical and mental health, they are eventually able to understand their HIV-status as a growth-producing experience that helped to strengthen their sense of self.

Reckoning with Death

In everyday life, it is common to set goals for the future, typically without doubting that one's life will progress to old age. Yet for African American women diagnosed with HIV, many of whom are between the ages of 20 and 39, future planning shifts drastically. Life has more of a finite meaning and becomes far more precious. One's initial reaction to her HIV status begins with shock, denial and despair, and is characterized by a state of disconnection from the world (Dunbar & Mueller, 1995, 1998; Nicholas, 1985). The process of reckoning with death is

TABLE 1. Stages of Adjustment Among African American Women

Stage of Adjustment	Description
Reckoning with death	Marks the beginning of healing and acceptance. Initial reaction begins with shock, denial, despair, and disconnecting. Life is perceived as finite.
Life affirmation	Begins with a realization of the choice to live or to give up, and is marked by a "fighting spirit" and a renewed sense of self-efficacy.
Creation of meaning	Alters conceptions of life and creates new meaning by examining life, working through unresolved past issues, and reframing negative life experiences.
Self-affirmation and redefining relationships	Involves reconnecting with others, making amends, and saying good-bye. Requires examining relationships and redefining each based on contributions, and reconnecting with the world and giving back to society. Concludes with tying together loose ends and making final plans.

very painful and is associated with feelings of hopelessness, depression, and rage. These feelings might be magnified and sustained as a result of the isolation most African American women usually experience after initially receiving the diagnosis. This baseline isolation can impede access to moral support from family, and social and mental health supports from health and human service providers (Havens & Mellins, 1996). In a study on HIV infected African American women, Bedimo et al. (1998) observed difficulty in disclosing HIV status to both family and significant others. The hidden or secretive nature of African American women diagnosed with HIV usually stems from fear of rejection and the stigma associated with the disease (Russell & Smith, 1999), and much of the shame and stigma that African American women feel results from being infected with a disease associated with promiscuity, illicit drug use, and death (Land, 1994). In addition, guilt and shame about behaviors associated with the acquisition of HIV can impede effective communication about their HIV diagnosis, further isolating women from social supports (Havens & Mellins, 1996).

Reckoning with death for African American women with HIV first requires engaging in self-analysis to examine beliefs, fears, strengths and desires, past choices, attitudes, and behavior. It is a time of reevaluation that can bring the individual to fuller conscious recognition of who they are as a person. The process initially involves feelings of confusion, distress, and self-devaluation (Nichols, 1985). The self-reflection that is involved can deepen their sense of psychological chaos and can seem counterproductive. African American women living with HIV/AIDS usually experience lowered self-esteem, shifts in identity and values, as well as estrangement and isolation from families and loved ones.

Reckoning with feelings of death is also critical to making choices that lead to transcendence. As women reckon with the realities of death, some of the feelings that they experience include dependence, fear, sadness, vulnerability, distrust, depression, hopelessness and anger (Kubler-Ross, 1969; Nichols, 1983, 1985). According to Dunbar and Mueller (1995), women might feel a lack of self-efficacy, a sense of helplessness, and self-loathing, each of which can lead to self-destructive behaviors. In accordance with the process of transcendence, reckoning with death marks the beginning of healing, and acceptance of having an HIV-positive diagnosis.

The culmination of emotions emanating from learning of their HIV-positive status can lead to either the internalizing or projecting of feelings. Internalized feelings lead to withdrawal, depression, and sometimes suicide attempts. Women who project their feelings onto others may have anger that is directed towards family members, loved ones, and caretakers. Additionally, the overwhelming emotional reaction to an HIV-positive diagnosis can lead to sexually acting out, or an increase in intravenous drug use. However, researchers have indicated that the psychiatric distress that African American women living with HIV experience is correlated with the mode of HIV transmission. For example, Goggin, Engelson, Rabkin, and Kotler (1998) observed that women whose HIV risk factor was sexual contact were more than five times more likely to be diagnosed with Hypoactive Sexual Desire Disorder than women who contracted HIV through IDU. Hence, as African American women make a mental transition from a state of despair to acceptance of their HIV-positive status, their mental health status is very erratic. However, for many African American women, a strong sense of isolation accompanies the introspection that is required to accept one's HIV status. The ability to directly confront issues associated with their HIV-positive status usually involves isolation from others and the fear of tomorrow. Moving through this process is the beginning of an awareness of one's own power and inner strength. Also, African American women might reckon with the thought of dying whenever they have symptoms of AIDS or when friends or partners have these symptoms.

In addition to coping with the realities of testing HIV-positive, African American women living with HIV must also deal with the external realities of life, such as feeding their children, going to work, and managing their health care. Many women deal with this paradox by putting their day-to-day functions on "automatic pilot" while directing psychic energy inward (Dunbar & Mueller, 1995). The recognition and resolution of death as the inevitable consequence of HIV/AIDS requires African American women to shift from future-focus to present-focus, which typically involves reordering priorities. For example, Russell and Smith (1999) conducted a preliminary phenomenological study describing the experiences of five African American women diagnosed with HIV. Results from their research indicated that these women lived with no future, just a "now"; and their lives consisted of only the present and death. This awakened recognition of death resulting from an HIV-positive diagnosis sustains reconstruction of time (Dunbar & Mueller, 1998). Time becomes very precious and many African American women living with HIV/AIDS who were involved in unhealthy or nonproductive behavior see their status as an opportunity to "get their acts together."

As the medical sequelae of HIV illness increase, so does the pressure to communicate with family members about their illness, and the need to plan for children's future. According to Havens and Mellins (1996), mothers with advancing HIV illness commonly have difficulty communicating effectively with their children about their illness. For example, in a study of 40 HIV-infected mothers, Mellins and Ehrhardt (1995) found that the majority had not disclosed their serostatus to their children, particularly when children were 12 or younger.

Life Affirmation

At some point during the process of introspection there comes a realization of the choice to live or to give up, and life takes on a different meaning (Dunbar & Mueller, 1998). This begins life affirmation. "All you can think about when you're first diagnosed is anger and sadness. Then you've got to make a choice. I chose to stick around . . ." (Kurth, 1993, p. 67). Dunbar and Mueller (1998) espoused that women who make a conscious decision to live a full life despite their HIV-positive status sometimes encounter the greatest amount of grief when reckoning with death. However, after reckoning with the realities of having a disease that ultimately ends in death, women commit to life redefined (Dunbar & Mueller, 1995). African American women living with HIV/AIDS who recognize their own strength and choose survival are moving through the levels of transcendence. This component is marked by a "fighting spirit" and a desire and willingness to regain control over life. Actions that manifest this sense of control include active involvement in the care of realities, and social activism. These behaviors emerge from a renewed sense of self-efficacy, and in turn, they enhance and strengthen one's sense of self.

Dunbar and Mueller (1995) stated that as a result of having affirmed their will to live, many women have turned frustration into action in order to help themselves and others, and describe this component in terms of their frustration with the unresponsive medical community and social service system. However, the desire for action does not occur as quickly as the women infected would like, especially because time is of the essence for these women.

Creation of Meaning

Once a woman has chosen life, it is necessary to alter conceptions of how long they will live and what this life will be like, oftentimes with finding new meaning. Dunbar and Mueller (1998) identified a period of life review as the first step in finding new purpose. This stage involves examining and working through unresolved past issues, which means reviewing past histories of trauma and abuse and reframing these painful incidents into experiences that have helped to shape them into stronger women. The initial stage of this process can be very painful. It involves letting go of previously held goals and dreams, and forces them to examine based on quality of life rather than longevity. African American women usually experience a resurgence of spirituality, a redefined sense of self, and a renewed sense of purpose (Cohen, 1990). Nichols (1985) described this stage as one in which African American women have a new stable identity characterized by the acceptance of HIV/AIDS and the limitations associated with this illness. Many women describe a greater appreciation for life, having come through the grief.

Self-Affirmation and Redefining Relationships

It is very difficult to discuss what occurs in the stage of self-affirmation for African American women with HIV/AIDS in isolation of their relationships. This is particularly because self-affirmation and self-affirming behaviors for these women require that they examine the positive and negative aspects of each relationship, and redefine each relationship in light of the attributes that contribute to quality of life.

African American women at this stage of transcendence experience a more positive sense of self. Some women view their positive status as a time to take care of themselves, whereas in the past their focus had been on the care and well-being of others. This also requires accepting care from others and sometimes asking others for help. Self-affirmation is also a time of life review, which sometimes involves reconnecting with others, making amends, and saying good-bye. These women cope with this disease by living one day at a time, and with a reassessment of the values of courage, commitment, concern for others, and an appreciation for quality rather than quantity of life (Dunbar & Mueller, 1995). In addition, "individuals begin to feel less victimized by life and less egocentric, deriving satisfaction from altruistic and community activities" (Cohen, 1990, p. 100). Ultimately, African American women living with HIV/AIDS who are on the path of transcendence grow to accept death in the context of accepting life as they have lived it.

With their new outlook on life, African American women must work on resolving and re-clarifying relationships with family, friends, and acquaintances (Dunbar & Mueller, 1998). This component also refers to the knowledge of one's profound connection to the world. It incorporates the dualities of *strength* in the context of need for help and support; *insight*, often greater than those who provide help; and *aloneness*, yet connection to all living things (Dunbar & Mueller, 1995), which requires the ability to both give and take. For women living with HIV, this connection takes many forms. For some, this connection is within a small community–the neighborhood picnics, PTA meetings, church, etc. For other women the community is larger. It is within this stage that African American women embrace the concept of public speaking and educating others regarding the behavioral risks of HIV/AIDS. Additionally, women in this stage begin to see themselves as survivors rather than victims.

From the day of diagnosis, African American women with HIV/AIDS are confronted with the terminal nature of their illness. Women might require assistance in completing unfinished business, tying together loose ends, writing wills, and making plans for their funerals. In the final stage of HIV illness, loss of parental functioning becomes paramount as the care of younger children might be left to older adolescents or young adult family members (Havens & Mellins, 1996). At this stage, parents should identify and designate friends or family members as guardians of their children, and identify appropriate and safe times associated with their physical and mental health when primary care of children should be shifted. Havens and Mellins (1996) reported that an existing marker for when the care of children is transferred is of greatest importance in those parents who develop AIDS-related dementia. Often, children experience the changes in their mothers' mental status without a clear understanding of the etiology or implications of these changes. If parents develop AIDS-related psychiatric disorders (such as mania or psychosis), their disinhibited or disorganized behavior can be dangerous to children in their care.

IMPACT OF SIGNIFICANT OTHERS ON MENTAL HEALTH

Just as African American women living with HIV/AIDS are impacted by the disease, so are family members and significant others. These women must cope with mental health issues associated with their illness as do their family members and significant others, especially since it is from these networks that African American women with HIV/AIDS must draw strength and support. In addition to being informed of the HIV-positive status of their loved ones, family members must also cope with the terminal effects of the virus, and the possibility of having to be physically and financially responsible for meeting the health care needs of their loved ones and their children.

Some of the stress African American women living with HIV/AIDS experience is partially due to the impact of their diagnosis on their children. The cyclical impact and effects that African American mothers living with HIV have on their children and vice versa has profound health and mental health implications. For example, according to Key and DeNoon (1996), children with an HIV-positive mother were significantly more withdrawn, had more problems with attention, and were more frequently depressed. Additionally, compared with children with asymptomatic mothers, the children of symptomatic mothers were significantly more anxious and/or depressed. As such, a mother's concern about the mental status of her children compounds the physical and mental health-related problems. According to Land (1994), if children are infected as a result of the mother's HIV-positive status, the guilt can be overwhelming. If their children are healthy, women feel guilty about the prospect that they will die and leave their children behind.

The placement of children following the death of their mother is a particularly challenging task for families and all persons involved. Havens and Mellins (1996) identified this process as *permanency planning*, and concluded that communication about HIV illness and permanency planning is closely intertwined with difficulties in one area being reflected in the other. Effective permanency planning requires the disclosure of HIV-positive status to the individuals selected to assume the children's care. Havens and Mellins (1996) found that "family-based permanency planning that actively involves the children, particularly teenagers, is much more likely to have a successful outcome than that which ignores or excludes the affected young people" (p. 220).

Disclosing one's HIV-positive status to other family members and significant others is a very difficult process, especially for African American women who struggle more than White HIV-positive females and HIV-positive African American males (Bedimo et al., 1998; Evans, Kell, Bond, & McRae, 1998). Disclosure means informing parents, children, siblings, extended family members, and friends about one's HIV status. Responses to and feelings of families of African American women with HIV vary tremendously. Cohen (1990) explained that families and significant others experience feelings that are very similar to those of African American women infected with HIV/AIDS. Bonuck (1993) identified six possible reactions of family members to a loved one's diagnosis: social stigma and isolation, fear of contagion, fear of infection, fear of abandonment, guilt, and psychological and physical fatigue.

Much of the social stigma that African American family members experience comes from their communities. Many African American communities have been reluctant to acknowledge the threat of AIDS. Land (1994) believes that this reluctance is due to the majority culture's tendency to associate Black communities with deviant behavior, and the conservative stance that the church takes on matters of sexual behavior and drug use. Additionally, acknowledging the existence of HIV/AIDS and its methods of transmission tends to affirm racist stereotypes associating African Americans communities with such criminal behavior as substance abuse and prostitution. As a result, the lack of support in many African American communities to infected women and affected families causes these individuals and families to secretively shoulder the caregiving responsibilities.

Family members are usually placed in the role of caregivers for African American women infected with HIV/AIDS. There are times when family members are required to provide health care and psychological support to African American women who are gravely ill. Psychological and physical fatigue are common reactions among family members with caregiving responsibilities of women with HIV. The manifestations of HIV/AIDS present a myriad of physical and psychological challenges. As a result, family members spend a significant amount of time visiting social service agencies, medical specialists, and health care facilities for assistance with treatment and medication. Because African American families have a strong desire and commitment to care for their own, family members are the primary care takers who assist with all activities of daily living of their loved ones. These day-to-day demands are overwhelming if respite is not available from other family members or community resources.

In order to provide optimal assistance and sustain the support of African American women infected, support services within and outside of the community are required to assist caregivers. Also, families must be relentless in their pursuits of seeking requisite resources to aid in the care of their loved one and to assist with the day-to-day caretaking responsibilities. Financial assistance programs, individual and family therapy, support groups, and home-care services are only a few resources that are essential to meeting the physical and mental health needs of African American women with HIV/AIDS. These resources help to alleviate stress on the women infected and caregivers, and contribute to optimal family structuring.

Bereavement, in conjunction with family reconfiguration, is very important process that begins when women enter the final stage of AIDS and persist long after the loved one has died (Havens & Mellins, 1996). With parental death, grieving children and adolescents help to reconfigure existing families, during a time when extended families are also mourning the loss of the loved one. Much of the social support services that were available to families by virtue of the parent's HIV/AIDS diagnosis either diminish or disappear following the parent's death. Usually, African American children and adolescents who are orphaned by AIDS are moving from one situation of poverty to another, with the responsibility for the care of these children falling on families with limited financial resources. In situations where children and adolescents move into non-family foster care, they are required to make the difficult adjustment into new and unfamiliar families with life styles that are sometimes totally different from those to which they are accustomed. Both reconfigured and foster families must assume the care and responsibility of children who are experiencing substantial emotional trauma and behavioral problems, and some of whom exhibit failing academic function.

IMPLICATIONS FOR PRACTICE

Service efforts for African American women living with HIV/AIDS must be systematically and carefully designed (Land, 1994). Clinicians working with women infected and families affected by HIV must draw from service models emphasizing empowerment in outreach and psychoeducation, both of which should be conceived and designed within the context of African American women's culture. Culturally relevant treatment should provide messages that are tailored to the specific needs and concerns of this population. Clinicians must also have expertise in the mental health concerns associated with the course of HIV illness among African American women and be aware of issues associated with substance abuse and other high-risk behavior specific to these women.

Culturally sensitive programs should be designed to decrease isolation, self-blame, and guilt. Support groups have the potential to empower African American women living with HIV/AIDS by reducing isolation and facilitating the development of strong relationships among members. Because time is required to build authentic relationships, groups should be ongoing. Sessions should be interactive, using techniques such as behavior rehearsal, role-plays, and guided imagery. Participants should be encouraged to teach and listen to one another. In addition to group content, group cohesion is very crucial to the success of the support group, which should be contextually relevant to the lives of the participants. To the extent possible, an HIV-positive African American woman should serve as a co-facilitator of the group. The group process should not be limited to designated parameters, but include the varying issues of participants involved.

Clinicians might also be required to assist African American women with preparing for death. This can be done by developing video or audio tapes, letters, and/or poems to leave for their loved ones. Women might also want to discuss their funeral arrangements. As African American women prepare for death, clinicians should encourage them to involve at least one family member or significant other with whom they feel close and who would like to be informed of their wishes. Planning for final arrangements can be a very difficult and emotionally draining experience; however, women should be encouraged to openly discuss their thoughts and feelings about death and dying, and of becoming dependent on others for care.

Individual therapy and support groups should also be formulated and available for children, other family members and significant others as well. These resources are especially important because these are the individuals who are called upon to provide caregiving tasks, and deal with many of the physical and mental health related issues that confront African American women living with HIV/AIDS. As such, culturally sensitive services are needed. Land (1994) proposed support groups for caregivers that provide information on the disease course and care of the HIV-infected individual, as well as other social supports that might be helpful. As mentioned above, these groups should fit the needs of those involved and should not be limited by any set parameters.

Because of the mental health implications that exist for children, it is important that they are placed in a therapeutic setting that would allow them to process their feelings and concerns. This can include individual therapy or family therapy that includes their mother. Additionally, children would benefit from being in social situations that involve other children whose mothers are living with HIV/AIDS. In addition to children being able to develop friendships, they are also able to understand that there are others who are living with similar situations.

CONCLUSION

African American women are confronted with myriad physical and mental health issues after learning of their HIV-positive diagnoses. Not only does having this disease affect the mental health of these women, but their mental health has been proven to have an impact on the course of the disease (Land, 1994). For example, depressed women are far more likely to get colds which can ultimately lead to pneumonia. Therefore, it is extremely important that clinicians have an understanding of the various issues that exist and have a working knowledge of ways to assist these women in navigating psychosocial pitfalls that usually accompany HIV. Hence, mental health clinicians working with African American women living with HIV/AIDS and their families must have the following specialized skills:

1. an understanding of the natural history of HIV infection in women, including potential nervous system effects of illness progression;
2. an understand of psychiatric co-morbidity in African American women who are drug dependent; and
3. an empathetic understanding of the impact of HIV on family structure and mental health functioning.

Clinicians with these requisite skills can assist in enhancing the quality of life for African American women living with HIV/AIDS, their children, other family members and significant others.

REFERENCES

Angell, M. (1991). A dual approach to the AIDS epidemic. *The New England Journal of Medicine, 324,* 1498-1500.

Atkins, B., & Hancock, A. (1993). AIDS: A continuing challenge for rehabilitation professionals. *American Rehabilitation, 19*(3), 30-34.

Bedimo, A. L., Bennett, M., Kissinger, P., & Clark, R. A. (1998). Understanding barriers to condom usage among HIV infected African American women. *Journal of the Association of Nursing AIDS Care, 9,* 48-58.

Bonuck, K. A. (1993). AIDS and families: Cultural, psychosocial, and functional impacts. *Social Work in Health Care, 18*(2), 75-89.

Breitbart, W., McDonald, M. V., Rosenfeld, B., Monkman, N. D., & Passik, S. (1998). Fatigue in ambulatory AIDS patients. *Journal of Pain Symptom Management, 15,* 159-167.

Bright, P. E., Arnett, D. K., Blair, C., & Bayona, M. (1996). Gender and ethnic differences in survival in a cohort of HIV positive clients. *Ethnicity and Health, 1*, 77-85.

Centers for Disease Control and Prevention (2000). *HIV/AIDS among African Americans. National Center for HIV, STD and TB Prevention.* Available: www.cdc.gov/hiv/pubs/facts/afam.htm.

Centers for Disease Control and Prevention (2001). *U.S. HIV and AIDS cases reported through June 2000,* Mid year edition Vol. 12, No. 1. Available: www.cdc.gov/hiv/stats/hasr1201.htm.

Cohen, M. A. A. (1990). Biopsychosocial approach to the human immunodeficiency virus epidemic. *General Hospital Psychiatry, 12*, 98-123.

Deering, M. J. (1993). Designing health promotion approaches to high-risk adolescents through formative research with youth and parents. *Public Health Reports, 108(Suppl. 1)*, 68-77.

Dunbar, H., & Mueller, C. W. (1995). Women and HIV: The process of transcendence. *Arete, 20*, 6-15.

Dunbar, H. T., & Mueller, C. W. (1998). Psychological and spiritual growth in women living with HIV. *Social Work, 43*, 144-155.

Evans, B. A., Kell, P. D., Bond, R. A., & McRae, K. D. (1998). Racial origin, sexual lifestyle, and genital infection among women attending a genitourinary medicine clinic in London. *Sexual Transmitted Infections, 74*, 45-49.

Goggin, K., Engelson, E. S., Rabkin, J. G. & Kotler, D. P. (1998). The relationship of mood, endocrine, and sexual disorders in human immunodeficiency virus positive (HIV +) women: An exploratory study. *Psychosomatic Medicine, 60*, 11-16.

Havens, J. F., & Mellins, C. A. (1996). Mental health issues in HIV-affected women and children. *International Review of Psychiatry, 8*, 217-225.

Kalichman, S. C., Williams, E. A., Cherry, C., Belcher, L., & Nachumson, D. (1998). Sexual coercion, domestic violence, and negotiating condom use among low-income African American women. *Journal of Women's Health, 7*, 371-378.

Key, K., & DeNoon, D. J. (1996, November 4). Depression in children with HIV infected mothers may be overlooked. *AIDS Weekly Plus.* 20-22.

Kubler-Ross, E. (1969). *On death and dying.* New York: Macmillan.

Kurth, A. (1993). *Until the cure: Caring for women with HIV.* New Haven, CT: Yale University Press.

Land, H. (1994). AIDS and women of color. *Families in Society: The Journal of Contemporary Human Services.* Milwaukee: Families International.

Linn, J. G., Poku, K. A., Cain, V. A., Holzapfel, K. M., & Crawford, D. E. (1995). Psychosocial outcomes of HIV illness in male and female African American clients. *Social Work in Health Care, 21*, 43-60.

McCain, N. L., & Zeller, J. (1994). Research priorities for psychosocial aspects of nursing care in HIV disease. *Journal of the Association of Nurses in AIDS Care, 5*, 21-26.

Mellers, J. D. C., Marchand-Gonad, N., King, M., Laupa, V., Frankel, S., & Schmit, T. (1994). Mental health of women with HIV infection: A study in Paris and London. *European Psychiatry, 9*, pp. 241-248.

Mellins, C. A., & Ehrhardt, A. A. (1995). *Stress, social support and psychosocial functioning in HIV-infected mothers and children.* Paper presented at the HIV Infection and Women: Setting a New Agenda Conference. Washington, DC.

Nichols, S. E. (1983). Psychiatric aspects of AIDS. *Psychomatics, 24,* 1083-1089.

Nichols, S. E. (1985). Psychosocial reactions of persons with the acquired immunodeficiency syndrome. *Annals of Internal Medicine, 103,* 765-767.

Orr, S. T., Celentano, D. D., Santelli, J., & Burwell, L. (1994). Depressive symptoms and risk factors for HIV acquisition among black women attending urban health centers in Baltimore. *AIDS Education and Prevention, 6,* 230-236.

Rabkin, J. G., Johnson, J., Lin, S. H., Lipsitz, J. D., Remien, R. H., Williams, J. B., & Gorman, J. M. (1997). Psychopathology in male and female HIV+ and negative injecting drug users: Longitudinal course over 3 years. *AIDS, 11,* 507-515.

Russell, J. M., & Smith, K. (1999). A holistic life view of human immunodeficiency virus: African American women. *Journal of Holistic Nursing, 17,* 331-346.

Siegel, K., Ravels, V. H., & Gorey, E. (1998). Barriers and pathways to testing among HIV-infected women. *AIDS Educational Prevention, 10,* 114-127.

Sowell, R. L., & Seals, B. F. (1997). Quality of life in HIV-infected women in the south-eastern United States. *AIDS Care, 9,* 501-512.

Van Servellen, G., Sarna, L., Nyamathi, A., Padilla, G., Brecht, M. L., & Jablonski, K. J. (1998). Emotional distress in women with symptomatic HIV disease. *Issues in Mental Health Nursing, 19,* 173-188.

Vedhara, K., Schifitto, G., & McDermott, M. (1999). Disease progression in HIV-positive women with moderate to severe immunosuppression: The role of depression. *Behavioral Medicine, 25,* 43-47.

Chronic Pain Syndromes
and Violence Against Women

Kathleen Kendall-Tackett
Roberta Marshall
Kenneth Ness

SUMMARY. Chronic pain is a common form of disability, and is often reported among women with a history of victimization. In the present study, we combine six pain symptoms into a measure of self-reported pain, and compare women who have experienced child or domestic abuse with those who do not report such a history. A sample of 110 female patients (57 abused, 53 non-abused controls) was drawn from an adult primary-care practice of 905 patients in a small, affluent, predominantly Caucasian community in northern New England. The subjects ranged in age from 18 to 88 (M = 47). Subjects completed a self-administered questionnaire that was used clinically as part of the new-patient work-up. Women who reported either child or domestic abuse were signifi-

Kathleen Kendall-Tackett, PhD, is a Research Associate at the Family Research Laboratory, University of New Hampshire, and a Fellow of the American Psychological Association. Roberta Marshall, MSN, ARNP, is a nurse practitioner in cardiology at the Veterans Administration Hospital, West Palm Beach, Florida. Kenneth Ness, MD, PhD, is an internist with a specialty in infectious disease at the Good Samaritan Hospital in West Palm Beach, Florida.

Address correspondence to: Kathleen Kendall-Tackett, PhD, Family Research Laboratory, 126 Horton Social Science Center, University of New Hampshire, Durham, NH 03824 (E-mail: kkendallt@aol.com).

The authors wish to thank the members of the Family Research Lab's weekly seminar for their helpful comments and suggestions.

[Haworth co-indexing entry note]: "Chronic Pain Syndromes and Violence Against Women." Kendall-Tackett, Kathleen, Roberta Marshall, and Kenneth Ness. Co-published simultaneously in *Women & Therapy* (The Haworth Press, Inc.) Vol. 26, No. 1/2, 2003, pp. 45-56; and: *Women with Visible and Invisible Disabilities: Multiple Intersections, Multiple Issues, Multiple Therapies* (ed. Martha E. Banks, and Ellyn Kaschak) The Haworth Press, Inc., 2003, pp. 45-56. Single or multiple copies of this article are available for a fee from The Haworth Document Delivery Service [1-800-HAWORTH, 9:00 a.m. - 5:00 p.m. (EST). E-mail address: getinfo@haworthpressinc.com].

45

cantly more likely to report pain symptoms than women in the control group. There was no significant difference between women who had experienced domestic abuse vs. child abuse alone. These findings held true even after controlling for depression. *[Article copies available for a fee from The Haworth Document Delivery Service: 1-800-HAWORTH. E-mail address: <getinfo@haworthpressinc.com> Website: <http://www.HaworthPress.com> © 2003 by The Haworth Press, Inc. All rights reserved.]*

KEYWORDS. Chronic pain, victimization, child abuse, domestic abuse

Women who have experienced child or domestic abuse often have poorer health than their non-abused counterparts–and these effects last long after the abuse has ended. These women see doctors more often and have higher patterns of health care use. In an HMO sample, Felitti (1991) found that 22% of his sample of child sexual abuse survivors had visited a doctor 10 or more times a year compared with 6% of the non-abused control group. High health care use was also noted in a study of women who had been battered or raped as adults (Koss, Koss & Woodruff, 1991). Severity of the abuse experience was the most powerful predictor of number of physician visits and outpatient costs (Koss et al., 1991).

In addition to office visits, health care use can include hospitalizations and surgery. Women who have experienced child or domestic abuse were also more likely to have had repeated surgeries (Arnold, Rogers & Cook, 1990; Harrop-Griffiths et al., 1988; Kendall-Tackett, Marshall, & Ness, 2000).

PAIN SYNDROMES

One factor that might be driving the higher patterns of health care use among adult survivors is the increased likelihood of one or more chronic pain syndromes. Chronic pain is a major form of disability, accounting for an estimated $125 billion each year in health care costs (Okifuji, Turk, & Kalauokalani, 1999), and it is common among victims of violence. In one recent study, pain was the most commonly occurring symptom in a community sample of child sexual abuse survivors (Teegen, 1999).

Pain is thought to be more common among survivors of violence because traumatic events appear to physiologically lower their pain thresholds (Kendall-Tackett, 2000). Neurons have the capacity to change function, chemical profile, or structure because of neuronal plasticity. Traumatic events can trigger these physiologic changes, and create a hypersensitivity to subsequent stimuli. Hypersensitivity often translates into increased pain. Some consider this hypersensitivity a major evolutionary advantage, in that it makes an individual more aware of potential danger. However, the increased pain that accompanies hypersensitivity makes day-to-day living difficult for women who have experienced violence (Woolf & Salter, 2000). It can limit the activities that women participate in, inhibit their ability to exercise, work, or perform basic household tasks, and make it difficult to care for children. Chronic pain can also interfere with sleep, making daytime fatigue a problem too. Indeed, chronic pain can influence every aspect of a woman's life.

Various types of pain have been studied with regard to past victimization. These studies are summarized below.

Headache, Back Pain, and Pelvic Pain

Previous studies have also noted high rates of chronic pelvic pain and severe PMS among adults survivors of childhood physical and sexual abuse (Harrop-Griffiths et al., 1988; Hudson, Goldenberg, Pope, Keck, & Schlesinger, 1992; Laws, 1993; Walling et al. 1994). Likewise, severe headaches have also been noted among women who had experienced physical, emotional or sexual abuse (Felitti, 1991; Hudson et al., 1992; Walling et al., 1994). Childhood abuse has even been related to whether surgery for back pain is successful. In a study of lumbar surgery, patients were questioned about five types of childhood trauma: sexual abuse, physical abuse, emotional abuse, parental substance abuse, and abandonment. Those reporting three or more types of abuse had a surgery failure rate of 85%, compared with a 5% failure rate among those with no history of trauma (Schofferman, Anderson, Hinds, Smith, & White, 1992).

Fibromyalgia Syndrome

Fibromyalgia syndrome (FMS) is chronic pain syndrome characterized by diffuse soft-tissue pain (Boisset-Pioro, Esdaile, & Fitzcharles, 1995). Two studies have recently considered the effects of childhood sexual abuse on the development of FMS. These studies found that

FMS is *not significantly more likely* among adult survivors of sexual abuse than it is among their non-abused counterparts. However, within the group of patients with FMS, those with a history of past abuse generally had a *worse experience* of the illness. Sexually abused FMS patients reported significantly more symptoms and pain than did non-abused FMS patients (Taylor, Trotter, & Csuka, 1995). Conversely, FMS patients were significantly more likely to report physical abuse during child or adulthood, or physical abuse in combination with sexual abuse than were the non-FMS patients (Boisset-Pioro et al., 1995).

Irritable Bowel Syndrome

Irritable bowel syndrome (IBS) has been the most-studied pain syndrome with regard to past victimization. In four studies that compared patients with IBS to those with organic gastrointestinal illnesses (e.g., ulcerative colitis), patients with IBS were more likely to report a history of threatened sex, incest, forced intercourse and frequent physical abuse than were patients in treatment for organic illness (Drossman et al., 1990; Talley, Fett, & Zinsmeister, 1995; Talley, Fett, Zinsmeister & Melton, 1994; Walker, Katon, Roy-Byrne, Jemelka, & Russo, 1993). The numbers are particularly striking in the study by Walker and colleagues. Patients with IBS had higher rates of lifetime sexual victimization (54% vs. 5%), *severe* lifetime sexual trauma (32% vs. 0%), and severe child sexual abuse (11% vs. 0%) than those with organic gastrointestinal illness (Walker et al., 1993). Even though most studies focus on sexual victimization, in one study, women with histories of physical abuse had the worst health outcomes (Leserman et al., 1996). Interestingly, patients whose abuse first occurred in childhood did not have worse health outcomes than those whose abuse first occurred as adults (Leserman et al., 1996).

Do patients report more pain because they are depressed? One recent study investigated the relationship between patient and psychiatric disturbance. Scarinci and colleagues (Scarinci, McDonald-Haile, Bradley, & Richter, 1994) found that IBS patients with a history of abuse had altered sensations of pain. Relative to the non-abused patients, abused patients had significantly lower pain threshold levels in response to finger pressure and significantly lower cognitive standards for judging stimuli as noxious. These results held even after controlling for psychiatric disturbance.

RESEARCH QUESTIONS

Previous research has done much to increase our understanding of the role of victimization in the development of chronic pain. However, previous studies are limited in that they tend to focus on one type of pain (e.g., irritable bowel syndrome). However, recent research on physiological correlates of past victimization strongly suggests that chronic stressors, such as child or domestic abuse, may lower the pain threshold overall. When only one type of pain is measured, we might miss the overall occurrence of pain. For example, when we ask only about IBS, but the patient has chronic headaches, we can underestimate the occurrence of pain as a symptom of past abuse. The present study combines six self-reported pain symptoms into a measure of self-reported pain, and compares women who have experienced child or domestic abuse with those who do not report such a history.

In the present study, we also have an opportunity to examine the relationship between pain and depression. Depression has been noted as a co-occurring symptom with both IBS and fibromyalgia, and is also common among victims of violence. The Scarinci et al. (1994) study described above indicates pain cannot be wholly explained by depression (i.e., depressed patients tending to describe worse symptoms). We can examine reporting of pain symptoms while controlling for self-reported depression.

Finally, since we report data from women who have suffered from child abuse vs. domestic violence, we have an opportunity to examine whether timing of the abuse experiences has any impact on symptoms. At least one previous study found that symptomatology did not differ significantly in those abused during childhood vs. adulthood (Leserman et al., 1996). In the present study, we have an opportunity to compare these two types of abuse.

METHOD

Participants

A sample of 110 female clients (57 abused, 53 non-abused controls) was drawn from an adult primary-care practice of 905 clients in a small, affluent community in northern New England. All clients in the sample were White. We first identified all clients who answered "yes" to at least one of two questions about either child or domestic abuse. We then gathered our control group of 53 non-abused clients by matching them for age with members of the abused group. The participants ranged in age from 18 to 88 ($M = 47$).

Of the 57 clients in the abused group, 27 indicated that they had experienced physical or sexual abuse as children, 20 indicated that they had experienced domestic abuse as adults, and 10 indicated that they had experienced both child and domestic abuse.

Questionnaire

The questionnaire was a five-page, 169 item, closed-ended, yes-no, self-administered questionnaire that was used clinically as part of the new-patient work-up. The questionnaire included the following: demographic information, past medical history; health maintenance; social history and victimization history ("Were you sexually or physically abused as a child?" and "Have you been the victim of domestic abuse as an adult?"). Depression was one item on a list of symptoms, in a yes-no format.

Six items that asked about pain in our questionnaire were combined into a measure of self-reported pain. These included "abdominal pain," "pain or stiffness in joints or muscles," "pain during urination," "arthritis," "back pain," and "severe headaches." These yes-no questions were scattered throughout the list of symptoms, and reflected a wide variety of chronic pains.

RESULTS

Pain Symptoms

When individual symptoms were compared, women who had been victimized were not significantly different from the non-victimized group, but all were in the predicted direction. These results are summarized in Table 1.

When the symptoms were combined, a significant difference did emerge. Women who reported either child or domestic abuse reported significantly more pain symptoms ($M = 2.2$; $F(1,82) = 5.91$, $p = .017$) *than those women in the control group ($M = 1.46$).*

TABLE 1. Individual Pain Symptoms

Symptom	Abused (n)	Non-abused (n)	χ^2	p
Abdominal pain	14	7	1.85	.174
Pain or stiffness in joints or muscles	28	21	.29	.59
Pain during urination	3	1	*	
Arthritis	19	10	2.67	.109
Back pain	30	21	2.17	.141
Severe headaches	20	16	.47	.495

*Cell sizes less than five

Depression

Women with a history of victimization were significantly more likely to report depression ($\chi^2 = 9.4, p < .002$) than their non-abused counterparts. When depression was entered as a covariate in the analysis of combined pain symptoms, there was still a significant difference between the women who had experienced victimization versus those who had not ($F(1,82) = 4.95, p = .029$).

There was no significant difference in depression between women who had experienced domestic abuse vs. child abuse alone ($F(2,44) = .975, p = .386$).

DISCUSSION

In the present study, we examined the relationship between past victimization and current reporting of pain symptoms. There were no significant differences between abused and non-abused women in reporting individual symptoms. However, when the symptoms were combined, there were significant differences. Combining these symptoms might have produced a more realistic estimate of occurrence of chronic pain in our sample; individual symptoms may have varied from woman to woman. Women with a history of victimization reported an average of slightly more than two pain symptoms. Some reported more musculoskeletal symptoms such as arthritis and back pain. Others reported more localized pain such as abdominal pain and painful urination.

There were no significant differences in symptoms between those abused in childhood vs. adulthood. This was not a complete surprise given the results of the Leserman et al. (1996) study, but it was somewhat surprising when we consider the relative vulnerability of children's vs. adults' brains. Since children's brains are still developing, we would expect more damage to occur if abuse happens during childhood. However, another possibility is that children's brains are more flexible, and may have been able to "re-wire" themselves in such a way that damage was minimized. This issue should also be revisited in future studies.

Chronic pain is also very much a women's health issue. Indeed, the overwhelming majority of patients with conditions such as irritable bowel syndrome, fibromyalgia, and severe recurring headaches are women. Many of these women also have a history of depression and past abuse. *And often women are the ones who have their pain symptoms dismissed.*

Why does this happen? There are several possible explanations. "Pain" is a highly subjective symptom, and physicians must rely upon patient self-report. Most of the pain syndromes described in previous studies fall under the general heading of "functional" illnesses–meaning that there are no laboratory or radiologic findings that confirm their existence. The lack of concrete lab findings, unfortunately, can also confirm physicians' stereotypes of female patients who use physical symptoms as a ploy for attention and sympathy. While these stereotypes are slowly changing, many women patients with vague, subjective symptoms such as pain still have to battle with their care providers to prove that their symptoms are real (Nechas & Foley, 1994).

Chronic pain is also quite resistant to traditional medical treatment, and physicians become frustrated with the lack of progress their patients make. In addition, chronic pain patients are often perceived as irritable and "difficult." All of these factors can contribute to a dismissive attitude by health care providers.

Depression and Pain

The presence of depression was not a surprising finding. As we have reported previously (Kendall-Tackett et al., 2000), depression is a common symptom of past victimization. In the present study, depression did not account for self-reported pain, but that is not the end of the story. Researchers are beginning to speculate that pain and depression might have a common underlying mechanism. In a study of patients with rheumatoid arthritis (RA), those who had had an episode of major depression, but who were not currently depressed, had worse pain from this organic condition than those who did not (Fifield, Tennen, Reisne, & McQuillan, 1998). Sleep abnormalities might also be involved in the relationship between pain and depression. In another study of RA patients, pain exacerbated sleeping problems, and both were thought to contribute to depression (Nicassio & Wallston, 1992).

Pain and depression share one other commonality. Two of the most effective treatments for depression–antidepressants and cognitive therapy–are also used in the treatment of pain. One way that antidepressants are thought to reduce pain is through regulation of sleep. Sleep disturbances, depression and pain are all related to brain levels of the neurotransmitter serotonin.

Study Limitations

We note some limitations in our study. The questionnaire we used was designed for clinical practice, and was not intended to be used as a research tool. Therefore, some of the questions had some limitations.

First, we might have had under-reporting of abuse history, possibly due to wording of the questions. For example, the question on domestic violence asked patients to identify themselves as "victims of domestic abuse." We might have had a higher rate of positive response if we had asked if they had ever been hit by a spouse or partner. The child abuse question was limited because it combined physical and sexual abuse. For both questions, we had limited information about the abuse itself including the identity of the perpetrator, the severity of abuse that occurred, the frequency and duration of the abuse experience, and the level of force that was involved. Each of these factors has been found to contribute to the severity of the abuse experience, which has been related to severity of symptoms in past studies (Golding, Cooper, & George, 1997; Leserman et al., 1996).

The measure of depression was also very limited. It is a single question that asked clients to indicate whether they were depressed. We have no information on severity or length of depression, and this approach relies on clients' identifying themselves as depressed. However, even with these limitations, the results are striking, with significantly more women identifying themselves as depressed in the abused than the non-abused group.

CONCLUSIONS

In this study, we found that women who had experienced family violence—as children or adults—were significantly more likely to report a wide variety of pain symptoms. Although depression was three times more likely among the abused women, its effects appear independent of self-reported pain.

There is increasing evidence that indicates that past abuse is one possible cause of chronic pain. In the wake of traumatic or chronically stressful events, the body learns to hyper-respond to stimuli, increasing the experience of pain. Treatment of pain in women with a history of child or domestic abuse should include ways to help the body "un-learn" its dysfunctional way of handling current stressors, thereby reducing their pain.

Relaxation techniques and biofeedback are examples of helping the body un-learn its dysfunctional patterns. When clients experience a body sensation as painful, they are instructed to relax that part of their body, rather than tensing it. Learning to relax the entire body can also help manage pain in a specific part. With biofeedback, clients learn to take conscious control over their bodies' reactions. In the case of chronic headaches, for example, clients are instructed in how to "move warmth" from the painful part of their body (e.g., their heads), to another part of their body, such as their hands. A machine provides feedback to let them know when they are having the desired reaction. Soon clients can create these responses without the machine. Both of these techniques teach women to be more aware of their bodies, how they work, and what are some of the early warning signs of impending pain.

Another approach involves educating clients who have been through traumatic events about the source of their pain. This can be empowering and validating, letting clients know that their pain is not "all in their heads." Cognitive therapy can also help in pain reduction. Learning to recognize the cognitive distortions that often accompany chronic pain (e.g., that pain means something is "seriously wrong") is an important step toward effective pain management. While underlying illness should be checked for and ruled out, learning that their chronic pain exists independent of an underlying illness can slow the cycle of multiple doctors' appointments, surgeries and treatments, and free them to find an approach that actually works.

Once adult survivors learn how their abuse experiences might have altered their sense of pain, they are in a position to do something about it. Relaxation techniques, biofeedback, education, and cognitive therapy can be combined with medications, physical therapy, and lifestyle changes. This multi-faceted, mind-body approach can help adult survivors manage pain, one of the most difficult symptoms of past abuse, and move toward healing their lives.

REFERENCES

Arnold, R.P., Rogers, D., & Cook, D.A.G. (1990). Medical problems of adults who were sexually abused in childhood. *British Medical Journal, 300,* 705-708.

Boisset-Pioro, M. H., Esdaile, J. M., & Fitzcharles, M. A. (1995). Sexual and physical abuse in women with fibromyalgia syndrome. *Arthritis & Rheumatism, 38,* 235-241.

Drossman, D., Leserman, J., Nachman, G., Li, Z., Gluck, H., Toomey, T., & Mitchell, M. (1990). Sexual and physical abuse in women with functional or organic gastrointestinal disorders. *Annals of Internal Medicine, 113,* 828-833.

Fellitti, V. (1991). Long-term medical consequences of incest, rape, and molestation. *Southern Medical Journal, 84,* 328-331.

Fifield, J., Tennen, H., Reisine, S., & McQuillan, J. (1998). Depression and the long-term risk of pain, fatigue, and disability in patients with rheumatoid arthritis. *Arthritis & Rheumatism, 41,* 1851-1857.

Golding, J. M., Cooper, M. L., & George, L. K. (1997). Sexual assault history and health perceptions: Seven general population studies. *Health Psychology, 16,* 417-425.

Harrop-Griffiths, J., Katon, W., Walker, E., Holm, L., Russo, J., & Hickok, L. (1988). The association between chronic pelvic pain, psychiatric diagnoses, and childhood sexual abuse. *Obstetrics and Gynecology, 71,* 589-594.

Hudson, J. I., Goldenberg, D. L., Pope, H. G., Keck, P. E., & Schlesigner, L. (1992). Comorbidity of fibromyalgia with medical and psychiatric disorders. *American Journal of Medicine, 92,* 363-367.

Kendall-Tackett, K. A. (2000). Physiological correlates of childhood abuse: Chronic hyperarousal in PTSD, depression and irritable bowel syndrome. *Child Abuse & Neglect, 24,* 799-810.

Kendall-Tackett, K. A., Marshall, R., & Ness, K. E. (2000). Victimization, healthcare use, and health maintenance. *Family Violence & Sexual Assault Bulletin, 16,* 18-21.

Koss, M.P., Koss, P. G., & Woodruff, M. S. (1991). Deleterious effects of criminal victimization on women's health and medical utilization. *Archives of Internal Medicine, 151,* 342-347.

Laws, A. (1993). Does a history of sexual abuse in childhood play a role in women's medical problems? A review. *Journal of Women's Health, 2,* 165-172.

Leserman, J., Drossman, D. A., Li, Z., Toomey, T. C., Nachman, G., & Glogau, L. (1996). Sexual and physical abuse history in gastroenterology practice: How types of abuse impact health status. *Psychosomatic Medicine, 58,* 4-15.

Nechas, E., & Foley, D. (1994). *Unequal treatment: What you don't know about how women are mistreated by the medical community.* New York: Simon & Schuster.

Nicassio, P. M., & Wallston, K. A. (1992). Longitudinal relationships among pain, sleep problems, and depression in Rheumatoid Arthritis. *Journal of Abnormal Psychology, 101,* 514-520.

Okifuji, A., Turk, D. C. & Kalauokalani, D. (1999). Clinical outcome and economic evaluation of multidisciplinary pain centers. In A. R. Block, E. F. Kremer, & E. Fernandez (Eds.) *Handbook of Pain Syndromes* (pp. 77-97). Mahwah, NJ: Lawrence Erlbaum Associates.

Scarinci, I. C., McDonald-Haile, J., Bradley, L. A., & Richter, J. E. (1994). Altered pain perception and psychosocial features among women with gastrointestinal disorders and history of abuse: A preliminary model. *The American Journal of Medicine, 97,* 108-118.

Schofferman, J., Anderson, D., Hinds, R., Smith, G., & White, A. (1992). Childhood psychological trauma correlates with unsuccessful lumbar spine surgery. *Spine, 17,* S1381-S1384.

Talley, N. J., Fett, S. L., & Zinsmeister, A. R. (1995). Self-reported abuse and gastrointestinal disease in outpatients: Association with irritable bowel-type symptoms. *American Journal of Gastroenterology, 90,* 366-371.

Talley, N. J., Fett, S. L., Zinsmeister, A. R., & Melton, L. J. (1994). Gastrointestinal tract symptoms and self-reported abuse: A population-based study. *Gastroenterology, 107,* 1040-1049.

Taylor, M. L., Trotter, D. R., & Csuka, M. E. (1995). The prevalence of sexual abuse in women with fibromyalgia. *Arthritis & Rheumatism, 38,* 229-234.

Teegen, F. (1999). Childhood sexual abuse and long-term sequelae. In A. Maercker, M. Schutzwohl, & Z. Solomon (Eds.) *Posttraumatic stress disorder: A lifespan developmental perspective* (pp. 97-112). Seattle: Hogrefe & Huber.

Walker, E., Katon, W., Roy-Byrne, P., Jemelka, R., & Russo, J. (1993). Histories of sexual victimization in patients with irritable bowel syndrome or inflammatory bowel disease. *American Journal of Psychiatry, 150,* 1502-1506.

Walling, M., O'Hara, M., Reiter, R., Milburn, A., Lilly, G., & Vincent, S.D. (1994). Abuse history and chronic pain in women: II. A multivariate analysis of abuse and psychological morbidity. *Obstetrics & Gynecology, 84,* 200-206.

Walling, M. K., Reiter, R. C., O'Hara, M. W., Milburn, A. K., Lilly, G., & Vincent, S. D. (1994). Abuse history and chronic pain in women: I. Prevalence of sexual abuse and physical abuse. *Obstetrics and Gynecology, 84,* 193-199.

Woolf, C. J., & Salter, M. W. (2000). Neuronal plasticity: Increasing the gain in pain. *Science, 288,* 1765-1768.

Eating Disorders Among Urban and Rural African American and European American Women

Cherie A. Bagley
Colleen D. Character
Lisamarie Shelton

SUMMARY. It is alleged that eating disorders are nonexistent in African American women and that eating disorder symptomatology occurs predominantly among White middle class women (Kumanyika, Wilson, &

Cherie A. Bagley, PhD, is affiliated with The University of Iowa, Department of Family Practice, College of Medicine. Colleen D. Character, PhD, is affiliated with Kent State University, Department of Human Development and Family Studies. Lisamarie Shelton, PhD, was research assistant and former graduate student at The University of Iowa, Department of Counseling Psychology (now at San Bernardino County Behavioral Health, Fontana, CA).

Address correspondence to: Cherie A. Bagley, Louis Stokes Cleveland Department of Veterans Affairs Medical Center, General Mental Health 51A, 10000 Brecksville Road, Brecksville, OH 44141 (E-mail: bagley.cherie@cleveland.va.gov).

This study was conducted through a grant from the College of Medicine at The University of Iowa. Organizational support was received from the Greater Atlanta YWCA, Spelman & Agnes Scott Colleges, Payne Memorial A. M. E. Church, YMCA of Waterloo, Allen Women's Health Center and numerous churches and social agencies in Waterloo and Atlanta. Gratitude is extended to all agencies and individuals involved in conducting and completing this research. Special thanks to The University of Iowa College of Medicine for financial sponsorship and to Dr. Craig Gjerde and Dr. Robert Oppliger, University of Iowa, Department of Family Practice, for statistical guidance.

[Haworth co-indexing entry note]: "Eating Disorders Among Urban and Rural African American and European American Women." Bagley, Cherie A., Colleen D. Character, and Lisamarie Shelton. Co-published simultaneously in *Women & Therapy* (The Haworth Press, Inc.) Vol. 26, No. 1/2, 2003, pp. 57-79; and: *Women with Visible and Invisible Disabilities: Multiple Intersections, Multiple Issues, Multiple Therapies* (ed: Martha E. Banks, and Ellyn Kaschak) The Haworth Press, Inc., 2003, pp. 57-79. Single or multiple copies of this article are available for a fee from The Haworth Document Delivery Service [1-800-HAWORTH, 9:00 a.m. - 5:00 p.m. (EST). E-mail address: getinfo@haworthpressinc.com].

Guilford-Davenport, 1993; Smolak & Striegel-Moore, 2001). This research attempted to identify differences in eating disorder symptomatology in African American and White American women. An eating disorder is a disability because it can damage the person physically, emotionally and socially. It can be undetected for years and society may reinforce the hidden disorder by being complimentary regarding the thin appearance of the person. The Eating Disorder Inventory (EDI) was used to measure psychological traits and symptom clusters associated with the understanding and treatment of eating disorders (Garner, 1990). Measures of self-esteem, depression and coping were also examined. Findings indicated differences between African American and White women on the Ineffectiveness scale of the EDI, differences between the urban/rural women on Ineffectiveness and Perfectionism, and differences in coping strategies and education among this sample group of women. Successful treatment usually involves psychotherapy and/or medication for depression. *[Article copies available for a fee from The Haworth Document Delivery Service: 1-800-HAWORTH. E-mail address: <getinfo@haworthpressinc.com> Website: <http://www.HaworthPress.com> © 2003 by The Haworth Press, Inc. All rights reserved.]*

KEYWORDS. Eating disorders, bulimia, anorexia, ethnic, African American, urban, rural

Research has predominantly involved White women in Western culture with little focus on other cultural groups. Current trends suggest that more ethnic people are being identified as anorexic or bulimic (Crago, Shisslak, & Estes, 1996; Schwartz, Thompson, & Johnson, 1982; Weiss, 1995; Wildes, Emery, & Simons, 2001). Osvold and Sodowsky (1993) suggested that DSM-IV-R criteria have utility for ethnic people but the cultural context must be recognized as part of the diagnosis (Williamson, 1990). The research reported here sought to examine the commonality of eating disorder symptomatology as well as the variant patterns that might exist between African American and White cultures and utilized DSM-IV criteria (American Psychiatric Association, 1987, 1994). This research goes beyond the traditional diagnoses to include unusual patterns of eating (Miller, 1991). Specifically, four primary questions and three secondary questions were proposed:

Primary:
1. What psychological eating disorder symptoms are found among women?
2. Are there healthy or unhealthy eating patterns?
   A. Are there ethnic differences in patterns of eating?
   B. What are the common and uncommon eating disorder factors among African American and White Women?
3. Are there differences associated with education level?
4. Are there geographic differences (rural, urban)?

Secondary:
5. How is depression related to eating?
6. How is self-esteem related to eating?
7. What type of help is useful in preventing or eliminating the symptoms?

THE ROLE OF ETHNICITY IN EATING DISORDERS

African American women manifest a variety of shapes and sizes. Generally the images that African American women hold for attractiveness is not in agreement with the prevalent thin body image presented by the media in the U.S. (Buchanan, 1993; Le Grange, Stone, & Brownell, 1998; Manley, Tonkin, & Hammond, 1988; Miller et al., 2000; Osvold & Sodowsky, 1993; Sanford & Donovan, 1985; Wolf, 1992). African Americans are less focused on dieting and more tolerant of weight than White women and weight is less connected to self-esteem (Kumanyika, Wilson, & Guilford-Davenport, 1993; Root, 1990; Thomas, 1987; Villarosa, 1994). Eating disorders are not apparent to significant others and eating is a common essential behavior. Acceptable reasons are given to forego a meal: not hungry or feeling well, plan to eat later, or ate while out. Frequently the person avoids eating at social functions and public places for fear of discovery of the disorder and to avoid elimination of food in a public domain. One can deny having a disorder with weight loss or gain and attribute the change to life circumstances or fluctuating hormones.

Women who purge do so privately in the bathroom. Evidence of an eating disorder is removed and rarely discovered. Workplaces and college campuses are instructed to discover the individual if aftereffects are found. Facilities take great lengths having staff watch the bathroom to discover who is leaving traces of regurgitation. Generally, agencies are looking to halt the behavior to prevent damage to their facilities or to prevent influencing others to do likewise. Punitive actions rather than a helpful attitude can contribute to the secrecy.

Culturally, food is always available for Black Women to increase environmental comfort. Food is involved at church gatherings, family reunions, holidays, Sunday dinners, special programs, and events. When food is absent from events, frequently there are invitations to "eat out." An eating disorder might be undetected for years. Society reinforces the disorder by endorsing the thin figure or athletic physique (Andersen, 1985; Gordon, 1990; Pipher, 1997). Black women celebrate with food, eating when happy or in discomfort. Black women in group therapy acknowledged food as comforting after a loss or due to life circumstances (Thompson, 1994).

Thomas (1987) examined body image satisfaction in 102 Black women and found dissatisfaction with their current weight status correlated with a desire for thinness or a more ideal figure and their weight was inversely correlated with satisfaction of body image. The result is similar to research on White women. Although there was a significant moderate relationship between self-esteem and body image in Thomas' research, a major finding was that body image satisfaction was highly related to the perception of significant male others. Husbands and boyfriends of Black women were influential in concerns with weight according to self-report. Kumanyika et al. (1993) studied 500 Black women at a health clinic and their attitudes toward weight. Black women did not perceive themselves as unattractive if they were overweight (Altabe, 1998). The research indicates a cultural component to obesity and few negative consequences for African American women (Cogan, Bhalla, Sefa-Dedeh, & Rothblum, 1996; LeGrange et al., 1998; Smolak & Striegel-Moore, 2001). Participants were aware of health risks involved with being overweight and many had experienced ineffective dieting. This research suggests that Black women might not maintain weight loss after dieting, and are less acquiescent to social pressure, particularly after age 45. Stressing the health benefits of weight loss would provide a better incentive for Black women than focus on an ideal body image (Kumanyika et al., 1993).

These cultural differences support the need for more research that will increase our knowledge and understanding (Crago et al., 1996; Davis & Yager, 1992; Root, 1990; Smolak & Striegel-Moore, 2001). Research projects which advocate including people of color must increase. Women are often rewarded for their physical appearance and femininity (Osvold & Sodowsky, 1993). Some research has suggested that Black women are protected against developing eating disorders due to healthy body size and less emphasis on physical acceptance (Osvold & Sodowsky, 1993; Root, 1990). To evaluate the cultural influence, one needs to know the level of acculturation of the individual to White culture. Counselors are encouraged to assist clients of all ethnicities with eating disorders in understanding the influence of White societal standards of health and thinness and refute them (Osvold & Sodowsky, 1993; Villarosa, 1994). Thompson (1994) interviewed African American, Latina, and White women and observed eating disorders occurred not out of vanity but as a reaction to coping with injustices in society, such as racism, sexism, or sexual abuse, and acculturation. Society does an injustice to women by describing them as seeking to look ideal when some women are actually attempting to numb painful experiences.

A study conducted with 2000 African American women concluded that African American women are at risk for eating disorders to the same degree as White women (Villarosa, 1994). Many Black women wrote letters admitting their battle with weight, body image, vomiting, and laxative use. Traditional African society has viewed the full figure as attractive and desirable (Cogan et al., 1996). This research found 71% of middle to upper class and highly educated women acknowledged the desire to be thinner. The stronger the Black identity, the less likely African American women were to develop eating disorders. Middle class African American women were more at risk because their ethnic identity was more susceptible to European American values or the thin ideal. Dieting behavior and exercise were frequent methods used to burn calories. Some women engaged in fasting and used laxatives to lose weight while a few vomited after eating. Researchers compared this data to a 1984 study of White women and concluded that African American women had higher levels of potentially dangerous eating behaviors. Black women were found to rely more heavily on laxative use than White women for weight loss. Many African Americans do not use traditional mental health services and this might influence the lack of evidence for eating disorders in the Black community. In order to receive a label one must first be diagnosed by the traditional health system (e.g., physician or therapist). Outreach might be necessary to substantiate what disorders are present (Root, 1990). This research study promotes this exploration.

METHOD

Participants

The 373 participants consisted of 168 women recruited from the Atlanta, Georgia area and 195 women from the Waterloo, Iowa area, including a pilot group of 10 University of Iowa graduate students. Waterloo and Atlanta were chosen as locations because it was thought that a sufficient number of Black women and White women could be recruited. Those sites were also chosen to measure urban-rural differences of perceptions of body image. The data collection sites were varied and participants were from colleges, churches, community groups and health centers. Recruitment involved circulating flyers, newspaper ads, letter writing, and personal appeal. Participants received $5 as incentive to complete the research. Suggestions by members of the pilot group were used to modify procedures for other participants, such as clarifying ambiguous questions.

The women's ages ranged from 18-55 years. For the total sample (N = 373), the mean age was 31 years. For research purposes, the women were assigned to (1) educated and (2) community subsamples. The educated subsample was defined as having more than two years of college education, a college degree, or currently matriculating in college. The community group consisted of women with high school diplomas/GEDs, high school and up to two years of college and not matriculating, or less than high school education. Fifty-two percent of the sample had a high school education or less and 45% were more educated. The marital status of the full sample was 50% single, 39% married and 10% divorced.

Overall, this sample group of women was not depressed, categorized in the minimal symptom range, and their self-esteem was intact. They can be considered as stable emotionally. Sixty-four percent of participants reported having stress.

Instruments

Eating Disorders Inventory-2 (EDI-2; Garner, 1990). This self-report instrument measures psychological symptoms associated with anorexia and bulimia nervosa. There are eight subscales including:

- Drive for Thinness (the pursuit of thinness)
- Bulimia (thoughts and acts of uncontrollable eating)
- Body Dissatisfaction (dissatisfaction with overall shape and size of parts of the body)
- Ineffectiveness (feelings of general inadequacy and lack of control of one's life, e.g., alone, insecure, not a worthwhile person, emptiness, and an inability to achieve one's standard)

- Perfectionism (belief that personal achievement should be superior, e.g., outstanding performance in the family, importance of approval from significant others, being the best, parental expectations of excellence, perfect performance and extremely high goals)
- Interpersonal Distrust (feelings of alienation and reluctance toward closeness)
- Interoceptive Awareness (confusion and apprehension in recognition and response to emotional states)
- Maturity Fears (desire to return to childhood)

and three provisional scales:

- Asceticism (seek virtue through spiritual ideals; e.g., self- restraint, self-discipline)
- Impulse Regulation (tendency toward impulsivity or recklessness), and
- Social Insecurity (belief that social relationships are unrewarding).

There are 91 items with a Likert response format with six response choices. There is also an EDI symptom checklist that includes symptoms, weight, and menstrual history. Scoring is based on weighted items from zero through three with three being the asymptomatic response. Internal Consistency reliability has been reported from .83 to .93 for eating disorder samples and from .65 to .91 for non-patients. Test-retest reliability from non-patient samples ranges from .65 to .92 for the eight subscales.

The Ways of Coping Scale (WCS; Folkman & Lazarus, 1980, 1988). This questionnaire is a 66-item survey that identifies thoughts and actions an individual uses to cope with a specific stressful encounter. Internal consistency reliability is reported from .61 to .79.

Beck Depression Inventory (BDI; Beck, 1978, Beck & Steer, 1993), is a 21-item instrument to measure the severity of depression. Participants rate recent symptoms on a Likert scale from one to four. Summed scores are categorized as: Minimal, Mild, Moderate, or Severe depression. Reliability is reported to range from .79 to .90.

Culture Free Self-Esteem Inventory (CFSEI-Form AD; Battle, 1992). This instrument measures perception of personal worth or self-esteem. Components measured are General, Social, and Personal self-esteem. The inventory contains 40 yes-no items. Scoring involves summation of items; higher scores indicate greater self-esteem. Form AD for adults was used. Test-retest reliability for women is .81 and .82.

Procedures

Each participant was provided with a packet of measures and group administration was provided at all sites (churches, colleges, libraries, malls, social agencies, women's health center, and YWCA). Three participants had individual administration. Instructions were provided orally to participants regarding each instrument. Participants were allowed to ask questions. Human Participants Information and consent forms were distributed and signed.

Data Collection

Data were collected from eight sites in both cities. The Greater Atlanta YWCA sponsored research in Atlanta and provided a different site across the city each day. Additional public sites were obtained by direct solicitation.

Data Analysis

The data were analyzed using the Statistical Analysis Package (SAS, 1990). Frequencies and means were computed on the demographic data and t-tests were used to analyze mean differences. Analyses of Variance with a $2 \times 2 \times 2$ design were conducted using race, geographic location, and education as independent variables with eating disorders, psychological factors related to eating disorders, coping styles, depression, and self-esteem as dependent variables. Pairwise comparisons using the Tukey test of difference followed significant differences noted by the ANOVA. Pearson product correlations were computed between the measures to determine relationship patterns among the data.

RESULTS

Demographics

In Atlanta (urban), there were 109 Black women and 59 White women. The Waterloo (rural) group consisted of 60 Black women and 145 White women. The Black women ($M = 33$ years) were, on average, older than the White women ($M = 30$ years) (see Table 1).

Among African Americans, 50% were single, 35% married and 13% divorced. For White women, 50% of the sample was single, 42% mar-

TABLE 1. Eating Disorders Inventory-2: Symptom Checklist

	Black	White	Urban	Rural	Comm.	Educ.	
Age (yrs.)	33	30	30	33	31	34	a*, b*, c**
AWPB	24.2	20.0	22.0	21.8	21.8	22.8	a**
ARD	22.5	19.4	20.0	21.3	20.6	21.0	a**
FB	18.8	16.3	17.8	17.4	17.3	18.3	
LAX	23.5	22.5	20.7	28.6	20.4	27.4	b*, c*
EX	39.7	38.8	42.3	36.9	39.7	39.0	
FP	18.3	17.1	15.9	18.4	15.3	20.3	c*
WP	1.4	5.7	3.5	5.8	2.4	8.9	a*
HPW	172.9	156.0	166.3	161.7	161.5	165.7	a***
LPW	131.6	124.4	130.0	126.2	126.4	127.0	a*
LW	148.5	137.5	143.0	142.5	139.9	145.9	a**
IW	139.0	128.0	134.4	132.0	131.3	134.4	a***
AW	168.0	148.0	159.0	155.7	155.7	159.0	a***

*p < .05, ** p < .01, *** p < .001

Black = African American
White = European American
AWPB = Age Weight Problems Began
ARD = Age First Restricted Diet
FB = First Binge
LAX = Age Laxatives First Taken
EX = Minutes of Exercise
FP = First Purge
WP = Worst Purge

HPW = Highest Past Weight
LPW = Lowest Past Weight
LW = Longest Weight
IW = Ideal Weight
AW = Actual Weight
a = Ethnicity
b = Urban-Rural
c = Education

ried, and 7% divorced. Marital status was impacted significantly by geographic location. The rural sample was more likely to be married (50%) than single (41%) or divorced (8%). The urban sample was mostly single (61%), married (25%), and divorced (12%).

There were no ethnic differences in stress, but there were differences between the urban and rural groups. More urban than rural women reported having stress. Depression was significantly different between the community group and the more educated group $(F(1, 365) = 5.82, p < .05)$. The Black community women and the more educated White urban women were more depressed than educated Black women $(F(1, 365) = 7.34, p < .01)$. Rural Black women were more depressed than urban Black women $(F(1, 365) = 4.96, p < .05)$.

More rural than urban women were postmenopausal, had hysterectomies, or were pregnant. One third of the women were taking prescribed medication.

Eating Disorders

Height was similar for both groups at an average height of 5'4". There were significant ethnic differences on all of the weight measures (see Table 1). The highest average past weight for Black women (172 lbs.) was higher than White women (156 lbs.; $t(303) = 3.62, p < .001$). The lowest mean past weight for Black women (132 lbs.) was also higher than White women (124 lbs.; $t(369) = 2.53, p < .05$). The average longest weight for Black women (149 lbs.) was higher than White women (138 lbs.; $t(298) = 2.95, p < .01$). The mean ideal weight for Black women (139 lbs.) was considerably higher than White women (128 lbs.; $t(366) = 4.85, p < .001$). Finally, the average actual weight was consistently higher for Black women (168 lbs.) than for White women (148 lbs.; $t(369) = 4.96, p < .001$). Black women actually weighed 20 pounds more and were heavier in their highest, lowest, longest and ideal weights than White women. There were no differences in those weights based on geographic region or level of education.

Weight problems began at a significantly earlier age for White women (20 years) than Black women (24 years; $t(241) = 3.00, p < .01$). Restricting food intake due to concerns of body size or weight was significantly different with White women restricting their diets at earlier ages (19 years) than the Black women (22 years; $t(275) = 3.14, p < .01$).

Purging behavior begins about age 17. There were significant ethnic differences with White women purging more frequently (6 times) than Black women (1 time; $t(23.6) = 2.09, p < .05$). The community group began the purge cycle at an earlier age (15 years; $t(28.1) = 2.58, p < .05$) than the more educated group (20 years).

There were no group differences in the use of laxatives or diet pills to control weight or get rid of food. There were differences in the ages laxatives were first taken with the urban women initiating use earlier (20 years) than the rural group (28 years; $t(36) = 2.28, p < .05$). The community group engaged in laxative use earlier (20 years) than the more educated group (27 years; $t(36) = 2.09, p < .05$). Diuretic use, minutes of exercise and age at first food binge were similar for all the women.

Urban educated White women had a greater drive for thinness than all other groups of women ($F(1, 365 = 4.07, p < .05$; see Table 2). The urban community White women were less likely to be bulimic than any of the other women ($F(1, 365 = 4.10, p < .05$). The urban community Black women were more likely to be bulimic than the more educated urban Black women ($F(1, 365 = 4.99, p < .05$).

TABLE 2. Eating Disorder Inventory-2: Psychological Symptoms Associated with Anorexia and Bulimia Nervosa

| | African American | | | | European American | | | | |
| | Urban | | Rural | | Urban | | Rural | | |
	Comm.	Educ.	Comm.	Educ.	Comm.	Educ.	Comm.	Educ.	
DT	5.6	4.2	5.2	6.0	5.8	7.9	5.6	5.6	abc*
B	2.4	1.2	1.8	1.8	.7	2.3	1.7	1.9	ac*, abc*
BD	8.3	7.2	7.4	8.9	7.9	8.2	7.4	7 1	
I	7.7	8.5	7.0	7.1	6.9	7.9	6.7	7.0	a*, b*
P	6.3	5.3	5.7	6.9	7.4	8.9	3.7	6.0	b***, c*, ab***, ac**
ID	6.9	8.6	7.6	7.9	7.7	8.7	7.8	8.2	c*
IA	4.7	3.0	5.3	3.2	3.6	5.2	3.6	3.9	ac**
MF	5.7	5.1	5.6	4.7	5.0	6.3	5.0	5.2	
A	4.1	2.3	3.9	2.1	3.3	3.6	2.9	3.0	c*, ac**
IR	4.5	.8	3.0	1.0	1.9	3.2	2.5	2.0	c***, ac***
SI	8.1	9.7	9.2	7.7	8.2	9.1	8.2	9.0	

*$p < .05$, ** $p < .01$, *** $p < .001$

DT = Drive for Thinness
B = Bulimia
BD = Body Dissatisfaction
I = Ineffectiveness
P = Perfectionism
ID = Interpersonal Distrust
IA = Interoceptive Awareness

MF = Maturity Fears
A = Asceticism
IR = Impulse Regulation
SI = Social Insecurity
a = Ethnicity
b = Urban-Rural
c = Education

African Americans experienced a higher degree of ineffectiveness than White women ($F(1, 365) = 5.44, p < .05$). There were greater feelings of ineffectiveness in the urban area than the rural area ($F(1, 365) = 3.71, p < .05$).

Urban women were more perfectionistic ($F(1, 365) = 13.63, p < .001$) than the rural women. The women with more education were also more perfectionistic than those with less education ($F(1, 365) = 5.20, p < .05$). Educated White women were most likely to be perfectionistic. Community White women were less perfectionistic than community Black women ($F(1, 365) = 8.89, p < .01$). Rural White women were less perfectionistic than rural Black women ($F(1, 365) = 15.92, p < .001$). White and Black urban women differed with Black women having less perfectionism. In addition, urban White women were more perfectionistic than rural women.

Eating disorders are more prevalent with higher education and the more education one receives the more skeptical or less trusting one becomes ($F(1, 365 = 4.88, p < .05$). Community Black women had more interoceptive awareness than more educated Black women. The community White women had less confusion in recognizing emotional states than community Black women. The more educated White women had more confusion in recognizing emotional states than the more educated Black women ($F(1, 365 = 9.29, p < .01$).

The community group focused on spiritual ideals ($F(1, 365) = 5.40, p < .05$) and were more impulsive than more educated women ($F(1, 365) = 11.15, p < .001$). Community Black women had greater impulsivity than all other groups. More educated Black women had less impulsivity than White women, regardless of education level ($F(1, 365 = 14.28, p < .001$. In addition, the community Black women had more impulsivity ($F(1, 365 = 14.28, p < .001$) and sought after spiritual ideals more than all other groups of women ($F(1, 365 = 8.88, p < .01$). White women, regardless of education level, were more impulsive than educated Black women ($F(1, 365 = 14.28, p < .001$). Educated White women sought after spiritual ideals or self-restraint more than educated Black women.

There were no ethnic, geographic, or educational differences in body dissatisfaction, maturity fears, and social insecurity. It would seem that education and race have a strong impact on psychological functions related to eating disorders.

Ways of Coping

African Americans differed from White women by detaching from situations ($F(1, 356) = 20.38, p < .001$), being more confrontive or aggressive ($F(1, 351) = 5.47, p < .05$), accepting their roles in problems that arise ($F(1, 360) = 22.51, p < .001$), and engaging in analytical problem solving efforts ($F(1, 356) = 13.66, p < .001$; see Table 3). Community women were more likely to distance, detach or minimize more than more educated women ($F(1, 354) = 11.20, p < .001$). The rural community women were more aggressive in coping behavior and acting on their environments than the more educated rural women ($F(1, 351) = 4.00, p < .05$).

Black women had more self-control than White women ($F(1, 356) = 17.76, p < .001$). Community Black women exercised more self-control than community White women or more educated women, regardless of ethnicity ($F(1, 356) = 4.80, p < .05$). The more educated rural women had less self-control than urban or rural community women and more educated urban women ($F(1, 356) = 4.86, p < .05$).

The community Black women accepted more responsibility than community White women or more educated Black and White women ($F(1, 360) = 9.44, p < .01$). The community women coped more with

TABLE 3. Ways of Coping, Beck Depression, and Culture Free Self-Esteem Group Scores

| | African American | | | | European American | | | | |
| | Urban | | Rural | | Urban | | Rural | | |
	Comm.	Educ.	Comm.	Educ.	Comm.	Educ.	Comm.	Educ.	
CC	7.2	6.6	8.2	5.6	5.6	6.3	6.7	5.9	a*, bc*
Dist	7.7	6.6	8.4	4.8	6.2	5.3	5.9	4.9	a***, c***
SC	10.7	10.3	12.3	7.9	9.6	10.1	8.7	8.7	a***, ac*, bc*
SSS	8.7	8.4	9.0	6.0	7.9	9.6	7.8	8.1	
AR	5.6	4.1	6.2	3.3	4.2	4.6	3.6	3.4	a***, c**, ac**
Esc	8.9	5.5	10.0	6.2	7.8	7.7	7.1	6.9	c**, ac**
PPS	10.2	9.9	10.3	9.0	8.5	8.3	8.4	8.6	a***
PR	13.1	11.2	12.2	10.3	6.5	7.1	8.2	8.1	a***
BDI	9.3	4.8	11.0	7.8	9.2	10.8	8.3	7.8	c*, ac**, ab*
CFS	23.8	20.7	24.0	22.5	23.3	23.3	23.5	24.2	c*, ac**

* $p < .05$, ** $p < .01$, *** $p < .001$

CC = Confrontive Coping
Dist = Distance
SC = Self Control
SSS = Seeking Social Support
AR = Accepting Responsibility
Esc = Escape Avoidance
PPS = Planful Problem Solving

PR = Positive Reappraisal
BDI = Beck Depression Inventory
CFS = Culture Free Self-Esteem Inventory
a = Ethnicity
b = Urban-Rural
c = Education

use of escape-avoidance than more educated women ($F(1, 349) = 10.08$, $p < .01$). Community Black women used more escape-avoidance than more educated Black women ($F(1, 349) = 10.10$, $p < .01$). Educated White and Black women used escape-avoidance similarly. Education affected these coping strategies: distance ($F(1, 354) = 11.20$, $p < .001$), accepting responsibility ($F(1, 360) = 8.17$, $p < .01$), and escape-avoidance. The community women were more likely than the more educated women to use detaching and escape-avoidance and more likely to accept responsibility.

Black women were more likely to use positive reappraisal than White women ($F(1, 354) = 57.24$, $p < .001$). There were no differences among the groups of women in seeking social support.

Depression and Self-Esteem

There was an educational impact on depression. The community women had a greater propensity toward depression than the more educated women $(F(1,365) = 5.82, p < .05)$. The more educated Black women were less depressed than the community Black or educated White women $(F(1, 365) = 7.34, p < .01)$. Rural Black women had greater levels of depression than urban Black women $(F(1,365) = 4.96, p < .05)$.

The community women had higher self-esteem than the more educated women $(F(1, 363) = 4.26, p < .05;$ see Table 3). Educated Black women had lower self-esteem than all of the other groups, although, on average, still in the intermediate range $(F(1, 363) = 11.99, p < .01)$.

The impact on each measure administered indicates that education influenced depression, self-esteem, coping and eating disorders tremendously (see Tables 2 and 3). Pearson correlations indicated a significant relationship between impulse regulation and escape-avoidance (r = .45). All correlations among eating disorder psychological factors were low to moderate. Depression significantly correlated with impulse regulation (r = .47) and interoceptive awareness (r = .50). Self-Esteem was moderately and inversely related to social insecurity (r = − .42).

DISCUSSION

What Psychological Eating Disorder Symptoms Are Found Among Women?

Eating disorder symptoms include ineffectiveness and perfectionism. The women experience being overwhelmed and have superior ideals and standards for achievement that might be unrealistic. These women exhibit more interpersonal distrust, social insecurity, and maturity fears than the normative Eating Disorder Group used in the development of the EDI. Ineffectiveness and perfectionism might result in greater stress and unrealistic expectations which, in turn, might lead to eating disorders. Subjective attractiveness and perfectionism has been linked to risk for disordered eating (Davis, Claridge, & Fox, 2000).

Participants in this study were similar to the nonpatient normative group in drive for thinness, bulimia, body dissatisfaction, perfectionism, interoceptive awareness, asceticism, and impulse regulation. When the total sample is compared to the normative group, the participants in our research experienced relationships as somewhat more tense and unrewarding, and they experienced feelings of insecurity with some desire to retreat to the security of childhood. They were experiencing a high degree of alienation and reluctance to form close relationships.

Are There Healthy or Unhealthy Eating Patterns?

There are healthy eating patterns. Unhealthy are extremes, such as frequent diet restriction, exercising at extremes, and purging, which lead to medical problems. Some participants noted purging frequently. Abnormal use of diet pills, diuretics and laxatives have unhealthy effects on the body. The effects might not appear immediately and weight loss provides immediate gratification. More focus regarding education on weight control with different populations should occur.

Are there racial differences in patterns of eating? There are racial differences in weights, eating patterns, and methods of weight control. Ideal weight differs by eleven pounds. White women prefer 128 pounds and Black women prefer 139 pounds as the ideal weights. Black women wish to be small, and White women even smaller. Since body image differs, it supports the idea of cultural relevance for the women in considering eating patterns. They differ in their lowest, longest, highest, actual, stable, and ideal weights with Black women consistently being higher and varying by seven to sixteen pounds.

White women tend to restrict their diets earlier than African Americans. White women acknowledged purging more frequently than Black women. Laxatives were used equally by both Black women and White women for weight control. Binging occurs early during the teen years and is common to both groups; White women begin earlier than Black women. Purging occurs at about the same age for each group. Purging occurs significantly more among White women and rarely among Black women. Black women and White women tend to use laxatives equally. Diet pill and diuretic use is similar among all groups. White women tend to restrict their diets more than Black women. Education for teenagers concerning nutrition and exercise is vastly important.

What are the common and uncommon eating disorder factors among African American and White Women? Black women acknowledge more feelings of ineffectiveness than White women. Black women had more feelings of inadequacy, worthlessness, and lack of control over their lives than White women. This is a critical component of eating disorders and relates to low self-esteem. This suggests that African American women recognize more of a struggle with inadequacy, worthlessness and control over life as it relates to an eating disorder than White women do.

Are There Differences Associated with Education Level?

There are psychological eating disorder symptoms associated with education levels. The community women used more asceticism and impulse regulation than the more educated women, and were more impulsive and likely to practice self-denial or restraint. There was also more difficulty interpreting bodily cues and managing impulses such as substance abuse, binging, etc. The more educated women were more interpersonally distrustful of others and more perfectionistic than the community women. This might be explained as the more knowledge one has gained, the more skeptical one becomes. More educated women were more critical or exacting in task accomplishment than the community women. The community women had higher self-esteem than the more educated women. The community women were more depressed than the educated women and the educated Black women were less depressed than all other groups.

Community women reported exercising more than more educated women. This might indicate that community women are more active or have greater concern with bodily shape and appearance or health concerns than more educated women. The use of diet pills was more frequent for community women than for women with more education. Those reporting indicated weekly use of diet pills most frequently.

Are There Geographic Differences (Rural, Urban)?

There were differences based on an urban-rural comparison. Urban women were more perfectionistic than rural women; that might relate to experiencing more pressure in striving. Urban women reported more feelings of ineffectiveness and reported experiencing more stress than rural women. Urban women also experienced stress more than rural women; that might be related to typical patterns of city life which include noise, congested travel, competition, and/or long waits.

The Black women in the rural area were, on average, mildly depressed. Rural Black women were more depressed than urban Black women. This might relate to Black women's being a significant minority in Iowa as opposed to Atlanta where there are significantly more Black women.

Laxatives were used significantly earlier for weight control by urban women than they were by rural women. This might indicate earlier concern in urban areas with body image and physical appearance. This is supported by urban women's stronger drive for thinness, perfectionism, and ineffectiveness. Urban women acknowledged binging as more often pleasurable than rural women did.

There were some demographic differences between urban and rural women. Urban women began their menstrual periods earlier than rural women did. More rural women had ceased having menstrual periods due to menopause, hysterectomy, or pregnancy than urban women. Urban women were more often single, although this might have been influenced by the use of two college sites for data collection. Urban women are more frequently divorced than rural women. Rural women were more likely to be married than urban women.

How Is Depression Related to Eating?

Depression in these women measured in the minimal range, but depression correlates moderately, with impulse regulation and interoceptive awareness. Research supports depression as highly related and a critical component of an eating disorder.

How Is Self-Esteem Related to Eating?

Self-esteem of the participants was in the average range. More educated Black women had lower self-esteem compared to others but still in the intermediate range. Yet the educated Black women were the least depressed when compared to all other women. The community women had higher self-esteem than more educated women. Self-esteem is related to eating as it inversely correlates with social insecurity. Research supports self-esteem as highly related to eating disorders; this study supports the relationship with a sample of nonpatients.

What Type of Help Is Useful in Preventing or Eliminating the Symptoms?

There is concern that clinicians do not recognize or diagnose eating disorders in Black and/or older women. The traditional focus of eating disorders has usually been advertised as young people, White middle class, or the golden girls disease (Browne, 1993; McCarthy, 1990; Root, 1990; Smolak & Striegel-Moore, 2001). Since young people get older, this might be a myth (Wolf, 1992). They still have perfectionistic ideas, body image concerns and extreme weight control methods. One does not get older and become eating ordered automatically. This research supports the idea of cultural differences and that symptoms of eating disorder can exist in an older or age varied population. It validates the onset of an eating disorder at the young adult phase when appearance and body image become important which supports the literature.

It might be useful for health providers to recognize that African American women might not seek to fit dimensions of the typical clinical weight charts and this standard might better depict the "thin ideal" of White women since there are vast differences between their ideal body images (Bowen, Tomoyasu, & Cauce, 1991). Differences in eating behavior might also exist due to social influences regarding women's eating, such as stress or regional location which supports Thompson's research (1994). It is useful to know that African American women with eating disorders might vary in their compensatory behaviors otherwise one might not recognize the symptoms. There might be less tendency for African Americans to purge. Concern with weight develops at a later age and ideal weight is perceived as higher than that for White women. This might have some implications for the typical weight chart which is encountered in health clinics and which tend to endorse a particular weight as the ideal health size and is more in keeping with White women's ideal weights. More emphasis is placed on laxatives for weight control in urban than in rural areas. White women restrict and purge more than Black women. Black women desire to be thin at 139 pounds and White women thinner at 128 pounds. All are based on an average height of five feet four inches for women. This supports the Villarosa finding that most women sought to be thin (Villarosa, 1994). Black women view themselves as attractive at higher weights than White women and the two groups endorse different weights at which they would be comfortable. However, neither average African Americans nor average White Americans are at their ideal weight. White women desire to be 20 pounds thinner and Black women 30 pounds thinner than their actual weights.

It would be helpful to conduct a thorough assessment to determine if clients are experiencing eating disorders. Culturally sensitive assessment involves recognizing food messages are cultural and the "Thin ideal" applies less to Black women as they often hear "Eat and Enjoy." Black women also believe they are still attractive at heavier weights (11 lbs.) that White women reject (Smolak & Striegel-Moore, 2001). Self-esteem is less a factor regarding weight for Black women which is generally unaffected to the degree that it is for White women who experience greater social pressure about being overweight. Gathering a relevant family and social history including attitudes toward eating, weight loss and control is important. Increased focus should be placed on binging behavior, body image, obesity and whether one is eating in response to inequalities in society or a general depression. For many women the thin ideal does not apply and is seen as shallow to view women as focused on bodies rather than with bodies, brains, and emotions. These results have implications for counselors. Black women with disordered eating would benefit from focus on issues of self-esteem; control in their life; and assessment for depression would be appropriate. The more educated Black woman may have less depression but identified greater self-esteem issues. They demonstrate stringent use of coping skills. European American women have greater susceptibility to societal pressure regarding weight and may benefit from focus on self-esteem; body image; reducing the role of external pressure and assessment for depression. They had the greater drive for thinness, endorsed smaller body sizes, and more perfectionistic values. Emphasis regarding weight is conveyed at a comparatively early age.

Treatment for eating disorders includes encouraging the person to express feelings and gets beyond the food issue to the core of the psychological dysfunction (Brouwers, 1994; Thompson, 1994). It would be helpful for health providers to develop culturally based strategies addressing socio-cultural values (e.g., sexism, racism, acculturation, abuse), issues involving extremes of weight, excess exercise, compensatory behavior, emotions, depression, self-esteem, coping and body image as they relate to eating (Boyd, 1993; Pipher, 1997; Thompson, 1994). Nutrition education and promoting healthy weight control might be most useful initiated at high school and college levels and continuing throughout the lifespan.

There is a need to cease using the term "fat" in the literature as this implies someone is researching the issue who has never struggled with an eating disorder. Inclusion of people of various weights as researchers; normal, thin, or heavy may provide varying perspectives. Multiracial treatment and research teams are recommended to broaden recognition and identification of eating disorders and increase comfort at seeking clinical treatment. Training counselors regarding eating disorders and ethnicity would be useful to improve detection. Although it is convenient to study populations at colleges and clinics, more field studies need to be achieved to examine how ethnic persons are affected in their context. Essentially the thin ideal is perpetuated by society and the myth that only White women are impacted by eating disorders should be dispelled. Addressing the health concerns of ethnic persons would likely have a positive impact on physical health of related dietary disorders that are prevalent in the Black community such as hypertension, diabetes, obesity, and coronary disease, in addition to issues of mental health.

In developing therapy approaches for working with women who have eating disorders, it is useful to review the coping strategies which they have found most effective. Black women used analytical problem solving more frequently and acknowledged their roles in situations. Black women use distance more than the White women suggesting minimization of a situation or efforts to detach and use more aggression. This might relate to ethnicity and finding ways to protect oneself in social interactions. Community participants also practice distance as a means of coping. Both Black women and less educated women might experience low status in social interactions. African Americans used self-control more than the White women. They put more effort into regulating their feelings and actions. This might indicate that Black women contend more with regulating emotions regarding situations than White women. Black women engaged in positive reappraisal more than White women, using focused problem solving more frequently to alter situations. This is regarded as a highly positive means of coping. Black women relied on these means of coping significantly more than White women. This might relate to the degree of conflict experienced in their environment and learning to respond in analytical ways, or it might recognize use of religion by Black women as the Positive Reappraisal scale includes the item "I prayed" about it. Seeking of social support was similar between the racial groups. The Community women relied more on distance, accepting or acknowledging their roles in problems and escape-avoidance of situations than the more educated group. Other scales were similar between the community and more educated women.

This study has limited generalizability since this was a normal population sampled for eating disorders. Though the urban and rural differences are noted, it may not be a precise difference as many of the participants in the rural area were in college temporarily, but may have established residence in an urban area.

The data collection sites differed significantly by education level ($\chi^2(80) = 209.39$, $p < .001$). One rural site and one urban site each differed from other sites in that most of the participants had not completed high school. Some participants in one of the urban settings had difficulty reading the survey and needed assistance. Correspondingly, one rural site and one urban site each had many participants with doctorates.

Urban-rural differences in menstrual histories might be due to data collection at a rural women's health center. Women were more frequently single than married. Differences in marital status might be influenced by sampling two colleges in the Atlanta/Decatur area where single young women are matriculating.

CONCLUSION

The research suggests that eating disorders are highly related to education, more concern with body image exists for urban women, and that there are racial differences in perceptions of ideal weight. Eating disorders are more prevalent among White women but Black women have less concern with being as thin as White women desire but still endorse a slender frame. Their perceptions of attractive body size are not equivalent but Black women should not be dismissed as lacking eating disorders. This study supports the literature which indicates Black women's acceptance of larger body size, and different perceptions of the ideal figure than White women. African Americans' eating relates more to feelings of inadequacy and might relate to compulsive eating. The coping styles of Black women also differ from White women: Black women tend to be more confrontive. Black women act more on their environment and exert more effort at resolving problems than White women. This is probably adaptive given the negative historical and current sociocultural treatment of Black Americans. The Black community women engaged more in bulimia than the more educated urban Black group. This does not fit the pattern of White women where the more educated White women experience the disorder. Educated urban women had a stronger drive for thinness than all other women. The White urban women also endorsed more perfectionism than women in the other groups.

This study was novel in that it used middle aged women with an age range from 18-55 years, averaging 45 years, with 95% of the women being 45 years old or younger. The mean age of this group of participants (31 years) was somewhat older than that of the participants in most of the eating disorder literature. Most studies focus on college or high school age people in their teens or twenties. This study expands the literature by including older women and African American women.

Eating disorders are multicultural and might manifest differently according to ethnicity, geographic location, and education level. It also appears that eating disorder symptoms can exist well beyond the teens and twenties. Development of healthy concepts and images regarding eating disorders should remain a priority.

REFERENCES

Altabe, M. (1998). Ethnicity and body image: Quantitative and qualitative analysis. *International Journal of Eating Disorders, 23*, 153-159.

American Psychiatric Association (1987). *Diagnostic and statistical manual of mental disorder* revised (3rd ed.). Washington, D.C.: Author.

American Psychiatric Association (1994). *Diagnostic and statistical manual of mental disorders* (4th ed.). Washington, D.C.: Author.

Andersen, A. (1985). *Practical comprehensive treatment of anorexia nervosa and bulimia.* Baltimore, MD: Johns Hopkins University Press.

Battle, J. (1992). *Culture-free self-esteem inventories* (2nd ed.). *Examiners Manual.* Austin, TX: Pro Ed.

Beck, A. T. (1978). *Beck depression inventory.* Philadelphia, PA: Center for Cognitive Therapy.

Beck, A. T., & Steer, R. A. (1993). *Beck depression inventory manual.* San Antonio, TX: The Psychological Corporation.

Bowen, D. J., Tomoyasu, N., & Cauce, A.M. (1991). The triple threat: A discussion of gender, class, and race differences in weight. *Women & Health, 17*, 123-143.

Boyd, J. A. (1993). *In the company of my sisters: Black women and self-esteem.* New York, NY: Dutton.

Brouwers, M. (1994). Bulimia and the relationship with food: A letters-to-food technique. *Journal of Counseling and Development, 73*, 220-222.

Browne, M. (1993, June). Dying to be thin. *Essence*, 86-87 and 124-129.

Buchanan, K. S. (1993). Creating beauty in Blackness. In C. Brown and K. Jasper eds. *Consuming passions: Feminist approaches to weight preoccupation and eating disorders.* Canada: Second Story Press.

Cogan, J. D., Bhalla, S. K., Sefa-Dedeh, A., & Rothblum, E. D. (1996). A comparison study of United States and African students on perceptions of obesity and thinness. *Journal of Cross-Cultural Psychology, 27* (1), 98-113.

Crago, M., Shisslak, C., & Estes, L. (1996). Eating disturbances among American minority groups: A review. *International Journal of Eating Disorders, 19*, 239-248.

Davis, C., Claridge, G., & Fox, J. (2000). Not just a pretty face: Physical attractiveness and perfectionism in the risk for eating disorders. *International Journal of Eating Disorders, 27*, 67-73.

Davis, C., & Yager, J. (1992). Transcultural aspects of eating disorders: A critical literature review. *Culture, Medicine and Psychiatry, 16*, 377-394.

Folkman, S., & Lazarus, R. S. (1980). An analysis of coping in a middle-aged community sample. *Journal of Health and Social Behavior, 21*, 219-239.

Folkman, S., & Lazarus, R. S. (1988). *Manual for the ways of coping questionnaire.* Palo Alto, CA: Consulting Psychologists Press, Inc.

Garner, D. M. (1990). *Eating disorder inventory-2. Professional Manual.* Odessa, FL: Psychological Assessment Resources, Inc.

Gordon, R. A. (1990). *Anorexia and Bulimia.* Cambridge, MA: Basil Blackwell.

Kumanyika, S., Wilson, J. F., & Guilford-Davenport, M. (1993). Weight-related attitudes and behaviors of Black women. *Journal of the American Diabetic Association, 93*, 416-422.

Le Grange, D., Stone, A. A., & Brownell, K. D. (1998). Eating disturbances in White and minority female dieters. *International Journal of Eating Disorders, 24*, 395-403.

Manley, R. S., Tonkin, R., & Hammond, C. (1988). A method for the assessment of body image disturbance in patients with eating disorders. *Journal of Adolescent Health Care, 9*, 384-388.

McCarthy, M. (1990). The thin ideal, depression and eating disorders in women. *Behavior Research Therapy, 28*, 205-215.

Miller, K. D. (1991). Compulsive overeating. *Nursing Clinics of North America, 26*, 699-705.

Miller, K J., Gleaves, D. H., Hirsch, T. G., Green, B. A., Snow, A. C., & Corbett, C. C. (2000). Comparisons of body image dimensions by race/ethnicity and gender in a university population. *International Journal of Eating Disorders, 27*, 310-316.

Osvold, L.L., & Sodowsky, G. R. (1993). Eating disorders of White American racial and ethnic minority American, and international women. *Journal of Multicultural Counseling and Development, 21*, 143-154.

Pipher, M. (1997). *Hunger pains: The modern woman's tragic quest for thinness.* New York: Ballantine.

Root, M. P. P. (1990). Disordered eating in women of color. *Sex Roles, 22*, 1-8.

Sanford, L. T., & Donovan, M. E. (1985). *Women and self-esteem.* New York, NY: Penguin Books, USA Inc.

Schwartz, D. M., Thompson, M. G., & Johnson, C. L. (1982). Anorexia nervosa & bulimia: The sociocultural context. *The International Journal of Eating Disorders, 1*, 20-36, Spring.

Smolak, L., & Striegel-Moore, R. H. (2001). Challenging the myth of the golden girl: Ethnicity and eating disorders. In R. H. Striegel-Moore & L. Smolak (Eds.), *Eating disorders: Innovative directions in research and practice* (pp. 111-132). Washington, DC: American Psychological Association.

Statistical Analysis Institute, Inc. (1990). *SAS/STAT users guide*, Version 6 (4th cd., Vol. 2). Cary, NC: Author.

Thomas, V. G. (1987). Body-image satisfaction among Black women. *The Journal of Social Psychology, 129*, 107-112.

Thompson, B. W. (1994). *A hunger so wide and so deep.* Minneapolis, MN: University of Minnesota.

Villarosa, L. (1994; January). Dangerous eating. *Essence, 24*, 19-21.

Weiss, M. G. (1995). Eating disorders and disordered eating in different cultures. *The Psychiatric Clinics of North America, 18* (3), 537-551.

Wildes, J. E., Emery, R. E., & Simons, A. D. (2001). The roles of ethnicity and culture in the development of eating disturbance and body dissatisfaction: A metaanalytic review. *Clinical Psychology Review, 21* (4), 521-551.

Williamson, D. A. (1990). *Assessment of eating disorders: obesity, anorexia, and bulimia nervosa.* Elmsford, NY: Pergamon Press.

Wolf, N. (1992). *The beauty myth.* New York, NY: Doubleday.

DORMANT
AND PART-TIME DISABILITIES

The Influence of Silent Learning Disorders
on the Lives of Women

Sara J. Hoffschmidt
Cheryl S. Weinstein

SUMMARY. Longstanding neurocognitive deficits such as learning disorders greatly influence development of a woman's personality, relationships, and educational and vocational attainment. In our clinical

Sara J. Hoffschmidt, PhD, is a post-doctoral fellow in neuropsychology at Harvard Medical School in the combined neuropsychology training program of Massachusetts Mental Health Center (MMIIC) and the Beth-Israel Deaconess Medical Center (BIDMC). Cheryl S. Weinstein, PhD, is Assistant Professor of Psychology of Harvard Medical School and Director of the Center for Cognitive Remediation at the Beth Israel Deaconess Hospital. She is also Assistant Director of Training in the neuropsychology training program of the MMHC and the BIDMC.

Address correspondence to: Sara J. Hoffschmidt, Massachusetts Mental Health Center/Harvard Medical School, 74 Fenwood Road, Boston, MA 02115.

[Haworth co-indexing entry note]: "The Influence of Silent Learning Disorders on the Lives of Women." Hoffschmidt, Sara J., and Cheryl S. Weinstein. Co-published simultaneously in *Women & Therapy* (The Haworth Press, Inc.) Vol. 26, No. 1/2, 2003, pp. 81-94; and: *Women with Visible and Invisible Disabilities: Multiple Intersections, Multiple Issues, Multiple Therapies* (ed: Martha E. Banks, and Ellyn Kaschak) The Haworth Press, Inc., 2003, pp. 81-94. Single or multiple copies of this article are available for a fee from The Haworth Document Delivery Service [1-800-HAWORTH, 9:00 a.m. - 5:00 p.m. (EST). E-mail address: getinfo@haworthpressinc.com].

practice, we increasingly see women with previously undiagnosed "silent learning disorders." Educational and career milestones, problems in the workplace, parenting a child with a learning disorder, and normal aging along with common medical conditions can exacerbate these "silent learning disorders." As a result, neurocognitive deficits might appear more pronounced as former ways of compensating for learning problems no longer are adequate. When such learning disorders are not detected, women and their therapists might not avail themselves of interventions that can help to treat the reading, visual-spatial, organizational, or other neurocognitive deficits, and indirectly help with patterns of anxiety, depression, and low self-esteem. In the present paper, we characterize women with silent learning disorders, discuss implications if disorders remain undetected, and present case examples. A model and strategies for detecting silent learning disorders also are presented. *[Article copies available for a fee from The Haworth Document Delivery Service: 1-800-HAWORTH. E-mail address: <getinfo@haworthpressinc.com> Website: <http://www.HaworthPress.com> © 2003 by The Haworth Press, Inc. All rights reserved.]*

KEYWORDS. Learning disorders, undiagnosed learning disorders, women

INTRODUCTION

Women's neurocognitive abilities influence their understanding of the world, their ability to connect with others, and educational and vocational achievement. The ability to attend to information, to process lengthy communication, and to inhibit distractions are essential components of interaction. If neurocognitive deficits are present (such as distractibility, language processing deficits, reduced attention span), the entire course of development will be affected (Weinstein, Seidman, Feldman, & Ratey, 1991). Although cognitive vulnerabilities ultimately create a lot of "noise" and interrupt therapeutic, family, educational, work, and social relationships (Sands & Ratey, 1986), many women find ways of compensating or "covering up" these areas of difficulty. As a result, such deficits (or "silent learning disorders") are quite painful because they might not be identified. Further, our culture compounds the struggle to compensate for neurocognitive difficulties by conveying the expectation that women be "superwomen," juggling the demands of a modern career along with more traditional roles of wife and mother.

It is our experience conducting neuropsychological evaluations in an outpatient hospital-based psychiatry department that women with "silent learning disorders" constitute a significant but often under-referred clinical population. In the current paper, we will: (1) characterize the clinical population of women with "silent learning disorders"; (2) discuss implications if learning disorders remain undetected and present case examples; and (3) provide a model and strategy for detecting and treating silent learning disorders.

Characterizing "Silent Learning Disorders"

We define a "silent learning disorder" as a previously undiagnosed learning disorder in which a neurocognitive function of attention, memory, planning and organization, visual-spatial processing, motor planning, or reading, spelling, mathematical, or writing skills is 1.5 standard deviations below intellectual functions. Further, these deficits cannot be accounted for by cultural, emotional, or socio-economical explanations. Women with silent learning disorders might struggle to work around these unacknowledged deficits. Because their difficulties are not readily apparent, problems in functioning might be commonly misattributed to laziness or failure to live up to potential. Problems in functioning also can be mistakenly ascribed to emotional factors such as depression, anxiety, or stress, but when a careful educational or neuropsychological evaluation is completed, it becomes clear that anxiety and depression are secondary to primary learning problems.

Implications of Silent Learning Disorders

Unfortunately one major consequence for women with silent learning disorders is continuous "misses" in understanding others. In other words, an individual with language processing problems is more likely to insert incorrect information that makes sense to her or him but might not have been presented. Attentional or auditory processing problems also can impede processing of social cues. Such miscommunications in processing and understanding the details of life can result in the failure to deepen relationships and determine what people mean when they say things. When such an error occurs in a therapeutic setting, the listener/therapist might not be aware of their patient's auditory processing problems. Thus, detail or processing errors can be interpreted as resistance or a defense. This unfortunately might lead the patient to blame herself, not fully appreciating the role of her learning disability.

Difficulties with processing also impact development of authenticity and mutuality, behaviors that are necessary for satisfying relationships (Jordan, Kaplan, Miller, Stiver, & Surrey, 1991). When successful, mutuality reflects genuine interest shown in another individual, most often accomplished through listening and paying attention. When one has a neurocognitive deficit that includes problems processing details, the communication flow that would lead to a deepening of relationship is now disrupted, and partners, therapists, teachers, co-workers, and friends might be left wondering "Are you with me?" or perhaps "Are you interested?" Nontraditional therapeutic interventions that can improve communication might be considered, such as writing down details of the session in the last ten minutes. Rather than taking the focus off of more emotional material, the latter approach can actually help the patient incorporate the ideas of therapy and improve the relationship.

Women in academic settings often face a complex interaction of silent learning disorders and other psychological and developmental issues. Students might present to the therapist with complaints of depressed mood, anxiety, and lowered self-image, and the focus of therapy can be separation from the family or improving ways of coping with stress. Rarely will a student say to a therapist, "I can't take notes in large classes because I miss critical details," or "I read slowly and can't finish assignments." Client One illustrates how both clients and therapists might focus more on emotional or family themes.

CLIENT EXAMPLE 1

RF, a twenty-six year old female graduate student from a prestigious college, was not having success in dealing with her anxiety after two years of intensive psychotherapy. Following years of treatment for cancer, her mother died when RF was in the seventh grade. Because her mother was so ill when she was learning to read, RF always thought that sadness about this contributed to anxiety when she was reading and writing. During the interview, however, we discovered that her father had atypical reading habits. He misread words during church services and his e-mail letters were "short blips of language." Although her father always encouraged her education, she saved her money for a neuropsychological evaluation that he perceived as a "narcissistic exercise."

On formal evaluation, RF appeared slightly anxious and provided psychological and emotional explanations when she had difficulty on testing. She was puzzled by her "slowness." Overall intellect was in the superior range, but RF appeared to have both a spelling disorder (10th percentile) and a reading disorder (1st percentile). Anxiety did not account for the slowed reading as the patient was unaware that her reading was slowed. A treatment shift occurred based on the neuropsychological evaluation. The meaning of RF's anxiety was expanded to include her experience of coping with a silent learning disorder. Specifically, it was hard to make decisions about her career and whether to pursue a graduate degree without anyone realizing how very hard she worked or commending her for her efforts.

Other women who are students might find they have exhausted their resources for coping with a silent learning disorder when they face major challenges such as graduate school admissions. A frequently heard issue is "If the law school ever knows that I read slowly, I'll never get in," or "I can't tell my professor I need extended time for an examination. He'll think I'm weak, and there will be no job recommendation." Client Two highlights such difficulties.

CLIENT EXAMPLE 2

Patient MB presented for neuropsychological evaluation questioning whether she had a learning disorder. She was in the process of applying to a highly competitive graduate program and was concerned that her grades, which were above average but not straight "As," would be reason to reject her. MB persisted in fearing that the current evaluation would reveal that she was "really dumb," even though learning difficulties were identified during a previous evaluation in her native country. Focusing on her perceived intellectual deficit, she presented with symptoms of anxiety and depression, and ignored that the prior evaluation had showed reading deficits in the context of very high intellect.

Results of our evaluation were consistent with her prior evaluation. Her verbal intellect was within the very superior range (> 99th percentile rank), yet her reading rate and comprehension were severely lowered (1st percentile rank and 12th percentile rank, respectively). Although she struggled with the knowledge that her reading was so low, a major intervention was accomplished in again reinforcing the excellence of her intellect. She also was able to focus on ways of coping with her deficits, in effect expanding treatment of her depression beyond medication to academic areas that were devastating to her self-esteem.

Once they leave school, women with silent learning disorders might conclude that learning problems are no longer an issue. In part, they hope that they will "outgrow" their learning problems (Hechtman, 1996). Unfortunately learning difficulties are likely to persist, manifesting themselves in the workplace. A woman might find herself working long hours to circumvent slowed reading, or continuously misunderstanding work assignments because of poor organization or mishearing details of a project. Such women can present to the therapist with complaints related to loneliness because there is no time for a social life. Frustration levels might increase as they see seemingly less intelligent individuals get promoted. Other women with silent learning problems might succeed, but interpersonal issues in the work environment are a source of significant stress. Because of the measures they take to compensate, they might be seen as rigid or demanding, as with Client Three.

CLIENT EXAMPLE 3

LP is a thirty-seven year old married mother of two children. She worked as a lawyer in an environment where there were specific rules to follow (e.g., preparing wills, contracts, etc.). She experienced significant success at work, but she had much difficulty working with her secretarial staff. Notably she was demanding and was prone to "blow up" when the necessary information was *not* in front of her. There were also problems at home where LP became particularly upset when there was not a plan for the day. While she prided herself in getting things done, it was particularly frustrating to her when her family did not follow a schedule. She was referred for a neuropsychological evaluation because of marital difficulties. LP's husband worried that LP was not aware of her behavior at work and the overflow of problems to the home environment.

On neuropsychological assessment, LP's intellect was well above average (84th percentile rank). She excelled on planning and problem solving tasks when the information was in front of her. In contrast, organization and planning skills on less structured tasks were markedly inefficient. This was seen on the copy of the Rey Osterrieth Complex Figure (Osterrieth, 1944) in which she started on the right side of space rather than the expected left side of space. She copied parts of the design rather than looking at the major organization components of the design ("the big picture"). This led to significant memory problems when she had to reproduce the design immediately after she drew it (see Figure 1).

Based on the neuropsychological evaluation, LP and her husband were referred for therapy to help them to better understand the meaning of LP's neurocognitive strengths and relative deficits. For LP, recognizing her difficulty problem solving when the information was *not* in front of her was important. She shared this with her staff who looked at her in a more empathic manner. She also could begin to address ways to work with staff to improve and take responsibility for her organization skills. At the same time, ways for LP to deal with organization problems at home were initiated. Her husband now understood her "demanding" behavior, and jointly they worked in therapy to problem solve in a more effective way.

Adult women can again confront silent learning problems when they see their children struggle and get diagnosed with a formal learning disorder. They often identify with their children's difficulties, and might experience feelings of both pain and guilt as they relive their own difficulties in their child's learning problems. At this point many women with silent learning disorders can better appreciate their own struggles, leading them to reassess their problems in learning. Specifically, questions might arise such as "Maybe I wasn't just talkative or a daydreamer because I was a girl. Maybe I had attention deficit disorder too!" or "Maybe math wasn't impossible for me just because I was a girl!"

Compounding their heightened awareness of their own learning problems, mothers of children with learning disorders can face great frustration when their children's teachers tell them to organize their children. Such a mother, with her own impaired organizational skills, might unfortunately be viewed as an unhelpful or disinterested parent. When impairments are more obvious, as in the case of multiple sclerosis or Parkinson's disease, parents are not typically expected to teach their child to work rapidly or get more organized. Yet, parents with other brain based difficulties, such as learning disorders with reduced organi-

FIGURE 1. Rey-Osterrieth Complex Figure Copy (top) and Immediate Recall (bottom) showing LP's poor organization and planning

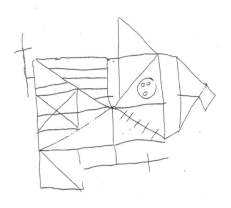

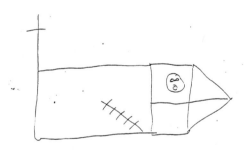

zation skills, often are asked to work with complex behavior reinforcement plans and other ways of teaching their children to get organized. We saw this dynamic in one mother who was having difficulty organizing her work and her family and described "getting organized as elusive as nailing Jell-O on a bulletin board." She often locked herself out of her home, and it was not unusual for her to leave her purse dangling on a restaurant chair. She commented, "Have you noticed that our society expects the woman of the family to be the glue that holds everyone's schedule together? I needed some glue to hold myself together." Therapy for these women must now include teaching organization skills to the mother and her family. This means teaching each family member to use a memory notebook in which they can all see everything they need to do for the day. It will also be important to calculate the amount of time it would take to do the task, the family member who is responsible for the activity, and a backup plan if there is a problem.

The process of aging leads yet another group of women to become more aware of silent learning problems when they are diagnosed with medical problems. When interviewed, they may say "I am in good health . . . with just a little hypertension" or "I only have thyroid problems" or "I only snore a little bit . . . just a little sleep apnea." In addition to medical problems that can impact neurocognitive functioning such as hypertension, hypothyroidism, sleep apnea, and diabetes, the normal aging process also can present changes in thinking. Older patients are likely to experience slower processing speed, and changes in estrogen levels due to menopause can lead to changes in executive functions such as directed attention, working memory, inhibition of inappropriate responses, and cognitive flexibility (Keenan, Ezzat, Ginsburg, & Moore, 2001). When these patients come to therapy with complaints of difficulties coping or feeling more easily stressed, it is important to review school records. After a neuropsychological assessment, it might become clear that there is a longstanding silent learning disorder. Up until this point, hard work and other ways of compensating have helped to disguise the disorder, but once even a mild medical problem develops, the deficit is more apparent. Unfortunately, the normal aging process makes it harder to circumvent longstanding deficits, and it appears that "a little reading disorder" plus mild hypothyroidism along with normal aging pushes the patient into overload (see Figure 2).

FROM VULNERABILITY TO DEFICIT: A MODEL FOR SILENT LEARNING DISORDERS

Figure 2 demonstrates the overload model where a confluence of seemingly mild problems leads to a deficit. A physician might look at each problem in isolation given the demands of managed care, and determine that the woman is stressed. This can lead to focused treatment that cannot address all relevant biological, psychological, and social factors.

The psychotherapist, however, is challenged to look at the big picture, and integrate all relevant factors that can contribute to learning problems. For example, a college student might work around slowed reading with success. She can, however, have premenstrual dysphoric problems, and at such times reading is extremely difficult. If the patient gets

FIGURE 2. From vulnerability to deficit: A model for silent learning disorders. The confluence of a silent learning disorder, normal aging, stress, and medical problems lead to more pronounced deficits and problems in functioning.

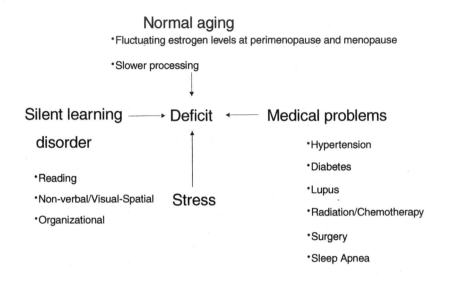

behind in school work, becomes stressed, and then depressed because of school difficulties, it is obviously important to address her depressed mood. At the same time, the astute therapist also looks for ways to support reading skills. For such a patient, even psychoeducation about the interplay among these neurodevelopmental, medical, and emotional factors can be useful and help to arrest her cycle of lowered functioning.

Another group that illustrates our model and is easily pushed into overload with undiagnosed learning problems are pre-term or low weight babies. Families of pre-term babies understandably are overjoyed that the child survives, but because in some ways these children have already exceeded expectations, neurodevelopmental cognitive problems may be overlooked. Unfortunately, research shows higher risk for impaired brain maturation in pre-term infants, and this is consistent with clinically observed behavioral and educational problems (Peterson et al., 2000). Client Four illustrates how underlying vulnerabilities that are most likely related to pre-term status lead to significant learning and emotional difficulties.

CLIENT EXAMPLE 4

AL presented for a neuropsychological consultation to determine whether neurocognitive factors were contributing to her disabling difficulties with anxiety and depression. She also reported long-standing difficulties with reading. During the interview, it became apparent that although she was successful in her job, AL felt helpless and demoralized from years of difficulty with concentration, thinking, depression, and anxiety. Notably, AL was born two and a half months premature, and her mother smoked during the pregnancy. AL's difficult childhood included shyness, bedwetting, and excessive worrying. As an adult, she had three inpatient psychiatric hospitalizations for depression. With great effort, she completed both undergraduate and graduate degrees. Neuropsychological testing revealed that in addition to depression and anxiety, AL had a significant neurodevelopmental learning disorder impacting attention, organization of information, and regulation of affect. Testing further indicated both reading and mathematics disorders, in contrast to her excellent intellect and strong verbal reasoning skills.

AL's prematurity is hypothesized to have influenced successful brain organization, leading to significant frontal network deficits in attention and organization of information as well as stress, depression, and anxiety. Prior to her evaluation, AL had focused more on the emotional aspects of her problems, with less of an appreciation for the major impact of her pre-term birth. Reframing her difficulties in this way allowed her to go back to therapy with a different focus; there was grieving about the circumstances of her birth to be done, but also less self-blame for her difficulties. The evaluation further helped AL to commend herself for her successes and better grasp how remarkable her educational achievements were in light of her learning disorders.

STRATEGIES FOR DETECTING
AND TREATING SILENT LEARNING DISORDERS

Therapists can begin to address silent learning disorders by expanding the questions that are asked in a diagnostic interview (see Table 1). This includes addressing biological vulnerabilities such as "Were you a bed wetter?" or "Did you have frequent ear infections in childhood?" Questions about early school experiences are particularly important such as "Did you have difficulty with your handwriting?" or "Were you a slow reader?" Problems can emerge at different grade levels. For example, the 4th grade is often a time when students are first asked to be more independent. During the seventh grade children with learning problems often have more difficulties as they change classes and the organization of a single classroom is removed. At the high school level the workload increases significantly and a foreign language might be introduced. Standardized test scores such as the PSAT and SAT can be particularly interesting measures to the clinician as an indication of reading abilities under timed conditions.

We find it productive to ask about the process of selecting a college, and whether parents or siblings went to similarly competitive settings. Oftentimes asking specifically about each sibling and where they went to school helps to contextualize the patient's experience in the family, giving clues about the possible presence of an undetected learning disorder. Another area of focus might be the transition to college, as a client with a silent learning disorder might report problems beginning in college, particularly when the support of family is removed and they are facing significantly less structure and less sleep.

Overall, a thorough intake interview and survey of symptoms highlighting signs of problems in learning will help detect silent learning disorders. This can be difficult for the therapist, particularly if the pa-

TABLE 1. Areas that may signal silent learning disorders

Speech and language: Circumstantial, rambling, or disorganized

Thinking: Perseverating, difficulty connecting thoughts, problems prioritizing information

Attention: Excessive daydreaming, difficulty doing two things simultaneously, distractibility, problems following directions, absentmindedness

Academic Skills: Poor reading, writing, spelling, and arithmetical skills, failure to achieve in school and career at predicted levels

Motor Functions: Hyperactivity, unexplained tremor, fidgeting, writing that is micrographic, poorly formed, or fragmented

Memory: Cannot recall recent events, complaints about poor memory, difficulty following directions, poor performance after a work promotion requiring new learning

Visual-spatial abilities: Gets lost, difficulty driving to new or familiar locations, poor manual skills, disorganized household and office

Emotions and Comportment: Apathy, irritability that is inappropriate to an incident, social learning problems and awkwardness, excessive shyness or a "loner," difficulty understanding humor and other social nuances

---

Source: Adapted from Howieson, D. B., & Lezak, M. D. (1992). The Neuropsychological Evaluation, in S. C. Yudofsky & R. E. Hales (Eds.), *American Psychiatric Textbook of Neuropsychiatry, 2nd Edition* (p.139). Washington, DC: American Psychiatric Press.

tient is focused on sharing painful experiences. Using a checklist such as the Wender Utah Scale (Wender, Reimherr, & Wood, 1985) or the Neuropsychology Symptom Checklist (Schinka, 1986) can be helpful to screen for learning problems. If a learning disorder is suspected, referral for neuropsychological evaluation might help to clarify the nature and degree of neurocognitive or neurodevelopmental deficit. The referral question also may include asking why a woman seems to be pushed into "overload" at this particular time of her life.

CONCLUSIONS

In our experience conducting outpatient neuropsychological evaluations, women with silent learning disorders represent an often overlooked clinical population. Too often, women "work harder," blaming themselves and attempting to compensate for long-standing neurodevelopmental problems. We have attempted to describe some instances in which silent learning disorders become more apparent as women develop and meet new challenges in school, at work, in the family, and with their health. Focusing on an interactive model, we proposed that neurocognitive vulnerabilities combined with life stressors, developmental milestones, normal aging, and medical problems might make it impossible for a woman to continue to cope as she is now truly experiencing deficits. We further suggested strategies for determining whether a complete neuropsychological evaluation can be helpful. It is our hope that incorporating awareness of silent learning disorders can dramatically alter the range and effectiveness of treatment interventions, helping patients to work through shame about their difficulties toward greater self acceptance.

REFERENCES

Hechtman, L. (Ed.). (1996). *Do they grow out of it? Long-term outcomes of childhood disorders.* Washington, DC: American Psychiatric Press, Inc.

Howieson, D. B., & Lezak, M. D. (1992). The Neuropsychological Evaluation, in S. C. Yudofsky & R. E. Hales (Eds.), *American Psychiatric Textbook of Neuropsychiatry, 2nd Edition* (p. 139). Washington, DC: American Psychiatric Press.

Jordan, J., Kaplan, A., Miller, J., Stiver, I., & Surrey, J. (1991). *Women's Growth in Connection.* New York: Guilford Press.

Keenan, P. A., Ezzat, W. H., Ginsburg, K., & Moore, G. J. (2001, February). *Prefrontal cortex as the site of estrogen's effect on cognition.* Poster session presented at the bi-annual meeting of the International Neuropsychological Society, Chicago, IL.

Osterrieth, P. A. (1944). Le test de copie d'une figure complexe. *Archives de Psychologie, 30*, 206-356.

Peterson, B. S., Vohr, B., Staib, L. H., Cannistraci, C. J., Dolberg, A., Schneider, K. C., Katz, K. H., Westerveld, M., Sparrow, S., Anderson, A. W., Duncan, C. C., Makuch, R. W., Gore, J. C., & Ment, L. R. (2000). Regional brain volume abnormalities and long-term cognitive outcome in pre-term infants. *Journal of the American Medical Association, 284*, 1939-1947.

Sands, S., & Ratey, J. J. (1986). The concept of noise. *Psychiatry, 49*, 290-297.

Schinka, J. A. (1986). *The Neuropsychological Symptom Checklist.* Odessa, FL: Psychological Assessment Resources, Inc.

Weinstein, C. S., Seidman, L. J., Feldman, J. J., & Ratey, J. (1991). Neurocognitive disorders in psychiatry: A case example of diagnostic and treatment dilemmas. *Psychiatry, 54*, 65-75.

Wender, P. H., Reinherr, F. W., & Wood, D. (1985). A controlled study of methylphenidate in the treatment of attention deficit disorder, residual type, in adults. *American Journal of Psychiatry, 142*, 522-547.

Part-Time Disabled Lesbian Passing on Roller Blades, or PMS, Prozac, and Essentializing Women's Ailments

Carmen Poulin
Lynne Gouliquer

SUMMARY. This paper discusses the role of the medical and psychiatric systems, as well as the pharmaceutical industry, in the social construction of women's hormonally-related ailments and their treatments. For some marginalised groups, *passing* as "normal" is a protection strategy against discrimination and maltreatment. Lesbians and *in*visibly disabled persons are examples of such groups. Given that the reproductive cycle and madness have been linked historically, women suffering from

Carmen Poulin, PhD, is Professor of Psychology and Director of Women Studies at the University of New Brunswick, Fredericton, New Brunswick, Canada. Lynne Gouliquer is currently completing her PhD in Sociology at McGill University, Montreal, Quebec, Canada.

Address correspondence to: Carmen Poulin, PhD, Psychology Department, University of New Brunswick, Bag Service # 45444, Fredericton, N.B. Canada E3B 6E4 (E-mail: carmen@unb.ca) or to Lynne Gouliquer, Sociology Department, McGill University, 855 Sherbrooke Street West, Montreal, Quebec, Canada H3A 2T7 (E-mail: lynne. gouliquer@ mcgill.ca).

The order of authorship was determined randomly as both authors contributed equally to the manuscript. The authors wish to thank Lucia Benaquisto, Bette Brazier, Bev Brazier, Jacquie Harvey, and Kristen Newman for their invaluable comments on earlier drafts of this paper. In addition, financial support from the Social Sciences and Humanities Research Council of Canada and the O'Brien Foundation, St. John, New Brunswick, Canada is gratefully acknowledged.

[Haworth co-indexing entry note]: "Part-Time Disabled Lesbian Passing on Roller Blades, or PMS, Prozac, and Essentializing Women's Ailments." Poulin, Carmen, and Lynne Gouliquer. Co-published simultaneously in *Women & Therapy* (The Haworth Press, Inc.) Vol. 26, No. 1/2, 2003, pp. 95-108; and: *Women with Visible and Invisible Disabilities: Multiple Intersections, Multiple Issues, Multiple Therapies* (ed: Martha E. Banks, and Ellyn Kaschak) The Haworth Press, Inc., 2003, pp. 95-108. Single or multiple copies of this article are available for a fee from The Haworth Document Delivery Service [1-800-HAWORTH, 9:00 a.m. - 5:00 p.m. (EST). E-mail address: getinfo@haworthpressinc.com].

95

disabling cyclical conditions might also be stigmatised. In this context, the dilemma between seeking treatment versus being labelled psychologically ill is expounded. *[Article copies available for a fee from The Haworth Document De-livery Service: 1-800-HAWORTH. E-mail address: <getinfo@haworthpressinc.com> Website: <http://www.HaworthPress.com> © 2003 by The Haworth Press, Inc. All rights reserved.]*

KEYWORDS. PMS, Prozac, disability, lesbian, premenstrual

Disability: According to the *Oxford Dictionary*, disability means "1. Physical incapacity, either congenital or caused by injury, disease, etc. 2. A lack of some asset, quality, or attribute, that prevents one's doing something. 3. A legal disqualification" (Allen, 1990, p. 331). Given that I am not a legal expert, I don't think I will comment on the latter definition, although I could probably ramble about how we regulate disabilities . . . but I wish to focus on the first two definitions, and how it relates to my reality. Let me introduce myself: I am a "half-out of the closet" lesbian who can "pass" for a heterosexual most of the time. I am also "fit" and "upbeat" for about 3/4 of the time; the last quarter of my time, I tend to hide in the closet . . . the "water closet," to be more precise. Why do I hang out in water closets? No, it is not for kinky sex, or because I am scared to come out. Rather, it's related to this disability thing, if I dare to call it this way. You see, this thing takes over my life. I hesitate to even admit to it. I mean, we all know about "outing" ourselves, and the discomfort that it can bring, but I'll risk telling you: It's linked to my menstrual cycle. OH DEAR! Not the dreaded PMS! Well, I suppose that according to some, it might be labelled as such. But let me explain: I don't get depressed, I don't get hostile, I don't even get grumpy. No, I just get digestion problems of the kind more commonly known to be associated with Irritable Bowel Disorder (IBD for short). Now which label is the safest? PMS or IBD? "It's all in your head, you know, you have . . . how can I say . . . a nervous digestive system." That's what the first GP I consulted told me.

But why consider this a disability? Well, I probably shouldn't, but during that time of the month, as the second Oxford definition of disability suggests, I exhibit "A lack of some asset, quality, or attribute, that prevents [me from] doing something" . . . like living my life! I don't mean to get too intimate, but I have severe diarrhea, painful cramps, I throw up, and most of the time, I am weak and dizzy because I cannot eat, although I still try to take various types of pain killers to help me manage. Not eating for two to four days is hard, not only because I get weak and dizzy, but because I love food! When I absolutely have to be in public, for instance to give a lecture, I try to determine which pain killer I might be able to keep down that day, which one will give me the least nausea, which one will be most effective to diminish the pain. Once I've ingested the medication and it stays down, I come out of the "water closet." While I feel weak and dizzy, I put on a good front: I put on make-up so that the colour of my face looks half normal, whatever that means. I move at half my regular speed, but for most of the time, I pass . . . I pass for a straight, healthy person.

When I consulted the medical profession about this condition, even though there is no "psychological" or "mental" symptoms associated with this "disability," I am paternalistically listened to and suggested to take Tylenol. More interestingly, the last doctor I consulted suggested Prozac. That had a "déjà vu" feel to it. Remember in the '60s when they used to prescribe Valium for "women's problems" and we rebelled against that? The experience, nevertheless, told me that maybe I should remain "in the closet" on that front. Heaven forbid! Next thing you know, I could be labelled as suffering from a mental disorder. After all, despite the lack of "scientific" evidence, a diagnosis for the so-called "premenstrual disorder" did make it into the *Diagnostic and Statistical Manual of Mental Disorders* (DSM-IV).

Discussing the issue with "like-minded" feminists can also be a drag. A common response is that I have simply bought into the social construction of PMS, which results in my developing this very painful syndrome. Another favourite is that I have been taking so many pain killers that my digestive tract is damaged: That's the chicken and the egg question, isn't it. The well-meaning feminist usually proceeds to tell me about the variety of alternative forms of medicine I should definitely be trying. Of course, much sympathy also accompanies these "supportive" comments. Now, don't get me wrong! I have nothing against alternative medicines. In fact, I have already explored some of these options.

There is menopause lurking around the corner. I am 42. If I make a prediction based on family patterns, I should be fully menopausal at 48. Can I wait until then? Will it be over then? Will I stop having this tendency to hide in closets?

So, where is the intersection between lesbianism and disability? Is being half out and passing, when it comes to proclaiming your lesbianism or disability, linked somehow? Does it have any theoretical meaning? Likely, but all I really want to say right now is that I would rather be out on both counts without having to deal with the discrimination, feeling like a disgrace to society, or feeling marginalised. I mean, it's no big deal, it's just my life. Oh and before I close, let me just add one thing: Whenever you see a woman zooming down the street with roller blades and knee pads, beware! She could be a "part-time disabled lesbian" passing for a "full-time straight and able person." You just never know!

INTRODUCTION

According to popular literature and many contemporary scientific journal articles, most women of reproductive age suffer from varying degrees of the Premenstrual Syndrome (PMS) (for reviews, see Parry, 1997; Poulin, 1991). PMS is defined as a menstruation-related mood and/or physical disorder (Elks, 1993; Hamilton, Parry, & Alagna, 1984; Mortola, 1993; Yonkers, 1997). Upon entering the 21st century, we would like to believe that science has brought us to new understandings, new knowledge, and effective treatments. However, science has found no definitive aetiology or treatment for PMS, despite the fact that it has been categorized as an "illness" or a "disability" for more than 50 years.

"Most discussions of disability begin with a laundry list of disabling conditions" (Finger, 1992, p. 87). PMS is also an umbrella for a long list of disabling conditions. More than 250 symptoms have been ascribed to PMS. According to Finger, a list is unavoidable for an understanding of disability; however, she also contends that the medical "laundry list" of terms limits our understanding because disability is largely a social construct.

In the present article, we examine the impact that dominant hegemonic traditions and institutions, such as religion, the medical profession, and the pharmaceutical industry, have had and still have on the conceptualisation of PMS, and women's lives. We begin by looking at the creation and definition of PMS and related constructs, and then examine the treatment approaches that have been used. We pay particular attention to the implications this has for women who struggle specifically with the *physical* manifestations of hormone-related ailments (e.g., endometriosis) and the invisible forms of disabilities it can represent. We conclude by returning to the concept of "passing," its benefits, and its costs.

The Creation of PMS

Given that PMS is a syndrome that afflicts women during their pre-menstrual phase, a confluence of the history of menstruation and of PMS can be defended (see Walker, 1997, for a parallel approach). This literature demonstrates the extent to which women's ability to menstruate has fascinated clerics, physicians, and scholars for thousands of years. For the most part, this fascination has been to the detriment of women.

To varying degrees, many religions denied women access to their "holy places," forbade their involvement in food preparation, and advocated abstinence from sexual intercourse during their menstrual periods (Elgin & Osterritter, 1973). The *Book of Leviticus* portrays menstruating women as unclean and untouchable, and commands women to perform cleansing rituals (Delaney, Lupton, & Toth, 1988). At one point, Christian doctrine viewed hysteria–which at the time was considered a malaise of the menstrual cycle–as the willful possession of the devil, and women were required to do atonement to rid themselves of it (Rodin, 1992). These religious taboos and doctrines not only limited women's movement and opportunities, they legitimated and cultivated negative menstrual myths (Delaney et al., 1988). Remnants of these limitations are still evident today in traditional religions (e.g., Christian, Islamic, and Jewish faiths).

Ancient Greeks were also concerned with women's reproductive biology (e.g., Pliny and Aristotle). An irregularity or a disorder of the menses was believed to cause madness or emotional anxiety in women (Walker, 1997). Hippocrates attributed mood and behavioural disorders to hysteria, the disease of the wandering uterus (Rodin, 1992; Severino & Moline, 1989).[1] To heal this condition, the Greeks tried to attract the womb back into place with smelling salts, and Hippocrates wrote of marriage and sexual intercourse as a cure (Rodin, 1992; Walker, 1997). Other treatments ranged from manual manipulations of the uterus, to the internal applications of leeches, and the cauterisation of women's reproductive organs (Walker, 1997). Women's psychology and their reproductive system continued to be linked as evidenced in the writing of von Feuchtersleben (1847) when he noted that some women suffered symptoms of mental uneasiness, irritability, and sadness during their menses.

As knowledge about women's anatomy advanced, the existence of the ovaries and their hormonal influence on women's menstrual cycle were identified. Accordingly, women's "madness" became attributed to dysfunctional hormones (Walker, 1997). In time, the menstrual cycle was anatomized into phases and the premenstrual phase came to stand on its own, separate from the menstrual or ovulation phases (Richardson, 1995). The premenstrual phase was identified as a period when negative symptoms (e.g., moodiness, anxiety, irritability) appeared. The symptoms were initially labelled as *premenstrual tension* (Frank, 1931; Horney, 1931/1967), but in the 1950s, the English physician, Dalton, re-cast and publicised the term, the *premenstrual syndrome* (PMS; Greene & Dalton, 1953). Dalton, who was considered an expert on PMS during the '60s and '70s, championed the idea that it was caused by a hormonal imbalance, and advocated natural progesterone as the treatment of choice.[2] Spanning more than 30 years, Dalton's research linked women suffering from PMS to an increased rate of violence and child abuse (1961), a predilection for accidents (1960), an increased frequency of hospital admissions of ill children (1970), and the occurrence of episodic psychiatric admissions (1959) and criminal activity (1980). By that time, PMS had become a common household term of the western world. While Walker (1997) contends that researchers have done a good job at identifying PMS symptoms that occur cross-culturally, the research is limited in terms of cultural variations regarding perceptions of PMS as an "*illness*" or a "*disability.*"

Treating PMS: The General Practice, or One-Size Fits All

Despite the uncertainty in the scientific community, many women report suffering from PMS, and those who seek medical intervention usually turn to their general practitioner. General practitioners tend to either prescribe some form of drug treatment, or refer women to other health care specialists, such as gynecologists or psychiatrists. One of the standard medical guides for general practitioners is the *Merck Manual of Diagnosis and Therapy*. First published in 1899 and now available in 17 languages, the *Merck Manual*, in fact, is believed to be the most widely used medical book in the world (Beers & Berkow, 1999).

In the *Merck Manual*, the premenstrual syndrome, subtitled *premenstrual tension*, can be found in the gynaecology and obstetrics section. Although it lists more than 30 symptoms associated with PMS, the *Merck Manual* reports that the most common complaints are mood alteration and psychological effects such as irritability, nervousness, lack of control, anger, and depression. Further, it suggests that the etiology of PMS is related to fluctuations in estrogen and progesterone (i.e., dysfunctional hormones). Under the heading "treatments," the *Merck Manual* advocates a symptom-based approach. For example, diuretics are recommended for fluid retention, counselling for stress, contraceptives for hormonal adjustments, and tranquillizers for irritability. However, the most recently introduced treatments, namely, fluoxetine and sertraline (brand names: Prozac and Zoloft, respectively), are heralded as "the most effective drugs in the management of both the psychological and physical symptoms of PMS" (Beers & Berkow, 1999, p. 1932). By this latter suggestion, the *Merck Manual* basically proposes that "one" drug, either Prozac or Zoloft, is suitable to treat all symptoms of PMS, whether physical or psychological.

Given its influential status, examining the beginnings of the *Merck Manual* is relevant here. The Merck Research Laboratories, official publishers of the *Merck Manual,* claim that it is published on a non-profit basis for the scientific community and public. Historically, the Merck & Company, in addition to conducting laboratory testing of samples for physicians for profit, sold many of the drugs prescribed in their manual (Merck & Co., 1899)! At this time, it would be interesting to identify and compare the financial players of Prozac and Zoloft, with those of the Merck Research Laboratories.

Prozac and the Pharmaceutical Industry

In the media, Prozac has been championed as the wonder drug for treatment of depression (e.g., Cowley, 1990, 1994; Farr, 1994). In the scientific literature, it is not only acclaimed as an effective treatment for depression and anxiety (Pinel, 1997), but also many other disorders (e.g., bulimia, anorexia, obsessive convulsive disorder, pain relief, PMS, Premenstrual Dysphoric Disorder–PMDD, panic disorder, dysthymic disorder, aggression, and panic disorder) (Messiha, 1993). Consequently, the impression is that Prozac is a "one-drug-fix-all."

Prozac is differentiated from previous generations of antidepressants in two important respects. First, it is considered to be relatively safe with few adverse side effects (*Consumer Reports*, 1998; Kramer, 1993). Second, Prozac is easier to administer because it does not require close medical monitoring. Although it does not treat all forms of depression, these two factors make it a more desirable, and easier to prescribe and administer. Cowley (1990) reports that "American physicians are writing or renewing 650,000 Prozac prescriptions every month" (p. 39) indicating its phenomenal popularity. In the 1990s, the level of sophistication with respect to the methodology of the clinical trials has increased, and the hegemonic argument that these drugs represent the "fix-all" solution has been increasingly and more tightly constructed (for attempts at taming down the message, see Fernandes, Por, & Evans, 1998; Prior, Gill, & Vigna, 1995; but see also Steiner, 1995).

The Politics of Advertising

Historically, drugs were often discovered by serendipity. The cost of developing any particular drug is enormous (i.e., 230 million dollars; Cohen, 1996). Today, much of this cost is taken on by pharmaceutical companies, and is incurred prior to the drug's release. The risks are high for these pharmaceutical companies because the success of any given drug is dependent on market forces. Consequently, pharmaceutical companies create consumer demand by using advertising to shape the social construction of a drug, its social acceptance, and its eventual financial success (Cohen, 1996). In 1985, Krupka and Vener found a high correlation between the leading prescription drugs filled and the leading drugs advertised. For example, Valium (diazepam), first introduced in 1963, was the most advertised drug in the world and became the number one selling drug of its time. While multi-million dollar advertising helps pharmaceutical companies realize a profit, it also adds to the social construction of the "condition" for which the drug was developed. In so doing, the words, slogans, and images used in the advertisements also shape the conceptualization and the experience of the condition itself.

Given the exorbitant cost for the development of new drugs, and the unpredictable market conditions, few companies are willing to invest the needed capital. This, of course, decreases the diversity of the research being conducted. Moreover, to protect their investments, the research of private enterprises is not open to public scrutiny. Therefore, it is not a public, democratic, or medical agenda per se that guides research but a profit motivated one.

Prozac is an example of a drug specifically developed for the treatment of depression by a profit-driven company (i.e., Eli Lilly). Prozac's popularity, especially amongst the general public, was not only influenced by direct consumer advertising, but also by a best-seller, *Listening to Prozac*, written by a psychiatrist (Kramer, 1993). Articles about the new generation of antidepressants (i.e., Prozac and Zoloft) in *MacLean's* (Nichols, 1994; Wood, 1994), and *Newsweek* (Cowley, 1990, 1994) also had a powerful influence.

In 1985, Krupka and Vener raised some ethical concerns that are still relevant for researchers and society today. They suggest that there is a potential for a particular drug to become a panacea: a drug used fad-like for a much wider range of conditions than that for which it was originally developed. For example, in the 1970s this was the case with Valium: Now the same phenomenon is occurring with Prozac and Zoloft. This can have positive outcomes, of course, but it can also have negative ones. For instance, Prozac has been described as a drug that alters the mind, and even the personality, of individuals (Kramer, 1993). If someone suffers from physical PMS symptoms and is prescribed Prozac, one of the side effects is a personality change? Even more significant is the corresponding neurological alteration associated with the use of Prozac.[3] At this point, we do not know the long-term effect of such a physiological change (Moline, 1993). Based on advertisements alone, it is impossible for consumers to understand how a particular drug produces change, know its actual efficacy, obtain a complete list of potential side effects, or gain full appreciation of the risks associated with a particular drug. This often requires the help of a health professional. How, then, do we know if the profit-driven and competitive forces of the marketplace are serving our best interests? How do we know that we are getting accurate and unbiased drug information?

Though the marketplace might represent a means for our society to develop drugs to help us deal with our ailments, its constant search and struggle for financial gain is problematic. In addition to the lack of access by public-representing-bodies in the research process, hardly any control is exerted over the profits made by multinational pharmaceutical companies. In other words, profits may or may not be reinvested in developing alternative drugs that have fewer side effects, or a narrower range of effects, especially when one drug monopolises the market for the treatment of countless medical conditions. Cohen (1996) also suggests that by trying to anticipate society's future pharmaceutical requirements and desires, the industry is actually creating the "need" without the "reason."

PMS or PMDD, Psychological or Physical Symptoms, Prozac or Prozac . . .

In general, PMS is defined as a condition that is reserved for milder physical symptoms and minor mood changes, whereas symptoms of dysphoria and lability of moods that seriously interfere with one's lifestyle are categorized as PMDD (Steiner, 1996). Thus, PMS is considered a common medical problem treatable by the general practitioner, whereas PMDD requires the attention of a psychiatrist. According to the *Diagnostic and Statistical Manual of Mental Disorders* (*DSM-IV*; American Psychiatric Association, 1994), PMDD is distinguishable from PMS by its characteristic pattern of symptoms, their severity and impairment, and the number of women it afflicts (*DSM-IV*, 1994). Schnurr, Hurt, and Stout (1994), however, argue that the difference between PMS and PMDD might not be discernable because the methods used to analyse symptom changes have not yielded consistent differences in severity of symptoms between women "with" and women "without" PMDD. Yet, the advocated treatment approach for both conditions is the same, so should there be a concern with specificity?

A similar issue relates to the differentiation between physical and psychological symptoms. The literature on the effectiveness of fluoxetine and sertraline, for example, suggests that the physical and psychological symptoms associated with PMS respond differentially to the drugs (e.g., Su et al., 1997; Wood, Mortola, Chan, Moossazadeh, & Yen, 1992). The etiology of these two classes of symptoms, in fact, may differ (Elks, 1993), but relatively little attention has been given to the physical symptoms.

Why has more research attention been given to the psychological aspects of PMS? Women's traditional role provides some clues. The conflation of PMS and PMDD, and of the psychological and physical symptoms of PMS feed into the social construction of women as mentally unstable. If the same medication can cure it all, then the lack of differentiation between these conditions increases. Further, women often report that the most disturbing symptoms are related to their moodiness and irritability, and the negative effects they have on others (Elks, 1993). As Elks suggests, "overt but controlled displays of anger by men are socially acceptable and expected; those by women are taken as evidence of a disorder" (1993, p. 505-506; see also Gottheil, Steinberg, & Granger, 1999, for an investigation of the impact this can have on the medical treatment men and women receive).

The stigma associated with psychiatric illness in our society, the conflation between PMS and PMDD, and the grouping of both psychological and physical symptoms under one single syndrome has serious consequences for the women who suffer from these various conditions. Suffering from any aspect of PMS, and "outing" this condition to the medical profession, means that one is at risk of being considered "mad" and thus having few treatment options to consider.

CONCLUSION

History suggests that across the centuries, women's medical problems have been systematically linked to the "malfunction" of the reproductive system, although the specific nature of this link has changed over time (e.g., the womb, the ovaries, the premenstrual phase, hormones, or neurotransmitters). Furthermore, the reproductive system has always been associated with one cardinal symptom group: psychological distress. Psychological distress has been promulgated as the hallmark of PMS (Stoppard, 1992), and the central defining characteristic of PMDD as denoted in the *DSM-IV* (1994). Hence, the linking of psychological symptoms with the menstrual cycle, and the quasi-total omission of attention to physical symptoms and their effects on the lives of women, is a historically recurring phenomenon. Consequently, many, if not most, doctors, researchers, and even women themselves, are powerfully affected by the following social belief: When a woman deviates from the prescribed feminine gender role, she must be mad, anxious, emotionally unstable, hysterical, or depressed because of her menstrual system. Women who are marginalized or feel estranged from this prescription for whatever reasons, have few options. Women are forced to choose between the closet or the diagnosis. Each can result in damaging consequences, whether it is being labelled mad or enduring discrimination. Women disabled by the invisible physical symptoms that are specifically linked to their hormonal cycle, or who have a lesbian lifestyle (see introductory story) might decide that it is safer to "pass" as healthy and straight, respectively. The invisibility of these conditions makes this possible, and fails to challenge the status quo.

NOTES

1. The term hysteria has since been metaphorically detached from its association with the womb and the menses, but still refers to an uncontrollable excitement of psychoneurotic origins (Allen, 1990).

2. Studies using a double-blind methodology have failed to demonstrate in a conclusive fashion that Progesterone is effective in treating PMS. It has been reported to potentially produce PMS-like symptoms, however (see Altshuler, Hendrick & Parry, 1995; Moline, 1993; and Mortola, 1994 for a coverage of this literature).

3. There is an increase in serotonin receptors in post-synaptic neurons due to the greater availability of serotonin, which is caused by the blocking of serotonin's re-uptake.

REFERENCES

Allen, R. E. (Ed.). (1990). *The concise Oxford dictionary of English (8th ed.).* Oxford: Clarendon Press.

Altshuler, L. L., Hendricks, V., & Parry B. (1995). Pharmacological management of premenstrual disorder. *Harvard Review of Psychiatry, 2,* 233-245.

American Psychiatric Association. (1994). *Diagnostic and statistical manual of mental disorders (4th ed.).* Washington, DC: Author.

Beers, M. H., & Berkow, R. (Eds.). (1999). *The Merck manual of diagnosis and therapy (17th ed.).* Whitehouse Station, N.J.: Merck Research Laboratories.

Cohen, D. (1996). The "new" mind medicines, A step toward the past? *Sociologies et Societies, 28* (2), 17-33.

Consumer Reports: A Division of Consumers Union. (1998). *Complete Drug Reference.* New York: Author.

Cowley, G. (1990, March 26). The promise of Prozac. *Newsweek,* 38-41.

Cowley, G. (1994, February 7). The culture of Prozac. *Newsweek,* 41-42.

Dalton, K. (1959, January 17). Menstruation and acute psychiatric illnesses. *British Medical Journal,* 148-149.

Dalton, K. (1960, November 12). Menstruation and accidents. *British Medical Journal,* 1425-1426.

Dalton, K. (1961, December 30). Menstruation and crime. *British Medical Journal,* 1752-1753.

Dalton, K. (1970, April 4). Children's hospital admissions and mother's menstruation. *British Medical Journal,* 27-28.

Dalton, K. (1980, November 15). Cyclical criminal acts in premenstrual syndrome. *The Lancet,* 1070-1071.

Delaney, J., Lupton, M. J. & Toth, E. (1988). *The curse: A cultural history of menstruation.* Chicago: University of Illinois Press.

Elgin, K. & Osterritter, J. F. (1973). *Twenty-eight days.* New York: David McKay Company.

Elks, M. L. (1993). Open trial of fluoxetine therapy for premenstrual syndrome. *Southern Medical Journal, 86,* 503-507.

Farr, M. (1994). Is everybody happy? The pushy politics of Prozac. *This Magazine, 28* (2), 28-33.

Fernandes, O., Por, C. P., & Evans, M. F. (1998). Is sertraline an effective therapy for premenstrual dysphoric disorder? *Canadian Family Physician/Le médecin de famille canadien, 44,* 765-767.

von Feuchtersleben, E. (1847). *The principles of medical psychology.* London: Sydenham Society.

Finger, A. (1992). Reproductive rights and disability. In J. A. Kourany, J. P. Sterba, & R. Tong (Eds.), *Feminist philosophies* (pp. 87-95). Englewood Cliffs, NJ: Prentice Hall.

Frank, R. T. (1931). The hormonal causes of premenstrual tension. *Archives of Neurology and Psychiatry, 26,* 2053-2057.

Gottheil, M., Steinberg, R., & Granger, L. (1999). An exploration of clinicians' diagnostic approaches to premenstrual symptomatology. *Canadian Journal of Behavioural Science, 31*, 254-262.

Greene, R., & Dalton, K. (1953). The premenstrual syndrome. *British Medical Journal, 1*, 1007-1014.

Hamilton, J. A., Parry, B. A., & Alagna, S. (1984). Premenstrual mood changes: A guide to evaluation and treatment. *Psychiatric Annuals, 14*, 426-535.

Horney, K. (1967). *Feminine psychology*. (H. Kelman, Trans.). London: Routledge and Kegan. (Original work published 1931).

Kramer, P. D. (1993). *Listening to Prozac*. New York: Viking.

Krupka, L., & Vener, M. (1985). Prescription drug advertising: Trends and implications. *Social Science and Medicine, 20*, 191-197.

Merck & Co. (1899). *Merck's 1899 manual of the materia medica*. New York: Merck & Co.

Messiha, F. S. (1993). Fluoxetine: A spectrum of clinical applications and postulates of underlying mechanisms. *Neuroscience & Biobehavioral Reviews, 17*, 385-396.

Moline, M. L. (1993). Pharmacologic strategies for managing premenstrual syndrome. *Clinical Pharmacy, 12* (3), 181-196.

Mortola, J. F. (1993). Applications of gonadotropin-releasing hormone analogues in the treatment of premenstrual syndrome. *Clinical Obstetrics & Gynecology, 36*, 753-763.

Mortola, J. F. (1994). A risk-benefit appraisal of drugs used in the management of premenstrual syndrome. *Drug Safety, 10* (2), 160-169.

Nichols, M. (1994, May 23). Questioning Prozac. *Maclean's, 107* (21), 36-41.

Parry, B. L. (1997). Psychobiology of premenstrual dysphoric disorder. *Seminars in Reproductive Endocrinology, 15*, 55-68.

Pinel, J. P. J. (1997). *Biopsychology (3rd ed.)*. Toronto: Allyn & Bacon.

Poulin, M. B. C. (1991). *Une recension des ecrits sur le syndrome premenstruel*. Montreal: Institut Philippe Pinel de Montreal.

Prior, J. C., Gill, K., & Vigna, Y. M. (1995). Fluoxetine for premenstrual dysphoria [Letter to the editor]. *The New England Journal of Medicine, 333*, 1152.

Richardson, J. T. E. (1995). The premenstrual syndrome: A brief history. *Social Science & Medicine, 41*, 761-767.

Rodin, M. (1992). The social construction of premenstrual syndrome. *Social Science & Medicine, 35*, 49-56.

Schnurr, P., Hurt, S., & Stout, A. (1994). Consequences of methodological decisions in the diagnosis of late luteal phase dysphoric disorder. In J. Gold and S. Severino (eds.), *Premenstrual dysphorias: Myths and realities*. Washington, DC: American Psychiatric Press.

Severino, S. K. & Moline, M. L. (1989). *Premenstrual syndrome: A clinician's guide*. New York: The Guilford Press.

Steiner, M. (1995). Fluoxetine for premenstrual dysphoria [Letter to the editor]. *The New England Journal of Medicine, 333*, 1153.

Steiner, M. (1996). Premenstrual dysphoric disorder. An update. *General Hospital Psychiatry, 18* (4), 244-250.

Stoppard, J. M. (1992). A suitable case for treatment? Premenstrual syndrome and the medicalization of women's bodies. In D. H. Currie & V. Raoul (Eds.), *Anatomy of gender: Women's struggle for the body* (pp. 119-129). Ottawa: Carleton University Press.

Su, T. P., Schmidt, P. J., Danaceau, M. A., Tobin, M. B., Rosenstein, D. L., Murphy, D. L., & Rubinow, D. R. (1997). Fluoxetine in the treatment of premenstrual dysphoria. *Neuropsychopharmacology, 16*, 346-356.

Walker, A. E. (1997). *The menstrual cycle.* New York: Routledge.

Wood, C. (1994, May 23). Prozac's prophet. *Maclean's, 107* (21), 41, 1p, 2c.

Wood, S. H., Mortola, J. F., Chan, Y. F., Moossazadeh, F., & Yen, S. S. (1992). Treatment of premenstrual syndrome with fluoxetine: A double-blind, placebo-controlled, crossover study. *Obstetrics & Gynecology, 80*, 339-344.

Yonkers, K. A. (1997). Anxiety symptoms and anxiety disorders: How are they related to premenstrual disorders? *Journal of Clinical Psychiatry, 58*(Suppl. 3), 62-69.

PERSONAL
AND INTERPERSONAL
CONCERNS FOR WOMEN
WITH DISABILITIES

SOCIAL CONSTRUCTION OF DISABILITY: IMPACT ON IDENTITY

Chronic Disease Health Beliefs and Lifestyle Practices Among Vietnamese Adults: Influence of Gender and Age

Barbara W. K. Yee
Ha T. Nguyen
Martin Ha

Barbara W. K. Yee, PhD, is Associate Professor, Department of Aging & Mental Health, Louis de la Parte Florida Mental Health Institute, University of South Florida. Ha T. Nguyen is a Post-Doctoral Fellow at the Sealy Center on Aging, University of Texas Medical Branch. Martin Ha is Executive Director of the Research Development Institute.

Address correspondence to: Barbara W. K. Yee, PhD, Department of Aging & Mental Health, Louis de la Parte Florida Mental Health Institute, University of South Florida, Tampa, FL 33612-3899 (E-mail: dragonboomer@aol.com).

This research was supported by a University of Texas Medical Branch intramural seed grant and School of Allied Health Sciences seed grant awarded to the first author.

[Haworth co-indexing entry note]: "Chronic Disease Health Beliefs and Lifestyle Practices Among Vietnamese Adults: Influence of Gender and Age." Yee, Barbara W. K., Ha T. Nguyen, and Martin Ha. Co-published simultaneously in *Women & Therapy* (The Haworth Press, Inc.) Vol. 26, No. 1/2, 2003, pp. 111-125; and: *Women with Visible and Invisible Disabilities: Multiple Intersections, Multiple Issues, Multiple Therapies* (ed: Martha E. Banks, and Ellyn Kaschak) The Haworth Press, Inc., 2003, pp. 111-125. Single or multiple copies of this article are available for a fee from The Haworth Document Delivery Service [1-800-HAWORTH, 9:00 a.m. - 5:00 p.m. (EST). E-mail address: getinfo@haworthpressinc.com].

111

SUMMARY. There is growing alarm about the dramatic increase of chronic diseases among more acculturated Vietnamese (Yee, 1999). There were 180 Vietnamese adults, stratified by gender and age: 93 males and 87 females; young (ages 18-34), middle aged (ages 35-58), and older (ages 59+). A MANOVA was performed with nine Chronic Diseases Risk subscales, health behaviors, acculturation, depression, and health locus of control as dependent variables. Significant main effects for age and gender were found, with female and older Vietnamese having more chronic disease risk knowledge. Younger Vietnamese engaged in more health behaviors, were more acculturated, less depressed, and had less external locus of control. Chronic disease prevention must take account of these intraethnic factors. *[Article copies available for a fee from The Haworth Document Delivery Service: 1-800-HAWORTH. E-mail address: <getinfo@haworthpressinc.com> Website: <http://www.HaworthPress.com> © 2003 by The Haworth Press, Inc. All rights reserved.]*

KEYWORDS. Vietnamese women, chronic disease risk, health behaviors, health promotion, acculturation, adults

After the fall of Saigon in 1975, slightly over a million Vietnamese refugees and immigrants resettled in the United States (Immigration and Naturalization Service, 2000). While the primary health focus has been on acute health conditions, such as tuberculosis and hepatitis infections in new Vietnamese arrivals, there is growing alarm about the negative health outcomes and dramatic increase in chronic diseases among more acculturated Vietnamese living in the United States (Yee, 1999).

The United Nations (1999) predicted that we must be prepared to deal with the growing impact of chronic disease and mental illnesses around the world. Good health is not only beneficial to individuals and their families, but it is sound economic policy (National Academy on an Aging Society, 1999a, b). Smedley and Syme (2000) highlighted that half of all mortality can be attributed to behavioral lifestyle factors. According to the MacArthur Foundation Study (Rowe & Kahn, 1998), lifestyle choices, rather than heredity, determined health and vitality during the elderly years. In order to make healthy lifestyle choices, one must have access to this health knowledge and have the financial, social, and personal resources to adopt and maintain these healthier lifestyle choices. A limited storehouse of knowledge regarding risks and symptoms of chronic diseases is a significant barrier to maintaining health during the later years. As a society, we have lessened the burden of chronic diseases for large segments of our population, however, significant ethnic and gender health disparities remain.

Poor health and its resulting disability is an accumulation of multiple and synergistic factors (Meng, Maskarinec, Lee, & Kolonel, 1999) that are exacerbated by poverty, discrimination, and poor access to basic health care over time (House & Williams, 2000). These societal disparities are found across and within ethnic groups. For instance, Hoyert and Kung (1997) found the entire range of health among Asian Americans, with Pacific Islanders reporting the poorest health while certain Asian Americans groups people with Asian Indian, Korean, and Japanese ancestry reported excellent health. In addition, Asian Americans who had the poorest health were those in the "Other API" category and Southeast Asian immigrants such as the Vietnamese, Hmong, Laotian, and Cambodian. Vietnamese women have the highest incidence of cervical cancer in the United States; a rate that is two and a half times the rate found among Hispanic women and nearly five times the rate for White women (Institute of Medicine [IOM], 1999; Miller et al. 1996). With regular PAP tests, early detection and treatment, deaths from cervical cancer can be eliminated. Breast cancer, while currently lower among Vietnamese women, may increase with acculturation to an American lifestyle and lead to high rates that are comparable to other American women in as little as one to two generations in the United States (Hernandez & Charney, 1998; Kaur, 2000; Ziegler et al., 1993). Newer immigrants such as the Vietnamese, however, have poorer preventive care (e.g., cancer screening) and health access that contribute to poorer health outcomes (Hoyert & Kung, 1997; Kuo & Porter, 1998; Yi, 1995).

The National Research Council found some startling health trends (Hernandez & Charney, 1998). Immigrant children experienced fewer acute and chronic health problems and had a lower prevalence of unintentional injuries than U.S. born children. By the third or fourth generation, the rates of risky behaviors are equal or exceeded the levels found among U.S. born, white adolescents. Cross-sectional studies have reported that immigrants who adopted a Western lifestyle and their American born relatives showed an increased incidence of chronic diseases that were epidemic in developed countries. With acculturation, changes in lifestyle behaviors (nutrition and diet, exercise, smoking and substance abuse, stress coping and adaptation) put immigrants at a higher risk for acquiring chronic diseases and disabling mental health conditions. The process of acculturation through changes in traditional health beliefs and lifestyle practices may have health promoting or health damaging effects that vary by gender in Vietnamese families.

DISEASE STATES OF POTENTIAL INTEREST

The Centers for Disease Control estimated that the state of Hawaii had the lowest age specific death rates in the nation (Hahn, Teutsch, Rothenberg, & Marks, 1990). They tracked preventable deaths in 1986 (i.e., stroke, coronary heart disease, diabetes, chronic obstructive pulmonary disease, chronic liver disease, and lung, breast, cervical and colorectal cancers) and found that the state of Hawaii had a 7% excess death rate for preventable deaths. The population of Hawaii, in comparison to other states, has a high proportion of people of Asian and Pacific Islander ancestry. Although Hahn et al. (1990) stated that controls for race did not significantly alter the state rankings, ethnicity/race may indirectly influence preventable health risks through acculturation and adoption of American lifestyle habits. The Honolulu Heart Program and the Japan Hawaii Cancer study found that the rate of coronary heart disease among Honolulu Japanese men was one-half the rate of white males in the Framingham study. The authors noted that this difference could not be explained by differences in baseline levels of serum cholesterol, blood pressure or cigarette smoking (Yano, Reed, & Kagan, 1985). Lipson and Kato-Palmer (1988) found that there was a three to four percent rate of diabetes for older people in Japan and a rate 20 to 22% of diabetes among Japanese Americans (highly acculturated) in Los Angeles. The authors concluded that Asians may have a genetic predisposition to diabetes that is expressed when they eat a typical American diet.

These studies suggested that additional explanatory variables must be identified. With acculturation to American lifestyles, native people and immigrants may have a predisposition to develop chronic diseases. Moderating and mediating factors such as social and behavioral (e.g., lifestyle practices, gender and culturally based stress responses, nutritional patterns, or levels of physical activity), psychological (e.g., locus of control, depression, self-reported health) and cultural factors (e.g., traditional health beliefs, acculturation, gender roles) may enhance our understanding of the excess rates of chronic diseases over and above what can be attributed to biomedical indicators (Idler & Benyamini, 1997; Singer & Ryff, 2001).

In order to better understand health promotion and disease prevention, culturally competent health survey instruments must be developed and tested in the Vietnamese population. The following study describes the development of a chronic disease health beliefs and lifestyle practices questionnaire with an examination of gender and age differences for an adult Vietnamese sample. Research questions include:

1. What do Vietnamese adults know about the risk factors for chronic diseases? (stroke, coronary heart disease, diabetes, chronic obstructive pulmonary disease, chronic liver disease, and lung, breast, cervical and colorectal cancers)?
2. Are there age differences in chronic disease risk knowledge and lifestyle practices, depression, language acculturation, and health locus of control?
3. Do Vietnamese men and women differ in their chronic disease risk knowledge and lifestyle practices, depression, language acculturation, and health locus of control?

This paper will conclude by suggesting ways in which chronic disease and their disabling outcomes can be reversed among the Vietnamese adult population.

METHOD

Participant Recruitment and Sampling Strategy

The U.S. Census estimated that there were approximately 395,632 Asian and Pacific Islander Americans (APIs) in the Houston-Galveston-Brazoria TX Consolidated Metropolitan Statistical Area (CMSA) in 1996 (Hooper & Bennett, 1998), most heavily in Harris county at 296,645 or 75% of the API population in this CMSA (Klineberg, 1996), with Vietnamese immigrants making up the majority group (30%) of APIs at approximately 100,000 to 130,500 in 1999. Like other rare populations, Vietnamese immigrants do not live in ethnic enclaves. Respondents were randomly selected from phone directories in Harris and Galveston counties and screened for Vietnamese surname households; however, this approach was terminated early since there was a high rejection rate from older respondents. Therefore, the primary sampling method was convenience sampling from Vietnamese mutual aid societies, refugee assistance centers, and from six Vietnamese apartment complexes scattered in the Houston-Galveston metropolitan area.

Procedure

Selection and training of Vietnamese interviewers. Fifteen interviewers and several backup interviewers bilingual in Vietnamese and English were trained over a 20 hour period. They were given an introduction to the study, trained on interviewing techniques, and reviewed the meaning of each question and procedures for the interview protocol. Each interviewer practiced interviewing family members, friends, and each other. Interviewers reviewed questions, clarifications, or confusions during training sessions. After interviewer training, face to face interviews were conducted with 180 Vietnamese respondents.

Interview procedures and methods. Upon initial contact with the household, household members were screened for age eligibility and selected by randomization table. Appointments and informed written consent were obtained from all respondents. The interviews were conducted in the homes of the respondents or in quiet rooms away from distractions at other sites selected by the respondents. After the interview, each respondent was thanked and given a $15.00 check as a token of appreciation.

Survey Instruments and Questionnaire

A survey protocol consisted of background and demographic questions, nine chronic disease health beliefs, and health behaviors questions. The survey protocol was available in English and Vietnamese; however, a large majority chose to do the interview in Vietnamese. The survey protocol was translated from English to Vietnamese by a set of translators. This Vietnamese version was back-translated to English by a different set of translators. A final Vietnamese questionnaire was the product of face-to-face discussions among the investigators and four translators of the survey questionnaire protocol. The goal of the translation procedures was to produce conceptual equivalence across instruments and survey items. Demographic variables included age, gender, year of arrival in the United States, family income, English language skills and competencies, and other questions.

Chronic Disease Risk & Symptom Questionnaire (CDRSQ). Chronic Disease Risk & Symptom Questionnaire (CDRSQ) instrument was developed and tested with Vietnamese respondents (Yee, 1997). The

CDRSQ assessed knowledge of risks and symptoms by respondents across nine chronic diseases (stroke, coronary heart disease, diabetes, chronic obstructive pulmonary disease, chronic liver disease, and lung, breast, cervical and colorectal cancers). The CDRSQ consisted of checklists of possible risks and symptoms for nine chronic diseases. Respondents were asked to select actual or suspected risk factors and symptoms for each chronic disease in response to the following questions:

> What risk factors contribute to increasing a person's chances of getting this disease?
> What are the symptoms of _____?

Only CDRSQ subscale scores consisting of the number of correctly identified risks for each chronic disease are reported in this paper. A 22-item checklist of known or suspected and false risks were created in each CDRSQ subscale in a random fashion to check for response biases, such as checking the whole list or randomly selecting items. The number of correct risk items that went into each CDRSQ checklist varied from 3 to 15 actual or suspected risks. Alpha reliability estimates in this sample were: stroke (15 items, $\alpha = .91$), coronary heart disease (9 items, $\alpha = .89$), diabetes (4 items, $\alpha = .25$), chronic obstructive pulmonary disease (3 items, $\alpha = .76$), chronic liver disease (4 items, $\alpha = .70$), and lung (5 items, $\alpha = .62$), breast (5 items, $\alpha = .43$), cervical (3 items, $\alpha = .56$) and colorectal (3 items, $\alpha = .35$) cancers. The CDRSQ is available in English and Vietnamese.

To permit comparison across the various CDRSQ subscales, scores for each CDRSQ subscale were calculated as percent correct of real risks (CDRSQ score = obtained number of correct items divided by total number of correct items). Then raw CDRSQ scores were standardized into T-scores ($M = 50$, $SD = 10$) based on the total sample means and standard deviations. A higher score on these subscales indicated a higher ability in identifying risks.

Healthstyle. This 24 item self test assessed behavioral lifestyle practices that are linked with seven of the ten leading causes of death in this country (U.S. Public Health Service, 1981). Lifestyle behaviors included smoking, alcohol or medication management, nutritional habits, exercise and fitness, job satisfaction and stress management, social relations, and safety. Each item response choice was weighted by the U.S. Public Health Service based upon contributions to maintaining health with high scores reflecting healthy behaviors and the range of possible scores from 0 to 71. For example, smoking items had the most health damaging weighted scores with dose (i.e., level of smoking) reflected in assigned weights. The alpha coefficient for the Healthstyle instrument was .74 across 24 lifestyle behavioral items for this sample.

Health Locus of Control. This health locus of control subscale was extracted from the Dimensions of Control Scale (DOCS) that measured control attributions regarding positive and negative outcomes across seven life domains: family relationships, relationships with friends, health, financial and living situations, intellectual functioning, and daily activities (Yee, 1997). The health locus of control variable was composed of eight Likert-type items (α = .59) that assessed the degree to which respondents agreed (i.e., 1-4 response options "not true at all" to "very true") with statements regarding their locus of control (i.e., internal, powerful others, luck or helplessness/lack of personal control) for positive and negative health outcomes (i.e., when healthy or sick). This health locus of control was scaled in the direction of externality by recoding the direction of two internal locus of control items. High scores indicated greater externality in locus of control attributions for health outcomes.

Kinzie Depression Scale. The Kinzie Depression scale (Kinzie & Manson, 1983) has been used successfully to discriminate between depressed patients and non-depressed individuals in the Vietnamese population. The depression scale contains 18 differentially weighted items and included dimensions of depression such as somatization of symptoms, or depressed feelings. A total possible score for this depression scale was 40 points, indicating high depression to the lowest possible depression score of 4. The alpha coefficient obtained for the Kinzie Depression Scale was .90 in this sample.

Language Acculturation. The English language acculturation variable was composed of seven items (α = .94) that tapped the respondents' English-speaking, writing, and reading ability. To illustrate, one item was "How well do you read English?" These Likert-type responses (i.e., very good, good, okay, fair, little, none) were recoded such that a higher score indicated a greater command of English skills and ability to communicate effectively in an English-speaking world.

RESULTS

Sample Characteristics

There were 180 Vietnamese adults in this sample who were 18 to 87 years of age, with a mean age of 47 years. There were 93 males and 87 females. All but two individuals arrived in the U.S. in 1975 or later. Family income ranged from $9,999 or less a year (43.4%) to $10,000-$40,000 or more (18.9%); more than a third of the sample (37.8%) refused to reveal their family income. The majority were married (59.4%), almost a third were single (31.7%), a smaller number widowed (6.7%), and small percentage separated or divorced (1.1%). The majority were Buddhist (43.4%), Catholic (41.7%), Protestant (9.4%), and other religion (5.6%).

Table 1 shows the sample distribution by age groups and was distributed in the following manner: 62 young adults (18-34 years of age), 58 middle aged adults (35-58 years), and 60 older adults (59+ years). Almost half (48.3%) of the respondents were female.

Raw CDRSQ scores were standardized into T-scores ($M = 50$, $SD = 10$) based on the total sample means and standard deviations. Table 2 presents the means and standard deviations by age and gender on each measure in the study. A Multivariate Analysis of Variance (MANOVA) was performed with nine CDRSQ subscales, Healthstyle, Acculturation, Depression, and Health Locus of Control as the dependent variables. Age, gender, and age by gender interaction were the independent variables.

Since the overall F-test (Wilks' Lambda) indicated significant multivariate main effects for age group ($F(26,328) = 5.82$, $p < .001$; Wilks' Lambda) and gender ($F(13,164) = 3.08$, $p < .001$), univariate analyses were examined across 13 measures (see Table 2 for a summary of univariate effects). No age by gender interaction effect was found.

TABLE 1. Summary of Sample Distribution by Age Groups and Gender

Age group (Years)	Gender Male	Female	Age M	SD
18-34	35	27	26.55	4.28
35-58	26	32	46.48	8.12
59+	32	28	68.93	6.56

TABLE 2. Summary of Effects Obtained by ANOVA (F-Ratios)

Variable	Age group					Gender		
	18-34	35-48	59+	F		Male	Female	F
	M (SD)	M (SD)	M (SD)			M (SD)	M (SD)	
Breast cancer	48.47 (8.13)	51.34 (9.99)	51.97 (11.42)	2.22		48.68 (8.99)	52.52 (10.64)	6.88**
Cervical cancer	50.32 (7.84)	51.04 (10.74)	50.43 (11.24)	0.32		47.94 (6.57)	53.25 (12.12)	13.36***
Heart disease	47.41 (9.83)	49.99 (10.44)	54.20 (8.60)	7.65***		50.31 (10.26)	50.76 (9.77)	0.10
Stroke	46.13 (9.14)	50.99 (10.79)	54.66 (8.11)	12.80***		49.37 (10.15)	51.82 (9.70)	3.07
Colorectal cancer	50.11 (10.28)	50.93 (10.27)	50.65 (9.56)	0.23		48.82 (9.39)	52.31 (10.35)	5.50
Lung cancer	48.24 (9.26)	49.70 (9.96)	53.59 (10.15)	4.80**		50.67 (10.18)	50.35 (9.86)	0.05
Diabetes	50.42 (9.75)	48.91 (10.08)	52.29 (10.10)	1.76		48.72 (9.37)	52.36 (10.39)	6.11**
Pulmonary disease	47.40 (8.34)	50.64 (10.63)	53.66 (10.08)	6.36**		49.64 (10.03)	51.49 (9.92)	1.63
Liver disease	47.23 (8.10)	50.90 (10.89)	53.57 (9.98)	6.58***		49.74 (9.77)	51.39 (10.21)	1.29
Healthstyle	50.08 (10.15)	47.98 (8.68)	43.48 (8.85)	8.20***		45.69 (10.52)	48.67 (8.36)	4.72*
Acculturation	23.97 (5.73)	17.34 (7.10)	11.94 (5.09)	62.44***		18.69 (7.13)	16.81 (8.36)	4.36*
Depression	5.05 (2.70)	7.48 (4.82)	9.14 (6.14)	11.39***		7.08 (5.22)	7.38 (4.83)	0.18
Locus of control	15.06 (2.79)	16.35 (2.96)	16.13 (2.30)	4.05**		15.38 (2.59)	16.31 (2.82)	5.46*

$*p < .05$, $**p < .01$, $***p < .001$

Scheffé analyses with adjusted alpha levels indicated that the youngest group obtained a lower depression score than respondents in the older groups; no gender effect was found for depression. As expected, the English language acculturation score was inversely related to age, with the oldest group (aged 59+) scoring significantly lower than the younger respondents (aged 18-58). English language acculturation scores were higher in men than in women. Healthstyle scores were also significantly related to age, and were lowest in the oldest group. In addition, an examination of the health locus of control indicated that the two older groups exhibited a stronger belief in external control than the youngest group. Responses to Healthstyle and Health Locus of Control questions indicated that females had significantly healthier behaviors than males. Vietnamese females were more external in their health locus of control attributions than the men.

Regarding the Chronic Disease Risk and Symptoms Questionnaire subscales, the youngest group (aged 18-34) was the least accurate in identifying risks for stroke and heart disease. They also had the lowest ability in identifying major risk factors that contributed to lung cancer, and liver and obstructive pulmonary diseases. In addition, a linear age difference was found with the oldest group (aged 59+) generally identifying more correct risk factors than the younger groups. With the exception of lung cancer, average scores were consistently higher in women than in men, especially for diabetes, breast and cervical cancer.

DISCUSSION

This study suggested that Vietnamese women are able to correctly identify a greater number of risks for breast, cervical, colorectal cancers, and diabetes, while engaging in healthier lifestyle practices than Vietnamese men. This finding is similar to gender differences found among other ethnic groups (Crosby & Yarber, 2001; Fagerli & Wandel, 1999; Fardy et al., 2000; Gallant & Dorn, 2001). There were no gender differences in knowledge of risks for stroke or heart disease, liver disease, lung cancer or chronic obstructive pulmonary disease in this Vietnamese sample. However, significant improvements can be made toward increasing the basic level of risk knowledge across preventable chronic diseases. There were some poorly recognized risks, such as diabetes or nutrition, which contributes to a higher risk across a number of chronic diseases. Without this basic health information, there will be an absence of health-promoting and help-seeking behaviors to improve prevention and detection during early phases of chronic diseases.

Gender differences were also found in English language acculturation, with men having significantly more English skills than women in this sample. English language based health media communications would not reach Vietnamese women, especially the middle aged and elderly women. Special interventions, such as ethnic language targeting and culturally competent chronic disease prevention and health promotion programming, must be implemented, funded and tested with older Vietnamese women.

Women had significantly more external attributions for their health outcomes than men did. Vietnamese men said that they had more personal control (internal locus of control) over their health. Vietnamese women in the sample were more likely to say that luck, powerful others, or that they did not have any personal control (helplessness) over their health status. These findings suggest that health promotion and disease prevention should be gender specific in order to be most effective (Yee, Mokuau, & Kim, 1999). For example, poor breast and cervical cancer preventive screening among Vietnamese women was associated with having a Vietnamese physician (McPhee et al., 1997). By linking the finding that Vietnamese women were more likely to say that powerful others (e.g., their doctors) contributed to their health with the finding that having a Vietnamese doctor was associated with poorer preventive cancer screening, our interventions must include educating Vietnamese physicians about the value of prevention since they exert such a powerful influence over the health of Vietnamese women. Our interventions may need to incorporate these cultural, social, and psychological factors to improve health promotion and disease prevention strategies for Vietnamese women.

There were significant age group differences in which the youngest adults (18 to 34 year olds) knew significantly less than the middle aged (34 to 58 year olds) and elderly (59+) adults about stroke/heart disease, lung cancer, chronic liver disease, and chronic obstructive pulmonary disease risks. The oldest Vietnamese group had significantly more knowledge than the middle age group regarding stroke/heart disease and lung cancer risks. The young adults reported that they engaged in healthier lifestyle practices than the middle aged or elderly Vietnamese. The middle aged Vietnamese reported that they engaged in healthier lifestyle practices than the elderly. Perhaps this trend is a result of acculturation, stage of the lifespan, or higher access to English language health promotion efforts. Significant improvements could be made towards increasing healthy behaviors among middle aged and elderly Vietnamese. In this adult Vietnamese sample, chronic disease risk knowledge and health behaviors go in opposite directions. This is a paradox that must be explored in a future study. There may be a discrepancy between knowledge about chronic disease risks, self-reporting of these health behaviors, or enactment and maintenance of health behaviors. In other words, chronic disease prevention must examine the causal relationships between chronic disease knowledge, self-reported and observed health behaviors, and health outcomes over time. This is a limitation of the current study.

There is one clear primary prevention implication for the Vietnamese adult population (Yee, 1999). Limited knowledge of risks and symptoms is a critical barrier to seeking help in early developmental phases of disease pathways when these diseases can be prevented, cured, and managed most effectively. Women have a longer life expectancy than men and bear the brunt of disabilities brought about by chronic diseases in later life.

Future studies must refine the Chronic Disease Risk and Symptoms Questionnaire to include gender related chronic and disabling diseases, such as prostate or ovarian cancers, lupus or arthritis, and test the efficacy of a gender specific questionnaire. Further refinements of the Vietnamese translations could be conducted to improve conceptual equivalence across gender, generation and cohort, with the development of a more cost-effective and innovative sampling strategies to enhance research with this rare population.

REFERENCES

Crosby, R. A. & Yarber, W. L. (2001). Perceived versus actual knowledge about correct condom use among U.S. adolescents: Results from a national study. *Journal of Adolescent Health, 28,* 415-420.

Fagerli, R. A. & Wandel, M. (1999). Gender differences in opinions and practices with regard to a "healthy diet." *Appetite, 32,* 171-190.

Fardy, P. S., Azzollini, A., Magel, J. R., White, R. E., Schmitz, M. K., Agin, D., Clark, L. T., Bayne-Smith, M., Dohn, S., & Tekverk, L. (2000). Gender and ethnic differences in health behaviors and risks factors for coronary disease among urban teenagers: The PATH program. *Journal of Gender Specific Medicine, 3,* 59-68.

Gallant, M. P., & Dorn, G. P. (2001). Gender and race differences in the predictors of daily health practices among older adults. *Health Education Research, 16,* 21-31.

Hahn, R. A., Teutsch, S. M., Rothenberg, R. B., & Marks, J. S. (1990). Excess deaths from nine chronic diseases in the United States, 1986. *Journal of the American Medical Association, 264,* (20), 2654-2659.

Hernandez, D. J. & Charney, E. (Eds.) (1998). *From generation to generation: The health and well-being of children in immigrant families.* Washington, DC: National Academy Press.

Hooper, L. M., & Bennett, C. E. (1998). The Asian and Pacific Islander Population in the United States: March 1997 (update). *Current Population Reports (P20-512, PPL-08).*

House, J. S., & Williams, D. R. (2000). Paper Contribution B: Understanding and reducing socioeconomic and racial/ethnic disparities in health. In B. D. Smedley & S. L. Syme (Eds.), *Promoting health: Intervention strategies from social and behavioral research* (pp. 81-124). Institute of Medicine, Washington DC: National Academy Press.

Hoyert, D. L., & Kung, H. C. (1997, August 14). Asian or Pacific Islander mortality, selected states, 1992. *Monthly Vital Statistics Report, 46(1),* Hyattsville, MD: National Center of Health Statistics.

Idler, E. L., & Benyamini, Y. (1997). Self-rated health and mortality: A review of twenty-seven community studies. *Journal of Health and Social Behavior, 38,* 21-37.

Institute of Medicine (1999). *The unequal burden of cancer.* Washington, DC: National Academy Press.

Immigration and Naturalization Service (2000). *This month in immigration history–July 1979. http://www.ins.usdoj.gov/graphics/aboutins/history/july79.htm.*

Kaur, J. S (2000). Migration patterns and breast carcinoma. National Action plan on breast cancer workshop on multicultural aspects of breast cancer etiology. *Cancer Supplement, 88,* 1203-1206.

Kinzie, J. D., & Manson, S. (1983). Five years experience with Indo-Chinese refugee psychiatric patients. *Journal of Operational Psychiatry, 14,* 105-111.

Klineberg, S. L. (1996). *Houston's Ethnic Community, 3rd Edition.* Houston, TX: Rice University.

Kuo, J., & Porter, K. (1998). Health status of Asian Americans: United States, 1992-1994. *Advance Data from Vital and Health Statistics, #298,* Hyattsville, MD: National Center for Health Statistics.

Lipson, L. G., & Kato-Palmer, S. (1988). Asian Americans, *Diabetes Forecast, 41,* 48-51.

McPhee, S. J., Stewart, S., Brock, K. C., Bird, J. A., Jenkins, C. N. H., & Pham, G. Q. (1997). Factors associated with breast and cervical cancer screening practices among Vietnamese American women. *Cancer Detection and Prevention, 21(6),* 510-521.

Meng, L., Maskarinec, G., Lee, J., & Kolonel, L.N. (1999). Lifestyle factors and chronic diseases: Application of a compositie risk index. *Preventive Medicine, 29,* 296-304.

Miller, B. A., Kolonel, L. N., Berstein, L. Young, Jr., J. L., Swanson, G. M., West, D., Key, C. R., Liff, J. M., Gover, C. S. Alexander, G. A., Coyle, L., Hankey, B. F., Gloecker Ries, L. A., Kosary, C. L., Harras, A., Percy, C., & Edwards, B. K. (Eds.) (1996). *Racial/Ethnic Patterns of Cancer in the United States 1988-1992.* Bethesda: National Cancer Institute, NIH Pub. No. 96-4104.

National Academy on an Aging Society (1999a, February). Is demography destiny? *The Public Policy and Aging Report, 9* (4), 1-14.

National Academy on an Aging Society and Center for Health Care Solutions (1999b, March). *Facts on low literacy skills*. FS-99-3.

Rowe, J. W. & Kahn, R. L. (1998). *Successful aging*. New York, NY: Pantheon Books.

Singer, B. H. & Ryff, C. D. (Eds.) (2001). *New horizons in health: An integrative approach*. Washington, DC: National Academy Press.

Smedley, B. D., & Syme, S. L. (Eds.) (2000). *Promoting health: Intervention strategies from social and behavioral research*. Institute of Medicine, Washington, DC: National Academy Press.

United Nations Population Division (1999). *An Aging World*. Organization of Economic Cooperation and Development, International Monetary Fund.

United States Public Health Service (1981). *Healthstyle Self Test*, Office of Disease Prevention and Health Promotion, U.S. Dept. of Health and Human Services, DHHS Pub. No. (PHS) 81-50155. Washington, DC: Government Printing Office.

Yano, K., Reed, D. M., & Kagan, A. (1985). Coronary heart disease, hypertension, and stroke among Japanese-American men in Hawaii: The Honolulu Heart Program. *Hawaii Medical Journal, 44,* 297-764.

Yee, B. W. K. (1997). Stroke, lung cancer, diabetes health beliefs and lifestyle practices of Vietnamese elders: Implications for Geriatric Rehabilitation. *Topics in Geriatric Rehabilitation, 13*(2), 1-12.

Yee, B. W. K. (1999). Influence of traditional and cultural health practices among Asian women. In *Agenda for Research on Women's Health for the 21st century. Volume 6*: (Pub. No 99-4390) (pp.150-165), National Institutes of Health, Office on Women's Health Research.

Yee, B. W. K., Mokuau, N., & Kim, S. (Eds.) (1999). *Developing Cultural Competence in Asian American and Pacific Islander Communities: Opportunities in Primary Health Care and Substance Abuse Prevention*, Cultural Competence Series, Volume V (DHHS Pub. No. (SMA) 98-3193), Special Collaborative Edition. Washington, DC: Center for Substance Abuse Prevention (SAMHSA), Bureau of Primary Health Care (HRSA) and Office of Minority Health (DHHS).

Yi, J. K. (1995). Acculturation, access to care, and use of preventive health services by Vietnamese women. *Asian American and Pacific Islander Journal of Health, 3,* 31-41.

Ziegler, R. G., Hoover, R. N., Pike, M. C., Hildesheim, A., Nomura, A. M., West, D. W., Wu-Williams, A. H., Kolonel, L. N., Horn-Ross, P. L., & Rosenthal, J. F. (1993). Migration patterns and breast cancer risk in Asian-American women. *Journal of the National Cancer Institute, 85,* 1819-1827.

Keep Moving:
Conceptions of Illness and Disability
of Middle-Aged African-American Women
with Arthritis

Scott I. Feldman
Georgina Tegart

SUMMARY. Black women continue to be disproportionately affected by most forms of chronic disease in the United States, yet current literature neglects Black women's constructions of chronic illness and disability. This paper explores arthritis as experienced by older African American women taking part in peer support groups within a health pro-

Scott I. Feldman, MA, is a doctoral student in clinical psychology at the University of Illinois at Chicago (UIC) specializing in disability studies. He is committed to the development of disability affirmative models of psychotherapy and psychological research. Georgina Tegart is a research specialist in the UIC psychology department. She is about to begin her Masters in Rhetoric on disability discourse.

The first author would like to thank Dr. Jim Rimmer and the Center on Health Promotion Research for Persons with Disabilities for the opportunity to facilitate the peer support groups on which this article is based (Centers for Disease Control Grant No. RO4/CCR514155-01). He would like to thank Elizabeth Cunniff and Julie Heitkamp for translating the printed word, and Emma Emam-Mulhin and her staff at the Health Sciences library for retrieving it from hiding. He is grateful to Georgina Tegart for her thoughtful collaboration in the conceptualization and composition of this article. Most of all, both authors would like to acknowledge the women whose lives and perspectives have helped them to think more deeply about the meaning of our own disabilities.

Address correspondence to: Scott Feldman (E-mail: sif@uic.edu).

[Haworth co-indexing entry note]: "Keep Moving: Conceptions of Illness and Disability of Middle-Aged African-American Women with Arthritis." Feldman, Scott I., and Georgina Tegart. Co-published simultaneously in *Women & Therapy* (The Haworth Press, Inc.) Vol. 26, No. 1/2, 2003, pp. 127-143; and; *Women with Visible and Invisible Disabilities. Multiple Intersections, Multiple Issues, Multiple Therapies* (ed: Martha E. Banks, and Ellyn Kaschak) The Haworth Press, Inc., 2003, pp. 127-143. Single or multiple copies of this article are available for a fee from The Haworth Document Delivery Service [1-800-HAWORTH, 9:00 a.m. - 5:00 p.m. (EST). E-mail address: getinfo@haworthpressinc.com].

motion program. Early discussions focused on motivations for health behavior change, particularly the desire to lose weight and fear of disability. Subsequent discussions revealed these women's struggles to renegotiate their central roles within their extended families. In contrast to dominant cultural notions, group members did not distinguish between their personal health and that of their relations and communities. The paper concludes with an examination of the strengths and liabilities of this communal orientation, along with the potential for conflict with traditional health promotion interventions. *[Article copies available for a fee from The Haworth Document Delivery Service: 1-800-HAWORTH. E-mail address: <getinfo@haworthpressinc.com> Website: <http://www.HaworthPress.com> © 2003 by The Haworth Press, Inc. All rights reserved.]*

KEYWORDS. Arthritis, chronic illness, African-American women, communal worldview, peer support groups, meanings of disability

You've just got to keep moving. If you get in a chair, you just stiffen up and end up staying there. (Group participant)

A dearth of research exists on minority women's experiences of health, illness, and disability (Hanna & Rogovsky, 1992; Klonoff, Landrine, & Scott, 1995; Lillie-Blanton, Parsons, Gayle & Dievler, 1996), despite the striking health discrepancies between White and minority populations in the United States. Minority populations experience higher rates of incidence, prevalence, mortality and physical and emotional impact of a variety of diseases, including all forms of chronic disease such as cardiovascular disease, asthma, stroke, cancer, diabetes, and arthritis (Office of Disease Prevention and Health Promotion [ODPHP], 2000). The lack of research impedes health promotion interventions that are both relevant and sustainable in low-income minority communities. It also limits our knowledge and understanding of models of health, illness and disability among diverse populations.

Two competing paradigms drive current research in disability and chronic illness (Hedlund, 2000), the traditional medical model and the alternative social model shaped by the disability rights movement. According to the medical model, disability is a physical, cognitive, or emotional deficit residing within the individual. Research guided by this model, sometimes called the personal tragedy model, focuses on medical interventions, drug regimes, and diagnostic and classification systems of disability. The social model of disability, in contrast, rejects the reduction of disability to individual deficit (Fine & Asch, 1988; Longmore, 1995). It conceptualizes disability as constructed through societal attitudes, policies, and practices (Hahn, 1985, 1993, 1996; Morris, 1991; Oliver, 1996). These attitudes determine what is considered a disability and to a large degree the social, political, and economic consequences for people with disabilities (Hahn, 1993; McDermott & Varenne, 1995). Within the social model, interventions should be aimed at forging systems change to remove political-economic, physical, communicative, and attitudinal barriers to full participation in society (Heumann, 1993; Shakespeare & Watson, 1997; Swain, Finkelstein, French, & Oliver, 1993). Thus, the medical model locates the problem of disability within the individual, whereas the social model locates it in social structures.

The relevance of the medical and social models to the experience of disability in minority populations has been questioned. The medical model has been criticized for ignoring the cultural and social dimensions of disability and illness (Bayne-Smith, 1996). The social model and the disability rights movement have been criticized for opening rifts between people with disabilities and their non-disabled communities, and for marginalizing minorities with disabilities within the movement (Humphrey, 2000). Both the medical and social models, with their clear demarcations between person and environment, might be at odds with the more collectivistic worldviews of many U.S. minorities, including African-Americans. Within both discourses, the perspectives of Black women with chronic illness are rarely heard.

With such concerns in mind, the first author approached the task of facilitating two peer support groups of people with osteoarthritis. These groups were part of a comprehensive health promotion intervention designed to reduce, through exercise sessions, nutrition training, and peer support, the number of lifestyle-related secondary health conditions in individuals with disabilities. According to the Centers for Disease Control and Prevention, arthritis affects more than 42 million Americans, making it the leading cause of disability in the United States (CDC, 1999). The CDC is predicting that by 2020, arthritis will affect 59.4 million people in the United States, most of them women, and most of them of lower income (Helmick, Lawrence, Pollard, Lloyd, & Heyse, 1995; Leigh & Fries, 1991). The participants with arthritis with whom the first author worked in this program were predominantly middle-aged African-American women from working-class backgrounds. They all were experiencing substantial pain and functional impairment, including severely limited mobility. All also were significantly overweight (180-300 lbs), reflecting an additional inclusion criterion for the program.

The first author's interest in working with this group emerged from his own experience of disablement in early adulthood and subsequent search for meaning and identity in his newly configured self and social circumstances (Clay, 1999; Feldman, 1997, 1998). Through this process, the first author has become increasingly aware of the complex interactions among the particulars of his impairment (blindness), its societal representations and repercussions, and the expectations and privileges attending his other status characteristics, particularly as a White, highly formally educated male. The profound shifts in attitudes and values he has undergone during this process have sensitized him to the contextual nature of truths and the need for care in not imposing his beliefs about what is important on others who may or may not share these beliefs.

The first author wanted to allow the support group participants freedom to discuss their experiences of disability in whatever terms they chose. An ecological framework (Bronfenbrenner, 1986), with its incorporation of personal, interpersonal, and structural factors, seemed suited to this purpose. Accordingly, the first author introduced this general framework during the first session and referred back to it periodically to help chart the wide-ranging nature of each group's discussions. This avoided privileging a priori a particular level of analysis (as the medical and social models do) and allowed the women's own understandings to emerge.

KEEP IT MOVING: THE PEER GROUP EXPERIENCE

Participants attended the health promotion program for three hours a day, three days a week. On two of these days, the peer support group met for 90 minutes. Between 4 and 8 people typically attended. Participants had substantial contact with one another during the other components of the program. Moreover, based on pilot data that identified transportation as a potential barrier (see Rimmer, Rubin & Braddock, 2000), several members were bussed to and from the program, providing additional opportunities for member interaction. Members of both groups elected relatively early to share phone numbers so that they could provide encouragement and support to one another between sessions. The program staff encouraged this, as we saw the benefits that members were deriving from the support of this newly emerging community. Group conflicts sometimes emerged from or were continued during such contacts and served as fruitful material for subsequent group meetings (Boyd-Franklin, 1991).

The group format was relatively unstructured, with topics emerging from group discussions. The first author began each session by asking members about issues that remained from the previous session or that had emerged in the interim. Typically, one or two dominant themes occupied most of the day's discussion. During certain sessions, the first author taught specific skills relevant to the topic at hand, such as relaxation and guided imagery for pain management. The first author ended each session by briefly summarizing the discussion and highlighting any issues that seemed unresolved and might warrant further attention.

Early group discussions focused on the women's motivations for participating in the program. Most group members came to us by referral by their doctors who suggested that participating in our program could help to increase their mobility, decrease their pain, and control their blood pressure and blood sugar. To the women, too, these seemed like good reasons. Prior to beginning the program, many reported having difficulty walking a block or climbing a flight of stairs. The trek from the weight room to the support group was manifestly laborious for some. Most reported being in severe pain from arthritis most or all of the time, in spite of the fact that all were on some form (usually forms) of pain medication. Some members periodically got up during group to stretch, and it was not unusual to find a member who was close to falling asleep after taking a strong dose of pain medication. Group members endorsed increasing mobility and energy, decreasing pain, and improving general health as important motivations for changing their exercise and nutrition habits.

Two other reasons evoked even stronger emotional reactions from the group. First was the desire to lose weight. Group members vividly described the prejudice and discrimination that they experienced on account of their weight. To be visibly overweight in these women's communities was to be subject to jeers from youths in passing cars. It was to be asked, through wordless stares or cutting remarks from passersby, "How could you let yourself get this way?" One group member remarked that "prejudice against fat people is the last openly acceptable one in our society" (Quinn & Crocker, 1998). Such powerful messages are often internalized (Hall, 1995). In one discussion, several members disclosed that because of their appearance they did not look at themselves in mirrors and avoided looking at other reflective surfaces like store windows. *In spite of these experiences and the emotional pain associated with them, these women disclaimed social pressure as a motivator of their desire to lose weight.* As one member put it, "But I'm not doing this because of them. I'm doing it for myself."

The second focus in these early discussions was fear of disability. Most group members did not consider themselves to be disabled nor to have a disability; rather they had a medical condition. As one member said, "I have a knee problem. I am not disabled." To group members, being disabled would mean using a wheelchair or "being unable to do anything" to care for oneself. As one member put it, "it's a very negative thing–something I don't want to be." Few group members had ever had to use a wheelchair, although several expressed fears about needing to use one in the future if their condition worsened. Members agreed that imagining such a feared self (Cross & Markus, 1991) was a major motivator for changing their health behaviors. The desire to avoid or discontinue use of a walking cane also emerged in these discussions. Those members who used canes expressed feeling self-conscious and did not want others "to see me this way." For some, this had meant reducing their contact with friends and other members of their communities (Herskovits & Mitteness, 1994).

The unique power of the wheelchair was apparent even in its absence. In one discussion, members shared their difficulties getting through grocery stores without becoming fatigued and needing to rest. A member shared the idea of carrying around a light folding chair that one could set down to rest every aisle or so as needed. The first author appeared to be the only person present who saw the irony in this solution, working as he does alongside physically disabled students and faculty who move about with ease in their powered wheelchairs. When the first author in a later session introduced the example of his research mentor who has quadriplegia and uses a wheelchair, group members expressed admiration but nevertheless seemed unable to identify with her. To them she remained an "other" who was inspiring by virtue of her presumed greater misfortune as reflected in her use of a wheelchair.

Disability was not a part of most of these women's identities. Nevertheless, in common with other people with moderate to severe arthritis (CDC, 1994a), they experienced significant physical symptomatology and functional impairment. Moreover, arthritis posed a major challenge to their most valued roles (Ralston, 1997). The nature of this challenge and how group members dealt with it emerged as salient issues during subsequent discussions.

Most of the women in our groups had left work and were receiving disability benefits. This had clearly changed their status within their communities, as well as in society at large. They described being approached by people in their neighborhoods who demanded to know why they were not working for a living. Social welfare workers assumed either that they were faking disability or that because they were disabled they were not capable of any form of productive activity. Those few members who continued to work described being forced to make choices between feeding themselves and their children and paying for costly medications and medical procedures, because they had been forced by welfare policy to forfeit federal medical benefits.

Caregiving roles clearly continued to be central in these women's lives and identities. They took great pride in having helped to raise various members of their extended families, while lamenting those who had "gone wrong," such as by turning to drugs or gangs. The women remained highly involved in providing for their children, grandchildren, and other members of their extended kinship networks. For those who were not working, disability income received by them and, often, by other family members was judiciously used to meet the family's needs. Several members provided housing for sub-families within the extended family system, such as a daughter, son-in-law, and their children. These women regularly watched grandchildren, grand nieces and nephews, and other family members while the parents worked (Winston, 1999).

Nor were their investments restricted to their extended families. Members expressed concerns about the health of their communities and their people. They discussed their fears that changes in patterns of parenting were contributing to a generation of undisciplined Black youth and their distress at the physical and social decline of their neighborhoods. My initial impulse (consistent with my individualistic worldview) was to label such discussions as diversions from or perhaps masked forms of more personal material. Yet, judging by the intensity and recurrence of such themes within both groups, they appeared to be quite central to the women's subjective well-being.

These women's sense of connection to their extended families and communities provided a rich framework of meaning for their lives and help to buffer their identity and self-esteem against the losses that they had experienced. At the same time, many expressed feeling strained to try to meet their families' and communities' expectations of them. Several spoke of the difficulty of attending to their personal needs, particularly finding ways to pace themselves. One of our participants, for example, split time between working two jobs and looking after her children and grandchildren. She spoke of wanting to carve out time for herself but finding that there was always something more demanding to occupy her. The women talked about wishing that family members, especially adult sons living at home, would help more with household tasks like cleaning. They expressed difficulties setting boundaries with relatives who wanted them to look after children or help out with other aspects of extended family functioning.

These women experienced a press to minimize their pain and disability in order to fulfill their traditional role obligations. They reported that family and friends could not relate to their distress about their pain and limited mobility and quickly tired of hearing about it. "They don't care" was a common sentiment. These circumstances were exacerbated by the non-apparent nature of these women's conditions. They reported that many people, including family members, openly questioned the reality and severity of their pain and associated functional limitations (Barshay, 1993). One member summarized the group's attitude by saying, "Just because they can't see it doesn't mean it's not there."

A few members, believing themselves incapable of meeting the expectations of their families and communities, had physically and socially withdrawn. A common pattern was to spend long hours in bed watching television and eating. This pattern was associated with a deepening cycle of inactivity and depression. For these women, the depression became as or more disabling than their arthritis (Husaini & Moore, 1990; Penninx, Beekman, Ormel, & Kriegsman, 1996). They subsequently reported that one of the most important aspects of the program was that it got them out of the house, providing structured activities through which they could reengage with others. On those mornings when members struggled with pain and lethargy, they reported that it was this structure, and especially the human contact that it afforded them, that convinced them to come in anyway. As one member put it, "I thought of seeing you all here and this got me out of bed."

DISCUSSION

This paper reports the first author's experiences with two peer support groups of people with arthritis, predominantly middle-aged African-American women, taking part in a health promotion program.

These women's perceptions of their illness experience challenge traditional notions of health, illness, and disability and call for the development of more inclusive models to guide intervention.

Toward a Communal Model of Health

A communal orientation to health and illness emerged from the group discussions about disability and illness. Much of the women's expressed concerns focused on the perceived health and disease of their relationships, families, and communities. They saw these issues as integral rather than peripheral to personal well-being. Black feminist scholars have emphasized the importance of avoiding dualistic thinking, stressing instead a "both and" orientation (Collins, 1990; Williams, 1999). Within this perspective, the medical versus social model debate may be seen to artificially separate person from environment. Within African communalist philosophy, self, nature, and the world are perceived to be part of a spiritual whole (Nobles, 1972). This communalist orientation persists in contemporary African-American culture and is manifest in a concern for the well-being of the family and community and a sense of self as inextricably linked to these (King & Ferguson, 1996).

King and Ferguson (1996) note how such a communalist orientation serves as the basis for self-expression and empowerment for African-American women and helps to buffer the corrosive effects of race and gender oppression. "In essence, we find [B]lack women cultivating a sensibility and an aesthetic based on the capacity to build community" (King & Ferguson, 1996, p. 40). African-American women have been observed to serve pivotal roles in their families and communities, in fact, in society at large (Pinderhughes, 1994). Poor, middle-aged African-American women in particular often are responsible for caring and providing for multiple generations within their extended familial networks (Boyd-Franklin, 1991). Particularly within the context of an individualistic dominant culture, and a legacy of race and class oppression that challenges the integrity of Black families and communities, many African-American women may find themselves shouldering disproportionate responsibility for sustaining their families and communities (King & Ferguson, 1996; Ralston, 1997). This is reinforced by internalization of societal stereotypes of Black women as strong matriarchs (Greene, 1994a; McNair, 1992).

Hines (1988) notes how these demands can come into conflict with these women's often deteriorating health due to the cumulative effects of poverty and oppression. Ralston (1997) cautions that older African-American women who do not balance the demands of their social roles with self-care can ultimately negate any positive health effects that these roles might have.

In empirical studies, many people report that acquiring a disability triggers an exploration of personal values and priorities and a renegotiation of social roles as the person encounters obstacles to old patterns and ways of doing things (Collins, Taylor, & Skokan, 1990; Fife, 1994). Many of the participants in our groups had been socialized to attend to the needs and demands of others and had not been encouraged to actively explore and assert their own needs. Thus, it is noteworthy that these women committed several hours three days a week to attend a program that focused on their own physical and emotional health. In the peer support groups, members supported one another in coming to view their personal issues and needs as important. They gave one another praise for making positive changes in their lives and thereby learned to praise and reward themselves. During one of the last sessions of our first group, when the first author asked members to reflect on what they felt they had gained from our work together, they expressed having been encouraged by the group to "take care of ourselves."

These women continued to report, however, resistance by their extended families to any changes in their traditional roles. Further, those women who desired to resume work encountered major obstacles in the social welfare system. Boyd-Franklin (1989) has developed a multi-systems model of intervention with African-American families that addresses the key role of the extended family and broader social systems that impinge on family functioning. Similarly, Olkin (1999) stresses the importance of incorporating both familial and professional support networks into interventions with clients with disabilities. Use of such models in the present context might have ultimately proved to be more effective in leading to sustained improvements in these women's quality of life.

In addition to personal and familial intervention models, these women's understandings of the essential interconnections among self, family, community, and society emphasize the value of community level intervention. Health promotion interventions often make use of an empowerment model to change individual health behavior. Self-empowerment, control, and personal autonomy have been reliably linked to better physical, social, and mental health in the health promotion literature. Riger (1993), however, has noted that empowerment rhetoric is individualistic and champions the traditionally masculine concepts of mastery, power, and control over traditionally feminine concerns of communion and cooperation. Rather than do away with an empowerment approach, it is important to build a framework for understanding how the principles of empowerment can contribute to wellness in communities subscribing to a more communal worldview. Wallerstein (1992) describes community empowerment as a social action approach to change. A community empowerment approach would promote equality of resources, encourage community equity and capacity to address environmental conditions related to health, and focus on enhancing and supporting naturally occurring helping behavior (Neighbors, Braithwaite, & Thompson, 1995). For example, interventions utilizing a community empowerment framework might include introducing a "buddy" system whereby community members could help people with arthritis with physically demanding tasks such as grocery shopping or catalyzing a grass roots movement to convince local businesses to make their properties more accessible. Barlow and Williams (1999) demonstrated the effectiveness of a community empowerment approach with older people with arthritis.

The Dilemma of Health Promotion Efforts for People with Disabilities

Our participants held strongly negative views of disability. For most of them, disability was a state of helplessness and dependency to be avoided at all costs. They hoped by changing their health behaviors to forestall or reverse their physical decline towards this assumed state of total incapacity. Most of them experienced significant increases in mobility and decreases in pain during the course of the program. They expressed feeling greater control over their lives and feeling less depressed and anxious. These outcomes were consistent with their goals and also with those of the health promotion program. At the same time, all of the women continued to experience significant symptoms, functional impairment, and disability associated with their conditions. Given the progressive nature of arthritis (CDC, 1994b), it is likely that such effects will persist and potentially increase, rather than decrease, with time.

Participants were similarly motivated to exit the social category of the overweight. Most of them lost some weight during the program, although hardly enough to move them into a range of weight considered normal. If their personal experiences with prior weight loss efforts, along with normative data from empirical studies (Cogan & Ernsberger, 1999), are any guide, this weight loss, too, might be, for most of them, difficult to sustain.

The health promotion program explicitly promoted a model of healthy living with disability (Rimmer, 1999). In contrast, participants perceived health and disability to be on opposite ends of a continuum, and their participation in the program only seemed to reinforce this notion. This was, after all, the model held by the doctors who referred them, the social welfare system on whom most depended for their income and medical insurance, and doubtless most members of their extended family networks and communities. These women were much more likely to find a program like ours that focuses on changing their health behaviors than one that would change their environments to fit their new physical abilities. Substantially more societal resources are committed to efforts toward individual prevention and cure than into making the environment more suitable for the millions of people who sustain chronic conditions. As the number of people living with chronic illnesses and disability continues to grow with the aging of the population and, ironically, improvements in medical technology, the effects of this disparity will mount. Researchers must continue to search for ways that health promotion programs can embrace positive views of disability while promoting healthy living.

Including Black Women's Voices in Disability Discourse

The disability rights movement had little presence in the lives of the group members. They did not view the organized disability community as one with which they identified, nor did they appear to have a language for labeling their many experiences of what would be termed, from a social model perspective, disability oppression. These included the categorical approach of the social welfare system and its association of disability with an inability to work, the equation within society of one's value with the ability to work, and social pressure to try to pass as non-disabled. These women were struggling to make sense of such experiences from the traditional lens on disability within the dominant culture and their communities.

The disability rights movement might not have reached these women for several reasons. First, as noted earlier, the disability rights movement has been slow to embrace issues of ethnic diversity. Some people with disabilities within the African-American community perceive it as a predominantly White movement. Like the women's and Afrocentric movements that preceded it, the disability rights movement has challenged dominant cultural constructions of disability while replicating other forms of oppression. Second, the disability rights movement has been slow to incorporate the issues and concerns of persons with non-apparent disabilities. People with visible disabilities and their issues dominate much of the movement's discourse, although significant changes are taking place in this regard. Third, the independent living model that is at the heart of this movement essentially embraces the individualistic values of the dominant culture. Maximal autonomy and self-determination are stressed as core values. Advocacy is aimed at the ideal of creating circumstances in which people can live independently in the community with the assistance of people outside of their familial and social networks. Such values and goals can come into conflict with the communal orientation and worldview of many African-American women. The movement might be seen as threatening to pull African-Americans away from the familial and cultural networks that have been so critical to their survival in a hostile, racist society (Greene, 1994b).

Minority women make up a large and growing segment of the disability community. It is essential for the growth of the disability movement that these women's concerns be incorporated into its conceptions of the disability experience and of quality of life as the goal of social change efforts. True integration could result in an approach that poses an even more substantial challenge to the dominant cultural view of disability as a degraded form of life, or, if especially severe, a fate worse than death (Ditto, Druley, Moore, Danks, & Smucker, 1996).

CONCLUSION

Models of illness and disability influence public policy, funding priorities, research initiatives, community interventions, and societal attitudes. They guide discourse and debate. But models that fail to adequately capture real life experiences and values cannot direct and guide our efforts meaningfully. African-American women seem especially at risk inasmuch as existing models of illness and disability do not address their unique needs and perspectives. At risk too, then, are the families and communities in which they play such a pivotal role (Shenk, Croom & Ruiz, 1998). By anchoring models of illness and disability in these women's unique familial, cultural, and sociopolitical circumstances, we can produce health promotion interventions that are maximally relevant and sustaining. Moreover, by listening to the voices of older African-American women with chronic illness, we can learn more about the limits and potentialities of our constructions of ourselves as abled or disabled.

REFERENCES

Barlow, J. H., & Williams, B. (1999). "I now feel that I'm not just a bit of left luggage": The experiences of older women with arthritis attending a Personal Independence Course. *Disability & Society, 14* (1), 53-64.

Barshay, J. M. (1993). Another Strand of Our Diversity: Some Thoughts from a Feminist Therapist with Severe Chronic Illness. *Women & Therapy, 14* (3/4), 159-169.

Bayne-Smith, M. (Ed.). (1996). *Race, gender, and health.* Thousand Oaks, CA: Sage Publications, Inc.

Boyd-Franklin, N. (1989). *Black families in therapy: A multi-systems approach.* NY: Guilford Press.

Boyd-Franklin, N. (1991). Recurrent themes in the treatment of African-American women in group psychotherapy. *Women & Therapy, 11* (2), 25-40.

Bronfenbrenner, U. (1986). Ecology of the family as a context for human development: Research perspectives. *Developmental Psychology, 22* (6), 723-742.

Centers for Disease Control and Prevention. (1994a). Arthritis prevalence and activity limitations–United States, 1990. *Morbidity and Mortality Weekly Reports, 43*: 433-438.

Centers for Disease Control and Prevention. (1994b). Current trends prevalence of disabilities and associated health conditions–United States, 1991-1992. *Morbidity and Mortality Weekly Reports, 43*, 730-731, 737-739.

Centers for Disease Control and Prevention. (1999). *Chronic diseases and their risk factors: The Nation's leading causes of death.* US Department of Health and Human Services.

Clay, R. A. (1999). Four psychologists help others to see. *APA Monitor, 30,* 3.

Cogan, J. C., & Ernsberger, P. (Eds.) (1999). Dying to be thin in the name of health: Shifting the paradigm. *Journal of Social Issues, 55* (2) [Special Issue].

Collins, P. (1990). *Black feminist thought: Knowledge, consciousness, and the politics of empowerment.* London: Unwin Hyman Ltd.

Collins, R. L., Taylor, S. E., & Skokan, L. A. (1990). A better world or a shattered vision? Changes in life perspectives following victimization. *Social Cognition, 8* (3), 263-285.

Cross, S., & Markus, H. (1991). Possible selves across the life span. *Human Development, 34* (4), 230-255.

Ditto, P. H., Druley, J. A., Moore, K. A., Danks, J. H., & Smucker, W. D. (1996). Fates worse than death: The role of valued life activities in health-state evaluations. *Health Psychology, 15* (5), 332-343.

Feldman, S. (1997). I am choosing blindness: Personal reflections on the need for a functional definition. *Braille Monitor,* February.

Feldman, S. (1998, August). Reconciling identities: Thoughts on psychology and disability. Paper presented at the annual meeting of the American Psychological Association, San Francisco, CA.

Fife, B. L. (1994). The conceptualization of meaning in illness. *Social Science Medicine, 38* (2), 309-316.

Fine, M. & Asch, A. (1988). Disability beyond stigma: Social interaction, discrimination, and activism. *Journal of Social Issues, 44* (1), 3-21.

Greene, B. (1994a). African American Women. In: L. Comas-Díaz and B. Greene (Eds.) *Women of Color: Integrating ethnic and gender identities in psychotherapy.* New York, NY: Guilford.

Greene, B. (1994b). Lesbian women of color: Triple jeopardy. In L. Comas-Díaz & B. Greene (Eds.). *Women of color: Integrating ethnic and gender identities in psychotherapy.* New York, NY: Guilford.

Hahn, H. (1985). Toward a politics of disability: Definitions, disciplines, and policies. *Social Sciences Journal, 22* (4), 97-105.

Hahn, H. (1993). The potential impact of disability studies on political science (as well as vice versa). *Policy Studies Journal, 21*, 740-751.

Hahn, H. (1996). Anti-discrimination laws and social research on disability: The minority group perspective. *Behavioral Sciences and the Law, 14* (1), 41-59.

Hall, C. C. (1995). Beauty is in the soul of the beholder: Psychological implications of beauty and African American women. *Cultural Diversity & Mental Health, 1* (2), 125-137.

Hanna, W. J., & Rogovsky, E. (1992). On the situation of African-American women with physical disabilities. *Journal of Applied Rehabilitation Counseling, 23* (4), 39-45.

Hedlund, M. (2000). Disability as a phenomenon: A discourse of social and biological understanding. *Disability & Society, 15*, 765-780.

Helmick, C. G., Lawrence, R. C., Pollard, R. A., Lloyd, E., & Heyse, S. (1995). Arthritis and other rheumatic conditions: Who is affected now and who will be affected later? *Arthritis Care and Research.*

Herskovits, E. & Mitteness, L. (1994). Transgressions and sickness in old age. *Journal of Aging Studies, 3*, 327-340.

Heumann, J. E. (1993). Building Our Own Boats: A Personal Perspective on Disability Policy. In L. O. Gostin & H. A. Beyer (Eds.), *Implementing the Americans with Disabilities Act: Rights and Responsibilities of all Americans.* Boston, MA: Pauh Publishing.

Hines, P. (1988). The family life cycle of poor Black families. In: B. Carter & M. McGoldrick (Eds.), *The Changing Family Life Cycle: A Framework for Family Therapy* (2nd ed.). New York: Gardner Press.

Humphrey, J. C. (2000). Researching disability politics, or, some problems with the social model in practice. *Disability & Society, 15* (1), 63-85.

Husaini, B. A., & Moore, S. T. (1990). Arthritis disability, depression, and life satisfaction among Black elderly people. *Health and Social Work, 15*, 253-260.

King, T., & Ferguson, S. (1996). "I am because we are": Clinical interpretations of communal experience among African American Women. *Women & Therapy, 18* (1), 33-46.

Klonoff, E., Landrine, H., & Scott, J. (1995). Double jeopardy: Ethnicity and gender in health research. In H. Landrine (Ed.), *Bringing cultural diversity to feminist psy-*

chology: Theory, research, and practice (pp. 335-360). Washington, DC: American Psychological Association.

Leigh, J. P., & Fries, J. F. (1991). Occupation, income, and education, as independent covariates of arthritis in four national probability samples. *Arthritis and Rheumatology, 34*, 984-94.

Lillie-Blanton, M., Parsons, P. E., Gayle H., & Dievler, A. (1996). Racial differences in health: Not just Black and White, but shades of gray. *Annual Review of Public Health, 17*, 411-418.

Longmore, P. K. (1995). The second phase: From disability rights to disability culture. *The Disability Rag & Resource, 16* (5), 4-11.

McDermott, R., & Varenne, H. (1995). Culture as disability. *Anthropology & Education Quarterly, 26* (3), 324-348.

McNair, L. (1992). African American women in therapy: An Afrocentric and feminist synthesis. *Women & Therapy, 12* (1/2), 5-19.

Morris, J. (1991). *Pride against prejudice.* Philadelphia: New Society Publishers.

Neighbors, H. W, Braithwaite, R. L., & Thompson, E. (1995). Health promotion and African-Americans: From personal empowerment to community action. *American Journal of Health Promotion, 9* (4), 281-287.

Nobles, W. (1972). African philosophy: Foundations for Black psychology. *African Philosophy*, 23-36.

Office of Disease Prevention and Health Promotion. (2000). *Healthy People 2010: Understanding and Improving Health: Second Edition.* U.S. Department of Health and Human Services.

Oliver, M. (1996). *Understanding disability: From theory to practice.* New York, NY, USA: St. Martin's Press, Inc.

Olkin, R. (1999). The personal, professional and political when clients have disabilities. *Women & Therapy, 22* (2), 87-103.

Penninx, B. W. J. H., Beekman, A. T. F., Ormel, J., & Kriegsman, D. M. W. (1996). Psychological status among elderly people with chronic diseases: Does type of disease play a part? *Journal of Psychosomatic Research, 40* (5), 521-534.

Pinderhughes, E. (1994). Foreword. In L. Comas-Díaz & B. Greene (Eds.), *Women of color: Integrating ethnic and gender identities in psychotherapy* (pp. xi-xiii). New York: The Guilford Press.

Quinn, D., & Crocker, J. (1998). Stigma of Overweight. In J. Swim & C. Stangler (Eds.). *Prejudice: The target's perspective.* San Diego, CA: Academic Press.

Ralston, P. A. (1997). Midlife and older Black women. In J. M. Coyle (Ed.). *Handbook on women and aging.* Westport, CT: Greenwood Press.

Riger, S. (1993). What's wrong with empowerment? *American Journal of Community Psychology, 21* (3), 279-292.

Rimmer, J. H. (1999). Health promotion for people with disabilities: The emerging paradigm shift from disability prevention to prevention of secondary conditions. *Physical Therapy, 79* (5), 495-502.

Rimmer, J. H., Rubin, S. S., & Braddock, D. (2000). Barriers to Physical Activity in African-American Women with Physical Disabilities. *Archives of Physical Medicine and Rehabilitation, 81*, 182-8.

Shakespeare, T. & Watson, N. (1997). Defending the social model. *Disability and Society*, *12*, 293-300.

Shenk, D., Croom, B., & Ruiz, D. (1998). The voices of wise older women: African American women aging after Jim Crow. In R. J. F. Elsner (Ed.). (1998). *Voices of experience: Listening to our elders*. Symposia from the ninth annual student convention in gerontology and geriatrics. Athens, GA: Privately printed.

Swain, J., Finkelstein, V., French, S. & Oliver, M. (Eds.) (1993). *Disabling barriers enabling environments*. London: Sage Publications.

Wallerstein, N. (1992). Powerlessness, empowerment, and health: Implications for health promotion programs. *American Journal of Health Promotion*, *6* (3), 197-205.

Williams, C. B. (1999). African American women, Afrocentrism and feminism: Implications for therapy. *Women & Therapy*, *22* (4), 1-16.

Winston, C. (1999). Self-help for grandmothers parenting again. *Journal of Social Distress and the Homeless*, *8*(3), 157-165.

To Be or Not to Be Disabled

Monique Williams
Wendy Schutt Upadhyay

SUMMARY. This narrative consists of two sections that describe the experience of a graduate student with a learning disability. The first section documents the first author's process of coming to understand and accept the positive and negative impacts of her learning disability. This author explains how others (e.g., parents, teachers, therapists, coaches) have exhibited a natural tendency to underestimate the pervasiveness of the disability. The second section reflects the experience of the first author's coach in working with the first author around her learning disability. Potential implications for therapists working with learning disabled clients are also discussed throughout the article. *[Article copies available for a fee from The Haworth Document Delivery Service. 1-800-HAWORTH. E-mail address: <getinfo@haworthpressinc.com> Website: <http:// www.HaworthPress.com> © 2003 by The Haworth Press, Inc. All rights reserved.]*

Monique Williams, PsyD, completed her doctoral work in clinical psychology at the Illinois School of Professional Psychology-Chicago. She has a primary emphasis in child and family therapy, with a specialty in learning disabilities and trauma work. She is currently completing her post-doctoral work at Challenger/Bridgeview Extended Day Schools in Chicago. Wendy Schutt Upadhyay, PsyD, completed her degree in clinical psychology at the Illinois School of Professional Psychology-Chicago. She currently lives in Madison, WI, where she is an adjunct faculty member doing after-hours crisis work with U. of Wisconsin students. Her main interests are in treating eating disorders, self-injury, and trauma.

Both authors wish to acknowledge the editing, guidance, and feedback of Scott Feldman, MA, Cheryl Huff, MEd, Kirsten Lombard, Matt Ross, and Christopher L. Johnson. The first author also wants to acknowledge Wendy Schutt Upadhyay for her excellent job of capturing her voice by maintaining some of the inherent inconsistencies and choppiness of my writing and thought processes due to my learning disability.

The authors may be contacted by calling (773) 929-6009 or e-mailing: <wendyay@ charter.net>.

[Haworth co-indexing entry note]: "To Be or Not to Be Disabled." Williams, Monique, and Wendy Schutt Upadhyay. Co-published simultaneously in *Women & Therapy* (The Haworth Press, Inc.) Vol. 26, No. 1/2, 2003, pp. 145-154; and: *Women with Visible and Invisible Disabilities: Multiple Intersections, Multiple Issues, Multiple Therapies* (ed: Martha E. Banks, and Ellyn Kaschak) The Haworth Press, Inc., 2003, pp. 145-154. Single or multiple copies of this article are available for a fee from The Haworth Document Delivery Service [1-800-HAWORTH, 9:00 a.m. - 5:00 p.m. (EST). E-mail address: getinfo@haworthpressinc.com].

KEYWORDS. Learning disability, therapy, minimization, invisible disability, disabled

> "To finally recognize our own invisibility to to finally be on the path toward visibility."
> —Mitsuye Yamada

Original quote: "To finally recognize our own invisibility is to finally be on the path toward visibility."–Mitsuye Yamada (1993).

Who copied this quote? I am a 26-year-old, 5th-year, doctoral student in clinical psychology, who has secured a full-time internship for the final year of my program. I often struggle to explain the multiple components of my learning disability and their pervasive effects on my life as a whole. Besides having the complex task of putting the effects of my disability into words, I am also concerned about how my professional reputation could be compromised if I was to share just how disabling my disability can be. I do not want others to assume I am incompetent by judging me based on my need for accommodations.

This is the first paper I have truly enjoyed writing because I was able to dictate my thoughts to an assistant who then transcribed them. Essentially, I have a visual-motor processing integration problem. In practical terms, this means that I have trouble retaining material I read to myself. I manage to retain about 90% of the material when I read along while someone else reads aloud. Because my executive functioning is also compromised, I have difficulty planning and organizing. Additionally, my ability to put my thoughts into writing is greatly affected. Another factor complicating my situation is that my processing speed and ability to function varies widely from hour-to-hour and day-to-day. Given that it varies so inconsistently, I never know how well I'll be able to process information at any particular time. My poor fine and gross motor skills make it difficult for me to write or do other physical activities with precision. For instance, as you can tell by the copying of the quote at the beginning of this article, my handwriting compares to that of a young child. Due to this motor difficulty, I trip and bump into even the most obviously-placed things with great frequency. While occasionally amusing to myself and others it often leaves me bruised, battered, and feeling very frustrated.

I am conscious of the fact that when I focus on the negative impacts of my disability throughout this paper, you might miss the overall richness of my experience. I fear you will pity me instead of seeing how my learning disability can be an asset, a vital part of my identity that I would not relinquish. Through a process of introspection that began with my diagnosis at the age of eighteen, I less often minimize my disability. I now see it as positively enhancing my life as well as creating barriers throughout it. I feel, however, that societal pressures make it easy for people to minimize invisible disabilities, and difficult for them to remain open to the positive aspects inherent in them. I challenge you to embrace both the negative and positive parts of my experience. My story will undoubtedly bring you full-force into my daily world of chaos, excitement, hopefulness, and struggle. I am willing to give you the privilege of this glimpse, and to take some personal risk via my disclosures in my sincere hope that you will pass along your increased understanding and awareness to others.

I can't believe I woke up at 10:00 instead of 9:00 again this morning! I'm getting fed up with the fact that I can't remember to set my alarm. This morning I barely had time to take a shower. I got out of the shower, quickly threw on my clothes and went online while I was making my breakfast. I downloaded my e-mails from my reader, which contained the letter that she and I composed yesterday. The only problem was—I couldn't find where the downloaded e-mail was stored because I couldn't think of the file's name. Finally, fifteen minutes later, I was able to locate it and print it out as I was packing my bag to leave. Just as I was heading out the door, I realized I didn't have my keys so I spent 10 minutes searching and finally found them under my couch. Upon heading out the door again, I remembered I didn't have my book and notebook for class. By this point, I was getting very angry with myself since I knew I saw them earlier this morning; I finally found them after 5 minutes. On the way out this time, I saw my hairbrush on the coffee table and realized I still hadn't brushed my hair. I brushed my hair and on this attempt to leave, I realized I just lost the keys I had managed to find only minutes ago. Argh!! Finally, I saw them on the coffee table halfway under a piece of paper, grabbed them and clung to them as if my life depended on it. Stumbling over a few books, I finally made it out the door on this attempt. I caught a cab, barely made it to school on time and had to put the rest of my errands on hold until after class. Oops! I just realized that I forgot to put on my deodorant today.

Could you imagine if you had to tell your teacher, boss, or family member that this was the process you went through each morning just to leave the house? To be honest, I can't either! It seems quite overwhelming now that I look at it in writing. This is often just a fraction of the experience that someone with a learning disability may face in daily life. This aspect of my disability is very frequently overlooked. For many years I thought that everyone went through similar morning rituals. I now know differently and have learned to make adjustments to this routine.

Fortunately for me, this horrendous ritual started to change for the better about one and a half years prior to the writing of this article. A big impetus for this change came with my increased awareness of my disability, and the negative reactions I received from my boyfriend, friends, and acquaintances. Nearly one and a half years ago, I became increasingly aware that my disability affected my capacity to organize my life and complete my daily living tasks. Through this rewarding and tedious process, I have been able to uncover practical solutions that enable me to function in the world with more confidence and competence. Now, for the first time in my life, I actually have a fairly functionally-organized apartment. I now use a system of labeling and color coding, and have an assistant come in to help maintain this arrangement. For example, I have my bookcases organized in a way such that each category or topic has a certain standard sticker. This system works for me because I can process pictures more easily than words. A sticker with a picture enables me to locate books faster and put them away more quickly as well. For the first time in my life I actually have organized bookshelves. Another method I now incorporate is that of list-keeping. For example, I keep a checklist attached to the mirror in my bathroom to remind me to brush my teeth, brush my hair, put on deodorant, take a shower, and wash my hands. The time required for completion of my morning routine has been cut substantially by attaching my keys and my palm pilot directly to my purse. I no longer spend hours each week hunting for them.

Prior to being diagnosed with a learning disability, I attempted to normalize the behaviors I have just mentioned to you. I believed I was just lazy, clumsy, or disorganized. This attempt to minimize my disability worked quite well for years; after all, I had the support of my family and several educators who also wanted to believe the problems were simply motivational and not organic/biological. All this changed, however, when I entered college and slowly came to understand the truth about what was happening with me. I do, indeed, have a learning disability. In the next part of the paper, I will show you just how commonly others minimize my disability, causing me a great deal of frustration and confusion about my own disability identity.

In April of 1998, I entered into therapy with a therapist to work on issues pertaining to interpersonal relationships, separation-individuation, and disability identity development. Discussing my invisible disability was a complicated undertaking because my disability is very abstract, inconsistent, and hard to explicitly define, especially with my inability to articulate clearly at times. In treatment, whenever I mentioned my disability, it seemed that we always strayed to other topics. When I tried to bring it back to the topic of disability, we strayed again. In contrast, my therapist was able to validate my experiences around interpersonal relationships and separation-individuation issues. This led me to believe there was something different and difficult with respect to the disability topic. At the time, I was unclear which of us had the difficulty with the topic. Since I did not feel like he was able to validate my experience or provide empathic mirroring around my disability, I tried to get him to understand it in a more concrete way. For instance, I brought in writing samples to demonstrate to him that I really did have a disability. He responded to this by saying that he makes similar mistakes at times, leaving me feeling further invalidated.

Nine months into my treatment, I began dating a man who is blind with whom I still have a relationship. Through the early phases of our courtship, I became more sensitized to issues related to my own disability. Thus, the focus of my therapy sessions quickly became more centered on disability issues. I can recall several instances when I was talking about the impact of my and my boyfriend's disabilities on my life. My therapist responded by asking specific questions about how my boyfriend coped with his disability. For example, he asked how someone who is blind would shop for food and walk around in Chicago. This upset me because the emphasis shifted from me and my experiences to how my boyfriend functioned with his disability. My then-therapist's reaction was most likely a product of our culture, societal norms, and the difficulty that many people have understanding that invisible disabilities can be just as debilitating as visible disabilities.

Throughout my life, I have experienced many others who have minimized my difficulties, refused to believe the extent of the impact of the learning disability, and refused to validate my experiences. An example of this occurred only a few months ago when my mother said I shouldn't discuss my learning disability, that I was a perfectly normal, beautiful girl, that there was nothing wrong with me, and that I shouldn't talk negatively about myself.

When my parents learned that my boyfriend was blind, they responded with great concern about my wellbeing and our relationship. When we visited my family, I heard many statements like, "Please help him out, the poor thing . . . He looks so frail. Oh, the horrible thing that happened to you (referring to his vision loss at age 20)." My parents feared that I would have to spend the rest of my life taking care of him and meeting all his basic needs. Of course, what they could not see, was that my boyfriend was fully functional in the world, effectively making it through a prestigious clinical psychology doctoral program while navigating the city of Chicago along the way. He makes it around with much more ease and competence than I could ever wish for myself. In fact, he is the one in our relationship that is not directionally-challenged. Regarding my therapy, my parents assumed it would be my boyfriend who would need therapy to cope with his disability. It never made any sense to them that I felt a strong need for my own personal therapy. I feel my parents and many other people harbor misconceptions that if you can't see, touch, feel, and observe a problem outright, it really doesn't constitute a problem. It may be viewed as an inconvenience, but rarely is it seen as a life-altering set of conditions with which to cope.

Right before I graduated from college, I received insight into why my parents had minimized the disability aspect of my difficulties for all those years. A month before I graduated from college, my mother relayed to me that my fourth-grade reading resource teacher told both of my parents not to expect much from me and that I probably wouldn't even make it through college. This teacher viewed my situation as so negative that she had already given up hope for my future academic success. My parents reacted to this information by offering me increased assistance to ensure my academic success. They provided whatever help I needed and we never directly discussed the possibility of my having a learning disability. They realized I needed extra help but had little societal support and were unwilling to label me as disabled (a natural and compassionate response). However, I realized that I needed much more assistance than did most of my peers. I remember how humiliated I felt having to ask my mother to read for me during high school. My difficulties with learning, my need for assistance, and my parents' avoidance of the learning disability issue left me feeling stupid and inadequate. Thus, my parents, with the best of intentions, attempted to fix my disability rather than to help me learn to cope with and accept all aspects of it.

During one therapy session, I felt particularly determined to talk about the positive aspects of my disability. Up to this point in therapy, I had focused almost exclusively on the barriers and struggles I had endured as a result of my disability. When I returned from an APA conference where the American Psychology Association of Graduate Students (APAGS) Committee for Students with Disabilities convened for the first time, I felt a growing confidence to view my disability in positive ways. This was a unique opportunity to meet other people with both visible and invisible disabilities who were living very productive and fulfilled lives. I found myself vacillating between feeling positive about my disability and feeling very frustrated and angry at having to be faced with its effects on a daily basis. This made my therapy all the more complicated. Up until that point, I had shied away from talking about the positive aspects of my disability with my therapist because I didn't feel like he was able to resonate with me at a level I needed. I had real questions about whether or not he would be able to understand me and felt a strong sense of discomfort about what his reaction might be. Despite my fears, I did finally discuss how my disability helped me learn to be more flexible, creative, and resilient in the ways I approached my life and the people in it.

Approximately halfway into one particular session, my therapist asked me a question: "Let me see if I understand this right. If you had a miracle pill that could take away your disability, you wouldn't take it?" Without hesitating I said, "No." Then I tried to explain that I wouldn't take a miracle pill because I feel that my disability is a major part of my self identity and if I took that away I would lose a major part of who I am as a person. Not feeling heard, I continued by mentioning that if my boyfriend had an option for such a miracle pill, he also would refuse it for the same reasons. That my therapist appeared shocked would be an understatement. He then launched into a mini-dissertation about how he could not understand why I wouldn't take such a pill. For example, he explained that he had a "trick knee" (a condition with intermittent knee pain) and if there was a pill to get rid of that condition, he would have taken it without hesitation.

From his response, I was immediately aware that he did not and could not understand why I would decline such an option. In future telephone conversations and sessions with him, his interpretation always remained the same: that I was denying the struggles and barriers of my disability. I even tried to explain to him that getting rid of my disability would be more comparable to him getting rid of his maleness or changing his ethnic identity than his getting rid of a "trick knee." Since we could not bridge this impasse and come to a satisfactory resolution of this issue, I decided to seek out a new therapist.

Fortunately, I was able to locate a competent new therapist who seemed to try very hard to understand me, my disability, and its impact on my overall functioning. In the beginning of my work with this therapist, she, too, asked many questions about my boyfriend's disability. I was intent, however, on not repeating the cycle of defending him, while neglecting my own feelings about my disability. I chose to express my anger from the outset whenever this occurred, and clearly reiterated the need for me to focus on myself. This prevented us from reaching a similar impasse that I had with my first therapist. Despite this, we have had our share of empathic breaks that have caused me ongoing frustration. For example, she occasionally spent several minutes of my sessions checking on the accuracy of my bill. She even asked me to check my records and call her back in an attempt to determine the accuracy of the billing. What she continually failed to understand was that I was unable to keep track of this due to my disability. However, I was willing to speak up about my anger and frustration at her insensitivity to my organizational difficulties. Since that time, no such incident has occurred.

I have been able to learn how to get my needs met through this therapeutic relationship. Even though I know my current therapist is probably going to make more empathic breaks around my disability, I feel confident that she and I will be able to talk them through. Additionally, I feel she is able to own her part of our interactions. She admits when empathic breaks occur and validates my experience of them. This type of interaction is a new and liberating experience for me.

DISCUSSION:
WRITTEN FROM THE PERSPECTIVE OF MY COACH

Being a clinical psychology doctoral student myself, having finished my training and having nearly completed my dissertation, I understand very well the struggles inherent in being a graduate student. This type of intensive, all-consuming, and highly-demanding program can take its toll on even the most well-equipped, intelligent, and dedicated student. For students like the first author, who enter such programs with disabilities added to the equation, it is a daunting and cumbersome challenge to say the least. I have gained valuable insights into how Ms. Williams' learning disability has impacted her self-esteem, her personal and professional relationships, and her progress through a rigorous doctoral program. I initially became aware of the first author's disability in my second year of our program, and shortly thereafter, agreed to work with her as a "tutor/proofreader." Four years later, I am still working with her, albeit in a much more expanded version of my original role. As the first author learned more about her own disability, I also went through a parallel process of learning how to meet her needs. This gradual expansion has shifted my role into one of a coach, schedule-tracker, organizer, advocate, as well as that of tutor, editor, and proofreader.

For anyone who is or will potentially be tutoring someone, or working with clients or supervisees that have learning disabilities, there are some traps or pitfalls to avoid. I will share some of them with you in hopes that you will learn from my mistakes and initially-misguided attempts to help. The first trap, and perhaps the most common, is that of attempting to "fix" or "solve" some aspects of the disability. For example, many times in proofing the first author's work, I found that the same spelling, structural, and grammatical errors occurred repeatedly. I made notes of the errors, and assumed that by teaching her why I made the corrections, she would be able to incorporate this new information into her future work. That did not happen. I found myself becoming more and more frustrated because my methods of teaching were not helping. What I failed to realize at that time was that I was never hired to be her teacher. Secondly, such grammatical and syntax errors were a by-product of her learning disability—and therefore, could not be unlearned or relearned. *I* was the one who needed to adapt *my* method of proofreading so that I could take her words and her thoughts and put them together meaningfully onto paper. Once I surrendered the notion of teaching, correcting, developing new systems, and fixing her disability, my work with the first author transitioned into a much more satisfying and understanding working relationship. She and others with learning disabilities need help coping and adapting to limits imposed by their disabilities and by societal reactions to them. They do not need people to try to help them "overcome" their disabilities; this would be about as easy a task as "overcoming" one's gender or ethnic identity.

Another trap that I fell into was working with an individual without knowing her first as a person. Not knowing her living environment, what has or has not worked for her in the past, or what she thinks and feels about having her disability, meant that I was developing strategies that would work only for myself, but that were entirely ineffective in helping her. I had to learn to comprehend her perspective, and learn her way of understanding and processing information. This has been essential for developing ideas that can truly make a difference in her life. For example, each time we talk, I now go through a daily checklist of tasks to be completed and add new tasks to the list, which helps to jog her memory and ensures important things do not get easily missed as they did in past coaching sessions.

I now understand that having a learning disability is not all about continual struggle and despair. Rather, it is a part of who Ms. Williams is, a part of her life which can be just as positive as it can be negative. Her bursts of creative genius, dedication, and ongoing optimism about the world and her clients, have had nothing less than a powerfully moving and enduring impact on me as a person, a therapist, and a friend. I look forward to the chance to navigate the world with her for many years to come. I also encourage those in the women's therapy community to embrace women with invisible disabilities, to help them to have their voices be heard, and to eliminate any sense of shame that may accompany them into our therapy offices, our supervision offices, or even our telephone coaching/tutoring sessions. These women too often attempt to "pass-for-well," so that they can avoid negative reactions and disbelief from others, as well as avoid their own shame and possible self-hatred (Barshay, 1993). With time and through educating others via a strengths-based approach, however, I believe these women can be considered "well" just as they are, and the fear or belief that something is wrong with them can be dispelled.

REFERENCES

Barshay, J. M. (1993). Another strand of our diversity: Some thoughts from a feminist therapist with severe chronic illness. *Women & Therapy, 14* (3/4), 159-169.

Yamada, M. (1993). The importance of un-learning. In G. Steinem (Ed.), *Revolution from within: A book of self-esteem* (pp. 109). Boston, MA: Little, Brown and Company.

ACCOMMODATION IN EDUCATION AND EMPLOYMENT: APPLICATION OF THE AMERICANS WITH DISABILITIES ACT

ADA Accommodation of Therapists with Disabilities in Clinical Training

Hendrika Vande Kemp
Jennifer Shiomi Chen
Gail Nagel Erickson
Nancy L. Friesen

Hendrika Vande Kemp, PhD, was Professor of Psychology at Fuller Theological Seminary and instructor for the course *Theological, Cultural & Therapeutic Issues in Disability.* Jennifer Shiomi Chen is a PsyD candidate with special interest in multiculturalism and disability. Gail Nagel Erickson is a PsyD candidate with interest in disability training for medical and mental health professionals. Nancy L. Friesen, a PhD candidate, serves as a Learning Disability Specialist at California Polytechnic University in Pomona and has a special interest in disability and personality development.

Address correspondence to: Hendrika Vande Kemp, Graduate School of Psychology, Fuller Theological Seminary, 180 N. Oakland Ave., Pasadena, CA 91101-1714.

[Haworth co-indexing entry note]: "ADA Accommodation of Therapists with Disabilities in Clinical Training." Vande Kemp, Hendrika et al. Co-published simultaneously in *Women & Therapy* (The Haworth Press, Inc.) Vol. 26, No. 1/2, 2003, pp. 155-168; and: *Women with Visible and Invisible Disabilities: Multiple Intersections, Multiple Issues, Multiple Therapies* (ed: Martha E. Banks, and Ellyn Kaschak) The Haworth Press, Inc., 2003, pp. 155-168. Single or multiple copies of this article are available for a fee from The Haworth Document Delivery Service [1-800-HAWORTH, 9:00 a.m. - 5:00 p.m. (EST). E-mail address: getinfo@haworthpressinc.com].

SUMMARY. The authors discuss the need for reasonable accommodation at clinical practicum, clerkship, and internship sites. They summarize the key types of disability legislation and data on general compliance with the Americans with Disabilities Act. They discuss accommodation needs in the classroom and the clinic, focusing on time, space, and procedural accommodations; accommodations in test administration procedures; and accommodations for mental illness and substance abuse. They end with a plea for APA-accredited half-time internships to permit equal access for women with fatigue-related disabilities that involve the need for regular rest and a reduced schedule. *[Article copies available for a fee from The Haworth Document Delivery Service: 1-800-HAWORTH. E-mail address: <getinfo@haworthpressinc.com> Website: <http://www.HaworthPress.com> © 2003 by The Haworth Press, Inc. All rights reserved.]*

KEYWORDS. Reasonable accommodation, clinical training, Americans with Disabilities Act, invisible disability, internship

INTRODUCTION:
THE DISABILITY SPECTRUM AND INVISIBILITY

Three Types of Disability Legislation

The term "disability" applies to a wide spectrum of Americans. At one extreme are those persons covered by "a complex system of *insurance and welfare legislation* [which] guarantees benefits to people with disabilities who are unable to work" (Bonnie, 1997, p. 2). The federal Social Security Disability Insurance program (SSDI) provides income to those who were gainfully employed before becoming unable to work. The federal Social Security Income program (SSI) provides income to those who become disabled whether they have previously worked or not. Those who qualify as disabled under these entitlement laws are persons whose disabilities justify "withdrawal from the labor force" (p. 3). Two other groups of persons qualify as disabled under laws that stress opportunities and civil rights for those who need assistance in entering the work-place or in successfully remaining there. "*Vocational rehabilitation* (VR) statutes provide rehabilitative services to people with disabilities to enable them to compete in the labor market" (p. 1). Finally, a series of "*antidiscrimination statutes,* such as the [1990] Americans with Disabilities Act (ADA)" seek to "facilitate equal access to employment for those who seek it" (p. 1; Summaries of key legislation may be found on the United States Department of Justice home page at http://www.usdoj.gov/crt/ada/cguide.htm). Here, the law assumes "that the person with a disability *is* able to work and is entitled to any reasonable accommodation that would enable [her] to do so" (Bonnie & Monahan, 1997, p. 151).

Compliance with Requests for Reasonable Accommodation

The ADA is grounded in the principle of *reasonable accommodation,* which involves the implicit assumption that disability is socially constructed (Fine & Asch, 1988), and can be "deconstructed" by providing a less disabling environment. Harlan and Robert (1998) note that ADA recognizes that "work environments are the result of choices about how work is accomplished" (p. 398), and that there is frequently nothing "essential" about standard work environments, procedures, schedules, and attendance requirements. Accommodation involves alterations in these job functions or job-related contexts. These investigators found that in a large civil service system

> accommodations in the physical environment–furniture, parking, adaptive equipment, and surroundings–are the least likely to be denied, whereas requests for changes in the social work environment–work schedules, job functions, and personal assistance–are most likely to be denied. (p. 420)

Roessler and Sumner (1997) found that major corporate employers regarded the following requests as reasonable: "flexible scheduling, assistive/adaptive equipment, special parking, physical change of office space, . . . and temporary assignment of job duties to a co-worker to accommodate sick leave" (p. 31). The same employers regarded as *unreasonable* those "accommodations [that] included work at home, afternoon rest and nap periods, transportation to work, and provision of a support person" (p. 33).

Harlan and Robert (1998) found that employers were more likely to grant accommodation requests from professional workers than those from "clerical, service, and blue-collar workers" (p. 422). Roessler and Sumner (1997) suggest that "cost, negative reactions of other employees, disruption of work schedules, and threats to supervisory control are significant employer concerns" (p. 33).

Employees and supervisors are often ignorant about disability law and institutional accommodation policies. Harlan and Robert (1998) found that even when employers have official policies and procedures for providing reasonable accommodation, "most employees with disabilities and their frontline supervisors are not familiar with these procedures" (p. 409). Thompson, Bethea, and Turner (1997) report that fewer than 18% of 400 faculty members at a southeastern university were familiar with Section 504 of the Rehabilitation Act of 1973 and only half of the faculty members were familiar with the ADA. When professional and academic psychologists, supervisors at training sites, and directors of clinical training remain uninformed, they create an obstacle course for the would-be-therapist with a disability.

Invisible Disabilities

Many women are plagued with invisible disabilities that include the *physical and mental fatigue* that accompanies auto-immune disorders such as fibromyalgia and lupus, chronic fatigue syndrome, neuromuscular disorders, chronic heart and lung disease, mild traumatic head injury, and the enervating side effects of chemotherapy and radiation. Frequently invisible disabilities also involve *pain*, which is itself invisible (Olkin, 1999; Vande Kemp, 1993, 2001) and exacts the toll of fatigue and alienation from others. Other women suffer from *difficulties in information processing* which accompany learning disabilities, fibromyalgia, post-concussion syndrome, and chronic fatigue.

These invisible disabilities pose special problems. A woman is not likely to suffer discrimination based on an unidentified invisible disability, but an unacknowledged disability cannot be accommodated. Harlan and Robert (1998) report that "employees with non apparent disabilities have the most difficulty in convincing their employers that they are covered by the ADA" (p. 410). Such persons are caught in a classic bind: "If they do not satisfactorily establish the severity of their condition, they relinquish their right to reasonable accommodation. Conversely, if they succeed in convincing their employer that they have a disability, they may be penalized in other ways" (p. 411). Often they resort to invisible accommodations: They work in the evening and on week-ends to make up for time lost to rest and the added time required to accomplish ordinary tasks; they lower their achievement goals; they spend personal money on ergonomic aids and assistive technology because they don't qualify for third-party payments (see Smith, 1998).

FOCUS: THE CLINICAL TRAINEE WITH A DISABILITY

Psychologists with Disabilities

A number of professionals have addressed the issue of what psychologists should know about persons with disabilities (Bruyère & O'Keeffe, 1994; Olkin, 1999). Few professionals have specifically addressed the problems that occur when it is the academic psychologist, psychotherapist, or supervisor herself who has a disability. The four authors of this paper are all clinicians with disabilities requiring accommodation under the ADA. All of us have invisible disabilities that include fibromyalgia, learning disability, and mild traumatic brain injury. One of us has cerebral palsy. Another also suffers from the visible effects of childhood rheumatoid arthritis that qualify her for SSI and SSDI benefits. The issues we will raise emerged in part out of our personal accommodation needs in the academic and clinical settings. They also reflect the experiences of practicum students, clerks, and interns from southern California, and from intern applicants who responded to an inquiry on the list-serve for The Association of Psychology & Postdoctoral Internship Centers (APPIC).

The Dilemma of the Clinical Trainee with a Disability

Clinical trainees who have disabilities often find themselves in an untenable position. It is virtually impossible to qualify for disability benefits under entitlement programs, and it is especially difficult to qualify for *permanent partial disability* under SSI or SSDI legislation (Pryor, 1997). A college graduate with a genuine functional disability might find herself unable to work full-time without an accommodation; she doesn't have the option of falling back on entitlement programs–she *must* work; and she does not have the "fate control" power (Carson, 1969) fully to implement her civil rights under the ADA. She has internal and external resources that have led to previous academic success: intelligence, competence, autonomy, and solid interpersonal skills. A career as a psychotherapist or counselor offers her the opportunity for flexible working hours in a controllable setting. She in fact closely resembles the disability rights advocates who initiated the ADA, "a law providing employment protection only for those capable of competitive employment. To be protected, an individual must be able to compete with other applicants and employees in spite of having a disability" (Bell, 1997, pp. 204-205). The law assumes that "an employer and an applicant or employee with a disability work together to identify the most appropriate form of reasonable accommodation, on the assumption that the person with the disability has the self- awareness, knowledge, and communication skills required to guide an unenlightened employer through the accommodation process" (p. 205). This negotiation process involves reciprocity and mutual respect, conditions often lacking in the practicum, clerkship, and internship settings which feature a clear power differential between a trainee and the supervisor who must respond to her request for accommodation.

Problems at clinical out-placements are often difficult to resolve, especially at the pre-internship level, because women are uncertain about whether to take their accommodation request to their academic institution or to the off-campus clinical training site. Student service personnel in academic institutions, who should be advocates for their off-campus students, often have not dealt with the unique demands of clinical training settings nor developed the habit of negotiating with their off-campus peers. Students placed in off-campus sites for only a few hours a week find it difficult to negotiate yet one more system and to determine to whom to present their accommodation request. Trainees frequently encounter supervisors and faculty advisors who "pass the buck" and diffuse responsibility, delaying the accommodation process for months.

APPIC recently addressed the accommodation issue for internship sites by printing a newsletter article on the responsibilities of training directors (Khubchandani, 1999). This, however, served only as a minimal introduction to the requirements of ADA and the process of negotiating for reasonable accommodations. The APA Committee on Disability Issues in Psychology (CDIP, 1998) also recently produced a *Site Visitor Training Manual* with case vignettes on disabilities. But CDIP limited its vignettes to blindness and visual impairment, deafness, HIV/AIDS, learning disabilities, and spinal cord injuries. ADA requires not only *reasonable accommodation* but also the avoidance of *disparate treatment and disparate impact* (Goodman-Delahunty, 2000). Olkin (1999) documented a variety of ways that supervision subjects trainees with disabilities to disparate treatment. The *Site Visitor Training Manual* (CDIP, 1998) does provide extensive guidelines for avoiding disparate treatment and disparate impact, and for providing reasonable accommodation.

Currently Available Accommodations at Training Sites

Despite the obvious need–virtually all investigators agree that approximately 15% of Americans have a disabling condition–disability is not a standard part of clinical training in diversity. We found that of the 618 internship sites recently listed on the APPIC web-site, only 81 listed a disabilities rotation. An in-depth survey of 74 of those sites revealed that 2 had no disabilities emphasis and 22 focused on children's developmental disabilities. Of the remaining 50 sites, only 3 dealt with disabilities other than those presented in the case vignettes of the *Site Visitor Training Manual* (CDIP, 1998): disability law, chronic pain, and disability compensation screening. The picture is even bleaker when we examine how training sites accommodate clinicians with disabilities.

Olkin and Bourg (2001) surveyed 120 practica/internship sites in the greater San Francisco Bay Area. They found that among the responding sites (46%), more than 50% involved travel to less accessible secondary sites; nearly all sites had a floor not accessible by elevator; 20% lacked handicapped parking; 25% had no ramps; 81% had no automatic door openers; most had outside doorways at least 36" wide, but often inside doorways less than 32" wide. These investigators found that access was particularly poor for trainees with sensory impairments. Of the reporting sites, only 16% had Braille signage; 38% had emergency alarms with both visible and audible warnings; 12% had elevators with Braille and audible signals; 78% provided no TTY [Telecommunication Device for the Deaf]; even fewer listed TTY numbers on letterhead.

Caoile, Gainey, and Williamson (1998) gathered accessibility data on 22 practicum and clerkship sites in southern California. Of these, 13 were generally accessible, 7 had access limitations, and 2 were essentially inaccessible. These researchers found that some sites lacked a lounge or resting area; many had file storage areas without room to maneuver a wheelchair and with files stored too high for wheelchair access (a problem that can be solved by using horizontal file cabinets); many involved travel of more than 300 yards between buildings (which poses problems for the mobility impaired); some had violent or disabled clients who require physical assistance from the clinician (thus assuming able-bodied clinicians); many focused on neuropsychological testing, which requires object manipulation, a nearly impossible task for clinicians with certain types of motor weakness or spinal cord and neck injuries; many sites involved other testing that entails intact vision or hearing.

Hauser, Maxwell-McCaw, Leigh, and Gutman (2000) focused specifically on access and accommodation issues for deaf and hard-of-hearing students. They found that deaf applicants consistently experience "inappropriate questions, comments, or challenges to their competency based on interviewers' negative perceptions of deafness or Deaf people" (p. 570).

NECESSARY ACCOMMODATIONS

The Hauser et al. (2000) report highlights the first process in which students with disabilities encounter illegal discrimination: the personal interview used to screen applicants for admission to graduate school or acceptance at internships and clinical training sites. It is impossible to determine how frequently disability leads to rejection of applicants, but Olkin and Bourg (2001) found that 70% of the sites they surveyed had neither employees nor students with physical or sensory disabilities in the past three years. Under ADA hiring guidelines, applicants for graduate school and internships who have identified disabilities should "be asked the same questions in interviews as are other applicants," and "if the disability would seem to interfere with or prevent performance of job-related functions," interviewers may ask "special questions about how these activities would be performed" (p. 572). However, other screening, especially at the graduate school admissions level, should focus only on essential functions of the job of professional psychologist. Crewe (1994) attempted to identify these essential requirements, but there are currently no adequate operational definitions of these functions, which makes it difficult for both trainees and clinical supervisors to determine whether an accommodation request is reasonable.

Classroom Accommodations

Coble, Williams, Fraguli, and Ghiselli (1998) summarized various accommodations that apply to the classroom, most of which can be found in various ADA resources. Registrars should provide priority registration so that students with disabilities can schedule classes around medication schedules and rest periods, arrange for textbooks to be read onto tape, and request alterations in the building (external and internal access, maintenance schedules for elevators) or the class-room environment (lighting, temperature, and allergy controls; access to electrical outlets for computers and assistive devices; comfortable seating and suitable writing surfaces). Registrars and curriculum committees should ensure that required courses are not scheduled only in exhausting intensive formats, or at only one time. Instructors should make course materials available in such alternative formats as large print, Braille, computer diskette, audiotape, and campus web; and they should print exams with additional white space for writing. They should facilitate the taping of lectures and make available copies of their lecture notes and visual aids. They should not cancel scheduled class breaks, which provide essential rest and change in position for those susceptible to mental fatigue or muscle pain. They must, when necessary, adapt testing procedures to permit testing in a quiet room, with the option of using a computer, and with provision for additional time and rest breaks. Student service officers must be easily accessible physically and by TTY devices, and they should publicize accommodation procedures and provide note takers, scribes and editors, tutors, sign language interpreters, and assistive hearing devices. Producers of videotapes for clinical training should provide closed-captioning for the deaf and complete transcripts that can be brailled for blind students.

Clinic Accommodations

We discuss here several special situations covered neither by standard guidelines for classroom accommodation nor by the *Site Visitor Training Manual* (CDIP, 1998), focusing both on the needs of clinical trainees and problems posed for the supervisor.

Time, Space, and Procedural Accommodations. Neither APPIC nor APA has at this point addressed one of the most frequently needed accommodations for persons whose primary symptoms are *physical and mental fatigue*: a part-time schedule. Only a few half-time internships are accredited under APA's policy: APPIC listed only 5, among the 618 sites listed in 2001. As a result, women with invisible disabilities are deprived of their legal right to equal access to an APA-approved internship. Until women wage and win the legal battle for equal access, trainees will need to negotiate other ways to manage fatigue. Supervisors must be willing to accommodate by negotiating for rest periods and naps in trainee schedules, and providing a comfortable place to rest or sleep: minimally a couch in an employee lounge or the trainee's office, ideally a private sound-proofed room with a cot or bed. Supervisors must also set clear standards regarding tardiness and absences, and keep records on all trainees, so that such standards don't have disparate impact on trainees with disabilities, who report that they are often held to more stringent standards than are their able-bodied peers. Although attendance and punctuality are generally regarded by the Equal Employment Opportunity Commission (EEOC) as essential job functions, modifications of these standards do constitute reasonable accommodations in professional settings (Goodman-Delahunty, 2000).

Many ambulatory trainees have neurological and muscular disabilities that affect their capacity to walk long distances or to carry heavy or bulky objects. These trainees should be provided with handicapped parking spaces and a personal desk or other storage space directly in their work area so that they do not have to carry personal computers, testing materials, and client files.

Supervisors should assure that standard clinic procedures do not present additional obstacles. Students report on one clinic with videotaping procedures that required them to rearrange furniture to place it within camera range and then to go to another floor to turn on the camera in a room without space to maneuver a wheel-chair. A key to this equipment room had to be retrieved from a vertical file cabinet. These tasks were unnecessarily time-consuming and difficult for mobility-impaired clinicians. In addition, students had to memorize three unique security codes for three different non-automatic doors, presenting both cognitive and physical challenges. Supervisors would not permit a student to bring her own camera, thus illegally refusing a highly reasonable accommodation request.

Accommodations to Testing Procedures. Psychometric experts have given considerable thought to the appropriateness of modifying test administration procedures for clients with disabilities (see American Educational Research Association, American Psychological Association, & National Council on Measurement Education, 1999; Fischer, 1994; Nester, 1993; Sandoval, 1998). Much less has been written about whether it is appropriate to modify these procedures for test *administrators* with disabilities. The CDIP (1998) *Site Visitor Training Manual* suggests modified procedures for blind interns, but does not address test administration issues for deaf interns. But difficulties in test administration are not limited to interns with sensory disabilities. The challenges of test administration and scoring, especially for neuropsychological batteries, seriously cast doubt on the assumption that for the job of clinical psychologist "aptitude requirements (spatial, form, and clerical perception, motor coordination, finger and manual dexterity, eye/hand/ foot coordination, and color discrimination) are set at the middle third of the population or lower" (Crewe, 1994, p. 18) and that mathematical ability need only lie in the middle third. Many interns with physical disabilities will be unable to administer a complete neuropsychological battery; interns with learning disabilities may have difficulties with various aspects of test administration and with accurate recording and scoring. Psychometric experts will have to determine whether routine modifications in test administration procedures to accommodate the psychologist are appropriate. Supervisors and accrediting agencies must determine whether test administration is an essential element of training, since it is not an essential element of the job of the clinical or counseling psychologist, who frequently relies on a psychometrician to administer and score tests. The CDIP (1998) *Manual* does not suggest waiver of the testing requirement as a reasonable accommodation, but this should be given serious consideration: Interns *can* be evaluated on their ability to write an integrated assessment report and to establish a diagnosis based on testing results.

Accommodations for Mental Illness and Substance Abuse. Perhaps the most difficult accommodation requests are those relating to mental disabilities (Bonnie & Monahan, 1997). Relying on several previous reviews of the literature, Hantula and Reilly (1996) summarized the range of disabling conditions associated with mental illness: "difficulties with: the range of concentration, screening out environmental stimuli, maintaining stamina throughout the work day, managing time pressure and deadlines, initiating interpersonal contact, focusing on multiple tasks simultaneously, and responding to negative feedback" (p. 110). Most of the items in this list appear to refer to essential functions for the clinical and counseling psychologist (stamina is an obvious exception). While supervisors have legal obligations to offer reasonable accommodations for disability, Frame and Stevens-Smith (1995) note that they also have legal and ethical obligations to clients under the principle of nonmaleficence and the obligation to "monitor students' personal and professional development" (p. 119). Interpersonal and professional difficulties of impaired therapists may subject training institutions to malpractice lawsuits. These authors offer a "model monitoring and dismissal process" (p. 124) that should be implemented long before students are allowed to apply for internships. Under this model, the following characteristics gleaned from the literature are regarded as essential to the task of the counselor: "open . . . flexible . . . positive . . . cooperative . . . willing to use and accept feedback . . . aware of impact on others . . . able to deal with conflict . . . able to accept personal responsibility . . . and able to express feelings effectively and appropriately" (p. 124).

It is appropriate for internship supervisors to accommodate mental disabilities by offering the intern the usual medical leave time for appointments with a psychotherapist or psychiatrist and permitting short breaks to take medications. To determine whether the intern can perform essential job functions, supervisors should base their judgment on the same data used to evaluate other interns: audio- and video-tapes of therapy and assessment sessions and first-hand observation. "Disagreements then can be focused on specific incidents rather than on global concerns about the supervisee, and can be adjudicated by a consultant with expertise in disability" (Olkin, 1999, p. 326). If supervisors remain focused on clearly delineated clinical skills, they can evaluate the intern without concentrating on the disability. Case law has established that "no exceptions need be made regarding compliance with conduct standards. Violation of conduct standards is always a justifiable basis for discipline or discharge, and non-compliance may render an employee disqualified for employment" (Goodman-Delahunty, 2000, p. 201). This criterion is especially significant in cases of alcoholism and substance abuse. The law is clear that substance abusers "must adhere to the same standards of conduct as other nondisabled employees even when poor performance or behavior is caused by or related to the drug use or alcoholism" (p. 201).

FINAL COMMENTS

We recommend that directors of clinical training at graduate school and in training centers become familiar with every aspect of the ADA. Training directors must gather data about compliance with accessibility, responses to requests for reasonable accommodation, and patterns of disparate treatment at all training sites to ensure that disabled students are matched with appropriate sites. Training directors must become advocates for trainees with disabilities, facilitating rather than hindering the accommodation process. APPIC and the APA Committee on Accreditation have a legal obligation to provide all potential applicants with equal access to an APA-accredited internship, and must begin now to accredit half-time internships.

REFERENCES

American Educational Research Association, American Psychological Association, & National Council on Measurement Education. (1999). *Standards for educational and psychological testing*. Washington, DC: American Educational Research Association.

Bell, C. G. (1997). The Americans with Disabilities Act, mental disability, and work. In R. J. Bonnie & J. Monahan (Eds.), *Mental disorder, work disability, and the law* (pp. 203-220). Chicago: The University of Chicago Press.

Bonnie, R. J. (1997). Introduction to work disability and mental health law. In R. J. Bonnie & J. Monahan (Eds.), *Mental disorder, work disability, and the law* (pp. 1-10). Chicago: The University of Chicago Press.

Bonnie, R. J., & Monahan, J. (Eds.). (1997). *Mental disorder, work disability, and the law.* Chicago: The University of Chicago Press.

Bruyère, S. M., & O'Keeffe, J. (Eds.). (1994). *Implications of the Americans with Disabilities Act for psychology.* Washington, DC: American Psychological Association.

Caoile, J. D., Gainey, M. H., & Williamson, R. (1998, September). *Disabilities Task Force: Updated evaluation of practicum and clerkship sites for disabled clinicians.* Pasadena, CA: Graduate School of Psychology, Fuller Theological Seminary.

Carson, R. (1969). *Interaction concepts of personality.* Chicago: Aldine.

Coble, A. C., Williams, M., Fraguli, J., & Ghiselli, N. A. [APAGS Task Force on Disability]. (1998, August). *Symposium: Disability culture and the field of psychology–The student view-point.* Presented at the annual convention of the American Psychological Association, San Francisco, CA.

Committee on Disability Issues in Psychology. (1998). *Site visitor training manual: Case vignette on disability.* Washington, DC: American Psychological Association.

Crewe, N. M. (1994). Implications of the Americans with Disabilities Act for the training of psychologists. *Rehabilitation Education, 8,* 9-16.

Fine, M., & Asch, A. (1988). Disability beyond stigma: Social interaction, discrimination, and activism. *Journal of Social Issues, 44,* 3-21.

Fischer, R. J. (1994). The Americans with Disabilities Act: Implications for measurement. *Educational Measurement: Issues and Practice, 13* (3), 17-26, 37.

Frame, M. W., & Stevens-Smith, P. (1995). Out of harm's way: Enhancing monitoring and dismissal processes in counselor education programs. *Counselor Education & Supervision, 35,* 118-129.

Goodman-Delahunty, J. (2000). Psychological impairment under the Americans with Disabilities Act: Legal guidelines. *Professional Psychology: Research & Practice, 31,* 197-205.

Hantula, D. A., & Reilly, N. A. (1996). Reasonable accommodation for employees with mental disabilities: A mandate for effective supervision? *Behavioral Sciences and the Law, 14,* 107-120.

Harlan, S. L., & Robert, P. M. (1998). The social construction of disability in organizations. *Work & Occupations, 25,* 397-435.

Hauser, P. C., Maxwell-McCaw, D. L., Leigh, I. W., & Gutman, V. A. (2000). Internship accessibility issues for deaf and hard-of-hearing applications: No cause for complacency. *Professional Psychology: Research & Practice, 31,* 569-574.

Khubchandani, A. (1999, November). The ADA and internships: Your responsibilities as internship and postdoctoral agency directors. *APPIC Newsletter, 24,* 10-1, 21-22.

Nester, M. A. (1993). Psychometric testing and reasonable accommodation for persons with disabilities. *Rehabilitation Psychology, 38,* 75-85.

Olkin, R. (1999). *What psychotherapists should know about disability.* New York: Guilford Press.

Olkin, R., & Bourg, E. (2001, January). *Data on accessibility of practica and internship sites in the SF Bay Area.* Paper presented at the National Multi-Culturalism Summit-II, Santa Barbara, CA.

Pryor, E. S. (1997). Mental disabilities and the disability fabric. In R. J. Bonnie & J. Monahan (Eds.), *Mental disorder, work disability, and the law* (pp. 153-198). Chicago: The University of Chicago Press.

Roessler, R. T., & Sumner, G. (1997). Employer opinion about accommodating employees with chronic illnesses. *Journal of Applied Rehabilitation Counseling, 28,* 29-34.

Sandoval, J. (Ed.). (1998). *Test interpretation and diversity: Achieving equity in assessment.* Washington, DC: American Psychological Association.

Smith, D. C. (1998). Assistive technology: Funding options and strategies. *Mental & Physical Disability Law Reporter, 22,* 115-123.

Thompson, A. R., Bethea, L., & Turner, J. (1997). Faculty knowledge of disability laws in higher education: A survey. *Rehabilitation Counseling Bulletin, 40,* 166-180.

Vande Kemp, H. (1993). Adrift in pain, anchored by grace. In J. Lee (Ed.). *Storying ourselves: A narrative perspective on Christians in psychology* (pp. 261-291). Grand Rapids, MI: Baker Book House.

Vande Kemp, H. (2001). The patient-philosopher evaluates the scientist-practitioner. In B. D. Slife, R. N. Williams, & S. H. Barlow (Eds.), *Critical issues in psychotherapy: Translating new ideas into practice* (pp. 171-185). Thousand Oaks, CA: Sage.

Obsessive Compulsive Disorder in the Workplace: An Invisible Disability

Angela Neal Barnett
Lorre Leon Mendelson

SUMMARY. In this paper we examine the role of obsessive-compulsive disorder (OCD) in the workplace lives of women. Classified as a disability under the Americans with Disabilities Act (ADA), the secrecy associated with the disorder makes it invisible to everyone except the women who suffer from it. Left untreated and without appropriate forms of support and accommodation, OCD often creates difficulties in the working lives of women. However, with appropriate treatment, education, and support, women with OCD are successful and bring unique and valuable assets to their jobs. Case studies and a recent court case are used to illustrate our recommendations. *[Article copies available for a fee from The Haworth Document Delivery Service: 1-800-HAWORTH. E-mail address. <getinfo@haworthpressinc.com> Website: <http://www.HaworthPress.com> © 2003 by The Haworth Press, Inc. All rights reserved.]*

Angela Neal-Barnett, PhD, is in the Clinical Psychology Department at Kent State University. Lorre Leon Mendelson, BA, is the founder and a disability consultant at en-LIGHTNING Consulting.

Address correspondence to: Angela M. Neal-Barnett, Department of Psychology, Kent State University, 118 Kent Hall, Kent, OH 44242-0001 (E-mail: aneal@kent.edu).

Identifying features and names have been changed to protect the confidentiality of clients.

[Haworth co-indexing entry note]: "Obsessive Compulsive Disorder in the Workplace: An Invisible Disability." Neal-Barnett, Angela, and Lorre Leon Mendelson. Co-published simultaneously in *Women & Therapy* (The Haworth Press, Inc.) Vol. 26, No. 1/2, 2003, pp. 169-178; and: *Women with Visible and Invisible Disabilities: Multiple Intersections, Multiple Issues, Multiple Therapies* (ed: Martha E. Banks, and Ellyn Kaschak) The Haworth Press, Inc., 2003, pp. 169-178. Single or multiple copies of this article are available for a fee from The Haworth Document Delivery Service [1-800-HAWORTH, 9:00 a.m. - 5:00 p.m. (EST). E-mail address: getinfo@haworthpressinc.com].

169

KEYWORDS. Obsessive-compulsive disorder, American with Disabilities Act, accommodation, anxiety

Carolyn Humphrey, an otherwise excellent employee, compiled a history of tardiness and absenteeism because of grooming and dressing rituals that took hours, sometimes all day. Humphrey, a medical transcriber, sued the Modesto hospital that fired her, claiming the obsessive trait that drove her relentless primping had not been accommodated, as required by the Americans with Disabilities Act. A federal judge in Fresno threw her out of court. But a three-judge panel of the 9th U.S. Circuit Court of Appeals decided last month that Humphrey has a good point and sent her case back to Fresno for trial. (Walsh, 2001, p. 1)

Caroline Humphrey suffers from obsessive-compulsive disorder (OCD). Characterized by recurrent thoughts and behaviors, OCD interrupts the daily working lives of millions of Americans (National Institutes of Mental Health (NIMH), 1994). Yet, because so many employers and co-workers are unaware of the disorder, its consequences, and its treatments, supervisors and co-workers often see women with obsessive-compulsive disorder as disorganized, unproductive, bizarre, or strange. As a result, the work environment can become hostile, and the worker might be reprimanded, and in some cases, terminated.

In this paper we examine the role of OCD in the working lives of women. Classified as a disability under the Americans with Disabilities Act (ADA; United States Justice Department, 1990), OCD is virtually invisible to everyone except the women who suffer from it. Left untreated and without appropriate forms of support, OCD often creates difficulties in the workplace. However, with appropriate treatment, education, and support, women with OCD bring unique and valuable assets to their jobs.

WHAT IS OBSESSIVE COMPULSIVE DISORDER?

Obsessive-compulsive disorder (OCD) is an anxiety disorder characterized by recurrent thoughts (obsessions) and behaviors (compulsions). Common obsessions include fear of contamination from germs, dirt, etc., imagining having harmed self or others, imagining losing control of aggressive urges, intrusive sexual thoughts or urges, excessive religious or moral doubt, forbidden thoughts, a need to have things "just so" and a need to tell, ask, or confess (American Psychiatric Association, 1994). In response to the obsessions, individuals develop rituals known as compulsions. Compulsions temporarily reduce the anxiety associated with the obsessive thoughts (*DSM-IV*, 1994). Common compulsions include washing, repeating, checking, touching, counting, ordering/arranging, hoarding, saving, and praying (*DSM-IV*, 1994). Individuals with the disorder find themselves caught up in a cycle of tension and tension-reduction. Obsessions produce anxiety that is relieved by the compulsions. However, the relief is short-lived and the cycle repeats itself (NIMH, 1994).

Psychiatrist Judith Rapoport characterizes OCD as hiccups in the brain (1989). Once the obsessions and compulsions start, most people find it difficult to make them stop. OCD equally affects men and women. Epidemiological studies indicate that approximately 2% of the United States population suffers from the disorder, making OCD more prevalent than schizophrenia, panic disorder, or bipolar disorder (NIMH, 1994; Obsessive Compulsive Foundation, 2001). Most individuals with OCD experience other anxiety problems as well. Panic disorder and social phobia as well as various forms of depression frequently co-occur with OCD (*DSM-IV*, 1994; March, Frances, Carpenter, & Kahn, 1997).

Over the past 10 years, new advances have occurred in the treatment of OCD. Empirical research demonstrates that a combination of cognitive behavior therapy and serotonin reuptake inhibitors (SRIs) medication is effective in the treatment of the disorder (March et al., 1997). The treatment advances allow people with OCD to lead full and productive lives. Similar to other individuals with chronic conditions, individuals who are successfully managing their OCD can experience an exacerbation of symptoms or relapse (Gravitz, 1998).

For every woman who is being successfully treated for OCD, there are thousands more who are unaware that their behavior has a name. These women suffer in silence and go to great lengths to conceal their compulsions from family, friends, and co-workers. The secrecy and shame associated with the intrusive thoughts and behaviors prevent many women from seeking assistance (Gravitz, 1998; Obsessive-Compulsive Foundation, 2001).

IS OCD A DISABILITY?

OCD is a treatable mental disorder. For this reason, many people are skeptical as to whether it should be classified as a disability. According to the ADA (United States Justice Department, 1990), the term "disability" means, with respect to an individual (a) physical or mental impairment that substantially limits one or more of the major life activities of such individual, (b) record of such an impairment, or (c) being regarded as having such an impairment. Within the workplace, individuals with disabilities are to be provided with job opportunities in which the person can "perform the essential job functions with or without a reasonable accommodation" (United States Department of Justice, 1990).

A June 1999 ruling by the United States Supreme Court placed some restrictions on who could seek coverage under this landmark law. The particular ruling involved twin sisters from Spokane, Washington, Karen Sutton and Kimberly Hinton, who were turned down for pilot jobs at United Air Lines because of their extreme nearsightedness. The twins failed to meet the airline's minimum requirement for uncorrected visual acuity of 20/100. When they sued under the ADA, the justices ruled that the law did not cover people who can correct their disabilities and manage as well as most other people (Biskupic, 1999).

This interpretation of the ADA can place women with OCD in a precarious position. Advances in the treatment of OCD allow many women to lead healthy, productive lives. They can go for months or years being relatively symptom free. As such, these women might be deemed by their employers not to be eligible for accommodations because the disability has been corrected. Yet as previously mentioned, individuals with OCD experience periods of relapse. An exacerbation of one's symptoms might require the worker to seek additional treatment to obtain and/or maintain successful employment thus qualifying for reasonable accommodations.

We began this article with the story of Caroline Humphrey, a women who was fired from her job because of what her employer and the press characterized as "excessive grooming habits" ("How much accommodation?" 2001; Walsh, 2001). Ms. Humphrey's case illustrates how and why OCD is a disability, the reluctance some employers have to view it as such, and the need to continue to accommodate it.

According to newspaper and court documents, Ms. Humphrey was employed as a medical transcriptionist in a hospital from 1986 to 1995. In 1989, Ms. Humphrey began to experience problems getting to work on time or at all due to grooming compulsions. The compulsions included rinsing her hair for up to an hour, brushing her hair and if it didn't feel "just right," rewashing it, dressing very slowly, and pulling out strands of her hair to make sure nothing was in it ("How much accommodation?" 2001; Walsh, 2001).

In June 1994, her tardiness and absenteeism led to a "Level I" disciplinary warning. She was required to call her supervisor before she was due to be at work if she was going to be late or absent. Humphrey's obsessions and rituals only grew worse after the warning, and neither her attendance or her compliance with the requirement to call in improved. In December 1994, she received a "Level III" warning after having four tardy days and one unreported absence in two weeks. ("How much accommodation?" 2001)

After the second warning, Ms. Humphrey was referred to the EAP counselor. The EAP counselor neither diagnosed nor treated her for OCD. Instead time management tips were given. Ms. Humphrey did not suspect that the problem might be psychological/psychiatric in nature until she saw an episode of the Oprah Winfrey show on attention deficit disorder in 1995.

In May 1995, she asked if she could see a psychiatrist for an evaluation. The doctor diagnosed her with obsessive-compulsive disorder and informed her employer that this was directly contributing to her lateness. He stated that he felt he could treat her, but treatment might take time. He also informed the employer she would qualify under the Americans with Disability [sic] Act.

During her treatment, Humphrey was given an accommodation of being able to work any time of the day on days she was scheduled. Humphrey continued to have difficulties with this and requested by email that she be permitted to work from home "as a lot of other transcriptionists are doing." Her request was denied on the grounds that employees involved in any disciplinary action were ineligible to be a home-based transcriptionist [sic]. The response also stated that when she was at work, her performance was of high quality. After two more absences, Humphrey was fired. When she was told this, she asked if she could take a leave of absence instead. This was denied. ("How much accommodation?" 2001)

Ms. Humphrey then sued the hospital under the ADA (United States Department of Justice, 1990). In the initial ruling, the federal court judge threw the case out. Her employer argued that under the ADA, a disability is any impairment that substantially hinders a major life activity and that Ms. Humphrey was not disabled within the meaning of the statute (Walsh, 2001). Ms. Humphrey's attorneys filed an appeal. The U.S. 9th Circuit Court of Appeals found that Ms. Humphrey was a "qualified individual" under the ADA as long as she was able to perform the essential functions of her job "with or without reasonable accommodation." Either of two potential reasonable accommodations might have made it possible for Ms. Humphrey to perform the essential functions of her job: granting her a leave of absence or allowing her to become a "home-based transcriptionist." The Court concluded that it "would be inconsistent with the purposes of the ADA to permit an employer to deny an otherwise reasonable accommodation because of past disciplinary action taken due to the disability sought to be accommodated." Thus, Humphrey's disciplinary record does not constitute an appropriate basis for denying her a work-at-home accommodation ("How much accommodation?" 2001).

The Circuit Court's ruling allows Ms. Humphrey to sue her former employer for discrimination under the ADA. The case was scheduled go to trial later in 2001.

OCD IN THE WORKPLACE

Similar to Caroline Humphrey, many women with OCD realize that their rituals are excessive but are unaware that the behavior is a disorder. The guilt, shame, and secrecy that accompany the compulsive behavior seal their lips. Rather than sharing with their supervisors that they were late because it took them "3 hours to check and recheck the locks, windows, and doors" or "they kept redriving the route to check for bodies" or "they couldn't leave until they really felt clean," women with OCD might simply excuse their behavior with a simple "I just couldn't get it together this morning." Such a reply might make matters worse.

Within the workplace, undiagnosed, misdiagnosed, and improperly treated OCD results in absenteeism and lower productivity. Recent estimates indicate that OCD and other anxiety disorders cost the United States labor force 4.2 billion dollars in lost wages, productivity, and medical expenses ("New ADAA Study Shows," 1999). Each year these costs continue to rise.

A major contributor to the rising cost of OCD in the work place is employees' and employers' lack of knowledge about the disorder. Caroline Humphrey's OCD was misdiagnosed and therefore, improperly treated for 6 years. By the time the proper diagnosis was made, she had received several reprimands and during the course of treatment was terminated from her job ("How much accommodation?" 2001).

In most work environments, emphasis is placed on performance, not process. Thus workers with undiagnosed OCD and their supervisors focus on the *consequences* of their compulsive behavior (e.g., absenteeism, chronic tardiness, low productivity, failure to complete work) rather than the compulsive *behavior* itself. These consequences can be interpreted as lack of focus, disorganization, or an inability to manage time. As a result, women with undiagnosed/misdiagnosed OCD might be referred for coaching or time management sessions. The problems persist, increasing the workers' compulsions, and the employers' dissatisfaction and frustration with the workers increases. In many cases, the women are terminated. This scenario might repeat itself in several work settings until the disorder is properly diagnosed.

OCD education and awareness programs in the work place can significantly reduce the financial and emotional cost of the disorder on the U.S. labor force. Employees and employers might recognize the symptoms earlier and seek appropriate help sooner. Early recognition and assistance increases the likelihood that a work environment can be created that allows the person with OCD to succeed.

The issues differ when helping women who are properly diagnosed and receiving treatment. The focus shifts to advocacy and empowerment. In the second author's work as a disability counselor and advocate, she finds many women are unsure and uncomfortable about seeking and asking for accommodations related to their disorder. Many women fear their OCD will be used against them. Key to empowering women with OCD is the knowledge that OCD qualifies as a disability under the ADA. With appropriate accommodations, women with OCD can be successful in whatever careers they have chosen.

The content of the obsessions and the nature of the compulsion differ among women. Each woman with OCD has her own "prescription" for her OCD, her own rules and rituals. For instance, one woman might have thoughts (obsessions) of running over people while she is driving and the ritual or compulsion might be to go back and check to make sure there is no blood in the road or bodies laying where she ran over a bump. Another might seek reassurance from a passenger that she has not hit someone.

For these reasons, the specific accommodations an employer makes must be tailored to the individual. The accommodations made for a woman who constantly seeks reassurance would differ than those made for a woman who checks. Examples of accommodations include modifying work schedule, avoiding rush hour traffic, encouraging and/or facilitating use of public transportation instead of driving, job sharing, telecommuting, taking breaks at work more frequently, having a mentor at work, and allowing time off to meet with a therapist or psychiatrist (which may be covered under sick leave). Whatever the accommodation, its creation should be a collaborative effort between the employee with OCD and her employer. Such collaborations promote open communication and further facilitate the OCD workers' sense of ownership, independence, and recovery.

CLIENT EXAMPLES

Dani was a 32-year-old woman with OCD. Although in treatment, Dani's ability to drive was limited to a 3-mile area. Once she passed that point, she began retracing her route to make sure she had not hit anyone. Dani received a wonderful job offer, but it was 10 miles from her home. Rather than turn it down, Dani, her disability advocate, and her prospective employer sat down and reviewed the options. A transportation service was available through the county's disability services department.

The disability services department denied Dani's application because she had a valid driver's license. With encouragement from the second author and a letter of support from her prospective employer, Dani appealed and was granted access to service. Dani thrived in her new position and was eventually promoted to department director. Furthermore Dani continued treatment and now drives to work 3 days a week.

Open communication between the worker with OCD and a prospective employer can also lead to a decision not to accept a position. This was the case with Lisa who recently turned down the position of executive assistant to the vice-president of a high profile grant foundation.

During the interview, Lisa learned that the vice-president created his schedule on a daily basis, not in advance. In addition, Lisa, whose obsessive thoughts included the fear of throwing out something important, would be required to take notes at staff meetings and "separate the wheat from the chaff." Lisa evaluated her skills and decided she would work most effectively with a more stable schedule. Because of this and the difficulty in determining what is the chaff and what is the wheat, Lisa decided this was not the right job for her. When she shared her decision and the reasoning behind it, the Human Resource officer concurred. Impressed with Lisa's skills and candor, she then hired her for another position within the foundation that better complemented Lisa's needs and skills.

CONCLUSION

Recently, the second author was contacted by a therapist who said, "I have a female client with OCD, what type of work can she do?" The reply was swift and strong: "Anything she wants." As therapists, rehabilitation counselors, and advocates, we have many tools at our disposal to assess and evaluate work and the work environment. Ultimately, the most important information about vocational choice for women with OCD comes from the women themselves. The key is focusing on the whole person, not just on the OCD. If a woman with OCD knows what type of work she wants to do, what type of work she loves, and has insight into her OCD, with support, appropriate accommodations, and a sense of empowerment, she will succeed.

REFERENCES

American Psychiatric Association. (1994). *Diagnostic and statistical manual of mental disorders* (4th ed.). Washington, DC: Author.

Biskupic, J. (1999, June 23). Supreme Court limits meaning of disability. *Washington Post*, p. A1.

Gravitz, H. L. (1998). *Obsessive-compulsive disorder: New help for the family*. Santa Barbara, CA: Healing Visions Press.

How much accommodation does the ADA require? (2001, April). *Labor and the law: News and current events from the IRRA section on labor and employment law (LEL)*. Retrieved May 31, 2001 from http://www.irra.uiuc.edu/newsletters/LEL%20Newsletters/2001/2001-04.htm.

March, J. S., Frances, A., Carpenter, D., & Kahn, D. A. (1997). The expert consensus guideline series: Treatment of obsessive-compulsive disorder. *The Journal of Clinical Psychiatry, 58* (4), 3-20.

National Institute of Mental Health. (1994). *Obsessive-compulsive disorder*. Rockville, MD: Author.

New ADAA study shows anxiety disorder cost nation 42 billion a year in 1990 (1999). *ADAA Reporter, 10* (3), 1, 8.

Obsessive Compulsive Foundation (2001). What is OCD? New Haven, CT: Author. Retrieved March 1, 2001 from http://www.ocfoundation.org.

Rapoport, J. L. (1989). *The boy who couldn't stop washing: The experience and treatment of obsessive-compulsive disorder.* New York: E. P. Dutton.

United States Department of Justice. (1990). Americans with Disabilities Act: ADA Home Page. Retrieved March 1, 2001 from http://www.usdoj.gov/crt/ada/ adahom1.htm.

Walsh, D. (2001). Compulsive grooming a true disability? Perhaps. *The Sacramento Bee.* Retrieved April 21, 2001 from http://www.sacbee.com/news/news/old/ local02_20010314.html.

SEXUALITY ISSUES:
"WHO?!," "NO!" AND "HOW?"

Representations of Disability and the Interpersonal Relationships of Women with Disabilities

Danette Crawford
Joan M. Ostrove

Danette Crawford, BA, and Joan M. Ostrove, PhD, are affiliated with the Department of Psychology, Macalester College, St. Paul, MN.

Address correspondence to: Joan M. Ostrove, Department of Psychology, Macalester College, 1600 Grand Avenue, St. Paul, MN 55105 (E-mail: ostrove@macalester.edu).

The authors are particularly grateful to the women who shared their time and experiences by participating in this project. The research for this study was supported by a Keck Student-Faculty Collaboration Grant from Macalester College. They would also like to thank Alice Adams for her helpful comments on an earlier draft of this manuscript.

Portions of this paper were presented at the Multicultural Conference and Summit II (The Psychology of Race/Ethnicity, Gender, Sexual Orientation, and Disability: Intersections, Divergence, and Convergence), January, 2001.

[Haworth co-indexing entry note]: "Representations of Disability and the Interpersonal Relationships of Women with Disabilities." Crawford, Danette, and Joan M. Ostrove. Co-published simultaneously in *Women & Therapy* (The Haworth Press, Inc.) Vol. 26, No. 3/4, 2003, pp. 179-194; and: *Women with Visible and Invisible Disabilities: Multiple Intersections, Multiple Issues, Multiple Therapies* (ed: Martha E. Banks, and Ellyn Kaschak) The Haworth Press, Inc., 2003, pp. 179-194. Single or multiple copies of this article are available for a fee from The Haworth Document Delivery Service [1-800-HAWORTH, 9:00 a.m. - 5:00 p.m. (EST). E-mail address: getinfo@haworthpressinc.com].

SUMMARY. This paper explores the relation between societal representations of disability and the intimate relationships of women with disabilities. The study confirmed that views of people with disabilities as incompetent and helpless, intellectually challenged, super-capable and asexual, continue to influence the lives of women with disabilities. Most of these stereotypes were encountered by women with different types of disabilities, suggesting that these categories are fairly universally applied. With respect to intimate relationships, the women had had a wide variety of both positive and negative experiences. A common disability experience seemed to have an important positive influence on sustaining close intimate relationships. Relatedly, the lack of this similarity was, in many cases, perceived as a major impediment to relationships with the able-bodied. *[Article copies available for a fee from The Haworth Document Delivery Service: 1-800-HAWORTH. E-mail address: <getinfo@haworthpressinc.com> Website: <http://www.HaworthPress.com> © 2003 by The Haworth Press, Inc. All rights reserved.]*

KEYWORDS. Disability, women, social construction, relationships

In general, people with disabilities have been systematically isolated from the rest of society (see, e.g., Davis, 1997). Historically, the rates of institutionalization of people with many different kinds of disabilities has been extremely high (Biklen, 1988). In addition, structural and social barriers mean that many disabled people[1] live circumscribed lives, systematically confined to the places–and/or to the information–that is accessible to them (Kaye & Longmore, 1997). These realities have produced a segregated society with respect to disability that both results from and perpetuates cultural stereotypes of disability. It also serves to exclude analysis of disability oppression from U.S. social and cultural discourse. It is the intention of this paper to examine the nature of the social construction of disability, and to demonstrate the ways in which these constructions affect the interpersonal relationships of women with disabilities.

In our culture, disability is negatively social constructed. Social constructionism posits that disability is the result of the interaction between societal oppression and bodily impairment (Wendell, 1996). People with disabilities are defined as much by the cultural narratives surrounding their impairment as they are by their individual characteristics. For example, historically, people with disabilities have been characterized as demonic and depraved (Florian, 1982; Fries, 1997). In addition, people with disabilities are often represented exclusively by their medical condition (Olkin, 1999). Modern notions of the disabled are predicated on images of helplessness, vulnerability, asexuality, and perpetual child-like innocence (Gartner & Joe, 1987; Haller, 2000; Pelka, 1997).

Conversely, examples of "the disabled hero" permeate our collective understanding of disability. Disabled people are viewed as heroes and/or super-capable if they have performed extraordinary physical feats despite their limitations (Clare, 1999; Olkin, 1999). This social construction perpetuates a hierarchy of disability that places White, heterosexual, physically independent men on the top rung, and physically dependent women–particularly Women of Color–in the lower echelon (Asch & Fine, 1997; Fine & Asch, 1988). Additionally, individuals with disabilities experience great internalized pressure to conform themselves and their behavior to that of their able-bodied counterparts (Hershey, 1993; Panzarino, 1994). This cultural conception that individuals with disabilities should be able to transcend their limitations (Kriegel, 1987) and accept any social barriers as simply a part of their life can be both psychologically destructive and serve as an excuse to leave social and physical barriers intact. Persons with disabilities who are unable to care for themselves independently and those whose physical appearance differs from the expected norm experience particularly high levels of social ostracism (Olkin, 1999; Solomon, 1993). For individuals who do not meet these high standards related to independence, psychological research has postulated that these negative social experiences are a direct result of the cultural belief that individuals whose lives contradict societal expectations of disability are incapable or unworthy of meaningful relationships (Moore & Feist-Price, 1999).

While the negative social constructions of disability–and their implications for interpersonal relationships–have deeply affected both men and women, the interpersonal and relational consequences have been particularly salient for women (Fine & Asch, 1988; Morris, 1996). Disabled women have endured discrimination and social oppression in the areas of health care, employment, sexuality and other social relationships. Women with disabilities are also disproportionately affected by our cultural emphasis on bodily perfection for women. Women with disabilities are often treated as less desirable than their able-bodied counterparts–especially when compared to mythical standards of beauty (Rintala et al., 1997). Their median income is significantly less than their male counterparts' and substantially below the poverty line (Fine & Asch, 1988; Olkin, 1999). Feminist and other progressive movements have largely failed to incorporate these issues into their agendas (Morris, 1996). Mainstream liberal feminisms' focus on independence and personal autonomy contributes significantly to a general lack of understanding of the issues facing disabled women. Also, isolation and loneliness due to lack of mainstream acceptance remains a pervasive issue for women with disabilities (Asch & Fine, 1997; Fine & Asch, 1988; Krotoski, Nosek, & Turk, 1996).

Our cultural discourse regarding the sexuality of persons with disabilities is a particularly salient example of the ways in which particular social constructions dramatically affect the lives and relationships of disabled women. The psychological scholarship regarding sexuality and disability has historically been medicalized and geared to rehabilitation professionals (Rowe & Savage, 1987). This work often constructs the sexuality of disabled persons as "inappropriate" or nonexistent, characterizations that are reflective of cultural attitudes in general. Rehabilitation programs for adults who become disabled perpetuate a belief in the asexuality of the disabled with devastating consequences for their clients (Morris, 1996). Individuals often lack the resources and information to adapt their sexual lives to their newly disabled bodies (Matthews, 1983). Lack of information, services, and support can have a devastating impact on intimate relationships. Many couples simply cannot endure the strain of adjusting independently to the life-changing consequences of disability. This transition is particularly difficult when cultural notions of disability exclude the possibility of sexual freedom and intimacy.

Another pertinent issue in the literature on sexuality and disability is the sexual exploitation of disabled women. An extremely high percentage of developmentally disabled women will experience sexual violence at least once before their twenty-first birthday (Stromsness, 1993). The vast majority of the survivors receive no medical, psychological, or legal services. A number of personal accounts (e.g., Sheldon, 1993) illustrate both the pervasiveness and emotionally devastating impact of this violence. Women with physical disabilities are also particularly vulnerable to sexual exploitation (Stromsness, 1993). This increased susceptibility has been linked to a lack of social experience. When this decreased cultural knowledge is combined with a deep desire to share closeness, disabled women become easy targets. Obviously, in some cases, physical limitations also prevent these individuals from adequately defending themselves (Stromsness, 1993). The threat of violence makes many women believe that they are too vulnerable to leave the safety and security of their parents' homes for a more independent lifestyle (Hendey & Pascall, 1998). This cycle of violence and abuse solidifies social constructions of women with disabilities as helpless and dependent. There is a great irony in being depicted as asexual while simultaneously enduring extreme sexual violence and brutality.

The issues just discussed concerning societal views generally and issues of sexuality more specifically present clear obstacles to sustaining and acquiring reciprocal intimate relationships for disabled women. As stated previously, women with disabilities are often considered less desirable potential partners than their able-bodied peers (Fine & Asch, 1988). Women with cognitive and learning disabilities experience higher rates of marriage and other significant relationships than do visibly physically disabled women (Gill, 1996). Gill (1996) has postulated that these statistics demonstrate the impact of narrow societal conceptualizations of beauty on the perceived desirability of physically "imperfect" women. Also women with disabilities are devalued as potential mates because of assumptions regarding their universal incapability. Specifically, these women are seen as unable to carry out traditional gender roles ascribed to them, including caring for children, maintaining households and securing employment (Gill, 1996). Most importantly, women with disabilities are thought to be unable to contribute to meaningful reciprocal relationships. Gay and lesbian advocates often dismiss women with disabilities as the helpless antithesis of everything they are trying to accomplish in disrupting conventional gender roles in relationships (Klein, 1992). Even in childhood, disabled persons are discouraged from seeing themselves as viable relational partners. Girls are often encouraged to pursue their education based on the societal belief that scholarly pursuits are the only way to integrate themselves meaningfully into the world (Nemeth, 2000).

The concept of "settling" also predominates the literature regarding relationships for women with disabilities. Women with disabilities who choose to partner with another individual who is also disabled are often constructed as having accommodated themselves to the best option available to them. Although many women do end up in less than desirable relationships, the vast majority who choose partners do so based on their genuine feelings for one another (Gill, 1996). Mutual understanding and a sense of kinship appear to be key factors in these relationships.

Regardless of their choices of partners, women with disabilities who find intimate relationships face great obstacles to their success. Negotiating a mutually satisfactory sexual experience can be complicated by the ingenuity that is sometimes required to overcome physical disabilities (Mairs, 1997). If a partner is required to provide intimate personal assistance, relationship boundaries can be blurred to such an extent as to undermine the quality of the relationship as a whole. Current government policies also serve as obstacles to meaningful relationships for the disabled. Marriage penalties often force individuals with extensive disabilities to choose between vital health care and cohabitating with their chosen partners (Gill, 1996; Waxman, 1993). Despite the financial penalties, many individuals have chosen to share households. These couples either experience extreme financial difficulties or must defraud the government by hiding their living arrangements. This economic oppression is particularly salient when both partners are disabled. Waxman (1993) noted that in these cases government support is cut in half, making even the most subsistence of livings virtually impossible.

Social stereotypes, lack of government resources, and an overall absence of social support can combine to make a woman with a disability particularly dependent upon her intimate relationship. Theorists have postulated that this reliance contributes to the increased incidence of sexual, emotional, and physical abuse experienced by women with disabilities (Gill, 1996; Pelka, 1997; Sobsey, 1994). Social isolation and loneliness diminish the opportunities a woman has to meet potential partners. Additionally, women with disabilities may feel compelled to prove themselves as sexual beings (Gill, 1996). All of these factors can compel disabled women to stay in relationships that have abusive components.

Theoretical and empirical investigations at the nexus of sexuality, intimate relationships, and the social construction of disability have been limited, particularly in psychology. A study by Barron (1997) demonstrated that young women with physical disabilities are subjected to negative social constructions regarding disability such as assumptions of intellectual incapacity, inability to mother and/or have children, asexuality, and general helplessness. The author argues that construction of disabled women as passive children is a self-fulfilling stereotype. Only one research study (Rousso, 1996) directly explores the impact of social constructions of disability on sexual development and expression. This study focused on adolescent girls and the impact of their parents' internalization of societal attitudes about disability on the children's subsequent sexual development. Individuals whose parents did not feel that their sexual options would be limited by their disability were more likely to achieve healthy sexual development. Our research endeavor combines both of these works by exploring the impact of social representations of disability on intimate relationships. Our research goals are two-fold:

1. to illuminate the ways in which disability is represented in contemporary U.S. society through the experiences of disabled women themselves, and
2. to explore the relationship between these societal messages and the relationships of women with disabilities.

METHOD

Participants

Nineteen adult women who have visible physical and/or sensory disabilities that result in functional impairment participated in one to two hour interviews. Disabilities that are immediately apparent upon interaction were chosen in order to explore the impact of such visibility. Eighteen participants were Caucasian and identified either as European-American, or did not state an ethnic identity. One individual identified as Laotian. Eighteen participants were heterosexual and one identified as a lesbian. Participants experienced a variety of disabilities, including multiple sclerosis, blindness, deafness, spina bifida, cerebral palsy, and polio. The participants demonstrated wide-ranging diversity in terms of their class backgrounds, which ranged from upper middle class to poverty. Thirteen of the women were living below the poverty line. Ten of the women were currently in relationships with partners. All but two had had an intimate relationship at some time in their adult lives.

Procedure

Flyers and newsletter bulletins were distributed to over fifty disability-related organizations across the state of Minnesota, with a particular focus on the Minneapolis-St. Paul metropolitan area. Additionally, participants were recruited via a research subject e-mail list compiled by the State of Iowa, Department of Education, Special Education Parent Consultant. A third source of contacts was provided by a web site focused on issues surrounding independent living. Participation was unpaid and voluntary.

An open-ended series of questions related to disabilities, sexuality and interpersonal relationships were asked in an interview format. All interviews were tape-recorded either through the use of a tape recorder or through a device attached to the researcher's phone. Five interviews were conducted in person, and fourteen were carried out over the telephone. Interviews were then transcribed and checked by the interviewer for accuracy. Field notes for the interviews provide context of the interviews, nonverbal reactions of participants (when available), and reactions of the interviewer. Anecdotally, many of the participants expressed a greater willingness to be open and honest as a result of the first author's disability.

The interviews were coded using mutually agreed-upon themes developed by the two authors. Themes related to social construction of disability (e.g., asexuality, intellectually challenged, helplessness), interpersonal relationships (e.g., good and bad experiences with disabled partners, good and bad experiences with able-bodied partners, exploitative/abusive experiences), and sexuality (e.g., sources of information, sexuality and sexual relationships, messages about being sexual) were identified as either present or absent in each of the transcripts. The primary coder's reliability with the resolved/expert codes was .91.

RESULTS

The women interviewed noted a variety of negative social constructions and images of people with disabilities. These included beliefs that people with disabilities are universally intellectually challenged (mentioned by 11 participants), asexual (11 participants), super capable (2 participants), helpless and incompetent (10 participants), and invisible (2 participants). No doubt as a function of these societal attitudes, the women mentioned being treated with condescension (13 respondents), pity (5 respondents), and other negative responses. Treatment as intellectually challenged was mentioned by 11 respondents. As articulated by one woman, assumptions regarding the cognitive inferiority of the disabled are prevalent and often accompanied by infantilizing behavior on the part of able-bodied people:

> Well, just the fact that they assume that if you are not able to walk, they assume you are retarded. It is crazy. It is very difficult knowing that you have a documented intelligence test that indicates that you have superior intelligence and they treat you like they do–talk

down to you. (Betty[2], a 50-year-old woman with polio and a brain injury)

Two individuals described instances of being treated as super-capable. Able-bodied individuals often pigeonhole their disabled counterparts as either cognitively incompetent or super capable. "Well, I think probably some of the greatest stereotypes are because you are blind you are either retarded or you can do everything" (Elizabeth, a 48-year-old woman who is blind).

Eleven of the women interviewed highlighted images of the disabled as asexual. Thirteen of the participants also noted the ways in which negative assumptions regarding their sexuality resulted in dismissive treatment. Diane (age 51, who is blind and has spina bifida), said, "It seems as though most people thought of us as asexual. I don't know if other people have run into that, but I have. No matter what age group we are in they seemed surprised when I talk about boys and being attracted." Paula, who is 47 and has multiple sclerosis and fibromyalgia, noted the impact that an exacerbation of her illness had on the perceptions of others regarding her sexuality,

> It has been over 3 years since I have had any kind of a significant other. Okay? So, my sexuality hasn't been addressed [since being in a wheelchair] . . . 'Oh so you are in a wheelchair?'. . . I actually finally told one guy 'just because I'm disabled and my legs don't work doesn't mean . . . my vagina [doesn't work].'

Twelve participants mentioned isolation and loneliness as consequences of their disabilities. One woman poignantly illustrated how being treated as invisible contributes to this experience:

> They [strangers] treat me like a ghost standing there. When I try to get into conversations, and oh this is the worst thing, they say this all the time. When I ask them what they are saying, they say 'Oh nothing, it is okay' and they won't repeat it because to them it is not worth repeating. To me it is like gold. I still want to know. (Carol, a 57-year-old woman who is deaf.)[3]

Elizabeth's experience underscores the ways in which isolation is perpetuated by invisibility: "When I go to our bank, [the people there] are like stones. You walk into the bank and you'll sit there and you'll wait and you'll wait . . . and then people will walk right past you and get help." Betty also highlighted how lack of accommodation and mutual understanding contributes to the isolation of people with disabilities: "Now I prefer to stay home. I would rather not go out for dinner even. I don't like the accessibility issues and I seclude. I stay home on my off time."

The women interviewed had vastly different experiences in terms of whether or not they were able to sustain a mutually satisfying and reciprocal relationship with either able-bodied or disabled partners. Eleven participants mentioned at least one good experience with an able-bodied partner. Kathy, who is 38 and became quadriplegic in a car accident, details the survival of her relationship despite discouragement from rehab professionals.

> Everyone told us to get a divorce and told me to go on welfare and [said] our marriage would never last . . . Finally [my husband] told them to shut up–that he didn't want to hear any more about it. He looked at us as a couple . . . and has been very supportive.

Six of the women interviewed reported negative experiences with able-bodied partners, many of which could be considered exploitive and/or abusive. Carol's experience illustrates how disability is used as a convenient mechanism for mistreatment:

> When my husband and I would double date–they were hearing–and when we parked to neck he would park under a street light so that the light would be shining on my face and not his so he could talk to the others in the car without my knowing what he was saying. And I never knew that until we were married 10 or 15 years already before I found out. And they joke about this.

Seven of the women described good experiences with disabled partners. "He [my husband] is very caring. He is gentle and he is very loving . . . and he is willing to take care of me" (Gloria, a 40-year-old woman with cerebral palsy and spina bifida).

All of the women who mentioned good experiences with disabled partners also stated that the fact that both of them had disabilities affected their relationship in a positive manner. As Betty said, "It does make a difference. We accept each other. We are more aware of the disability and we are more aware of people needing their space." Conversely, nine of the women interviewed mentioned bad experiences with a partner who also had a disability. In some of these cases, a less significantly disabled partner would use disability as a manipulative tool in much the same way their able-bodied counterparts had. As Diane said,

> He [my husband] did some pretty nasty things that would not have gotten past me if I could see . . . it was hard to know what was head games or if his sight really was changing that much . . . it was really scary . . . he also used it as a power trip, kind of like 'hey you have to do this for me,' even though he was fully capable of doing it himself.

Other women also reported that their partners were able to get away with abusive conduct on the basis of their disability either because of cultural stereotypes regarding the disabled or as a result of manipulation on the part of the offender. This trend was eloquently encapsulated by Frieda, who is 21 and has spina bifida. She noted that, "In the middle of the relationship, he became abusive, so that was kind of bad . . . this guy was really abusive to me, and he understood enough not to hit me . . . he acted like he didn't understand, but I knew he did." Frieda went on to explain that her reports of abuse went unheeded because authorities believed that her boyfriend was incapable of understanding the consequences of his actions.

Six of the participants mentioned abusive and/or exploitative experiences at the hands of significant individuals in their lives other than their partners. One participant recalled,

> When we were in school, she'd [my sister] walk on the other side of the hall just to avoid me . . . she would have parties on Friday night during football season . . . and she'd say 'You're staying in your room tonight because I don't want my friends to know I have a sister with a disability'. . . I was in my room in the dark, I couldn't even have lights on. (Isabel, a 50-year-old woman with spina bifida)

Many participants expressed a belief that, aside from outright experiences of mistreatment related to their disabilities, able-bodied people exhibited an overall lack of interest and/or ability to participate in mutually satisfying relationships. This assertion was most starkly articulated by Carol who expressed bewilderment when asked to name an able-bodied individual who truly understood her experience as a disabled woman. She said, "Who really understands my disability? My mom was determined to make me talk and she succeeded. But to understand deafness? I don't know, I don't know anyone who understands."

The vast majority of individuals who highlighted this lack of awareness coped by affiliating themselves primarily with the disability community. Eleven participants stated that they either preferred to spend time in or experienced the majority of their intimate connections within the disabled community.

> I found myself beginning social recreation as an adolescent among other blind people . . . because I didn't have a very good time in high school. Things were a little bit better my senior year, but by and large it was just something to get through. And so I just got through it and got that kind of stimulation among other blind people. (Nancy, who is blind and is in her forties)

In addition to finding stimulation–and sometimes refuge–within a community of other people with disabilities, the women clearly articulated the personal attributes and attitudes they developed for handling issues related to disability. Fifteen of the women focused on their own independence, resilience and determination. Feelings of self-worth and an ability to dismiss insensitive individuals were also cited by 15 women as being integral to a positive adjustment. Julia, a 37-year-old woman with cerebral palsy, described the situation this way: "You have to know who you are and you have to be able to stand up and say it and take the flack because there are going to be people out there who are going to try to get you not to fight, but that's just kind of the reality." Another woman said, "I'm not ashamed to be in a wheelchair . . . If they do [feel sorry for me] then I don't think they are a friend of mine, therefore I don't really need them. I have enough friends" (Alice, a 62-year-old woman with multiple sclerosis). And Frieda insisted, "I'm not different. I'm not different. I just sit in a piece of metal."

DISCUSSION

The present study confirmed that views of people with disabilities as incompetent and helpless, intellectually challenged, super-capable and asexual, continue to influence the lives of women with disabilities. Notably, most of these stereotypes were encountered by women with different types of disabilities, suggesting that these categories are fairly universally applied. With respect to intimate relationships, the women had had a wide variety of both positive and negative experiences. Notably, a common disability experience seemed to have an important positive influence on sustaining close intimate relationships. Relatedly, the lack of this similarity was, in many cases, perceived as a major impediment to relationships with the able-bodied.

Participants spoke poignantly about their pervasive isolation and loneliness. Many participants espoused that their disabilities–or attitudes toward them–at least to some extent limited their ability to access meaningful social interactions. Participants' frustration with this situation was tied to their unwillingness to participate more actively in society at large. Thus a vicious cycle is activated which serves to further isolate individuals with disabilities and solidify stereotypes relating to their social maturity and competence.

The high levels of isolation and rejection experienced by the women in this study made positive intimate relationships with able-bodied individuals all the more salient. In describing fulfilling mutual connections with able-bodied partners, these women emphasized the unique level of awareness attained by their mates. Importantly, though, most of the women interviewed lived or worked almost exclusively with disabled people. This segregation may have precluded the kind of sustained intimate contact necessary for the establishment of long-lasting relationships with able-bodied people. The continued segregation of individuals with disabilities both from society and our cultural discourse serves to perpetuate these limitations on relationships. Lack of integration of individuals with disabilities prevents the daily interaction necessary for both disabled and able-bodied individuals to learn to negotiate the delicate balance between two cultures.

The major limitation of this study was our inability to represent the full range of diversity among women. Issues surrounding sexual orientation could not be considered because only one woman self identified as a lesbian. Relatedly, the issues experienced by woman of color who are also disabled are not represented in this study. The "multiplicity of oppression" experienced by these women undoubtedly has a significant impact on their relationships. Without exploring these issues in a more diverse sample, we cannot know the ways in which having privilege in certain areas mediates the experience of disability, or the ways in which additional experiences of oppression change the experience of disability. In addition, it will be important to explore the issues addressed in this study among men, in an effort to understand more fully the gendered nature of experiencing disability.

This study is one of the few to investigate systematically the connections between societal representations of disability and disabled women's interpersonal relationships using the voices of women with disabilities themselves. We hope that future research will explore more thoroughly the implications of the ways in which disability is constructed for other aspects of interpersonal experience and for well-being in general. The experiences of the women in this study also underscore the need to foster stronger alliances between disabled and able-bodied people.

NOTES

1. Both the terms "people with disabilities" and "disabled people" are used throughout this paper. Many disability rights activists believe that the term "people with disabilities" puts the person first without undue focus on their medical condition. Other disabled individuals, particularly in the UK, assert that "disabled person" should be used to highlight the salience of disability oppression. The use of both terms is meant to recognize and support both perspectives.
2. All names are pseudonyms.
3. Carol, who is prelingually deaf, communicates by speaking and lip reading, does not know American Sign Language, and is not part of the Deaf community. Many people in the Deaf community consider themselves to be part of a linguistic minority group and a distinct culture, and do not consider themselves disabled. It seemed reasonable to include Betty in this study of women with disabilities given her lack of affiliation with Deaf culture. For further discussion of the Deaf community and the disability community, see Davis (1995) and Wendell (1996).

REFERENCES

Asch, A. & Fine, M. (1997). Nurturance, sexuality and women with disabilities. In L. J. Davis (Ed.), *The disability studies reader* (pp. 241-259). NY: Routledge.

Barron, K. (1997). The bumpy road to womanhood. *Disability & Society, 12*, 223-239.

Biklen, D. (1988). The myth of clinical judgment. *Journal of Social Issues, 44*, 127-140.

Clare, E. (1999). *Pride: Disability, queerness and liberation.* Cambridge, MA: South End Press.

Davis, L. J. (1995). *Enforcing normalcy: Disability, deafness and the body.* London: Verso Press.

Davis, L. J. (1997). *The disability studies reader.* NY: Routledge.

Fine, M., & Asch, A. (1988). Beyond pedestals. In M. Fine & A. Asch (Eds.), *Women with disabilities: Essays in psychology, culture and politics* (pp. 1-39). Philadelphia: Temple University Press.

Florian, V. (1982). Cross-cultural differences in attitudes towards disabled persons: A study of Jewish and Arab youth in Israel. *International Journal of Intercultural Relations, 6,* 291-299.

Fries, K. (Ed.) (1997). Introduction to *Staring back: The disability experience from the inside out* (pp. 1-13). New York: Penguin Books.

Gartner, A., & Joe, T. (Eds.) (1987). Introduction to *Images of the disabled, disabling images* (pp. 1-7). NY: Praeger Publishers.

Gill, C. (1996). Dating and relationship issues. In D. Krotoski, M. Nosek, & M. Turk (Eds.), *Women with physical disabilities* (pp. 117 123). Baltimore, MD: Paul H. Brookes Publishing Co.

Haller, B. (2000). If they limp, they lead? News representations and the hierarchy of disability images. In D. O. Braithwaite & T. L. Thompson (Eds.), *Handbook of communication and people with disabilities: Research and application* (pp. 273-288). Manwath, NJ: Lawrence Erlbaum Associates.

Hendey, N., & Pascall, G. (1998). Independent living: Gender, violence and the threat of violence. *Disability & Society, 13,* 415-427.

Hershey, L. (1993). Coming out in voices. In L. Holcomb & M. E. Willmuth (Eds.), *Women with disabilities: Found voices* (pp. 9-19). New York: The Haworth Press, Inc.

Kaye, H. S., & Longmore, P. K. (1997). *Disability watch: The status of people with disabilities in the United States.* Oakland, CA: Disability Rights Advocates.

Klein, B. S. (1992). We are who you are: Feminism and disability. *Ms., 3,* 70-74.

Kriegel, L. (1987). The cripple in literature. In A. Gartner, & T. Joe (Eds.), *Images of the disabled, Disabling images* (pp. 31-47). NY: Praeger Publishers.

Krotoski, D. M., Nosck, M. A., & Turk, M. A. (Eds.) (1996). *Women with physical disabilities: Achieving and maintaining health and well-being.* Baltimore, MD: Paul H. Brooks Publishing Company.

Mairs, N. (1997). Carnal Acts. In K. Fries (Ed.), *Staring back: The disability experience from the inside out* (pp. 51-62). NY: Penguin Books.

Matthews, G. F. (1983). *Voices from the shadows: Women with disabilities speak out.* Toronto: Women's Educational Press.

Moore, C., & Feist-Price, S. (1999). Societal attitudes and the civil rights of persons with disabilities. *Journal of Applied Rehabilitation Counseling, 30,* 19-24.

Morris, J. (Ed.) (1996). *Encounters with strangers: Feminism and disability.* London: The Women's Press.

Nemeth, S. (2000). Society, sexuality, and disabled/able-bodied romantic relationships. In D. O. Braithwaite & T. L. Thompson (Eds.), *Handbook of communication and people with disabilities: Research and application* (pp. 193-222). Manwath, NJ: Lawrence Erlbaum Associates.

Olkin, R. (1999). *What psychotherapists should know about disability.* NY: Guilford.

Panzarino, C. (1994). *The me in the mirror.* Seattle, WA: Seal Press.

Pelka, F. (1997). *The ABC-CLIO companion to the disability rights movement.* Santa Barbara, CA: ABC-CLIO.

Rintala, D. H., Howland, C. A., Nosek, M. A., Bennett, J. L., Young, M. E., Foley, C., C., Rossi, C. D., & Chanpong, G. (1997). Dating issues for women with physical disabilities. *Sexuality and Disability, 15,* 219-242.

Rousso, H. (1996). Sexuality and a positive sense of self. In D. M. Krotoski, M. A. Nosek, & M. A. Turk (Eds.), *Women with physical disabilities: Achieving and maintaining health and well-being* (pp. 109-116). Baltimore, MD: Paul H. Brookes.

Rowe, W. S., & Savage, S. (1987). *Sexuality and the developmentally handicapped: A guidebook for the health care professionals.* Queenston, Ontario: The Edwin Mellen Press.

Sheldon, M. (1993). An open letter to health and mental health care professionals from a survivor of sexual exploitation. In L. Holcomb & M. E. Willmuth (Eds.), *Women with disabilities: Found voices* (pp. 133-139). NY: The Haworth Press, Inc.

Sobsey, D. (1994). *Violence and abuse in the lives of people with disabilities: The end of silent acceptance?* Baltimore, MD: Paul H. Brookes.

Solomon, S. (1993). Women and physical distinction: A review of the literature and suggestions for intervention. In L. Holcomb & M. E. Willmuth (Eds.), *Women with disabilities: Found voices* (pp. 91-106). NY: The Haworth Press, Inc.

Stromsness, M. (1993). Sexually abused women with mental retardation: Hidden victims, absent resources. In L. Holcomb & M. E. Willmuth (Eds.), *Women with disabilities: Found voices* (pp. 139-153). NY: The Haworth Press, Inc.

Waxman, B. (1993). Girls: It is time to publicize our sexual oppression. *The Disability Rag: Special Issue on Sexuality and Disability.* pp. 28-33.

Wendell, S. (1996). *The rejected body: Feminist philosophical reflections on disability.* London: Routledge.

"People Tell Me I Can't Have Sex": Women with Disabilities Share Their Personal Perspectives on Health Care, Sexuality, and Reproductive Rights

Lori Ann Dotson
Jennifer Stinson
LeeAnn Christian

SUMMARY. Much of the information "known" about the personal beliefs and experiences of women with developmental disabilities, their needs, desires, and sexual practices, have been gleaned from second-hand accounts and speculation. Utilizing direct interviews, this study was designed to assess women's level of knowledge, their access to resources and their feelings of control over choices concerning their bodies. Further, this study sought to examine the impact that disability

Lori Ann Dotson, MA, is a doctoral student in clinical psychology at the Fielding Institute. Additionally, she is a therapist at SHIELDS for Families, Inc., in South Central Los Angeles. Jennifer Stinson, BA, is a doctoral student in clinical psychology at the California School of Professional Psychology, Los Angeles. She is also a behavior consultant at the Institute for Applied Behavior Analysis (IABA). LeeAnn Christian, PhD, is the Research Director at IABA.

Address correspondence to: Lori Ann Dotson, 1788 S. Garth Avenue, Los Angeles, CA 90035.

The authors wish to extend their gratitude to the participants of this study for their candor and courage. Additionally, they would like to thank IABA for their continued support of relevant research and commitment to improving the lives of people with developmental disabilities.

[Haworth co-indexing entry note]: " 'People Tell Me I Can't Have Sex': Women with Disabilities Share Their Personal Perspectives on Health Care, Sexuality, and Reproductive Rights." Dotson, Lori Ann, Jennifer Stinson, and LeeAnn Christian. Co-published simultaneously in *Women & Therapy* (The Haworth Press, Inc.) Vol. 26, No. 3/4, 2003, pp. 195-209; and: *Women with Visible and Invisible Disabilities: Multiple Intersections, Multiple Issues, Multiple Therapies* (ed: Martha E. Banks, and Ellyn Kaschak) The Haworth Press, Inc., 2003, pp. 195-209. Single or multiple copies of this article are available for a fee from The Haworth Document Delivery Service [1-800-HAWORTH, 9:00 a.m. - 5:00 p.m. (EST). E-mail address: getinfo@haworthpressinc.com].

has on sexuality from the women who experience it. Implications for future research are discussed. *[Article copies available for a fee from The Haworth Document Delivery Service: 1-800-HAWORTH. E-mail address: <getinfo@haworthpressinc.com> Website: <http://www.HaworthPress.com> © 2003 by The Haworth Press, Inc. All rights reserved.]*

KEYWORDS. Women, developmental disabilities, sexuality

In the past decade, increasing attention has been given to women with developmental disabilities and their unique needs regarding sexuality (Williams & Nind, 1999). Historically, women with developmental disabilities have been an invisible group. They have been segregated in institutions and denied their identities as women, mothers, and sexual beings. While many positive changes have occurred, women with developmental disabilities still face conflicting stereotypes, which portray them as either asexual, childlike and dependent, or oversexed, undiscriminating and "easy" (Olney & Kuper, 1998; Tilley, 1998; Williams & Nind, 1999). These stereotypes are harmful because they lead either to the belief that a woman's sexual expression can be ignored or that it must be suppressed.

While many barriers continue to exist for the sexual expression of women with developmental disabilities, it is encouraging that they are being increasingly recognized and discussed. However, studies are most often presented from the perspectives of service providers, parents and advocates. First-hand accounts and opinions from women with developmental disabilities are largely absent from the literature. In an innovative study, British researcher McCarthy (1998) interviewed several women with developmental disabilities, asking questions about their feelings towards their bodies, health and reproduction and how much control they had over choices concerning their bodies. Her findings indicated that women had a lot to say about their experiences when given the opportunity. Many expressed dissatisfaction with their bodies, did not regard their bodies as a source of pleasure and felt they had little control over important choices in their lives, such as what type of contraception to use, if any. McCarthy's study (1998) demonstrated a need to set aside theories and assumptions and listen to the actual experiences of women with developmental disabilities.

Gynecological health care is an essential component of both general health maintenance and sexuality. Yet, gynecological exams can pose various problems for many women with developmental disabilities. Doctors might be unfamiliar with the cognitive needs of women with developmental disabilities and might not explain things in language that is easy to understand (Welner, 1997). They also might address questions and give information to accompanying parents or caregivers instead of speaking directly to their patients.

Doctors can be insensitive to the anxiety that many women feel when subjected to a Pap smear. This invasive procedure is anxiety producing for many women without disabilities. Women with developmental disabilities might experience heightened anxiety if they do not know what to expect, are not treated with respect and understanding by their doctors, or if they have histories of sexual abuse (Welner, 1997). Women with developmental disabilities face a much higher risk of sexual abuse than women without disabilities. It has been estimated that as many as 70% of women with developmental disabilities have experienced some form of sexual abuse in their lifetimes (Petersilia, 2000). Traumatic memories of abuse can be evoked during the gynecological exam causing many women to avoid the exam altogether, thus putting themselves at higher risk for undiagnosed health problems. As a result, some women with developmental disabilities experience so much anxiety that they require sedation in order to get a Pap smear. Unfortunately, this can be a costly procedure. It might be difficult for women to obtain adequate insurance coverage for health care services (Welner, 1997).

Breast exams are another important component of the complete gynecological exam. To aid in the early detection of cancerous lumps, women need to learn to do breast self-exams each month. As indicated by a lack of inclusion in the literature, many women with developmental disabilities do not receive adequate education about breast self-exams due to the same barriers that limit access to routine Pap smears. This procedure can be explained in language they do not understand or it might be overlooked with the assumption that they will not understand or lack the skills to learn or perform the monthly procedure.

Sex remains an uncomfortable topic to directly discuss in both disability and mainstream culture. Literature on this topic predominantly focuses on the attitudes of parents and support staff and how negative attitudes may contribute to poor supports for sexual expression. There also have been many studies on the high rate of sexual abuse for women with developmental disabilities and the difficulty of detecting and reporting abuse (Olney & Kuper, 1998; Petersilia, 2000; Schaller & Feiberg,

2000). Studies of this nature are invaluable in examining shortcomings and seeking solutions for better service provision. However, it is unclear how women with developmental disabilities perceive these problems.

Furthermore, homosexuality, and sexual acts such as anal intercourse and oral sex are often ignored or mentioned only superficially in the literature (Williams & Nind, 1999). Studies of the attitudes of service providers indicate that these activities continue to be met with discomfort or disapproval from support staff (Scotti, Slack, Bowman, & Morris, 1996; Wolfe, 1997). Masturbation is another topic that may elicit negative responses from staff and parents or even be defined as a "problem behavior." Yet, it is likely that many women experience confusion and frustration related to orgasmic difficulty and would benefit from education and masturbation training. Ultimately, it remains unknown whether women with developmental disabilities feel limited in their means of sexual expression or whether they are even aware of a range of human sexual behaviors.

Women with developmental disabilities are commonly regarded as dependent, incapable of raising children and incapable of making appropriate choices regarding reproduction (Waxman, 1994). Thousands of women were involuntarily sterilized during the Eugenics Movements of the late nineteenth and early twentieth centuries in an effort to quell their sexuality and prevent the passing of "disabled" genes to offspring (Kempton & Kahn, 1991; Olney & Kuper, 1998; Wolfe & Blanchett, 2000). While involuntary sterilization is no longer legal, surgical sterilization is still presented as a viable option to minors and adult women with developmental disabilities and is legally performed on consenting patients (Nelson et al., 1999).

It has been suggested that contraceptive agents, such as birth control pills and Depo-Provera injections, are routinely dispensed with little or no explanation given to the women using them (McCarthy, 1998; Waxman, 1994). As with other issues of gynecological care, doctors might not use clear language to describe why and how contraceptives are used, what side effects to expect or present options for alternative forms of contraception. Parents and caregivers also can fail to provide adequate education regarding birth control. Thus, women with developmental disabilities might lack important information about using contraception and can even be unaware that they are using it (McCarthy, 1998; Waxman, 1994). This serves to perpetuate a lack of control over reproductive choices just as forced sterilization did in the past. Women also might be at higher risk of contracting sexually transmitted diseases if they do not receive education about specific forms of birth control, such as condoms, which prevent the transmission of bodily fluids (Welner, 1997). Furthermore, studies indicate that women who are unable to have children because of sterilization or birth control use might be at higher risk for sexual abuse if perpetrators know their actions will not be detected through pregnancy (McCarthy, 1998).

What do women with developmental disabilities think about having children? What are the ramifications of being denied this option? The present study was designed to assess women's level of knowledge, their access to resources and their feelings of control over choices concerning their bodies. Additionally, this study sought to examine the impact that disability has on sexuality from the women who experience it. It is imperative that we begin listening to the voices of women with developmental disabilities, not only to witness their experiences, but to begin meeting their needs.

METHOD

Participants

Eight women with developmental disabilities served as participants in this study. Their average age was 35 years old with a range of 32 to 40 years old. Seven of the participants were European American, and one participant was Latina. Few participants received psychotropic medications for challenging behaviors such as aggression, self-injurious behavior, and property destruction, but half (50%) received psychotropic medications for mental health problems. All participants received supported living, supported employment or behavior management day services from a human services agency in California.

Instruments

A Health and Sexuality Interview was developed to determine the women's knowledge and perceptions about their gynecological care, sexual activity, and reproductive decisions. The 103-item interview contained "yes/no" questions (e.g., "Do you know what a gynecologist is?"), as well as open-ended questions (e.g., "What does it mean to you when I say that someone is sexually active?"). Additionally, the interview contained several short statements such as, "My gynecologist talks to my staff person or parent during my exam" and "My gynecologist explains what is going to happen in ways that I can understand," that were endorsed as either "never true," "sometimes true," or "always true" by the respondent. Demographic information, such as age and services received, was collected during the interview and was verified through a review of case records. Ethnicity, diagnoses, and medication regimes were gathered from the records review. To the extent possible, other information gathered during the interview process also was verified through records review and/or support staff interview (e.g., doctor's name, last appointment, who made the appointments). The instrument was developed from a variety of sources (Matikka & Vesala, 1997; McCarthy, 1996, 1998; Welner, 1997; Williams & Nind, 2000) and is available from the first author.

Procedures

Health and sexuality interviews were scheduled with participants after consent was obtained. Interviews were conducted in a location convenient for the participant and one that ensured privacy, such as the agency's administrative offices or the women's homes. Administration of the Health and Sexuality Interview took approximately 30 to 45 minutes. To ensure consistency in interviewing, a scripted introduction was read to each participant at the beginning of the interview and the interview was audio taped. Additional instructions were provided directly on the interview form to ensure consistency across interviewers. For example, if in response to the question "Do you know what a gynecologist is?" the respondent said "no," the form instructed the interviewer as follows: "If no, we explain. 'A gynecologist is the special doctor women see every year to make sure their breasts and vaginas and other reproductive parts are healthy.' If the person is not familiar with the names of these body parts, use the drawing on the last page to indicate the breasts and genital area."

All interview questions were read to the participants and their responses were recorded on the interview form. As stated earlier, after completing the interviews, targeted information was verified through records reviews and support staff interviews. All participants' case records were maintained by the human services agency and were secured in the administrative offices.

Interobserver and procedural reliability were conducted by having another observer listen to the audiotape to verify that the interview was conducted according the provided instructions and that information recorded on the interview forms matched what was said on the audiotape.

If a discrepancy arose, the interviewer and observer listened to the tape simultaneously and together decided how to record the response. Both procedural and interobserver reliability revealed only minor deviations by interviewers, more as a result of minor modifications needed on the instrument, rather than interviewer variability.

RESULTS AND DISCUSSION

The results of the health care portion of the interview indicated that only three of the eight participants had been to the gynecologist in the previous year. One woman said she had never been, and four women said they had gone a long time ago. Additionally, the participants' staff could not provide the dates of their last exams, further indicating that reproductive health is a low priority for caregivers. Of those women who had been to the gynecologist, all indicated their doctors were friendly, but most reported that their doctors sometimes explained things in ways they couldn't understand. Only one woman had been both told about and instructed on conducting breast self-exams. She indicated, however, that she didn't really understand how to give herself a breast exam, and thus, did not do it regularly. One woman reported that she didn't know whom she could talk to if she had a problem or question about her body or her health.

In the portion of the interview designed to elicit responses about sex, many of the participants gave incomplete or incorrect answers to the question, "What does it mean to you when I say someone is sexually active." Responses included "interested in sex," "bad," "sick," "have sex every day with different partners," and "kissing." One participant reported that she didn't know the answer, and another requested that the question be skipped. Five of the women reported that they had had sex, or were currently sexually active. The participants learned about sex from a variety of places, including family members, school, and support staff. However, one participant reported that "nobody" has taught her about sex. Seven of the eight participants positively endorsed the statement "I have sexual feelings toward men." However, all of the women responded "never true" to questions about having sex with women or wanting to have sex with women, despite collateral information to the contrary. While most participants indicated that they had varying levels of control regarding their sexuality and reproductive health decisions, one participant indicated that said she did not have control over the choice of whether or not to have sex. She reported that staff controlled these decisions. Four women said they knew how to make themselves feel good by masturbating, although one expressed extreme shame about this topic. Two women indicated that they did not know how to make themselves feel good by masturbating. One woman said she had never masturbated and one passed on the question.

In regards to contraception and birth control, only one woman had never heard of birth control, and six of the women report they are currently using or have used contraception in the past. Six of the eight participants could describe what a sexually transmitted disease was and give examples. Half of the participants were unsure about whether or not they could become pregnant. Seven women reported that they had not been pregnant in the past, and one woman was unsure. Half of the participants reported that they'd like to become mothers someday.

What follows are the stories of the eight women we interviewed. To help understand or clarify some of their responses to the interview questions, collateral information from their support staff also is included. The women's names have been changed to protect their privacy.

Sara is a 35-year-old European American woman diagnosed with mild mental retardation and depressive disorder. As a woman who had lived and worked in a variety of places throughout her life, Sara was often perceived as "streetwise" and capable of advocating for herself within the social service system that provided her support. As reported by her support staff, Sara regularly voiced how important it was to her to be in control of her life at all times. She was known as an open person who frequently shared her sexual experiences with her closest support staff as a way of expressing that she did indeed have control of her life and could make her own choices. As such, it was not surprising to learn that Sara made her own doctor's appointments, went to the doctor without the support of a paid staff, and was knowledgeable about the purpose of Pap smears and clinical breast exams as well as about sexually transmitted diseases, birth control, and contraception. In fact, she astutely reported that she had to get Pap smears twice a year because her pap smears results frequently had been abnormal in the past. Not surprisingly, a repeated theme throughout Sara's interview was control. For example, when asked whether she felt that she had control over whether or not she had sex or used birth control or contraception, Sara emphatically insisted, "No one can control me. I don't like it." However, Sara's responses to questions regarding same-sex relationships were surprising based on her usual candidness. When asked whether she had sexual feelings towards women, had ever had sex with women, or was interested in having sex with women, she became agitated and said, "I'm not gay!" Outside the interview situation, Sara openly talked about the sexual relationship she and her female roommate shared as well as the relationship she had with her current boyfriend. Her later concern for who would have access to the answers she had given during the interview might explain her unwillingness to truthfully share her sexual experiences. Moreover, it seemed that Sara was adamantly denying a possible attraction to women because she had been told it was not appropriate or acceptable behavior. When asked about reproductive issues, Sara explained that she did not currently use birth control nor did she use barrier methods to prevent sexually transmitted diseases because her boyfriend was "fixed." It was interesting that she so faithfully got Pap smears twice a year and was knowledgeable about STDs, yet so naïve about the potential risks she was exposing herself to in this area. The most poignant moment of the interview came during a discussion of childbearing. When asked whether she thought her disability affected her sexuality, she icily replied, "No," but when asked if she might like to have a child one day, she quickly said, "No, because of my mental illness."

Mary is a 32-year-old European American woman diagnosed with moderate mental retardation, cerebral palsy, and a seizure disorder. The impression one got during Mary's interview was that she was embarrassed by and yet intrigued with the interview questions. She visibly struggled with embarrassment at the directness of some of the questions, but seemed to want to answer them. Perhaps after a lifetime of constant supervision by paid staff or family members, Mary finally saw an opportunity to share her feelings about an area that was not often openly discussed. With regard to her health care, Mary was unable to name the doctor who did her gynecological exams and reported that her caregiver made her doctor's appointments. Mary said her doctor was more likely to talk to her caregiver during her gynecological exam than directly to her. She also said her doctor sometimes used words that she didn't understand. Considering the sheltered life Mary has led in her family's home and then in a group home providing 24-hour support, Mary's lack of sexual activity was predictable. She said she had never been sexually active nor had anyone ever taught her about sex. Interestingly, Mary reported that she never had sexual feelings towards men or women, and was not interested in having sex with men nor women, but answered "So-so" when asked if she was satisfied with her level of sexual activity. She did report that she was always able to make herself feel good sexually by masturbating. Notably, when asked who did or would have control over the choice of whether or not she had sex, Mary said her boyfriend would control those choices. (One wonders where this perception comes from for a woman who has never had a sexual relationship.) Mary's lack of sexual experiences did not seem to thwart her knowledge about birth control or sexually transmitted diseases. Although her knowledge was not sophisticated, she at minimum knew that women took birth control pills so they wouldn't have a baby and that AIDS was a sexually transmitted disease. As anticipated based on her other answers, Mary had never used birth control or contraception. Mary did not know whether she was physically able to become pregnant, but her caregiver reported that she was able. When asked whether she thought her disability affected her sexuality, Mary seemed surprised and disturbed by this question and adamantly answered, "No." Poignantly, when asked if she would like to have children some day, she first said no, but under her breath said, "In my dreams." When asked what she meant by that, she said she actually would like having children, but that it was just a dream because people told her she never could.

Martha is a 33-year-old Latina woman diagnosed with mild mental retardation. She receives round the clock supportive employment and living services. Martha reported that she has a gynecologist, but is unsure when she last saw him. Her staff confirmed that it had been over a year since her last check-up, but could not provide a date. Martha reported that her gynecologist sometimes asks about her health and her body, and sometimes explains things in language she understands. She reported that she had never been informed about how to conduct a breast self exam (BSE), and was unaware of reasons for conducting a BSE, or for going to the gynecologist more than once a year. She defined being sexually active as being "bad" and "sick." When asked if she was happy about her level of sexual activity, Martha indicated that she was happy she didn't do "that thing." This theme continued throughout her interview, indicating that using birth control is "bad–not good." Further, she reported that she does not masturbate. Martha has a boyfriend, who is also developmentally disabled, and who receives twenty-four hour daily supportive services. Martha did not mention her boyfriend during the interview.

Crystal is a 39-year-old European American woman diagnosed with mild mental retardation, schizophrenia, and anxiety disorder. She receives in-home supporting living services a few hours a day. She is currently employed. Crystal identified her gynecologist by name, and reported that she is responsible for making appointments with her doctor. She reported that her doctor sometimes speaks in language she doesn't understand. She identified pregnancy as a reason that a woman should go to a gynecologist more than once a year. Crystal reported that she might have been pregnant in the past but was unsure, and stated that the doctor told her she "might have been because of having sex." Her support staff reported that Crystal last visited her gynecologist one and a half years ago for abnormal periods and because she was lactating. Crystal identified sexually active as meaning "hav[ing] sex with another person." Further, she identified herself as sexually active, and reported that she currently has one male sexual partner. Crystal is taking birth control pills and reported that she feels that she is in control of whether or not she takes them. However, she reported that she felt her doctor controlled what type of birth control she takes, and reported that she had not been informed about the potential risks and or side effects of the birth control pills she is taking. She reported that she has not used contraception to protect her from sexually transmitted diseases (STD). Crystal identified two sexually transmitted diseases when asked to list the ones she'd heard of. She did not, however, identify herpes, a sexually transmitted disease for which she is currently being treated.

Susie is a 40-year-old European American woman diagnosed with mild mental retardation and depression. She is currently employed, and receives minimal supportive living and supportive employment services, for a total of four hours of supportive services daily. Additionally, Susie sees a psychologist every other week to address her symptoms of depression. She identified her gynecologist by name, and reported that her last exam was eight months ago. She reported that her gynecologist is friendly, but doesn't always explain things in a language that she can understand, and reports that he doesn't notice if she's uncomfortable. Susie reported that she's been sexually active in the past, but is "waiting" to have sex with her current boyfriend. When asked if she felt her disability affected her sex life, she reported that she has never had an orgasm with a man, and expressed that she felt that men are "not patient." She reported that she knows how to make herself feel good sexually by masturbating but expressed a lot of concern about views other people have about masturbating. She reported that she had attended a class which included sex education information, and felt that she could utilize her staff, doctor or psychologist if she needed more information. Susie reported that her mother decided when she was nineteen or twenty that her tubes should be tied. Susie skipped the question which inquired about her desire to have a child. She reported that it's a "hard responsibility to have a kid."

Carol is a 38-year-old European American woman diagnosed with mild mental retardation, a seizure disorder, and hemiplegia. She is currently employed and receives supportive employment services ten hours a week, and supportive living services forty-two hours a week. She reported that her mother has a gynecologist but was unsure of whether or not she had one. She reported that she had never had a Pap smear, and that she "gathers it's painful." Reporting further, " [I] can't tolerate pain–[they] stick all that crap up inside you." Carol was unaware if she is at risk for breast cancer, had difficulty identifying any special risks for women in regard to the reproductive health. She reported that she had never been sexually active, and was happy about her current level of sexual activity "because you don't know where it's [sexual activity] going to lead." Carol requested to pass on the question regarding whether or not she knew how to please herself sexually by masturbating. Carol reported that she cannot have children because of "all the medication taken over the years." When asked if she desired having a child, she responded simply, "I can't for medical reasons." When asked if her disability affects her sex life, Carol indicated that her disability "slows me down in a lot of ways."

Jill is a 34-year-old European American woman with a diagnosis of mild mental retardation. She is currently employed and receives supportive living services 12 hours a week, and supportive employment services 14 hours a week. She identified her gynecologist by name, but could not remember when she last had a gynecological visit. She had difficulty identifying the reasons for gynecological check-ups and reported that she had neither been told nor instructed about how to do a breast self-exam. She reported that she had had one sexual partner in the last year. She reported that her mother introduced the concept of birth control to her, and described contraception as a way to "help protect to not have any kids." She reported that a side effect to taking contraception is that one "feel[s] sad–when you miss a pill you have to go through everything." Jill reported that she had never been pregnant and doesn't want to become a parent. She reported that she was unaware of whether of not she could get pregnant. However, she was aware of the status of her boyfriend, and indicated that he was sterile.

Rhonda is a 33-year-old European American woman diagnosed with Asperger's syndrome, and severe/recurrent major depressive disorder. She is employed and receives supportive living services nine hours a week, and supportive employment services twenty hours a week. Rhonda identified her gynecologist by name, and reported that she makes her own appointments. Rhonda's last visit was one month prior to the interview.

When asked why she goes to the gynecologist she replied, "I go to the gynecologist once a year. I have to make sure I don't have anything wrong with my reproductive system." She reported that her gynecologist always uses words that she understands, and that he explains things to her. She reported that if a woman has an abnormal Pap smear, or a yeast infection, she may need to go to the gynecologist more than once a year. She reported that she had been told about breast self-exams but never taught to perform one. She reports that she got information from other sources and learned how to do breast exams on her own. It is particularly disappointing that Rhoda was not taught this skill by her gynecologist since she is very interested in her physical health and has a history of good follow-through regarding health related behaviors. Rhonda reported that she is happy with her level of sexual activity and reported "I feel like I'm in control of my life." She identified several sexually transmitted diseases and was informed about how they're transmitted. She included herpes, a sexually transmitted disease for which she is being treated. Rhonda reported that she previously took birth control pills, and identified several side effects that resulted. She reported that she feels comfortable asking her staff and her doctor about contraception and reproduction issues. She also indicated that she utilizes the Internet for health related information. Rhonda reported that she'd like to have a child someday "but not now." She reported that she can get pregnant because she doesn't have her "tubes tied off." She reported "I vowed never to have them tied off."

CONCLUSIONS

In response to the invaluable personal information each woman in this study provided, we felt a strong need to make a relevant, reciprocal gesture. Thus, all participants were offered the chance to participate in a "Special Touch" Breast Self-Exam (BSE) Class sponsored by the Community Education Center of a local hospital. Two of the participants from this study were able to attend the class. Two of the woman declined to participate in the BSE class, and the remaining four women expressed interest in attending, but could not due to scheduling conflicts. An instructor that often volunteered at the Community Education Center taught the class. She was trained as a Special Touch BSE Instructor by the American Cancer Society. The instructor adapted the class for the women in the following ways: (1) the class time was lengthened from 1.5 hr to 2 hr; (2) information provided through lecture was minimized; (3) one-to-one instructor attention was maximized by a limited class size and (4) time spent in practicing with a breast model was increased.

Classes such as this one are a good first step in addressing the health needs of women with developmental disabilities. Additionally, same-sex and co-ed psycho-educational groups on other health, reproduction, and sexuality related topics would likely benefit women with developmental disabilities. Topics could include: friendship, intimacy, masturbation, non-conventional and safe-sex practices, co-habitation, sexual side-effects to medications, sexual exploitation, as well as social and protective skills and assertiveness training. Support staff and family members would also likely benefit from the availability of social support groups. Additionally, women with developmental disabilities should be included in the development and oversight of all programs and policies that impact their lives.

The lack of similar research in this area necessitates much trial and error in conducting this type of study. In hindsight, this interview included some language and formatting that was difficult for the participants to understand. For instance, asking participants to respond "never true," "sometimes true," or "always true" to negatively worded statements (e.g., "my gynecologist does not notice if I am uncomfortable") was universally problematic. This indicates a need to refine this interview tool for future use. An additional limitation was that the present research design excludes woman with lower cognitive abilities and verbal skills. Women with more severe disabilities are routinely absent from sexuality research studies due to a lack of appropriate tools and research designs. Unfortunately, these might be the women whose needs and experiences are least understood and most requiring of attention through research. It is imperative that future studies make efforts to include women with more severe disabilities. This might include utilizing sign language, photos, role-plays, naturalistic observation or possibly developing interactive computer programs as communication devices.

The invisibility of the special needs of women with developmental disabilities in research about sexuality is almost as insidious as the invisibility of people with developmental disabilities in other areas of research, as well as their general lack of representation in main-stream culture. Although we are aware that our inclusion of collateral information can be viewed as paternalistic, we have included it in the hopes that it may enrich others' awareness that women with disabilities, like those without, must make difficult decisions about self-disclosure, based on experienced and perceived biases. It is our hope that research such as this can begin to remove barriers to sexual expression, and challenge biases as they relate to gender, disability and sexuality. Further, this study aims to extend a budding dialogue regarding the importance of first person narratives, especially as it relates to the stories of people who have been previously denied a voice.

REFERENCES

Kempton, W., & Kahn, E. (1991). Sexuality and people with intellectual disabilities: A historical perspective. *Sexuality and Disability, 9*, 93-111.

Matikka, L. M. & Vesala, H. T. (1997). Acquiescence in quality-of-life interviews with adults who have mental retardation. *Mental Retardation, 35* (2), 75-82.

McCarthy, M. (1996). The sexual support needs of people with learning disabilities: A profile of those referred for sex education. *Sexuality and Disability, 14* (4), 165-278.

McCarthy, M. (1998). Whose body is it anyway? Pressures and control for women with learning disabilities. *Disability & Society, 13*, 557-569.

Nelson, R. M., Botkin, J. R., Levetown, M., Moseley, K. L., Truman, J. T., & Wilfond, B. S. (1999). Sterilization of minors with developmental disabilities. *Pediatrics, 104*, 337-340.

Olncy, M. F., & Kuper, E. V. (1998). The situation of women with developmental disabilities: Implications for practitioners in supported employment. *Journal of Applied Rehabilitation Counseling, 29*, 3-11.

Petersilia, J. (2000). Invisible victims. *Human Rights, 27*, 9-12.

Schaller, J. & Fieberg, J. (2000). Issues of abuse for women with disabilities and implications for rehabilitation counseling. *Journal of Applied Rehabilitation Counseling, 29* (2), 9-19.

Scotti, J. R., Slack, B. S., Bowman, R. A., & Morris, T. L. (1996). College student attitudes concerning the sexuality of persons with mental retardation: Development of perceptions of sexuality scale. *Sexuality and Disability, 14* (4), 249-263.

Tilley, C. M. (1998). Health care for women with developmental disabilities: Literature review and theory. *Sexuality and Disability, 16* (2), 87-102.

Waxman, B. F. (1994). Up against eugenics: Disabled women's challenge to receive reproductive health services. *Sexuality and Disability, 12* (2), 155-170.

Welner, S. L. (1997). Gynecologic care and sexuality issues for women with disabilities. *Sexuality and Disability, 15* (1), 33-40.

Williams, L., & Nind, M. (1999). Insiders or outsiders: Normalisation and women with learning difficulties. *Disability & Society, 14*, 659-668.

Wolfe, P. S. (1997). The influence of personal values on issues of sexuality and disability. *Sexuality and Disability, 15*, 69-90.

Wolfe, P. S., & Blanchett, W. J. (2000). Moving beyond denial, suppression and fear to embracing the sexuality of people with disabilities. *TASH Newsletter, 26(5)*, 5-7.

Sexual Options for People with Disabilities: Using Personal Assistance Services for Sexual Expression

Linda R. Mona

SUMMARY. Receiving Personal Assistance Services (PAS) for sexual activity is becoming of increasing importance to the disability community and to mental health professionals. PAS are defined comprehensively as well as how these services may relate specifically to sexual positioning for masturbation and partner sexually related activity. Conceptual and practical issues are explored within the framework of both disability and sexuality and guidelines for consumers and clinicians working with people with disabilities are offered. Specific issues discussed include defining the nature of PAS for sexual expression, identifying assistants who are open to facilitating sexual pleasure for people with disabilities, how to broach this topic with potential providers, safety and abuse concerns, and legal implications. *[Article copies available for a fee from The Haworth Document Delivery Service: 1-800-HAWORTH. E-mail address: <getinfo@haworthpressinc.com> Website: <http://www.HaworthPress.com> © 2003 by The Haworth Press, Inc. All rights reserved.]*

KEYWORDS. Disability, sexuality, personal, assistance, services

Linda R. Mona, PhD, is a psychologist at the World Institute on Disability.

Address correspondence to: Linda R. Mona, PhD, Behavioral Health (06/116B), VA Long Beach Healthcare System, 5901 East Seventh Street, Long Beach, CA 90822 (E-mail: LRMona@aol.com).

[Haworth co-indexing entry note]: "Sexual Options for People with Disabilities: Using Personal Assistance Services for Sexual Expression." Mona, Linda R. Co-published simultaneously in *Women & Therapy* (The Haworth Press, Inc.) Vol. 26, No. 3/4, 2003, pp. 211-221; and: *Women with Visible and Invisible Disabilities: Multiple Intersections, Multiple Issues, Multiple Therapies* (ed. Martha E. Banks, and Ellyn Kaschak) The Haworth Press, Inc., 2003, pp. 211-221. Single or multiple copies of this article are available for a fee from The Haworth Document Delivery Service [1-800-HAWORTH, 9:00 a.m. - 5:00 p.m. (EST). E-mail address: getinfo@haworthpressinc.com].

Although the sexual lives of people with disabilities have been discussed more readily by mental health professionals in recent years, there continues to be an emphasis placed upon sexual functioning more often than the social and psychological cultural influences (Mona & Gardos, 2000; Shuttleworth, 2000). Even though disability studies scholars, medical anthropologists, sociologists, sexual health educators, and other liberal arts academicians have begun to pay more attention to the socio-cultural contexts of the sexual lives of people with disabilities (Shakespeare, Gillespie-Sells, & Davies, 1996; Shuttleworth, 2000; Tepper, 2000b), the majority of clinical practitioners within the United States have delayed research efforts and revision of clinical treatment models that incorporate these notions. Given the fact that many people with disabilities often need to structure their life plans around public and governmental supports (e.g., Social Security benefits, Medicare), it becomes impossible to conceptualize their sexual life experiences outside of societal influences and socio-cultural norms (e.g., societal belief systems about disability and sexuality) within which they are immersed. Based upon this reality, it is clear that the lives of people with disabilities often intersect at personal and political junctures. That is, people with disabilities are invariably affected by political decisions and legislation that dictate eligibility for services and benefits. If this is true for most life aspects of disability, why should sexual expression and sexual activity depart from these domains?

The degree to which an individual with a physical, sensory, or cognitive disability is capable of exploring and expressing her/his sexuality can depend upon the ability to meet potential partners. Environmental and monetary factors (e.g., architectural barriers to social gatherings, lack of money for transportation and/or sign-language and voice interpreters) can prevent people with disabilities from exploring sexual relationships. In addition, the amount of assistance that individuals receive from others can affect one's access to being sexual with a partner as well as masturbation. This latter notion of receiving assistance with sexual activity, or sometimes termed "facilitated sex" (Earle, 1999), has become increasingly important to many people within the disability community (Mona, 1999, 2000; Tepper, 2000a).

This paper will address Personal Assistance Services (PAS) within the context of sexual expression. PAS will be defined comprehensively as well as how these services may relate specifically to sexual positioning for masturbation and partner sexually related activity. Conceptual and practical issues are explored within the framework of both disability and sexuality. Finally, guidelines for consumers and clinicians working with people with disabilities are offered.

PAS DEFINED

PAS have been defined as "involving a person assisting someone with a disability to perform tasks aimed at maintaining well-being, personal appearance, comfort, safety, and interaction with the community and society as a whole" (World Institute on Disability (WID), 1999). In other words, PAS, sometimes called attendant care, are the services of another person that people with disabilities use to assist them to perform, manage, and move through daily life. Please refer to Table 1 for examples of PAS service domains and activities (WID, 1999).

There are a variety of ways in which individuals may receive PAS. Different models of receiving PAS include: (1) receiving PAS informally, through family, friends; (2) receiving money through social service and publicly funded programs and paying a chosen provider; (3) being assigned an assistant from an agency; (4) paying out of pocket for services, and; (5) needing to be institutionalized to receive PAS. One of the greatest concerns of the disability community has been the struggle to have a choice in determining how, where, and with

TABLE 1. PAS Service Domains and Activity Examples

Domains of services	Activity examples
Personal Services	Eating, walking, getting in and out of chairs, getting to or using the toilet, taking medications, navigating grounds, sexual positioning
Paramedical Services	Respiratory care
Household Services	Preparing food, cleaning house, grocery shopping
Communication Services	Voice interpreter, sign language interpreter, reading
Transportation Assistance Services	Getting to and from home, school, work
Safety Assurance Services	On call services
Cognitive/Emotional Support Services	Managing schedules, time, interpretation of interpersonal interactions, cueing

(WID, 1999)

whom people receive PAS. Not surprisingly, the issue of choice of services is particularly relevant to sexual expression. To date, there is no nationally based PAS program which means that states vary in with the degree to which they offer services. For an overview of PAS service models visit the World Institute on Disability Website at http://www.wid.org.

Based upon general notions of PAS, sexual positioning certainly appears to be a component of personal daily life activity. The types of assistance that people with disabilities need around sexual expression might be unknown for both consumers and professionals working with this community. Given a variety of barriers, many people with disabilities have had few opportunities to engage in sexual activity with themselves or with partners. Thus, individuals might not know what activities they might or might not be capable of accomplishing if they have not had previous sexual experiences. Similarly, mental health professionals working with people with disabilities often have had limited training on sexuality issues and have no idea about how to begin conceptualizing these issues. Based upon clinical experience of the author, information obtained from group discussions from disability-related conferences/symposiums, and personal experience as a disabled person, an overview of possible PAS for sexual activity is offered within the context of specific impairments. See Table 2 for detailed information.

TABLE 2. Sexually-Related Activities Requiring PAS by Impairment Type

Impairment type	Activity example
Physical, mobility	Removing clothes, positioning for masturbation, positioning for partner sex, transferring in and out of wheelchair onto floor, couch, or bed, stimulating partners' body, stimulating own body, cleaning up and getting redressed, using birth control (e.g., condoms, diaphragm, birth control pill)
Visual	Preparation for sex (e.g., transportation to and from partner's location, purchasing appropriate condoms, discussion and interpretation of sexual positions often only drawn in books)
Hearing	Sign language interpretation during sexual activity with hearing partner, phone interpretation if TTY or other telecommunication services are not available
Developmental/cognitive	Cognitive and emotional interpretation of interpersonal interactions, cueing to remind people to use birth control, discussion of appropriate sexual boundaries with partners, decision making (e.g., when to be sexual and with whom)

PAS STATISTICS

The latest statistical information tells us that about 54 million people live with some level of disability (McNeil, 1997). An estimated 7.3 million adults living in the community are limited in their capacity to perform one or more of five basic activities of daily living (ADL) (e.g., bathing, transferring, dressing, eating, toileting) and more than half of this population, 3.7 million adults, require the assistance of another person in performing ADLs (Kennedy & LaPlante, 1997). Of those needing assistance with ADLs, around 61% are women (Kennedy & LaPlante, 1997). While statistics on the number of people with disabilities needing PAS to accomplish ADLs is available, we remain unclear about the number of people who use PAS.

A recent survey focusing on numerous issues related to PAS programs asked administrators whether or not sexual positioning would be an activity allowable to consumers under their program. Interestingly, sexual positioning was listed among other ADL activities on this particular survey. Of 255 publicly funded programs that either provide or fund PAS, 37 programs (14.5%), reported that they would allow funding to go towards sexual positioning (T. Bleecker, personal communication, March 14, 2001). According to T. Bleecker (personal communication, March 14, 2001), even though this is an important step in obtaining information on sexuality and PAS, it is important to keep in mind that the majority of respondents endorsing this item were part of consumer directed programs (i.e., programs that provide money to people with disabilities to use for the activities that they deem necessary). Thus, it is unclear whether or not the data are indicating the programs' support of PAS for sexual activity or support for consumers' decisions to pay providers for activities which they prioritize as important.

No information is available about the incidence of PAS for sexual activity. Three important questions appear to surface: (1) Is sexual activity an ADL? (2) If sexual activity is an ADL, how many people need PAS for sexual expression? and (3) How many people use PAS for such activity? We don't know the answers to these questions simply because the questions have not been considered or asked of consumers. While there are no definitive answers about sexuality and PAS from disability statisticians, assumptions can be made about those in need of such services. That is, based upon the fact that 3.7 million need some sort of personal assistance (Kennedy & LaPlante, 1997), it would seem plausible to conceive that a good percentage of these individuals might also need some sort of assistance for sexual activity. In order to explore these issues more clearly, definitions of PAS and specific assistance for sexual activity are warranted.

DISCUSSING PAS AND SEXUALITY

Identifying what types of PAS an individual might need for sexual expression and acknowledging that receiving this type of assistance might be a possibility are often the first hurdles in addressing this topic. Knowing how to discuss this topic with clients and assisting them with how to address this issue with their providers can be essential. The following are suggestions for consumers and/or mental health professionals working with this community.

Choosing a Provider

Finding an individual to assist with sexual expression can be a difficult and daunting task. Many people with disabilities who utilize family members or friends for the majority of their PAS might make efforts to hire a separate assistant for sexual activity. Some individuals have reported that having a Personal Assistant (PA) exclusively for sexual expression has helped to facilitate more "sacredness" around this activity. However, some clients with disabilities have conveyed to this author that they actually prefer having a familiar person, typically a friend, who can help with sexual activity. Based upon the fact that people with disabilities typically do the majority of training of their assistants, it is obviously important to find an individual that appears comfortable with the consumer as well as sexuality issues in general.

What and How to Say It

Even though the final choice of an assistant depends upon the comfort level of both the person with the disability and the provider, the initial discussion about the topic can be crucial. One easy approach is to include assistance with sexual activity among a variety of tasks when interviewing a potential assistant. This strategy implies that the consumer is comfortable with the topic and considers it to be just one of the activities with which assistance is needed. It is helpful to advise consumers to think about how they might talk about this topic (e.g., use of words, how to phrase conversation). Role-playing these scenarios with consumers can be helpful so that the most comfortable content and tone is reached.

Knowing what types of sexual assistance are needed is helpful prior to the first discussion with a potential PA. Once the topic has initiated, consumers might need to be prepared to answer more specific questions. However, given the numerous obstacles that prevent many people with disabilities from expressing their sexuality, opportunities to engage in such behavior might not have been available (Mona & Gardos, 2000). Thus, there seem to be two ways to approach this: explicitly or vaguely. For example, if an individual knows that she/he needs assistance with undressing and positioning to begin masturbating, this might be important information for the PA in making a decision about comfort level with the job. If an individual has not had opportunities to engage in self-pleasure in the past, a more indirect approach can be appropriate and could include stating that assistance is needed for activities around self-pleasure or masturbation.

Provider's Comfort

One of the most integral parts of receiving assistance with sexual expression is identifying a PA who is comfortable with assisting with these activities. Earle (1999) interviewed college students with disabilities and their PAs about PAS and sexual activity and revealed that while students identified assistance with sexuality as a *need*, PAs deemed it a *personal want*. Given this discrepancy in opinion, deciphering what is behind this difference in opinion becomes of interest. Some of the controversy seems to surround the nature of the sexual act and the role of the PA. Informal conversations with assistants have brought to light some of the concerns around facilitating sexual expression. According to some PAs, preparing consumers for sexual activity (e.g., removing clothes, positioning, and retrieving erotic materials) was considered to be less problematic than direct participation with stimulation (e.g., PA placing her/his hands on the consumer's hands to guide stimulation, helping two consumers with disabilities stimulate each other, guiding penile-vaginal/anal intercourse). Difficulties appear when there is confusion between "assisting with activities" and "engaging in activities." This gray area poses difficulties for both PAs and consumers. People with disabilities want access to their sexual expression and the supportive structures in their lives (e.g., PAs, architectural and communicative access, societal notions of disability and asexuality) often do not support these rights. However, some people with disabilities have had success in locating and hiring assistants for sexual expression. Suggestions to keep in mind when training a PA for sexual activity are listed in Table 3.

Engaging in Sexual Activity and Maintaining Intimacy

Even though having "an extra person in the room" can make the difference in terms of whether or not a person with a disability can participate in sexual activity, it can be awkward. It is true that people with many different types of disabilities receive daily assistance with very personal tasks (e.g., bowel/bladder care, menstrual care, eating) and that sexual assistance might, in fact, be simply one more activity to add to the list. However, given the importance of privacy during masturbation and the emotional intimacy within some partner sexual experiences, it is important to develop a system for maintaining intimacy.

During masturbatory activity in which a PA remains with the consumer, it may be important to have the assistant wear a hat, light a candle, or have some other type of symbol to recognize that this might be a private experience. Similarly, during sexual activity with a partner, establishing a means of maintaining intimacy (e.g., eye wink, saying certain words) can help with "keeping in the mood" as well as communicating the value of the relationship.

TABLE 3. Discussion Items and Related Examples for Training Personal Assistants to Facilitate Sexual Activity

Discussion items	Examples
Develop a concrete list of activities	Need assistance with removing clothes, masturbation, touching partner, using a condom or diaphragm
Establish boundaries and rules	Indicate how long PA stay in room, how will PA assist exactly, activities with which you do not want assistance
Agree upon a communication system within the sexual encounter	Establish particular words, hand signals, eye blinks
Partner involvement when both individuals have disabilities	Communicate with consumer's partner about her/his physical abilities, feelings about PA, what is her/his understanding of the PA involvement?

SAFETY ISSUES

Abuse and safety factors surface often when the topic of sexuality and disability is discussed (Ballan & Mona, 1999). Specific issues that are brought forth include vulnerability, consent to engage in sexual activities, and sexual abuse. Researchers have brought to light the incidence of physical and sexual abuse among people with disabilities, especially by care providers (Nosek, 1996). With this concern in mind, it is imperative to work with the disability community around issues of creating safe environments, meeting partners in safe areas, letting others know locations, etc. Although this might be routine within typical sex education courses and/or parenting messages, it is unclear how these messages trickle down to the people with disabilities given that many have not been exposed to general sex education (Mona & Gardos, 2000).

Of equal importance to abuse issues are safer sex practices. There is not only a dearth of sex education delivered to the disability community but also a lack of discussion about the importance of prevention of sexually transmitted diseases (STDs). A portion of discussions with people with disabilities around any topic related to sexuality must include information on STDs and/or prevention of unwanted pregnancy. Societal notions of asexuality and infantilization of people with disabilities have glazed over the fact that adults with disabilities have choices and rights that include sexual and reproductive health. Efforts targeted solely at prevention of abuse and safety issues run the risk of not acknowledging the sexual rights of people with disabilities. This community needs information and supports to make informed choices.

LEGAL ISSUES

People with disabilities as well as service providers have voiced legal concerns about sexuality and PAS. To date, this issue has not been reviewed from a legal or policy perspective. Service providers who work in structured living facilities and other institutional settings are placed between consumers who want to engage in sexual activities and administrators who are concerned about the legal ramifications of providing assistance with sexual expression. Whether people with disabilities are living in the community or within structured living environments, administrators and PAs may be questioning the legality of condoning PAS for sexual expression.

According to C. Sabatino (personal communication, November 3, 2000), attorney, "I am not an expert in this area but even if perfectly legal in theory, PAS for sexual activity would be a hot potato for policy makers if asked to clarify policy on it." Furthermore, C. Sabatino (personal communication, November 3, 2000) added that legal problems could arise because of the difficulty in making clear distinctions between helping an individual with sexual activity and participating in sexual activity. He further clarified that paying someone for participating in sexual activity is a crime. Thus paying an assistant might be tricky and that a policy in support of PAS for sexual activity would be complicated by sexual harassment laws which raise liability issues whenever expectations of sexual activity are tied to the work environment (C. Sabatino, personal communication, November 3, 2000).

CONCLUSIONS

Receiving assistance for sexual expression has been largely ignored as an advocacy issue in the disability community and understudied by professionals working with people with disabilities. Addressing sexual facilitation is important in acknowledging the sexual rights of people with disabilities as well as insuring that all individuals have access to basic human needs. With traditional rehabilitation models that psychology is advocating for self-reliance and independence, the important notion of interdependence for all individuals is lost. The reality is that people with disabilities often maintain their independence through their assistance from others and/or technology, and much of the disability community has redefined independence from "doing things by oneself" to "learning and understanding how to direct life." With this belief in mind, directing one's sexual life seems less of a stretch from the norm.

Public policy and psychological research in PAS and sexuality are greatly needed. Until data are available on this important issue that affects the largest minority group in the country, people with disabilities are left with their sexual rights in question and are reliant upon chance and good faith of PAs to get assistance with meeting their sexual needs. Even though it would be unheard of to not provide services for eating, bowel/bladder functioning, and/or menstrual care, it is still permissible to deny people with disabilities access to sexual care.

Mental health professionals are encouraged to become better educated about the sexual lives of people with disabilities including the social and political factors that affect quality of life of this community. It is also important for professionals to explore personal feelings around disability, sexuality, and facilitated sexual expression in particular. It is with joint efforts from consumers, advocates, and service providers that changes can be made that would insure that people with disabilities have full access to their sexual lives.

REFERENCES

Ballan, M. & Mona, L. R. (1999, November). *Sexuality across disability.* Paper presented at the American Association of Sex Educators, Counselors, & Therapists and the Society for the Scientific Study of Sexuality 1999 Joint Annual Meeting, St. Louis, MO.

Earle, S. (1999). Facilitated sex and the concept of sexual need: Disabled students and their personal assistants. *Disability & Society, 14*(3), 309-323.

Kennedy, J., & LaPlante, M. P. (1997). A profile of adults needing assistance with activities of daily living, 1991-1992. *Disability Statistics Report, 11.* Washington, DC: U.S. Department of Education, National Institute on Disability and Rehabilitation Research.

McNeil, J. M. (1997). *Americans with Disabilities: 1994-95.* U.S. Bureau of the Census. Current Population Reports, U.S. Government Printing Office, Washington, DC, 1997.

Mona, L. R. (November, 1999). *Having sex with assistance: The use of personal assistance services for sexual expression among people with disabilities.* Paper presented at the American Association of Sex Educators, Counselors, & Therapists and the Society for the Scientific Study of Sexuality 1999 Joint Annual Meeting, St. Louis, MO.

Mona, L. R. (2000, November). *Personal assistance services and sexual expression: A training for sex therapists and other professionals working with people with disabilities.* Invited continuing education workshop facilitated at the annual national meeting of the Society for the Scientific Study of Sexuality, Orlando, FL.

Mona, L. R., & Gardos, P. S. (2000). Disabled sexual partners. In L. T. Szuchman and F. Muscarella (Eds.), *Psychological perspectives on human sexuality* (pp. 309-354). New York: John Wiley & Sons.

Nosek, M.A. (1996). Sexual abuse of women with disabilities. In D. M. Krotoski, M. A. Nosek & M. A. Turk (Eds)., *Women with physical disabilities: Achieving and maintaining health and well-being* (pp. 153-173). Baltimore: Paul H. Brookes Publishing Co.

Shakespeare, T., Gillespie-Sells, K., & Davies, D. (1996). *The sexual politics of disability: Untold desires.* London: Cassell.

Shuttleworth, R. (2000). The search for sexual intimacy for men with cerebral palsy. *Sexuality and Disability, 18*(4), 263-282.

Tepper, M. S. (2000a, September). Facilitated sex: The next frontier in sexuality? *New Mobility, 11* (84), 20-24.

Tepper, M. S. (2000b). Sexuality and disability: The missing discourse of pleasure. *Sexuality and Disability, 18*(4), 283-290.

World Institute on Disability. (1999). *Personal assistance services 101: Structure, utilization and adequacy of existing PAS programs.* Oakland, CA: Author.

WORST CASE SCENARIOS: INTERSECTIONS OF GENDER, DISABILITY, ETHNICITY, CLASS AND SOCIAL DISAPPROVAL

Substance Abuse, Disabilities, and Black Women: An Issue Worth Exploring

Lula A. Beatty

SUMMARY. This paper presents information on the incidence and causes of substance abuse and disabilities in Black women, identifying common problems and risks. Drug abuse is technically a disability; however, there is little in the literature that jointly addresses issues of drug

Lula A. Beatty, PhD, is Chief of the Special Populations Office, National Institute on Drug Abuse, National Institutes of Health, Bethesda, MD.

Address correspondence to: Dr. Lula Beatty, 9007 Wallace Road, Lanham, MD 20706.

[Haworth co-indexing entry note]: "Substance Abuse, Disabilities, and Black Women: An Issue Worth Exploring." Beatty, Lula A. Co-published simultaneously in *Women & Therapy* (The Haworth Press, Inc.) Vol. 26, No. 3/4, 2003, pp. 223-236; and *Women with Visible and Invisible Disabilities: Multiple Intersections, Multiple Issues, Multiple Therapies* (ed: Martha E. Banks, and Ellyn Kaschak) The Haworth Press, Inc., 2003, pp. 223-236. Single or multiple copies of this article are available for a fee from The Haworth Document Delivery Service [1-800-HAWORTH, 9:00 a.m. - 5:00 p.m. (EST). E-mail address: getinfo@haworthpressinc.com].

addiction and disability. Black women are the second largest group of women with disabilities and one of the largest groups to suffer the consequences of drug use such as HIV/AIDS, a rising source of disability highly correlated with drug abuse. Psychiatric co-morbidities related to disabilities and drug abuse are identified. Implications for research and treatment are discussed. *[Article copies available for a fee from The Haworth Document Delivery Service: 1-800-HAWORTH. E-mail address: <getinfo@haworthpressinc. com> Website: <http://www.HaworthPress.com> © 2003 by The Haworth Press, Inc. All rights reserved.]*

KEYWORDS. Drug abuse, substance abuse, disabilities, Black women, co-morbidities

One of the most under-explored areas in drug abuse research is the relationship between substance abuse and disabilities. Of particular interest is the experience of substance use in Black women coping with disabilities. Empirical data on this topic is severely limited; therefore, we take the approach of exploring the likely significance of this issue to the field from what is known separately about drug abuse and disabilities in Black women. The key questions to be addressed are:

1. Are people with disabilities more susceptible to or at increased risk for drug abuse, and
2. Why do we suspect that a relationship among drug abuse, disabilities and Black women is worth investigating?

Implications for research and substance abuse prevention and treatment with Black women will be presented.

SUBSTANCE ABUSE IN BLACK WOMEN

In comparison to White women, Black women are less likely to use licit and illicit drugs (Substance Abuse and Mental Health Services Administration (SAMHSA), 1999). In fact, the great majority of Black women do not use drugs. Using data from the National Household Survey on Drug Abuse (NHSDA), Beatty (in press) found that Black women who do use drugs, similar to other women, are more likely to report using the licit drugs of cigarettes and alcohol followed by the illicit drugs of marijuana and cocaine. Use varies with age with generally more older women (26 years of age and over) using tobacco and alcohol and younger women (12-25 years of age) using marijuana. Women in the 26-35 age group are more likely to use cocaine. Young Black women are showing a steady increase in marijuana use (Beatty, in press) and anecdotal reports from the field suggest that Black and other ethnic minority women might be becoming increasingly involved with drug dealing and using.

Black women and White women do not differ in the degree to which drug use is experienced as a problem. Black people have a later onset of substance use with significant use starting in early or middle adulthood; moreover, they experience more problems as a result of drug use (Caetano, 1984; Harper, 2001; Herd, 1989). It is likely that this is true for Black women as well although it has been found that Black women may be at less risk for problems as a result of alcohol use (Herd, 1997).

Of greater concern than the use of drugs by Black women is the greater likelihood that Black women suffer more consequences as a result of their use. Severe consequences of drug abuse have been found for women and ethnic minorities, especially for alcohol use (e.g., Gordis, 1990; Rosenbaum, 1981). Women are more likely to suffer health and social consequences from drug use, including pregnancy complications and outcomes (Blumenthal, 1998), violence (Downs, Miller & Panek, 1993; Miller, 1998), child abuse and neglect (Walker, Zangrollo, & Smith, 1991), criminal justice involvement, health care utilization (Butz et al., 1993), psychiatric disorders and emotional ill health (Cottler, Abdallah & Compton, 1998; Lex, 1991) including posttraumatic stress disorder (Dansky, Saladin, Brad, Kilpatick, & Resnick, 1995) and greater vulnerability to HIV/AIDS infection. In addition, the stigma of drug abuse evidenced in social rejection and ostracism can be a bigger problem for Black women where family and community tolerance for female (and mother) addiction is speculated to be low.

HIV/AIDS has overwhelmingly become disproportionately experienced by Black women. Non-Hispanic Black women have the highest incidence of HIV/AIDS infection among women representing 62% of new AIDS cases in 1998 and 57% of all AIDS cases reported through 1999 (Centers for Disease Control and Prevention [CDC], 1999). Moreover, Black women have the highest proportion of babies with HIV and AIDS, with Black babies accounting for nearly three-quarters of babies with the infection or disease. AIDS has become one of the leading causes of death for Black women in the 25-44 age range, the prime years for family and work obligations. Although women are more likely to acquire HIV through heterosexual contact, injection drug use and sex activity related to drug use, e.g., exchange of sex for drugs and involvement with a male partner who is drug involved, are significant exposure routes for women (CDC, 1998; Singer, 1991). Black women may be at increased risk for exposure to the virus due to poor nutrition, exposure to other infections (Mondanaro, 1987), lifestyle (Edlin et al., 1994), neighborhood factors (Fullilove, Fullilove, Bowser, & Gross, 1990), and poverty and preference for crack cocaine (Sikkema, Heckman, Kelly, and the Community Housing AIDS Prevention Study Group, 1997).

DISABILITIES AND BLACK WOMEN

A disability refers to the state of being limited, due to a chronic mental or physical health condition, in the type or amount of activities that a person is expected to perform (LaPlante & Carlson, 1996). These activities or tasks vary according to age. For example, a child under the age of 5 who is not able to engage in play or an adult aged 18-69 years of age who is not able to work or keep house can be described as having a disability. Nearly 21% (20.6%) of the non-institutionalized population (53.9 million people) or one in five Americans met the criteria for disability as measured by the Survey of Income and Program Participation. Of this number, over 53% (28.6 million) were women and girls, 21.3% of the U.S. female population. Overall, women have more activity limitations than men due to longer longevity of women (see Jans & Stoddard, 1999).

The leading causes of disability for women are, in descending order, spine or back conditions, arthritis and allied disorders, heart diseases, asthma, orthopedic impairment of lower extremity, mental disorders, diabetes, and learning disability and mental retardation (Jans & Stoddard, 1999). Of these leading causes, Black people experience persistent disparities in the incidence and outcome of heart disease, asthma, and diabetes (Taylor & Braithwaite, 2001) and given poverty, violence, limited insurance and access to care issues, are likely to encounter more problems with the other leading conditions. Mental disorders include the psychiatric disorders of depressive, anxiety and substance use disorders. About 18% (17.9%) of women report a lifetime prevalence of substance abuse compared to about 35% (35.4%) of men.

Black women have the second highest rate of disability (21.7%) among all women, next to Native American women (21.8%). Differences by ethnicity are thought to occur because of socioeconomic disparities and cultural differences (Jans & Stoddard, 1999; LaPlante & Carlson, 1996). Although there is little research to understand the effect of gender and ethnicity on disability incidence and coping, there are other findings related to gender and disability that suggest that the experience of living with a disability might be more difficult or different for a Black woman. For example, Jans and Stoddard (1999) report that women with disabilities have lower labor force participation and lower income, are less likely to receive services from vocational rehabilitation, receive different career paths from vocational rehabilitation, are less likely to be married and more likely to be widowed, and are more vulnerable to certain kinds of physical, sexual, or emotional abuse than their peers with no disability (Nosek, Howland, & Young, 1997). Moreover, women with physical disabilities may be likely to experience abuse for longer periods of time and to be abused by health care providers, attendants or strangers (Nosek, Howland, & Young, 1997). Disturbingly, the Center on Emergent Disability (1997) suggests that women, given their higher rates of poverty, are disproportionately represented among emerging disabilities due to domestic violence, inadequate prenatal care, adolescent pregnancy, poor nutrition, and other factors. Many of these conditions are disproportionately experienced by a high number of Black women, particularly poverty, inadequate prenatal care, early pregnancy, and poor nutrition (Taylor & Braithwaite, 2001). We do not know, however, what these findings mean for substance use or abuse within the population of Black women with disabilities.

HIV/AIDS is a fast growing cause of disability in the country today although having HIV does not necessarily mean that one is limited in the ability to work or function independently. In a study supported by the National Institute on Disability and Rehabilitation Research, Sebesta and LaPlante (1996) examined "the diagnostic history of people living with HIV and its relation to function, disability, and labor force participation over time" (p. 1). Data were collected in 1991. The study participants were predominantly men (over 80%), People of Color (59%), and under 40 years old (69%). Nearly half of the women (48%) were African American, the largest subgroup of any gender by ethnic group configuration. Over three-quarters of the women (77.3%) were under 40 years old. Most of the women contracted the virus through heterosexual contact (40.2%) or injection drug use (38.6%) (as was previously stated there may be some overlap between the hetero-sexual contact group and the injection drug use). Nearly 70 percent of the women with HIV were functionally limited by their disease, even those who were classified as asymptomatic. Women were more likely than men to have been denied Social Security Disability Insurance (SSDI), to receive health coverage from public programs, to have re-ported feelings associated with depression at each stage of the disease, and to be unemployed. Analyses by ethnicity and gender were limited. Interestingly, Black women received SSDI more than other groups of women and less than all groups of men, and were denied SSDI more fre-quently than all other groups of women and all groups of men. As was indicated earlier, Black women are at much greater risk for HIV/AIDS than any other group in the country and are more likely to experience disabilities related to this condition.

CAUSES OF SUBSTANCE ABUSE IN WOMEN

There is growing consensus that factors related to trauma, stress, family and interpersonal relationships are predictive of drug abuse in women and racial/ethnic minority communities (Alegria et al., 1998; Hser, Anglin, & McGothlin, 1987; Russac & Weaver, 1995; Sanders-Phillips, 1998). Women entering drug treatment frequently present with histories of childhood sexual abuse, rape, or other violent trauma (Inciardi, Lockwood & Pottegier, 1993; Robles et al., 1998). Black and other ethnic minority women enter drug abuse treatment with more problems, with the most frequent being fear of loss of children, no alter-native care for children, fewer social supports, and severe health, em-ployment, educational and legal problems (Caetano, 1984, 1997; Lee, Mavis, & Stoffelmayr, 1991). Psychiatric comorbidities are also com-mon in women substance abusers (Cottler et al., 1998; Lex, 1991; McCauley et al., 1997; Ries, 1993) with the most frequent psychiatric problems being depression, affective disorders, anxiety disorders, and post-traumatic stress disorder (PTSD). Although analyses by gender and race/ethnicity are often limited in studies, Cottler et al. (1998) in-cluded a significant number of Black women (67%) in their study sug-gesting that the association between substance abuse and mental health problems is true for Black women as well.

Stressful life events and depression are linked to poorer health be-haviors in women (Leftwich & Collins, 1994). Stressful life events and negative experiences play a great role in substance abuse by Black women (Sanders-Phillips, 1998; Singleton, Harrell, & Kelly, 1986; Taylor, Henderson, & Jackson, 1991). Fullilove, Lown, and Fullilove (1992), who work with Black and other ethnic minority women, identify trauma and depression as key factors in women's drug abuse.

Although the relationship between substance use and sociodemographic variables is not fully understood (Kopstein & Gfrorerer, 1990), poverty and lower socioeconomic status is reportedly associated with greater drug use (Lillie-Blanton, Anthony, & Schuster, 1993) and consequences of use (Strickland, 2001). Married women (marriage can be used as an indicator of economic stability) are less likely than unmarried women to use illicit drugs or have problems with drinking or other drugs (SAMHSA, 1997, 1999). Employment and marital status were found to be correlated with drug use in Black women with unmarried and unemployed women reporting more smoking and use of marijuana and other illicit drugs (Beatty, in press). Black women are less likely to be married or to marry (Bennett, Bloom & Craig, 1989).

SUBSTANCE ABUSE, DISABILITIES, AND BLACK WOMEN

Substance abuse is by definition a disability. It has its own diagnostic category and persons who are dependent on drugs usually cannot adequately perform functional activities expected of them. Determining the relationship between substance abuse and other disabilities is challenging. Not much research on substance abuse is evident in the disabilities literature and concomitantly, there is little research on disabilities within the substance abuse literature. Moreover, seldom is substance abuse conceptually presented in the substance abuse literature as a disability. Johnstone (1998) characterizes disability studies as a relatively recent field that is now broadening to include a wider range of issues such as stigma and stereotyping. Disability studies and research seem to have focused largely on rehabilitation, occupational issues, and adjustment.

The two literature bases are separate and there may be little need for them to overlap or merge. Treatment providers may cross-read the literatures and acquire information they need from each. However, issues important to each group might not be addressed in the separate literatures. Clients can benefit from having professionals be aware of factors that can affect success in therapeutic interventions including vocational rehabilitation.

We know more about substance abuse and disabilities related to mental disorders. There is a well developed and growing body of knowledge showing the association between PTSD, depression, and substance use in women including Black women. For women, in many instances, the mental disorder precedes and seems to lead to substance abuse. For example, women who were sexually abused or raped are at increased risk for drug abuse and other self-destructive behaviors. Women with schizophrenia might be more likely to abuse substances and to be HIV-infected (Carey, Weinhardt, & Carey, 1995).

We do not know as much about the risk or experience of substance abuse in persons with other types of disabilities, e.g., persons with impairments, physically disabled due to violent trauma, outside of anecdotal reports (e.g., young Black adolescents with spinal cord injuries appear to be at risk for substance abuse according to some practitioners). It is possible that these other types of disabilities could serve as a protective factor against substance use and abuse in that persons affected might be getting services, attention, or coping skills and resources of some quality and intensity that directly or indirectly buffer them from abusing substances. Or other disabilities might place persons at increased risk for substance abuse due to attempts to cope with the stress, frustration, boredom, or negative mental states they experience.

Women with disabilities are less likely than men with disabilities to be married, more likely (one-third) to have children at home, and more likely to be living in poverty or below the poverty level. Parents with disabilities are economically and educationally disadvantaged, i.e., have lower incomes, higher rates of public assistance, higher high school drop-out rates, and lower college attendance. Fourteen percent of the parents with disabilities had at least one child with a disability (see Jans & Stoddard, 1999). In addition, women are more often the primary caregivers to persons with disabilities (Hoffman & Rice, 1996; National Alliance for Caregiving, 1997). This overall profile of poverty, low education, single parenthood, and responsibility for the care of others rings true of Black women with substance abuse problems. Caretakers might be at increased risk for substance abuse, particularly for alcohol and tobacco as a way of dealing with stress associated with caretaking (Minkler, Roe, & Robertson-Beckley, 1994).

Black women might be more prone to experiencing disabilities as a result of socioeconomic factors as well as the consequences and experiences that track drug use and involvement. For example, Black female addicts might be more likely to be triply diagnosed with substance abuse disorder, a psychiatric disorder, and other health problems such as HIV/AIDS, hypertension and diabetes. Black women captured in the disabilities population might be at high risk for substance abuse including the use of tobacco and alcohol.

IMPLICATIONS FOR RESEARCH AND TREATMENT

Research is needed to clarify the relationship between substance abuse and disabilities. The limited available data highly suggest that there are important questions to be explored including the following:

1. Are people with disabilities at increased risk for substance abuse? Are persons with multiple disabilities at increased risk?
2. Does having multiple disabilities change risk status for drug abuse?
3. Can a disability or certain disabilities be a protective factor(s) against substance abuse because, for example, of the responsiveness of the service delivery system?
4. Is appropriate and accessible information available on drug abuse prevention and treatment specific to the needs of persons with disabilities?
5. What do we know about substance abuse and persons receiving medications for disabilities that could be considered addictive?

Psychiatric disorders, poverty, stress, violence and trauma place women at greater risk for substance abuse. Within the next two decades, mental disorders will become the second leading worldwide cause of premature death and years lived with a disability; for women, unipolar major depression will become the single leading worldwide cause of premature death and years lived with a disability (Murray & Lopez, 1996). Therapy must be comprehensive to be effective with women. Drug treatment fails if it does not address psychiatric problems of women. Likewise, it would seem that therapy and support services for women with other disabilities that do not address a woman's drug problem or other psychiatric problem will not have long-term effectiveness. Research on disabilities and substance abuse in Black women is needed to clarify what assessment, prevention, treatment and service needs and approaches should be pursued.

The National Institute on Drug Abuse (NIDA) which supports the majority (85%) of the world's research on drug abuse has developed a research agenda for women that calls for research on antecedents, pathways, risk and protective factors involved in drug abuse by girls and women with emphasis on early identification and the full spectrum of prevention interventions; the impact of violence and victimization on the psychosocial development and psychosocial functioning of girls and women as it relates to drug abuse and dependence; and the co-existence of drug abuse and dependence with psychiatric disorders, especially PTSD, anxiety, depression and eating disorders. In addition, the NIDA is also encouraging research to better understand factors that contribute to health disparities experienced by racial/ethnic minorities. Disabilities are not explicitly mentioned in these initiatives, but they easily fit.

Paying attention to the possibility of substance use as a problem for women, especially Black women, can ensure that proper assessment, screening, and counseling can occur, and that staff working with these populations are knowledgeable and trained. Because overall drug abuse is low, however, in Black women (perhaps due to the protective factors of religion and family support), we cannot know if we should consider disability in Black women as a risk factor. Sensitively approaching these issues is mandatory so as not to further contribute to the stigma and marginalization that is already too frequently attached to being disabled, a substance abuser, or a Black woman.

REFERENCES

Alegria, M., Vera, M., Negron, G., Burgus, M., Albizo, C., & Canino, G. (1998). Methodological and conceptual issues in understanding female Hispanic drug users. In C. L. Wetherington & A. B. Roman (Eds.). *Drug addiction research and the health of women.* NIH Publication 98-4290, p. 21. Rockville, MD: National Institute on Drug Abuse.

Beatty, L. A. (in press). Changing their minds: Drug abuse and addiction in Black women. In D. R. Brown and V. M. Keith (Eds.), *In and out of our right minds: The mental health of African American women.*

Bennett, N. G., Bloom, D. E., & Craig, P. H. (1989). The divergence of Black and White marriage patterns. *American Journal of Sociology, 95,* 692-722.

Blumenthal, S. J. (1998). Women and substance abuse: A new national focus. In C. L. Wetherington & A. B. Roman (Eds.), *Drug addiction research and the health of women.* NIH Publication No. 98-4280. Rockville, MD: National Institute on Drug Abuse.

Butz, A. M., Hutton, N., Joyner, M., Vogelhut, J. Greenberg-Friedman, D., Schreibeis, D., & Anderson, J. R. (1993). HIV-infected women and infants. Social and health factors impeding utilization of health care. *Journal of Nurse-Midwifery, 38* (2), 103-109.

Caetano, R. (1984). Ethnicity and drinking in northern California: A comparison among Whites, Blacks, and Hispanics. *Alcohol and Alcoholism, 19,* 31-44.

Caetano, R. (1997). Prevalence, incidence, and stability of drinking problems among Whites, Blacks and Hispanics, 1984-1992. *Journal of Studies on Alcohol, 58,* 565-572.

Carey, M. P., Weinhardt, L., & Carey, K. B. (1995). Prevalence of infection with HIV among the seriously mentally ill: Review of research and implications for practice. *Professional Psychology: Research and Practice, 26,* 262-268.

Center on Emergent Disability. (1997). *Report from the Center on Emergent Disability.* Chicago: Institute for Disability and Human Development, University of Chicago at Illinois.

Centers for Disease Control and Prevention. (1998). *HIV/AIDS Surveillance Report, 10* (1).

Centers for Disease Control and Prevention. (1999). *Surveillance Report, Midyear edition, 11* (1).

Cottler, L. B., Abdalla, A. B., & Compton, W. M. (1998). Association between early or later onset of substance use and psychiatric disorders in women. In C. L. Wetherington & A. B. Roman (Eds.), *Drug addiction research and the health of women,* NIH Publication 98 4290. Rockville, MD: National Institute on Drug Abuse.

Dansky, B. S., Saladin, M. E., Brady, K. T., Kilpatrick, D. G., & Resnick, H. S. (1995). Prevalence of victimization and posttraumatic stress disorder among women with substance use disorders: Comparison of telephone and in-person assessment samples. *The International Journal of the Addictions, 30,* 1079-1099.

Downs, W. R., Miller, B. A., & Panek, D. D. (1993). Differential patterns of partner-to-woman violence: A comparison of samples of community, alcohol-abusing, and battered women. *Journal of Family Violence, 8,* 113-135.

Edlin, B. R., Irwin, K. L., Farrique, S., McCoy, C. B., Word, C., Serrano, Y., Inciardi, J. A., Bowser, B. P., Schilling, R. F., Holmberg, S. S., & the Multicenter Crack Cocaine and HIV Infection Study Team. (1994). Intersecting epidemics—crack cocaine use and HIV infection among inner-city young adults. *New England Journal of Medicine, 331,* 1422-1427.

Fullilove, M. T., Fullilove, R. E., Bowser, B., & Gross, S. (1990). Crack users: The new AIDS risk group? *Cancer Detection Prevention, 14,* 363-368.

Fullilove, M. T., Lown, E. A., & Fullilove, R. E. (1992). Crack 'hos and skeezers: Traumatic experiences of women crack users. *Journal of Sex Research, 29* (2), 275-287.

Gordis, E. (1990). Alcohol and women: A commentary by NIAAA. *Alcohol Alert, 10,* 1-3.

Harper, F. D. (2001). Alcohol use and misuse. In R. L. Braithwaite & S. E. Taylor (Eds.), *Health issues in the Black community* (2nd ed.). San Francisco: Jossey-Bass Publishers.

Herd, D. (1989). The epidemiology of drinking patterns and alcohol-related problems among U.S. Blacks. In D. Spiegler, D. Tate, S. Aitken, and C. Christian (Eds.), *Alcohol use among U.S. ethnic minorities*. NIAAA Research Monograph No. 18, DHHS, Publication No. (ADM) 89-1435, (pp. 3-50). Washington, DC: U.S. Government Printing Office.

Herd, D. (1997). Sex ratios of drinking patterns and problems among Blacks and Whites: Results from a national survey. *Journal of Studies on Alcohol, 58*, 75-82.

Hoffman, D., & Rice, D. (1996). *Chronic care in America: A 21st century challenge*. Princeton, NJ: The Robert Wood Johnson Foundation.

Hser, Y., Anglin, D., & McGothlion, W. (1987). Sex differences in addict careers, I: Initiation of use. *American Journal of Drug and Alcohol Abuse, 13*, 33-57.

Inciardi, J. A., Lockwood, P., & Pottegier, A. E. (1993). *Women and crack cocaine*. New York: McMillan.

Jans, L., & Stoddard, S. (1999). *Chartbook on women and disability in the United States*. An InFoUse Report. Washington, DC: U.S. Department of Education, National Institute on Disability and Rehabilitation Research.

Johnstone, D. (1998). *An introduction to disability studies*. London, England: David Fulton Publishers.

Kopstein, A., & Gfrorerer, J. (1990). Drug use patterns and demographics of employed drug users. Data from the 1988 household survey. In S. Gust, J. M. Walsh, L. B. Thomas, & D. J. Crouch (Eds.), *Drugs in the workplace: Research and evaluation data, Vol. II* (NIDA Research Monograph No. 100, pp. 11-24). Rockville, MD: National Institute on Drug Abuse.

LaPlante, M. P., & Carlson, D. (1996). *Disability in the United States; Prevalence and causes, 1992. Disability Statistics Report*. Washington, DC: U. S. Department of Education, National Institute on Disability and Rehabilitation Research.

Lee, J. A., Mavis, B. E., & Stoffelmayr, B. E. (1991). A comparison of problems-of-life for Blacks and Whites entering substance abuse treatment programs. *Journal of Psychoactive Drugs, 23* (3), 233-239.

Leftwich, M. J. T., & Collins, F. L. (1994). Parental smoking, depression, and child development: Persistent and unanswered questions. *Journal of Pediatric Psychology, 19*, 577-570.

Lex, B. W. (1991). Some gender differences in alcohol and polysubstance users. *Health Psychology, 10*, 121-132.

Lillie-Blanton, M., Anthony, J. C., & Schuster, C. R. (1993). *Journal of the American Medical Association, 269* (8), 993-997.

McCauley, J., Kern, D. E., Kolodner, K., Dill, L., Schroeder, A. F., DeChart, H. R., Ryden, J., Derogatis, L. R., & Bass, E. B. (1997). Clinical characteristics of women with a history of childhood abuse: Unhealed wounds. *Journal of the American Medical Association, 227*, 1362-1368.

Miller, B. A. (1998). Partner violence experiences and women's drug use: Exploring the connections. In C. L. Wetherington & A. B. Roman (Eds.). *Drug addiction and the health of women*. NIH Publication No. 98-4290. Rockville, MD: National Institute on Drug Abuse.

Minkler, M., Roe, K. M., & Robertson-Beckley, R. J. (1994). Raising grandchildren from crack-cocaine households: Effects on family and friendship ties of African-American women. *American Journal of Orthopsychiatry, 64* (1), 20-29.

Mondanaro, J. (1987). Strategies for AIDS prevention: Motivating health behavior in drug dependent women. *Journal of Psychoactive Drugs, 19* (2), 143-149.

Murray, C., & Lopez, A. D. (1996). *The global burden of disease*. Cambridge, MA: Harvard University Press.

National Alliance for Caregiving (1997). *Family caregiving in the United States: Findings from a national survey*. Bethesda, MD. Author.

Nosek, M. A., Howland, C. A., & Young, M. E. (1997). Abuse of women with physical disabilities: Policy implications. *Journal of Disability Studies, 8* (1-2), 157-176.

Ries, R. K. (1993). The dually diagnosed patient with psychotic symptoms. *Journal of Addictive Diseases, 12* (3), 103-122.

Robles, R. R., Marreo, C. A., Matos, T. D., Colon, H. M., Cancel, L. I., & Reyes, J. C. (1998). Social and behavioral consequences of chemical dependence. In C. L. Wetherington & A. B. Roman (Eds.), Drug addiction research and the health of women (NIH Publication No. 98-4290). Rockville, MD: National Institute on Drug Abuse.

Rosenbaum, M. (1981). Sex roles among deviants: The woman addict. *International Journal of the Addictions, 16*, 859-877.

Russac, R. J., & Weaver, S. T. (1995). Trends and theories concerning alcohol and other drug use among adolescent females. In R. R. Watson (Ed.). *Drug and Alcohol Abuse Reviews, Vol. 8: Drug and alcohol abuse during pregnancy and childhood*. Totowa, NJ: Human Press, Inc.

Sanders-Phillips, K. (1998). Factors influencing health behaviors and drug abuse among low-income Black and Latino women. In C. L. Wetherington & A. B. Roman (Eds.), *Drug addiction research and the health of women*. NIH Publication No. 98-4290. Rockville, MD: National Institute on Drug Abuse.

Sebesta, D. S., & LaPlante, M. P. (1996). *Disability statistics report. HIV/AIDS, disability, and employment*. Washington, DC: National Institute on Disability and Rehabilitation Research, U. S. Department of Education.

Sikkema, K. J., Heckman, T. G., Kelly, J. A., & the Community Housing AIDS Prevention Study Group (1997). HIV risk behaviors among inner-city African American women. *Women's Health: Research on Gender, Behavior, and Policy, 3* (3&4), 349-366.

Singer, M. (1991). Confronting the AIDS epidemic among IV drug users: Does ethnic culture matter? *AIDS Education and Prevention, 3*, 258-283.

Singleton, E. G., Harrell, J. P., & Kelley, L. M. (1986). Racial differentials in the impact of maternal cigarette smoking during pregnancy on fetal development and mortality: Concerns for Black psychologists. *Journal of Black Psychology, 12*, 71-83.

Strickland, T. L. (2001). Substance abuse. In R. L. Braithwaite & S. E. Taylor (Eds.), *Health issues in the Black community* (2nd ed.). San Francisco: Jossey-Bass Publishers.

Substance Abuse and Mental Health Services Administration (SAMHSA) (1997). *Substance use among women in the United States. (Analytic Series: A-3).* Rockville, MD: Office of Applied Studies, SAMHSA.

Substance Abuse and Mental Health Services Administration. (1999). *National household survey on drug abuse, main findings 1997.* Rockville, MD: Office of Applied Studies, SAMHSA.

Taylor, S. E., & Braithwaite, R. L. (2001). African American health: An overview. In R. L. Braithwaite & S.E. Taylor (Eds.), *Health issues in the Black community* (2nd ed.). San Francisco: Jossey-Bass Publishers.

Taylor, J., Henderson, D., & Jackson, B. B. (1991). A holistic model for understanding and predicting depressive symptoms in African-American women. *Journal of Community Psychology, 19,* 306-320.

Walker, C., Zangrollo, P., & Smith, J. (1991). *Parental drug abuse and African American children in foster care.* Report available from the National Clearinghouse for Alcohol and Drug Information.

Women with Physical Disabilities Who Want to Leave Their Partners: A Feminist and Disability-Affirmative Perspective

Rhoda Olkin

SUMMARY. Four domains of barriers for women with physical disabilities who are considering leaving a partner are outlined. These obstacles include (a) physical needs; (b) financial needs; (c) custody concerns; and (d) relationship issues. Disability policies can have direct bearing on the lives of women with disabilities, and hence on their freedom to choose to remain with or to leave a partner. *[Article copies available for a fee from The Haworth Document Delivery Service: 1-800-HAWORTH. E-mail address: <getinfo@haworthpressinc.com> Website: <http://www.HaworthPress.com> © 2003 by The Haworth Press, Inc. All rights reserved.]*

KEYWORDS. Women with disabilities, partners, disability-affirmative, disability barriers

Women with disabilities face significant barriers to their ability to leave a marital or partnership relationship. Such women, as members of

Rhoda Olkin is Professor of Clinical Psychology at the California School of Professional Psychology and is on the staff at Through the Looking Glass.
Address correspondence to: Dr. Rhoda Olkin (E-mail: Rolkin@alliant.edu).

[Haworth co-indexing entry note]: "Women with Physical Disabilities Who Want to Leave Their Partners: A Feminist and Disability-Affirmative Perspective." Olkin, Rhoda. Co-published simultaneously in *Women & Therapy* (The Haworth Press, Inc.) Vol. 26, No. 3/4, 2003, pp. 237-246; and: *Women with Visible and Invisible Disabilities: Multiple Intersections, Multiple Issues, Multiple Therapies* (ed: Martha E. Banks, and Ellyn Kaschak) The Haworth Press, Inc., 2003, pp. 237-246. Single or multiple copies of this article are available for a fee from The Haworth Document Delivery Service [1-800-HAWORTH, 9:00 a.m. - 5:00 p.m. (EST). E-mail address: getinfo@haworthpressinc.com].

a dual minority, can experience disadvantages in relationships based on being female and on being disabled. For example, women with disabilities are less likely to be employed than men with disabilities, and, when employed, earn less than do men with disabilities or women without disabilities (Houtenville, 2000a, 2000b). Most studies indicate higher rates of physical abuse (Kewman, Warschausky, Engel & Warzak, 1997; Nosek & Howland, 1997; Sobsey & Doe, 1991; Sobsey, Gray, Wells, Pyper, & Reimer-Heck, 1991) and sexual abuse (Finkelhor, 1984; Krents, Schulman, & Brenner, 1987; Nosek, 1995; Sobsey, Wells, Lucardie, & Mansell, 1995) for children and adults with disabilities compared to those without disabilities. In one large study women with disabilities reported a longer duration of abuse than did women without disabilities (Young, Nosek, Howland, Chanpong, & Rintala, 1997), and women with disabilities had in common specific vulnerabilities to abuse (Nosek, Howland, & Young, 1997). Thus, women with disabilities share unique factors that impinge on their freedom to enter and exit partnership relationships at will. Yet women with disabilities might wish to leave partners for all the myriad of reasons as do women without disabilities, such as dissatisfaction with the relationship, affairs of either partner, financial stresses, changes in employment, physical abuse, growing apart, etc.

The main purpose of this paper is to outline briefly some of the key obstacles for women with physical disabilities who are considering leaving a partner for any reason. These obstacles fall into four domains: (a) physical needs; (b) financial needs; (c) custody concerns; and (d) relationship issues. The ideas in this paper stem from clinical observations, from heterosexual women and to a lesser extent from lesbian women. To my knowledge there are no studies on women with physical disabilities and the dissolution of relationships, so the generalizability of these observations is unknown. In particular, the additional stigma and discrimination experienced by women of color and lesbian women can synergistically add complexity to both the relationship definition and the decision to exit the relationship (c.f., Green & Mitchell, 2002). A second purpose of this paper is to encourage the collation of stories from women with disabilities on the neglected area of romance, especially on how women with disabilities enter into and exit romantic partnerships. These stories are a necessary foundation for understanding the similarities and differences in the experiences of women with disabilities–lesbian or straight, of color or Caucasian–who are leaving partners.

PHYSICAL NEEDS

The first concern of a woman contemplating leaving a relationship relates to basic survival. A partner may be providing personal assistant services (PAS), such as helping a woman in and out of bed, on the toilet, in and out of the car, etc. Leaving the relationship means the need for immediate replacement of someone to provide these services. The partner supplying these services may not have been paid, and funding may not cover the amount of PAS needed to live independently. Thus the woman thinking of leaving the relationship can feel daunted by the need to find PAS, and anxious about her own survival without a partner. Even women who don't use PAS may share this concern. If a partner has been doing the laundry, carrying groceries from the car and putting them away, taking out the garbage, changing bed linens, fixing leaky toilets–i.e., the myriad daily chores of living–without the partner, someone is going to have to do these things. Paid help is an option for some women, but with a 66% rate of unemployment among people with disabilities, that option may be the exception. For a woman to pick up these extra tasks herself might strain her physical abilities, exacerbate her fatigue, and perhaps lead to secondary injuries. The question of who will put the garbage cans by the curbside for pickup and return them to the side of the house is not frivolous, but gets to the core of the vulnerability women with disabilities experience. As she makes the emotionally difficult decision to leave a relationship, these extra worries can make the choice to leave seem out of reach.

Assistive technology, such as wheelchairs, scooters, car lifts, automatic door openers, etc., break down with some regularity. Although each item might break only once or twice a year, among all of them something is broken frequently. For someone used to having a backup plan that involved a partner, the loss of this plan means a woman could be suddenly stranded (e.g., if the lift breaks and she can't get the wheelchair back in the car) or trapped (e.g., in her apartment until the automatic door opener is fixed). The knowledge that there is no longer someone with whom to share these travails can feel isolating and lonely.

The synergistic effects of aging and disability, and the uncertain future course of a disability, can add to a woman's trepidation about leaving a relationship. As she projects into her future she might perceive uncertainty about her own physical abilities and disability-related financial needs.

There might be a fear about falling or otherwise incurring an injury. A woman might be concerned that she would be unable to get help if she were hurt, or that a seemingly minor injury, when coupled with the disability, would be incapacitating. An injury could make her need for personal assistant services more acute, and more hours might be needed. Without the backup of a partner, falls and injuries can become major hindrances.

FINANCIAL NEEDS

There are many financial costs of physical disability, many borne by the person with a disability. For example, in a national survey of parents with disabilities, of the 69% who had made modifications to their homes for accessibility, 84% had paid for these modifications out of pocket (Toms Barker & Maralani, 1997). In that same study, of those who used adaptive baby care equipment, 66% had paid for the equipment with their own money. Costs of everything from shoe modifications to lift-equipped vans to maintenance and repair of assistive devices are considerable and constant. The loss of a partner's income can create financial hardship in light of these expenses. In additional to the expense, if a woman decides to move out of the abode she shares with a partner, moving to new quarters is an arduous task. The new housing might require the same modifications already made to the previous residence, with the attendant costs in money, time and energy involved in arranging for those modifications. Thus, a woman might be reluctant to leave, and wish her partner to leave. But if the two people owned a house together, for the woman with a disability to stay, she might need to buy out the partner's share of the house. These physical and financial factors impose constraints on the options in how the couple splits, at a time of emotional distress and upheaval.

Access to medical care is of concern for women with disabilities. If the woman is not working outside the home she might have been dependent on her partner's health insurance (for lesbian relationships, this is true only in the minority of cities with domestic partner laws), and face difficulty and considerable expense in obtaining health insurance on her own. She might be turned down for health, disability, and long-term care insurance unless she is in a group plan that cannot disallow anyone in the group. Even employed women with disabilities can worry about losing the second health insurance provided by a partner, and might not be able to switch jobs or leave a job without this backup insurance.

CUSTODY CONCERNS

Mothers with disabilities may have special fears related to custody, and these fears are by no means unfounded. Researchers have found that parents with disabilities experience prejudice about their rights or abilities to parent (Cohen, 1997; Conley-Jung & Olkin, 2001; Kirshbaum, 2000; Toms Barker & Maralani, 1997). In a national survey of almost 1,200 parents with disabilities, about 15% of the parents reported attempts to remove their children (Toms Barker & Maralani, 1997). Indeed, about 7% of over 300 undergraduate psychology majors did not think people with disabilities should be parents at all (Patterson & Witten, 1987). It seems that the stigma attached to disability encompasses a threat to the right to parent for persons with disabilities. Thus, the legal rights of parents with disabilities, especially in custody decisions, is a fundamental issue for all parents with disabilities. For a woman contemplating separation or divorce from an able-bodied partner, the concern over custody, especially with a partner who is asserting the wish for full custody, can be enough to stop a woman from leaving the relationship.

The fears about custody are magnified for lesbian women with disabilities, and again these fears are grounded in reality. The woman with a disability might be less likely than her able-bodied partner to be the birth parent, and her rights to adoption are curtailed, even in liberal states such as California. Protections for visitation and custody are reduced or nonexistent. This can leave her feeling precarious in the process of dissolution of the relationship, and even long after. A partner's threat to take sole custody, or to marry and have the husband adopt the child, carries considerable weight, and can intimidate the woman who wishes to leave. Adding to this base of legitimate fears, the additional disability concerns related to custody can terrify and perhaps dissuade the woman who wishes to leave a relationship.

RELATIONSHIP ISSUES

Leaving a relationship can mean a period of being alone, with all of the feelings and doubts that any woman might feel during this transition. The woman's parents might have their fears about their daughter's ability to live on her own, and they might convey their worry and concern in a way that underscores the woman's own doubts.

Women with disabilities can have special concerns about dating and sexuality and their prospects of finding another mate. The harsh truth is that many people are not interested in a romantic relationship with someone with a visible disability (DeLoach, 1994; Olkin & Howson, 1994). For those with an early-onset disability the memories of stigma and rejection in adolescence might be reawakened as the woman contemplates dating. Furthermore, "experiences of rejection may have curtailed opportunities for practice in friendships and romantic relationships. Thus there may be skill deficits related to how to present the disability to others, what to look for in potential partners, and how to develop a spectrum of relationships from acquaintance to friends to romantic partners" (Olkin, 1999, p. 224). Women with later onset disabilities might have no experience in dating as women with disabilities, and feel unattractive to potential partners.

Disability does not occur in isolation, but in the context of other personal factors. Older women with disabilities face both age and disability discrimination. Patterns of dating in lesbian communities or within various ethnic groups may augment or conflict with the norms of the disability independent living movement. For example, developing *families of choice* is common both to the lesbian and to the disability community. But the dissolution of a relationship can reverberate through that family, depriving the woman with a disability simultaneously of her partner and her family of choice.

Regardless of the age of disability onset there might be concerns about sexuality with a new partner. In addition to needing to feel attractive to a new partner, there can be logistical concerns. Most of the literature on sex and disability is in fact about the mechanics of sex (positions, erections, colostomy bags, etc.), but unfortunately this is at the neglect of psychosocial and interpersonal factors (Boyle, 1993; DeLoach, 1994). Talking with a new partner about positioning, birth control methods, and needed assistance can mean that spontaneity is not possible. The prospect of finding the right way of sexually relating to a new partner can be daunting. And, of course, dating in the age of AIDS presents its own terrors.

SUGGESTIONS FOR THERAPISTS

To understand the issues facing women with disabilities who are thinking of leaving partners it is first necessary to understand disability issues. The book *What Psychotherapists Should Know About Disability*

(Olkin, 1999) was written specifically for therapists with little or no training in disability issues, and was designed to provide the requisite foundation of understanding.

A second step is for therapists to become familiar with disability resources in their communities, in particular centers for independent living and accessible paratransit systems. Third, there are numerous useful Internet resources, two of which are the Center for Research on Women with Disabilities (CROWD; http://www.bcm.tmc.cdu/crowd/) and the government's Job Action Network (http://www.jan.wvu.edu/) for information on accommodating people with disabilities in the workplace.

Fourth, there is an emerging literature on people of color with disabilities. A few good references to get readers started are: (a) Asbury, Walker, Belgrave, Maholmes, and Green (1994), Belgrave (1998), and Kalyanpur, Keys, and Rao (1991) (African Americans with Disabilities); (b) Balcazar and Suarez-Balcazar (2001) and Smart and Smart (1992) (Hispanics with Disabilities); (c) D'Alonzo, Giordano, and Oyenque (1996) and Locust and Lang (1996) (American Indians with Disabilities); and (d) Chan, Lam, Wong, Leung, and Fang (1988) and Choi and Wynne (2000) (Asian Americans with Disabilities). And lastly, working to make changes to policies affecting women with disabilities and to the rights of parents with disabilities is the most powerful and durable tool therapists have.

CONCLUSIONS

In the previous sections four domains of barriers for women with physical disabilities contemplating leaving partners were outlined, including physical needs, financial needs, custody concerns, and relationship issues. The synergistic impact of these impediments can be considerable enough to reduce the woman's ability to choose freely whether to remain in the relationship or leave. It is not enough for well-meaning therapists to support a woman's right to choose whether to stay or go, when that choice is curtailed by policies and practical concerns. Policies on personal attendant services, health care, custody, disability and long-term care insurance, accessibility of housing and of transportation, can have direct bearing on the lives of women with disabilities, and improve or impede their freedom of choice.

It is possible that dyadic romantic relationships are not the best arrangements for women with disabilities. Their freedom to leave is compromised, and the high dissolution rate of relationships makes women with physical disabilities especially vulnerable to isolation. A safeguard is for women with disabilities to be part of a larger interdependent community, within which they might or might not be with partners. Women with disabilities might not ever enjoy the physical and economic means necessary for independence, and marriage and partnerships might be no more than temporary masks of this basic disempowered status.

REFERENCES

Asbury, C., Walker, S., Belgrave, F., Maholmes, V., & Green, L. (1994). Psychosocial, cultural, and accessibility factors associated with participation of African-Americans in rehabilitation. *Rehabilitation Psychology, 39*(2), 113-121.

Balcazar, F. E., Keys, C. B., & Suarez-Balcazar, Y. (2001). Empowering Latinos with disabilities to address issues of independent living and disability rights: A capacity-building approach. *Journal of Prevention & Intervention in the Community, 21*(2), 53-70.

Belgrave, F. Z. (1998). *Psychosocial aspects of chronic illness and disability among African Americans*. Westport, CT: Auburn House.

Boyle, P. S. (1993). Training in sexuality & disability: Preparing social workers to provide services to individuals with disabilities. *Journal of Social Work & Human Sexuality, 8*(2), 45-62.

Chan, F., Lam, C., Wong, D., Leung, P., & Fang, X. S. (1988). Counseling Chinese Americans with disabilities. *Journal of Applied Rehabilitation Counseling, 19*(4), 21-25.

Choi, K., & Wynne, M. (2000). Providing services to Asian Americans with developmental disabilities and their families: Mainstream service providers' perspective. *Community Mental Health Journal, 36*(6), 589-595.

Cohen, L. J. (1997). *Mothers' perceptions of the influence of their physical disabilities on the developmental tasks of children*. Unpublished doctoral dissertation, California School of Professional Psychology, Alameda. (Supported in part by the National Institute on Disability Research and Rehabilitation, Department of Education grant #H133B830076.)

Conley-Jung, C., & Olkin, R. (2001). Mothers with visual impairments or blindness raising young children. *Journal of Visual Impairment and Blindness, 91*(1), 14-29.

D'Alonzo, B. J., Giordano, G., & Oyenque, W. (1996). American Indian vocational rehabilitation services: A unique project. *American Rehabilitation, 22*(1), 20-26.

DeLoach, C. P. (1994). Attitudes toward disability: Impact on sexual development and forging of intimate relationships. *Journal of Applied Rehabilitation Counseling, 25*(1), 18-25.

Finkelhor, D. (1984). *Child sexual abuse: New theory and research*. NY: Free Press.

Green, R-J., & Mitchell, V. (2002). Gay and lesbian couples in therapy: Homophobia, relational ambiguity, and social support. In A. S. Gurman & N.S. Jacobson (Eds.). *Clinical handbook of couple therapy* (3rd ed.). New York: Guilford Publications.

Houtenville, A. (2000a). *Economics of disability research report #2: Estimates of employment rates for persons with disabilities in the U.S. by state, 1981-1999*. Ithaca, NY: Research & Rehabilitation Training Center for Economic Research on Employment Policy for Persons with Disabilities, Cornell University.

Houtenville, A. (2000b). *Economics of disability research report #3: Estimates of median household size-adjusted income for persons with disabilities in the U.S. by state, 1981-1999*. Ithaca, NY: Research & Rehabilitation Training Center for Economic Research on Employment Policy for Persons with Disabilities, Cornell University.

Kalyanpur, M., & Rao, S. S. (1991). Empowering low-income black families of handicapped children. *American Journal of Orthopsychiatry, 61*(4), 523-532.

Kewman, D., Warschausky, S., Engel, L., & Warzak, W. (1997). Sexual development of children and adolescents. In M. L. Sipski & C. J. Alexander (Eds.), *Sexual function in people with disabilities and chronic illness: A health practitioner's guide*. Gaithersburg, MD: Aspen.

Kirshbaum, M. (2000). A disability culture perspective on early intervention with parents with physical or cognitive disabilities and their infants. *Infants and Young Children, 13*(2), 9-20.

Krents, E., Schulman, V., & Brenner, S. (1987). Child abuse and the disabled child: Perspectives for parents. *Volta Review, 89*, 78-95.

Locust, C., & Lang, J. (1996). Walking in two worlds: Native Americans and the VR system. *American Rehabilitation, 22*(2), 2-11.

Nosek, M. A. (1995). Sexual abuse of women with physical disabilities. *Physical Medicine and Rehabilitation: State of the Art Reviews, 9*, 487-502.

Nosek, M. A., & Howland, C. A. (1997). Sexual abuse and people with disabilities. In M. L. Sipski & C. J. Alexander (Eds.), *Sexual function in people with disabilities and chronic illness: A health practitioner's guide*. Gaithersburg, MD: Aspen.

Nosek, M. A., Howland, C. A., & Young, M. E. (1997). Abuse of women with disabilities: Policy implications. *Journal of Disability Policy Studies, 8*, 157-176.

Olkin, R. (1999). *What psychotherapists should know about disability*. NY: Guilford Publications.

Olkin, R., & Howson, L. (1994). Attitudes toward and images of physical disability. *Journal of Social Behavior and Personality, 9*(5), 81-96.

Patterson, J. B., & Witten, B. (1987). Myths concerning persons with disabilities. *Journal of Applied Rehabilitation Counseling, 18*, 42-44.

Smart, J. F., & Smart, D. W. (1992). Cultural issues in the rehabilitation of Hispanics. *Journal of Rehabilitation, 58*(2), 29-37.

Sobsey, D., & Doe, T. (1991). Patterns of sexual abuse and assault. *Sexuality and Disability, 9*, 243-260.

Sobsey, D., Gray, S., Wells, D., Pyper, D., & Reimer-Heck, B. (1991). *Disability, sexuality, and abuse: An annotated bibliography*. Baltimore: Brookes.

Sobsey, D., Wells, D., Lucardie, R., & Mansell, S. (Eds.) (1995). *Violence and disability: An annotated bibliography*. Baltimore: Brookes.

Toms Barker, L. T., & Maralani, V. (1997). *Challenges and strategies of disabled parents: Findings from a national survey of parents with disabilities.* Oakland, CA: Berkeley Planning Associates.

Young, M. E., Nosek, M. A., Howland, C. A., Chanpong, G., & Rintala, D. H. (1997). Prevalence of abuse of women with physical disabilities. *Archives of Physical Medicine and Rehabilitation, 78 (Suppl),* S34-S38.

Prostitution and the Invisibility of Harm

Melissa Farley

SUMMARY. The harm of prostitution is socially invisible, and it is also invisible in the law, in public health, and in psychology. This article addresses origins of this invisibility, how words in current usage promote the invisibility of prostitution's harm, and how public health perspectives and psychological theory tend to ignore the harm done by men to women in prostitution. Literature which documents the overwhelming physical and psychological harm to those in prostitution is summarized here. The interconnectedness of racism, colonialism, and child sexual assault with prostitution is discussed. *[Article copies available for a fee from The Haworth Document Delivery Service: 1-800-HAWORTH. E-mail address: <getinfo@haworthpressinc.com> Website: <http://www.HaworthPress.com>* © 2003 *by The Haworth Press, Inc. All rights reserved.]*

KEYWORDS. Prostitution, domestic violence, rape, PTSD, torture

INTRODUCTION

Prostitution is sexual violence which results in economic profit for perpetrators. Other types of gender violence, such as incest, rape, and

---

Melissa Farley, PhD, is affiliated with Prostitution Research & Education, a sponsored project of the San Francisco Women's Centers, Inc., and with Kaiser Foundation Research Institute, Oakland, CA.

Address correspondence to: Melissa Farley, PhD, P. O. Box 16254, San Francisco, CA 94116-0254 (E-mail: mfarley@prostitutionresearch.com).

This article is dedicated to Andrea Dworkin, with love and great appreciation.

[Haworth co-indexing entry note]: "Prostitution and the Invisibility of Harm." Farley, Melissa. Co-published simultaneously in *Women & Therapy* (The Haworth Press, Inc.) Vol. 26, No. 3/4, 2003, pp. 247-280; and: *Women with Visible and Invisible Disabilities: Multiple Intersections, Multiple Issues, Multiple Therapies* (ed: Martha E. Banks, and Ellyn Kaschak) The Haworth Press, Inc., 2003, pp. 247-280. Single or multiple copies of this article are available for a fee from The Haworth Document Delivery Service [1-800-HAWORTH, 9:00 a.m. - 5:00 p.m. (EST). E-mail address: getinfo@haworthpressinc.com].

247

wife-beating, are hidden and frequently denied, but they are not sources of mass revenue. Like slavery, prostitution is a lucrative form of oppression of human beings. Many governments protect commercial sex businesses because of the monstrous profits. Institutions such as prostitution and slavery, which have existed for thousands of years, are so deeply embedded in cultures that they become invisible. In Mauritania, for example, there are 90,000 Africans enslaved by Arabs. Human rights activists travel to Mauritania to report on slavery, but because they do not observe the stereotype of what they think slavery should look like–if they don't see bidding for shackled people on auction blocks–they conclude that the Africans working (in slavery) in front of them are voluntary laborers who are receiving food and shelter as salary (Burkett, 1997).

In a similar way, if observers don't observe the stereotype of "harmful" prostitution, for example, if they do not see a teenaged girl being trafficked at gunpoint from one country to another, if what they see is a streetwise teenager who says, "I like this job, and I'm making a lot of money," then they don't see the harm. Johns (customers) go to Atlanta, Amsterdam, Phnom Penh, Moscow, Capetown, or Havana and see smiling girls and women waving at them. Customers decide that prostitution is a free choice.

The social and legal refusal to acknowledge the harm of prostitution is stunning. Normalization of prostitution by researchers, public health agencies, and the law is a significant barrier to addressing the harm of prostitution. For example, the International Labor Organization described prostitution as the "sex sector" of Asian economies in spite of citing their own surveys which indicated that, in Indonesia, 96% of those interviewed wanted to leave prostitution if they could (Lim, 1998). It makes no sense to oppose trafficking on the one hand, and promote the "consensual sex sector" or "commercial sex work" on the other. One cannot exist without the other; trafficking is the marketing of prostitution.

To assume that there is consent in the case of prostitution, is to disappear its harm. Social and legal assertion that there is consent involved in women's oppression is not new. Rape law, for example, commonly inquires whether or not the woman consented to any sexual act, rather than asking if the rapist obtained her freely given affirmative permission without verbal or physical coercion. In situations of domestic violence, the question is often "why did she agree to stay in the relationship?" rather than "how did he cut off her physical and psychological ability to safely escape?" And in cases of sexual harassment, the question is "did she invite, provoke, or welcome the behavior?" rather than "did he use his position of authority to compromise her ability to resist?" Just as we have not moved beyond the obstacle of consent for raped, battered, or sexually harassed women, so we are also still at ground zero where prostitution is concerned.[1] The line between coercion and consent is deliberately blurred in prostitution. The politician's insistence that prostitution is consensual parallels the john's insistence that mutuality occurs in prostitution.

In prostitution, the conditions which make genuine consent possible are absent: physical safety, equal power with customers, and real alternatives (Hernandez, 2001). One woman in Amsterdam described prostitution as "volunteer slavery," a description which reflects both the appearance of choice and the coercion behind that choice. Instead of the question "did she consent?" the more relevant question would be "did she have real alternatives to prostitution for survival?" As we will discuss below, it is a statistical, as well as an ethical, error to assume that most women in prostitution consent to it.

There is no mutuality of consideration or pleasure in prostitution. The purpose of prostitution is to make sure that one person is *object* to the other's *subject*, to make sure that one person does not use *her* personal desire to determine which sexual acts do and do not occur, while the other person acts on the basis of *his* personal desire. This is in stark contrast to non-commercial promiscuous, anonymous sex where both parties act on the basis of personal desire, and both parties are free to retract *without economic consequences* (Davidson, 1998).[2]

INVISIBILITY

Words which conceal harm lead to confusion about the real nature of prostitution. Some words in current usage make the harm of prostitution invisible: *voluntary prostitution* which implies that she consented when, usually, she actually had no other options to survive; *forced trafficking*, which implies that somewhere there are women who volunteer to be trafficked into prostitution; and *sex work*, which defines prostitution as a job rather than an act of violence against women. The term *migrant sex worker* blends prostitution and trafficking and implies that both are acceptable. The Chinese words *beautiful merchandise* benevolently conceal the objectification of women in prostitution. The expression *socially disadvantaged women* (ostensibly used to avoid stigmatizing prostitutes) removes any hint of the sexual violence which is intrinsic to prostitution.

Libertarian or postmodern ideology obscures the harm of prostitution, defining it as a form of sex. The harshest sexual exploitation in strip club prostitution has been reframed as *sexual expression* or *freedom to express one's sensuality by dancing*. Brothels are referred to as *short-time hotels, massage parlors, saunas*, and sometimes *health clubs*. Older men who buy teenagers for sex acts in Seoul call prostitution *compensated dating*. In Tokyo, prostitution is described as *assisted intercourse*.

Men who buy women in prostitution are called *interested parties* or *third parties*, rather than johns, which is what women call customers. Pimps are described as *boyfriends* or *managers*. One pimp recently referred to the *brief shelf life* of a girl in prostitution. What that means is that he knows the extent of the damage in prostitution, and realizes that she will not be saleable after a few years. In the United States, the expression *'ho* reflects the widely accepted view of all women, and especially Women of Color, as natural-born whores.[3]

Women in prostitution are called *escorts, hostesses, strippers*, and *dancers*. Sometimes these words are attempts by women in prostitution to retain some shred of dignity. The purpose of exposing these words is not to remove women's inherent dignity and worth, but to expose the brutal institution which harms them. What words can be used, without insulting women in prostitution? The expression sex worker implies that prostitution is an acceptable type of work (instead of brutal violence). We do not refer to battered women as "battering workers." And just as we would not turn a woman into the harm done to her (we don't refer to a woman who has been battered as a "batteree") we should not call a woman who has been prostituted, a "prostitute." We suggest retaining her humanity by referring to her as a woman who is *in prostitution*, who was *prostituted*, or who is *prostituting*. We also use the word "john" which is the word women themselves use to refer to customers.

The lines between prostitution and nonprostitution have become increasingly blurred. Since the 1980s, there has been huge growth in socially legitimized pimping in the United States. For example, the amount of physical contact between stripclub employees and customers has escalated since 1980. Customers can usually buy either a table dance or a lap dance where the dancer sits on the customer's lap while she wears few or no clothes and grinds her genitals against his. Although he is clothed, he usually expects ejaculation. The lap dance may take place on the main floor of the club or in a private room. The more private the sexual performance, the more it costs, and the more likely that violent sexual harassment or rape will occur.

Pervasive Invisibility of the Violence in Prostitution

Despite the fact that prostitution is an institution in which one person has the social and economic power to transform a human being into the living embodiment of a masturbation fantasy (Davidson, 1998), psychotherapists and the public alike collude in viewing prostitution as banal or denying its harm altogether.

Prostitution formalizes women's subordination by gender, race, and class. Poverty, racism, and sexism are inextricably connected in prostitution. Women are purchased because they are vulnerable as a result of lack of educational options, and as a result of previous physical and emotional harm. They are purchased on the basis of toxic ethnic and racial stereotypes.

For the vast majority of the world's prostituted women, prostitution is the experience of being hunted, dominated, harassed, assaulted, and battered. Prostitution is a gendered survival strategy which involves the assumption of unreasonable risks by the person in it. Most of us would not be willing to assume these risks.

A number of authors have documented and analyzed the sexual and physical violence which is the normative experience for women in prostitution, including Baldwin (1993, 1999); Barry (1979, 1995); Boyer, Chapman, and Marshall (1993); Chesler (1993); Dworkin (1981, 1997, 2000); Farley, Baral, Kiremire, and Sezgin (1998); Giobbe (1991, 1993); Hoigard and Finstad (1986); Hughes (1999); Hunter (1994); Jeffreys (1997); Karim, Karim, Soldan, and Zondi (1995); Leidholdt (1993); MacKinnon (1993); MacKinnon and Dworkin (1997); McKeganey and Barnard (1996); Miller (1995); Raymond (1998); Silbert and Pines (1982a, 1982b); Silbert, Pines, and Lynch (1982), Valera (1999); Vanwesenbeeck (1994); and Weisberg (1985). Silbert and Pines (1981, 1982b) reported that 70% of women suffered rape in prostitution, with 65% having been physically assaulted by customers, and 66% assaulted by pimps.

The physically and psychologically harmful effects of strip club prostitution have not been addressed. The level of harassment and phys ical assault of women in strip club prostitution has drastically increased in the past 20 years. Touching, grabbing, pinching, and fingering of dancers removes any boundary which previously existed between dancing, stripping, and prostitution (Lewis, 1998). Holsopple (1998) documented the verbal, physical, and sexual abuse experienced by women in strip club prostitution, which included being grabbed on the breasts, buttocks, and genitals, as well as being kicked, bitten, slapped, spit on, and penetrated vaginally and anally during lap dancing.

Sexual violence and physical assault are the normative experiences for women in prostitution. Silbert and Pines (1982b) reported that 70% of women in prostitution were raped. The Council for Prostitution Alternatives in Portland reported that prostituted women were raped an average of once a week (Hunter, 1994). In the Netherlands, 60% of prostituted women suffered physical assaults, 70% experienced verbal threats of physical assault, 40% experienced sexual violence, and 40% had been forced into prostitution and/or sexual abuse by acquaintances (Vanwesenbeeck, 1994). Most young women in prostitution were abused or beaten by pimps as well as johns. Eighty-five percent of women interviewed by Parriott (1994) had been raped in prostitution. Of 854 people in prostitution in nine countries (Canada, Colombia, Germany, Mexico, South Africa, Thailand, Turkey, United States, and Zambia), 71% had experienced physical assaults in prostitution, and 62% had been raped in prostitution. Eighty-nine percent of 854 people in prostitution from nine countries interviewed by Farley et al. (in press) stated that they wished to leave prostitution, but did not have other options. For these people, theorizing prostitution as consensual makes their desire to leave prostitution invisible. In another study, 94% of those in street prostitution had experienced sexual assault and 75% had been raped by one or more johns (Miller, 1995).

Summarizing the literature on different types of prostitution, Farley et al. (in press) have found that 100% of those in prostitution experienced sexual harassment which in the United States would be legally actionable in any other job setting. Sixty to ninety percent had been sexually assaulted as children. Seventy to ninety-five percent were physically assaulted in prostitution, and 60% to 75% were raped in prostitution. Seventy-five percent of those in prostitution had been homeless at some point in their lives.

Vanwesenbeeck (1994) found that two factors were associated with greater violence in prostitution. The greater the poverty, the greater the violence, and the longer one works in prostitution the more likely one is to experience violence. Like Vanwesenbeeck, we found that women who experienced the most extreme violence in prostitution were not represented in our research. It is likely that all of the aforementioned estimates of violence are conservative, and that the actual incidence of violence is greater than what is reported here.

The most relevant paradigm available in psychology for understanding the harm of prostitution is that of domestic violence. *Prostitution is domestic violence.* Giobbe (1991) compared pimps and batterers and found similarities in the ways they used extreme physical violence to control women, the ways they forced women into social isolation, used minimization and denial, threats, intimidation, verbal and sexual abuse, and had an attitude of ownership. The techniques of physical violence used by pimps are often the same as those used by batterers and torturers.

A majority of prostitution is pimp-controlled. Recruitment of young women into prostitution begins with what Barry (1995) has called *seasoning*–brutal violence designed to break the victim's will. After physical control is gained, pimps use psychological domination and brainwashing. Pimps establish emotional dependency as quickly as possible, beginning with changing a girl's name. This removes her previous identity and history, and additionally, isolates her from her community. The purpose of pimps' violence is to convince women of their worthlessness and social invisibility, as well as to establish physical control and captivity. Over time, escape from prostitution becomes more difficult as the woman is repeatedly overwhelmed with terror. She is forced to commit acts which are sexually humiliating and which cause her to betray her own principles. The contempt and violence aimed at her are eventually internalized, resulting in virulent self-hatred which then makes it even more difficult to defend herself. Survivors report a sense of contamination, of being different from others, and self-loathing which last many years after breaking away from prostitution.

Treatment approaches used by those who work with battered women are also applicable to prostituted women. The first goal must be to establish physical safety. This involves both client and therapist agreeing on the goal of leaving prostitution. Only after that has occurred (often by providing safe housing), can the initial stage of therapy proceed where issues of chemical dependence and acute PTSD are addressed.

Belton (1992) and Goodman and Fallot (1998) have discussed the need for intake inquiry regarding prostitution history. Unless screening questions are asked, prostitution will remain invisible. The questions "have you ever exchanged sex for money or clothes, food, housing, or drugs?" and "have you ever worked in the commercial sex industry: for example, dancing, escort, massage, prostitution, pornography, phone sex?" are now a routine part of the author's history-taking (Farley & Kelly, 2000).

The Invisibility of Racism and Colonialism in Prostitution

The racism which is inextricably connected to sexism in prostitution tends to be invisible to most observers. Women in prostitution are purchased for their appearance, including skin color and characteristics based on ethnic stereotyping. Throughout history, women have been prostituted on the basis of race and ethnicity, as well as gender and class.

Entire communities are affected by the racism which is entrenched in prostitution. The insidious trauma of racism continually wears away at People of Color, creating vulnerability to stress disorders (Root, 1996). Families who have been subjected to race and class discrimination might interface with street networks which normalize prostitution for economic survival. Legal prostitution, such as strip clubs and stores which sell pornography (that is, pictures of women in prostitution), tends to be zoned into poor neighborhoods, which in many urban areas in the United States, also tend to be neighborhoods of People of Color. Commercial sex businesses create a hostile environment in which girls and women are continually harassed by pimps and johns. Women and girls are actively recruited by pimps and are harassed by johns driving through their neighborhoods. There is a similarity between the abduction into prostitution of African women by slavers and today's cruising of African American neighborhoods by johns searching for women to buy (Nelson, 1993).

Compared to their numbers in the United States as a whole, Women of Color are overrepresented in prostitution. For example, in Minneapolis, a city which is 96% European American, more than half of the women in strip club prostitution are Women of Color (Dworkin, personal communication, 1997). African American women are arrested for prostitution solicitation at a higher rate than others charged with this crime.

Colonialism exploits not only natural resources, it objectifies the people whose land contains those resources. Especially vulnerable to violence from wars or economic devastation, indigenous women are brutally exploited in prostitution (for example, Mayan women in Mexico City, Hmong women in Minneapolis, Karen or Shan women in Bangkok, or First Nations women in Vancouver). The intersection of racism, sexism and class is especially apparent in sex tourism. Historically, colonialism in Asia and the Caribbean promoted a view of Women of Color as natural-born sex workers, sexually promiscuous, and immoral by nature. Over time, Women of Color have come to be viewed as "exotic others" and were defined as inherently hypersexual on the basis of race and gender (Hernandez, 2001). The prostitution tourist denies the racist exploitation of women in "native cultures," as in Bishop and Robinson's (1998) analysis of the Thai sex business: "Indigenous Thai people are seen as Peter-Pan-like children who are sensual and never grow up. Sex tourists believe that they are simply partaking of the Thai culture, which just happens to be 'overtly sexual.'" He might feel like a millionaire in a third or fourth world economy, and rationalize that he is helping women out of poverty. "These girls gotta eat, don't they? I'm putting bread on their plate. I'm making a contribution. They'd starve to death unless they whored" (Bishop & Robinson, 1998, p. 168).

The Thai perspective of this situation is diametrically opposed to that of the prostitution tourist: "Thailand is like a stage, where men from around the world come to perform their role of male supremacy over Thai women, and their white supremacy over Thai people" (Skrobanek cited in Seabrook, 1996, p. 89).

Racially-constructed ideas about women in sex tourism have a greater and greater effect on the ways Women of Color are treated at home. For example, Asian-American women reported rapes after men viewed pornography of Asian women (MacKinnon & Dworkin, 1997).

Once in prostitution, Women of Color face barriers to escape. Among these is an absence of culturally sensitive advocacy services in the United States. Other barriers faced by all women escaping prostitution are a lack of services which accommodate emergency needs such as shelters, treatment of drug/alcohol dependence, and treatment of acute post-traumatic stress disorder (PTSD). There is a similar lack of services to address long-term needs, such as treatment of depression and other mood disorders, complex post-traumatic stress disorder (CPTSD), vocational training, and long-term housing.

The Invisible Continuum: Child Abuse and Prostitution

The systematic nature of violence against girls and women is clearly seen when incest is understood as child prostitution. Use of a child for sex by adults, with or without payment, is prostitution of the child. When a child is incestuously assaulted, the perpetrator's objectification of the child victim and his rationalization and denial are the same as those of the john in prostitution. Incest and prostitution cause similar physical and psychological symptoms in the victim.

Child sexual abuse is a primary risk factor for prostitution. Familial sexual abuse functions as a training ground for prostitution. One young woman told Silbert and Pines (1982a, p. 488), "I started turning tricks to show my father what he made me." Dworkin (1997) described sexual abuse of children as "boot camp" for prostitution.

Most women over the age of eighteen in prostitution began prostituting when they were adolescents. du Plessis, who worked with homeless and prostituted children in Johannesburg, South Africa, reported that she could not refuse her agency's services to 21 year olds because she understood them to be *grown up child prostitutes* (Personal communication, 1997). Early adolescence is the most frequently reported age of entry into any type of prostitution. Boyer and colleagues (1993) interviewed 60 women prostituting in escort, street, strip club, phone sex, and massage parlors (brothels) in Seattle, Washington. All of them began prostituting between the ages of 12 and 14. In another study, Nadon, Koverola, and Schludermann (1998) found that 89% had begun prostitution before the age of 16. Of 200 adult women in prostitution, 78% began prostituting as juveniles and 68% began when they were younger than 16 (Silbert, 1982a).

The artificial distinction between child and adult prostitution obscures the continuity between the two. On a continuum of violence and relative powerlessness, the prostitution of a 12-year-old is more horrific than the prostitution of a 20-year-old, not because the acts committed against her are different, but because the younger person has less power. In other respects, the experiences of sexual exploitation, rape, verbal abuse, and social contempt are the same, whether the person being prostituted is the legal age of a child or the legal age of an adult. The antecedent poverty and attempts to escape from unbearable living conditions (violence at home or the economic violence of globalization) are similar in child and adult prostitution.

Multiple perpetrators of sexual abuse were common, as was physical abuse in the childhood of women in prostitution. Sixty-two percent of women in prostitution reported a history of physical abuse as children. Ninety percent of prostituted women had been physically battered in childhood; 74% were sexually abused in their families–with 50% also having been sexually abused by someone outside the family (Giobbe, Harrigan, Ryan, & Gamache, 1990). Of 123 survivors of prostitution at the Council for Prostitution Alternatives in Portland, 85% reported a history of incest, 90% a history of physical abuse, and 98% a history of emotional abuse (Hunter, 1994).

Prostituting adolescents grow up in neglectful, often violent families. Although not all sexually abused girls are recruited into prostitution, most of those in prostitution have a history of sexual abuse as children, *usually by several people.* Farley and Lynne (2000) reported that 88%

of 40 women prostituting in Vancouver had been sexually assaulted as children, by an average of five perpetrators. This latter statistic (those assaulted by an average of five perpetrators) did not include those who responded to the question "If there was unwanted sexual touching or sexual contact between you and an adult, how many people in all?" with "tons" or "I can't count that high" or "I was too young to remember." Sixty-three percent of those interviewed were First Nations women. One girl in prostitution said,

> We've all been molested. Over and over, and raped. We were all molested and sexually abused as children, don't you know that? We ran to get away. They didn't want us in the house anymore. We were thrown out, thrown away. We've been on the street since we were 12, 13, 14. (Boyer et al., 1993, p. 16)

Traumatic sexualization is the inappropriate conditioning of the child's sexual responsiveness and the socialization of the child into faulty beliefs and assumptions about sexuality which leave her vulnerable to additional sexual exploitation (Browne & Finkelor, 1986). Traumatic sexualization is an essential component of the grooming process for subsequent prostitution.

Some of the consequences of childhood sexual abuse are behaviors which are prostitution-like. A common symptom of sexually abused children is sexualized behavior. Sexual abuse may result in different behaviors at different stages of the child's development. Sexualized behaviors are likely to be prominent among sexually abused preschool-age children, submerge during the latency years, and then reemerge during adolescence as behavior described as promiscuity, prostitution, or sexual aggression.

The sexually abused child might incorporate the perpetrator's perspective into her identity, eventually viewing herself as good for nothing but sex, which is to say, she might adopt his view that she is a prostitute (Putnam, 1990). Survivors link physical, sexual, and emotional abuse as children to later prostitution. Seventy percent of the adult women in prostitution in one study stated that childhood sexual assault was largely responsible for their entry into prostitution (Silbert & Pines, 1982a). Family abuse and neglect were described as not only causing direct physical and emotional harm, but also creating a cycle of victimization which affected their futures. For example, one woman stated that by the time she was 17,

> . . . all I knew was how to be raped, and how to be attacked, and
> how to be beaten up, and that's all I knew. So when he put me on
> the game [pimped her] I was too down in the dumps to do any-
> thing. All I knew was abuse. (Phoenix, 1999, p. 111)

The constricted sense of self of the sexually abused child and the co-
ercive refusal of the perpetrator to respect the child's physical boundaries can result in subsequent difficulties in asserting boundaries, in
impaired self-protection, and a greater likelihood of being further sexually victimized, including becoming involved in prostitution (Briere,
1992).

The powerlessness of having been sexually assaulted as a child might
be related to the frequent discussions of control and power by women
who are prostituting. The emotional and physical helplessness of the
sexually abused child might be reenacted in the prostitution transaction,
with vigilant attention to the tiniest shard of control. Payment of money
for an unwanted sex act in prostitution can make the girl or woman feel
more in control when compared to the same experience with no payment of money. For example, one woman said that at age 17, she felt
safer and more in control turning tricks on the street than she did at
home with her stepfather raping her.

Pimps exploit the vulnerability of runaway or thrown-out children in
recruiting them to prostitution. In Vancouver, 46% of homeless girls
had received offers of "assistance to help them work in prostitution."
One 13-year-old who had run away from home was given housing by a
pimp, but only in exchange for prostituting. Ninety-six percent of the
adults interviewed by Silbert and Pines (1983) had been runaway children before they began prostituting. More than half of 50 prostituting
Asian girls aged 11 to 16 ran away because of family problems (Louie,
Luu, & Tong, 1991).

A survey of 500 homeless youths in Indianapolis reported that, at
first, only 14% acknowledged that they were working as prostitutes.
When the Indiana adolescents were subsequently asked nonjudgmental
questions about specific behaviors, they responded as follows: 32%
said that they had sex to get money; 21% said they had sex for a place to
stay overnight; 12% exchanged sex for food; 10% exchanged sex for
drugs; and 6% exchanged sex for clothes. In other words, a total of 81%,
not 14%, of these 500 homeless adolescents, were prostituting (Lucas &
Hackett, 1995).

Gay male adolescents' prostitution behavior is also likely to be a
reenactment of earlier sexual abuse. Homophobia plays a role in the

prostituting of gay young men in that gay youth may have been thrown out of their homes because of their sexual orientation. Furthermore, in many cities, prostitution was the only available entry into the gay community; it was an activity where boys could "practice" being gay. Thus, gay adolescent boys might develop an identity which links their sexual orientation to prostitution (Boyer, 1989).

HEALTH CONSEQUENCES OF PROSTITUTION

Violence-Related Physical Health Consequences of Prostitution

Although at first glance, the public health attention to HIV/STD infection includes the prostituted woman herself, on closer inspection it becomes apparent that the overarching concern is for the health of the customer: to decrease *his* exposure to disease. Aside from HIV/STD, the physical harm of prostitution to *her* is invisible. In spite of extensive documentation that HIV is overwhelmingly transmitted via male-to-female vaginal and anal intercourse, *not vice versa*, one of the misogynist myths about prostitution is that *she* is the source of infection. The exclusive focus on male customers' HIV risk–which ignores the psychological and physical violence to women–is a variant of this prejudice against prostituted women. Rape by customers is a primary source of HIV infection in women.

In the HIV literature from 1980 to 2000, most authors minimized or ignored HIV risk posed *by* the customer *to* the woman in prostitution. Most also failed to mention the option of escape from prostitution. For example, Karim et al. (1995) interviewed women who prostituted at a truck stop in South Africa. This group of researchers found that women were at *a higher risk for physical violence* when they insisted on condom use with customers, whose violence contributed to their relative powerlessness. Ignoring their finding that the women were at a higher risk for violence, the researchers recommended that women in prostitution learn negotiation and communication skills to reduce HIV risk. It seems tragically likely that this particular project (and others as well) might have resulted in additional injury, even death, to some women in prostitution.

Globally, the incidence of HIV seropositivity among prostituted women is devastating. Homeless children are at highest risk for HIV, for example, in Romania and Colombia. Piot (1999) noted that half of new AIDS cases are less than age 25, and that girls are likely to become infected at a much younger age than boys, in part because of the acceptance of violence perpetrated against girls and women in most cultures. The invisibility of women's HIV risk, as compared to men's risk, has resulted in a lack of attention to early HIV infection in women (Allen et al., 1993; Schoenbaum & Webber, 1993). Allen et al. (1993) investigated HIV risk-assessments in inner-city US women's health clinics and found that despite the presence of HIV infection across a broad age range for both sexes, early HIV infection (not yet AIDS) was "completely unrecognized among all adolescent, young adult, and older women" (p. 367).

STD and HIV have increased exponentially in the Ukraine and other former Soviet Union states since 1995. From 1987 to 1995, fewer than 200 new HIV infections per year were diagnosed in Russia. In the first six months of 1999, 5,000 new cases of HIV were reported (Dehne, Khodakevich, Hamers, & Schwartlander, 1999). In the city of Kaliningrad, one in three people infected with HIV was a woman, and 80% of the infected women were in prostitution (Smolskaya, Momot, Tahkinova, & Kotova, 1998). It is likely that this massive increase in HIV resulted from an extremely high rate of violence against women in Russia (Hamers, Downs, Infuso, & Brunet, 1998). Women in Russia are transformed into "office prostitutes" via job requirements to tolerate sexual harassment (or in the direct Russian translation, "sexual terror"; Hughes, 2000). In addition, political restructuring with control of state agencies held by criminals, extreme poverty, and collapse of healthcare systems contributed to the HIV pandemic in Russia (Hamers et al., 1998).

After two decades of research on HIV, the World Health Organization (1998) noted that *women's primary risk factor for HIV is violence* (Piot, 1999). Aral and Mann (1998) at the Centers for Disease Control, emphasized the importance of addressing human rights issues in conjunction with STDs. They noted that since most women enter prostitution as a result of poverty, rape, infertility, or divorce, public health programs must address the social factors which contribute to STD/HIV. Gender inequality in any culture normalizes sexual coercion, promoting domestic violence and prostitution, ultimately contributing to women's likelihood of becoming HIV-infected. Kalichman, Kelly, Shaboltas, and Granskaya (2000) and Kalichman, Williams, Cheery, Belcher, and Nachimson (1998) noted the coincidence of the HIV epidemic and domestic violence in Russia, Rwanda, and the USA.

Chronic health problems result from physical abuse and neglect in childhood (Radomsky, 1995), from sexual assault (Golding, 1994), battering (Crowell & Burgess, 1996), untreated health problems, overwhelming stress, and violence (Friedman & Yehuda, 1995; Koss & Heslet, 1992; Southwick, Yehuda, & Morgan, 1995). Prostituted women suffer from all of these. Many of the chronic physical symptoms of women in prostitution were similar to the physical consequences of torture. The lethal nature of prostitution is suggested by a 1985 Canadian study which found that the death rate of those in prostitution was 40 times higher than that of the general population (Special Committee on Pornography and Prostitution, 1985).

Prostituted women had an increased risk of cervical cancer and chronic hepatitis (Chattopadhyay, Bandyopadhyay, & Duttagupta, 1994; de Sanjose et al., 1993; Nakashima et al., 1996; Pelzer, Duncan, Tibaux, & Mebari, 1992). Incidence of abnormal Pap screens was several times higher than the state average in a Minnesota study of prostituted women's health (Parriott, 1994). Childhood rape was associated with increased incidence of cervical dysplasia in a study of women prisoners (Coker, Patel, Krishnaswami, Schmidt, & Richter, 1998). Women in prisons are frequently incarcerated for prostitution-related acts.

We asked 700 people in prostitution in 7 countries if they had health problems (Farley et al., 2000). Almost half of these people in Colombia, Mexico, South Africa, Thailand, Turkey, USA, and Zambia reported symptoms which were associated with violence, overwhelming stress, poverty, and homelessness.

Physicians' diagnoses of these 700 people in prostitution included tuberculosis, HIV, diabetes, cancer, arthritis, tachycardia, syphilis, malaria, asthma, anemia, and hepatitis. Twenty-four percent reported reproductive symptoms including sexually transmitted diseases (STD), uterine infections, menstrual problems, ovarian pain, abortion complications, pregnancy, hepatitis B, hepatitis C, infertility, syphilis, and HIV.

Without specific query about mental health, 17% of these 700 people in prostitution described severe emotional problems: depression, suicidality, flashbacks of child abuse, anxiety and extreme tension, terror regarding a relationship with a pimp, lack of self-esteem, and mood swings.

Fifteen percent reported gastrointestinal symptoms such as ulcers, chronic stomachache, diarrhea, and colitis. Fifteen percent reported neurological symptoms such as migraine headaches and non-migraine headaches, memory loss, numbness, seizures, and dizziness. Fourteen percent of these women and children in prostitution reported respiratory problems such as asthma, lung disease, bronchitis, and pneumonia.

Fourteen percent reported joint pain, including hip pain, bad knees, backache, arthritis, rheumatism, and nonspecific multiple-site joint pain.

Twelve percent of those who described health problems in prostitution reported injuries which were a direct result of violence. For example, a number of women had their ribs broken by the police in Istanbul, a woman in San Francisco broke her hips jumping out of a car when a john was attempting to kidnap her. Many women had their teeth knocked out by pimps and johns. Miller (1986) cited bruises, broken bones, cuts and abrasions which resulted from beatings and sexual assaults. One woman said about her health:

> I've had three broken arms, nose broken twice, [and] I'm partially deaf in one ear . . . I have a small fragment of a bone floating in my head that gives me migraines. I've had a fractured skull. My legs ain't worth shit no more; my toes have been broken. My feet, bottom of my feet, have been burned; they've been whopped with a hot iron and clothes hanger . . . the hair on my pussy had been burned off at one time . . . I have scars. I've been cut with a knife, beat with guns, two-by-fours. There hasn't been a place on my body that hasn't been bruised somehow, some way, some big, some small. (Giobbe, 1992, p. 126)

In the first phase of an in-depth review of chronic health problems resulting from prostitution, we interviewed 100 women and transgendered people in Vancouver, Canada, regarding their chronic health problems (Farley, Lynne, & Cotton, 2001). Seventy-five percent of these women reported injuries from violence in prostitution. Fifty percent suffered head injuries. The author has found that a majority of women in prostitution report traumatic head injuries inflicted by johns and pimps. Common symptoms were memory problems (66%), trouble concentrating (66%), headaches (56%), dizziness (44%), vision problems (45%), hearing problems (40%), balance problems (41%), aching muscles (78%), joint pain (60%), jaw pain (38%), and swelling of limbs (33%). Sixty-one percent of these respondents had cold/flu symptoms. Cardiovascular symptoms included chest pain (43%); pain/numbness in hands/feet (49%); irregular heartbeat (33%); shortness of breath (60%). In addition, 35% reported allergies and 32% reported asthma. Twenty-four percent reported both painful menstruation and vaginal pain. Twenty-three percent had breast pain.

Some of the health problems suffered by women in prostitution resulted from poverty. Although public health agencies in Bombay could obtain expensive drugs to treat HIV, they were unable to obtain antibiotics and other more "mundane" drugs to treat tuberculosis, which was the primary cause of death of women in prostitution (Jean D'Cunha, personal communication, 1997). Seventy percent of 100 prostituted girls and women in Bogota reported physical health problems. In addition to STD, their diseases were those of poverty and despair: allergies, respiratory problems and blindness caused by glue sniffing, migraines, symptoms of premature aging, dental problems, and complications of abortion (Spiwak, 1999).

Adolescent girls and boys in prostitution surveyed by Weisberg (1985) reported STD, hepatitis, pregnancies, sore throats, flu, and repeated suicide attempts. Women who serviced more customers in prostitution reported more severe physical symptoms (Vanwesenbeeck, 1994). The longer women were in prostitution, the more STD they reported (Parriott, 1994).

The Invisibility of Psychological Symptoms Among Women in Prostitution

The assault on women's sexuality in prostitution is overwhelming, yet invisible to most people. When women are turned into objects which men masturbate into (as prostitution has been described by Hoigard & Finstad, 1986), it causes immense harm to the person who is acting as receptacle.

> Prostitution and sexual liberation have got nothing to do with each other, they're exactly the opposite. I don't feel free with my body, I feel bad about it, I feel self-conscious. I don't really feel like my body's alive, I think of it more as bruised, as a weight. (Jaget, 1980, p. 112)

In all prostitution there is commodification of the woman's body. This commodification often results in internalized objectification, where the prostituted woman begins to see sexually objectified parts of her own body as separate from, rather than integral to her entire self. This process of internalized objectification leads to somatic dissociation, even in prostitution where there is no physical contact between the woman and the john. For example, Funari (1997) described the effects of peep show prostitution, where she worked in a mirror-walled booth, naked. A thick glass wall separated her from the men, and when the shutters went down men had to pay again in order to watch and masturbate. She wrote,

> At work, what my hands find when they touch my body is 'product.' Away from work, my body has continuity, integrity. Last night, lying in bed after work, I touched my belly, my breasts. They felt like Capri's [her peep show name] and they refused to switch back. When [her partner] kissed me I inadvertently shrunk from his touch. Shocked, we both jerked away and stared at each other. Somehow the glass had dissolved and he had become one of them. (Funari, 1997, p. 32)

In order to retain her self-respect, Funari resisted emotional connection with men who considered her to be essentially worthless. Yet she felt "poisoned" by the contempt of customers. Her sexual feelings for her boyfriend waned.

In an attempt to defend the self, women in prostitution at first might make a conscious decision to disconnect from parts of the body. Stating "I save my vagina for my lover," one woman performed only oral sex or masturbation (Pheterson, 1996). Over time, however, this piecing-out of parts of the body in prostitution (johns get this, lovers get that) results in somatoform dissociation, with the body numbed, considered not-me, the body a commodity, itself traumatically compartmentalized in the same way that traumatic affects and memories exist in states of dissociated consciousness. This disconnection between parts of the whole self is common among survivors of extreme trauma (Schwartz, 2000).

In prostitution, the continuous assaults on the body result in physical revulsion and retraumatization. One woman wrote about her body's response to repeated rape:

> I started getting physically ill whenever I turned a trick. My vagina closed on me again like it did when I was 15 years old [during a rape]. The men started getting real pissed off about that because it meant no intercourse . . . One night a man tried to force himself inside of me and damaged his penis in the process. (Williams, 1991, p. 77)

Most women who have been in prostitution for any length of time experience sexual dysfunction with their chosen partners. Feelings are disconnected from sexual acts. It becomes nearly impossible to view partners as anything but johns. One woman said,

> I felt like a prostitute every time I got into bed with him. I had lost myself in prostitution and had become so well established in my identity and role as a prostitute that once I had stopped I couldn't then relate to my lover as myself. (Perkins & Bennett, 1985, p. 112)

The same sexual trauma which occurs with women in prostitution also occurs with men. As one man said,

> [Prostitution] can destroy your sex life. I had a lover at one stage and there were times when I'd be having sex with him and I'd flash on to an old man that I'd had the night before and then I'd just have to stop, you know. (Perkins & Bennett, 1985, p. 152)

Dissociation occurs during extreme stress among prisoners of war who are tortured, among children who are being sexually assaulted, and among women being battered, raped, or prostituted (Herman, 1992). When one is prostituted for any length of time, a state of intense, unbearable fear develops. Dissociative disorders, depression, and other mood disorders were common among prostituted women in street, escort, and strip club prostitution (Belton, 1998; Ross, Anderson, Heber, & Norton, 1990; Vanwesenbeeck, 1994). Dissociation in prostitution results from both childhood sexual violence and sexual violence in adult prostitution. The dissociation which is necessary to survive rape in prostitution is the same as that used to endure familial sexual assault (Giobbe, 1991; Miller, 1986). Vanwesenbeeck noted that "dissociative proficiency" contributed to the professional attitudes among women in prostitution in the Netherlands (1994, p. 107). A Thai woman said, "You make yourself empty inside" (Bishop & Robinson, 1998, p. 47).

Most women report that they cannot prostitute unless they dissociate. Chemical dissociation aids psychological dissociation, and also functions as analgesic for injuries from violence. When women in prostitution do *not* dissociate, they are at risk for being overwhelmed with pain, shame, and rage. One woman said, "The disgust is difficult to deal with. I can deal with [the johns] individually but if I allow myself to think of them en masse I feel like grabbing a machine gun and mowing the lot down" (Wood, 1995, p. 29).

One woman described the gradual development of a dissociated identity during the years she prostituted in stripclubs:

> You start changing yourself to fit a fantasy role of what they think a woman should be. In the real world, these women don't exist. They stare at you with this starving hunger. It sucks you dry; you become this empty shell. They're not really looking at you, you're not you. You're not even there. (Farley, unpublished interview, 1998)

Another woman described a dissociative response to the trauma of prostitution:

> Prostitution is like rape. It's like when I was 15 years old and I was raped. I used to experience leaving my body. I mean that's what I did when that man raped me. I went to the ceiling and I numbed myself because I didn't want to feel what I was feeling. I was very frightened. And while I was a prostitute I used to do that all the time. I would numb my feelings. I wouldn't even feel like I was in my body. I would actually leave my body and go somewhere else with my thoughts and with my feelings until he got off and it was over with. I don't know how else to explain it except that it felt like rape. It was rape to me. (Giobbe, 1991, p. 144)

While the traumatic effects of rape are well established, the extremely high incidence of rape in prostitution, with resulting symptoms of PTSD, is not so well understood. One survivor said, "For the first few months I worked [in prostitution] I had a lot of nightmares involving mass numbers of penises" (Williams, 1991, p. 75).

Many years after escaping from prostitution, an Okinawan woman who had been purchased by US military personnel during the Vietnam war became extremely agitated and had visions of sexual abuse and persecution on the 15th and 30th of each month, those days which were Army paydays (Sturdevant & Stolzfus, 1992). Another woman described intrusive and physiologic hyperarousal symptoms of PTSD:

> I wonder why I keep going to therapists and telling them I can't sleep, and I have nightmares. They pass right over the fact that I was a prostitute and I was beaten with two-by-four boards, I had my fingers and toes broken by a pimp, and I was raped more than 30 times. Why do they ignore that? (Farley & Barkan, 1998, p. 46)

PTSD is common among prostituted women. In nine countries, Farley et al. (in press) found that 68% met criteria for a diagnosis of PTSD, a prevalence comparable to battered women seeking shelter

(Houskamp & Foy, 1991), rape survivors seeking treatment (Bownes, O'Gorman, & Sayers, 1991), and survivors of state-sponsored torture (Ramsay, Gorst-Unsworth, & Turner, 1993). These rates suggest that the traumatic consequences of prostitution were similar across different cultures.

There is a myth that escort and strip club prostitution are safer than street prostitution. This has not been verified by research. We compared street, brothel, and stripclub prostitution in two cities in Mexico, and found no differences in the incidence of physical assault, rape, childhood sexual abuse, or in the percentage of women who wanted to get out of prostitution. Furthermore, there were no differences in symptoms of PTSD among women in these three types of prostitution (Farley et al., in press). Prostitution is intrinsically traumatizing, wherever it occurs.

Vanwesenbeeck (1994) reported similar findings. She investigated emotional distress in women prostituting primarily in clubs, brothels, and windows. Although she did not measure PTSD, the symptoms she reported were similar to PTSD. Ninety percent of Vanwesenbeeck's group of prostituted women reported "extreme nervousness."

The johns' poisonous verbal assaults in all types of prostitution cause acute and long-term psychological symptoms. The verbal abuse in prostitution is normalized and is invisible. One woman said that over time, "It is internally damaging. You become in your own mind what these people do and say with you. You wonder how could you let yourself do this and why do these people want to do this to you?" (Farley, unpublished interview, 1997).

The physical violence of prostitution, the constant verbal humiliation, the social indignity and contempt, result in personality changes which have been described as complex posttraumatic stress disorder (CPTSD) (Herman, 1992). Symptoms of CPTSD include changes in consciousness and self-concept, changes in the ability to regulate emotions, changes in systems of meaning, such as loss of faith, and an unremitting sense of despair. Once out of prostitution, 76% of a group of women interviewed by Parriott (1994) reported that they had great difficulty with intimate relationships.

Unless human behavior under conditions of captivity is understood, the emotional bond between those prostituted and pimps is difficult to comprehend. The terror created in the prostituted woman by the pimp causes a sense of helplessness and dependence. This emotional bonding to an abuser under conditions of captivity has been described as the Stockholm Syndrome. Attitudes and behaviors which are part of this syndrome include:

1. intense gratefulness for small favors when the captor holds life and death power over the captive;
2. denial of the extent of violence and harm which the captor has inflicted or is obviously capable of inflicting;
3. hypervigilance with respect to the pimp's needs and identification with the pimp's perspective on the world (an example of this was Patty Hearst's identification with her captors' ideology);
4. perception of those trying to assist in escape as enemies and perception of captors as friends; and
5. extreme difficulty leaving one's captor/pimp, even after physical release has occurred.

Paradoxically, women in prostitution might feel that they owe their lives to pimps (Graham, Rawlings, & Rigsby, 1994).

Concepts in the Medical and Social Sciences Which Contribute to the Invisibility of Prostitution's Harm, and Which Inflict Additional Injury

The social invisibility of prostitution is the first barrier to grasping its harm. If the harm is not perceived, there is no possibility of healing the psychological damage which occurs as a result of being prostituted. Cotton and Forster (2000) surveyed psychology of women textbooks and found that eleven of fourteen texts published since 1995 failed to mention prostitution. When prostitution was mentioned, it was usually addressed as a "feminist debate" or as "work" rather than as violence.

Some have suggested that prostituted women in the sex businesses are "simply another category of workers with special problems and needs" (Bullough & Bullough, 1996, p. 177). In 1988, the World Health Organization defined prostitution as "dynamic and adaptive sex work, involving a transaction between seller and buyer of a sexual service" (cited in Scambler & Scambler, 1995, p. 18). Recent psychological and health sciences literature regularly assumed that prostitution is a vocational choice (Deren et al., 1996; Farr, Castro, DiSantostefano, Claassen, & Olguin, 1996; Green et al., 1993). The notion that prostitution is work tends to make its harm invisible (except perhaps for the need for labor unions). Once understood as violence, however, unionizing prostituted women makes as little sense as unionizing battered women.

Historically, there have been a number of medical, psychological, and "sexological" theories which not only make the harm of prostitution invisible, but which further blame women for their own victimization. In 1898, Lombroso and Ferraro suggested that prostitutes have a "demonic nature which is observable upon precise skull measurement." Damaging theories about why women prostitute are still in vogue. For example, some HIV researchers have represented women in prostitution as "vectors of disease," a concept akin to Lombroso's notion that prostitutes are demons. These views originate in Judeo-Christian formulations of women as sexually evil.

It seems to be titillating to theorize a mysterious perversity as a factor in entering prostitution. Urologist and criminologist Reitman wrote in 1931:

> Why does a woman fall in love with a pimp? It may be because she is a moron or a psychopathic personality, an eccentric ego. She may have either a superiority or an inferiority complex. It may be because she is poor and hungry or rich and bored. (p. 31)

Abraham speculated that "[The prostitute's] frigidity signifies a humiliation of all men . . . and her whole life is given up to this purpose" (Abraham, 1948, p. 361). Prostituted women do become sexually numbed, but Abraham reverses cause and effect. The woman in prostitution does not begin with the intention of humiliating men. Instead, she becomes sexually frozen in response to the accumulated traumatic effects of sexual and psychological violence. A similar numbing can occur in victims of state-sponsored torture.

Sexology, the study of sexuality, was built on the *uncritical acceptance of prostitution as an institution which expresses men's and women's sexuality*. Kinsey, Pomeroy, and Martin (1949) and Masters and Johnson (1973) worked in the late 1940s through the 1970s and articulated a sexuality which was graphically portrayed in *Playboy* magazine. The Playboy Press, for example, published Masters and Johnson's article, "Ten Sex Myths Exploded" (1973).

In 1954, Masters began "sexological studies" with prostitutes as subjects. His goal was to provide impotent men with orgasms by using women as sexual surrogates. Couched in scientific language, his work was prostitution. In a 1974 interview, Masters acknowledged that his cures of impotent men were largely a result of the efforts of the prostitutes he procured for them. Like Szasz (1980), we wonder why Masters was never prosecuted for pimping or procuring.

The psychological literature of the 1980s posited an essential masochism among battered women, a viewpoint which was later rejected for lack of evidence (Caplan, 1984; Koss et al., 1994). Yet it is still assumed that prostituted women have underlying personality characteristics which lead to their victimization. Rosiello (1993) described the inherent masochism of prostituted women as a "necessary ingredient" of their self-concept. MacVicar and Dillon (1980) suggested that masochism led to women's acceptance of abuse by pimps.

Other victim-blaming occurs when prostituted women are described as "risk takers," with the implication that they themselves provoked the violence and harassment aimed at them in prostitution (Vanwesenbeeck, de Graaf, van Zessen, Straver, & Visser, 1995). It was assumed that "risk-taking" prostituted women willingly exposed themselves to harm, although the histories of the "risk-takers" revealed that they had been battered and raped throughout their lives more frequently than the non-risk-takers. Risk-taking behavior was rarely interpreted as trauma-based repetition of childhood sexual abuse, or parental failure to teach self-protection.

It would be more appropriate to view all prostituted women as at-risk. It has been established that johns pressure women into unsafe sex (Farr et al., 1996). Women in prostitution were unable to prevent johns' demands for unsafe sex, and were often physically assaulted when they requested condoms (Ford & Koetsawang, 1991; Karim et al., 1995; Miller & Schwartz, 1995).

CONCLUSION

Women in prostitution consistently report that what is most painful is the invisibility of the harm done to them. When johns treat them as non-human, or when passersby contemptuously ignore them, their mental suffering is overwhelming. In order to end the human rights abuses of prostitution, it is necessary to make visible:

- lethal gender inequality;
- incest and other childhood sexual assault;
- poverty and homelessness;
- the ways in which racism and colonialism are inextricably connected with sexism in prostitution;
- domestic violence, including rape;
- posttraumatic stress disorder, depression, mood and dissociative disorders as consequences of prostitution;

- drug and alcohol addiction;
- the fact that prostitution is a global business which involves interstate and inter-country trafficking as necessary to its profitable operation;
- the ways in which economic development programs erode traditional ways of living and create vulnerability to prostitution;
- the need for culturally-relevant treatment; and
- the ways in which diverse cultures normalize and promote prostitution.

Stripping, exotic dancing, nude dancing, table dancing, phone sex, child and adult pornography, online prostitution, and Internet pimping of women and children (Hughes, 1999), lap dancing, massage brothels, and peep shows are different types of prostitution, but prostitution nonetheless. One's political perspective will determine whether prostitution is viewed primarily as a public health issue, as an issue of zoning and property values (in whose neighborhoods will strip clubs and pornography stores be zoned?), as vocational choice, as sexual liberation, as freedom of speech (does the webmaster have the right to sell Internet photographs of prostituted women being raped?), as petty crime, as domestic violence, or as human rights violation.

In the United States there is a lack of concern for women who enter prostitution because of educational neglect, childhood abuse and neglect, or lack of economic alternatives. Some women in prostitution do not *appear* to have been "forced." Distinctions which offer legal, financial, and social assistance only to those who can prove violent coercion, or who are under age eighteen, or who crossed international borders, fail to address the core of violence which is present in all types of prostitution. Legal responses to prostitution are inadequate if they fail to include johns as perpetrators, as well as pimps and traffickers.

A lack of attention to experiences of violence and sexual abuse has resulted in repeated failures of the health care system for all women (Dean-Patterson, 1999). Asthana and Oostvogels (1996) predicted that programs to assist those in prostitution would continue to fail unless significant changes were made to social and cultural systems which keep women in a position of subordination.

Demand creates supply in prostitution. Because men want to buy sex, prostitution is assumed to be inevitable, therefore "normal." Men's ambivalence about the purchase of women is reflected in the scarcity of research interviews with johns, their desire to remain hidden, and contradictory beliefs about prostitution. In interviews conducted by women prostituting in massage parlors, Plumridge, Chetwynd, Reed, and Gifford (1997) noted that, on the one hand, johns believed that commercial sex was a mutually pleasurable exchange, and on the other hand, they asserted that payment of money removed all social and ethical obligations.

White and Koss (1993) observed that violent behaviors against women have been associated with attitudes which promote men's beliefs that they are entitled to sexual access to women, that they are superior to women, and that they have license for sexual aggression. Prostitution myths are a component of attitudes which normalize sexual violence. Monto (1999) found that johns' acceptance of commodified sexuality was strongly associated with their acceptance of rape myths, violent sex, and less frequent use of condoms with women in prostitution. The relationship between attitudes toward prostitution and rape myth acceptance has been described by Cotton (1999). The positive correlation between attitudes toward prostitution and self-reported sexual violence has been described by Schmidt, Cotton, and Farley (2000). An acceptance of what has been described as nonrelational sexuality might be a contributing factor to the normalization of prostitution. Confusion regarding sex that is coercive/exploitative and sex that is positive human experience resulted in what Barry (1995) has called the prostitution of sexuality.

Until there is recognition that prostitution harms women, application of appropriate law will be impossible. Once recognition occurs, as for example in Sweden, governments can attack the spread of commercial sex businesses. The Swedish law (in effect since 1999) criminalizes pimps and johns, but not women in prostitution. The women are instead offered social services such as housing, medical treatment, psychotherapy, and job training.

Ultimately, major social change is necessary to end prostitution. Gender inequality, race discrimination, and poverty must be eliminated. But social change occurs in increments, with one small shift in attitude at a time. A high school teacher from Alabama contacted the Prostitution Research & Education website [http://www.prostitutionresearch.com] and described an annual school tradition–pimp and skank day. The teacher was gravely concerned about the effect on his students of this ritual which glamorized prostitution. He downloaded information from the website, and led a class discussion about prostitution. The students voted the tradition out, and two years later, it was still nonexistent.

NOTES

1. Thanks to Michelle J. Anderson, Associate Professor of Law, Villanova University School of Law, Pennsylvania, for clarifying how U.S. law regarding rape, sexual harassment and domestic violence is currently being interpreted.

2. Morrison, McGee, and Ruben (1995) observed that the most obviously intoxicated prostitutes appeared to be the most successful at attracting clients. They speculated that the reason for this was that women who appeared the most powerless and least capable of setting limits would attract men who wanted to "legitimize an act of sexual abuse by the payment of cash" (p. 293).

3. Donna M. Hughes contributed to this list of words which hide the violence of prostitution.

REFERENCES

Abraham, K. (1948). *Selected papers*, with introduction by Ernest Jones, translated by Douglas Bryan and Alix Strachey. London: Hogarth Press.

Allen, D., Lee, N., Schulz, S., Pappaioanou, M., Dondero, T., & Onorato, I. (1993). Determining HIV seroprevalence among women in women's health clinics. *American Journal of Public Health, 83,* 364-367.

Aral, S. O., & Mann, J. M. (1998). Commercial sex work and STD: The need for policy interventions to change social patterns. *Sexually Transmitted Diseases, 25,* 455-456.

Asthana, S., & Oostvogels, R. (1996). Community participation in HIV prevention: Problems and prospects for community-based strategies among female sex workers in Madras. *Social Science & Medicine, 43,* 133-148.

Baldwin, M.A. (1993). Strategies of connection: Prostitution and feminist politics. *Michigan Journal of Gender and Law, 1,* 65-79.

Baldwin, M.A. (1999). A million dollars and an apology: Prostitution and public benefits claims. *Hastings Women's Law Journal, 10,* 189-224.

Barry, K. (1979). *Female sexual slavery.* New York: New York University Press.

Barry, K. (1995). *The prostitution of sexuality,* New York: New York University Press.

Belton, R. (1992). *Prostitution as traumatic reenactment.* Paper presented at 8th Annual Meeting of International Society for Traumatic Stress Studies, Los Angeles, CA. October 22.

Belton, R. (1998). *Assessment, diagnosis, and treatment of prostitution trauma.* Paper presented at Prostitution: Critical Aspects of the Trauma. American Psychological Association 106th Annual Convention, San Francisco, August 17.

Bishop, R., & Robinson, L. S. (1998). *Night market: Sexual cultures and the Thai economic miracle.* New York: Routledge.

Bownes, I. T., O'Gorman, E. C., & Sayers, A. (1991). Assault characteristics and post-traumatic stress disorder in rape victims. *Acta Psychiatrica Scandinavica, 83,* 27-30.

Boyer, D. (1989). Male prostitution and homosexual identity. *Journal of Homosexuality*, *17*, 151-184.

Boyer, D., Chapman, L., & Marshall, B. K. (1993). *Survival sex in King County: Helping women out.* Report Submitted to King County Women's Advisory Board. Seattle: Northwest Resource Associates.

Briere, J. (1992). *Child abuse trauma: Theory and treatment of the lasting effects.* Newbury Park: Sage.

Browne, A., & Finklehor, D. (1986). Impact of child sexual abuse: A review of the research. *Psychological Bulletin*, *99*, 66-77.

Bullough, B., & Bullough, V. (1996). Female prostitution: Current research and changing interpretations. *Annual Review of Sex Research*, *7*, 158-180.

Burkett, E. (1997, October 12) God created me to be a slave. *New York Times Magazine*, 56-60.

Caplan, P. J. (1984). The myth of women's masochism. *American Psychologist*, *39*, 130-139.

Chattopadhyay, M., Bandyopadhyay, S., & Duttagupta, C. (1994). Biosocial factors influencing women to become prostitutes in India. *Social Biology*, 41, 252-259.

Chesler, P. (1993). A woman's right to self-defense: The Case of Aileen Carol Wuornos. *St. John's Law Review*, *66*, 933-977.

Coker, A., Patel, N., Krishnaswami, S., Schmidt, W., & Richter, D. (1998). Childhood forced sex and cervical dysplasia among women prison inmates. *Violence Against Women*, *4*, 595-608.

Cotton, A. (1999). *Attitudes toward prostitution and rape myth acceptance.* Unpublished Doctoral Dissertation, Pacific University School of Professional Psychology, Forest Grove, Oregon.

Cotton, A., & Forster, C. (2000, March 10). *Pornography and prostitution: A survey of psychology of women texts.* Paper presented at Association for Women in Psychology 25th Annual Meeting. Salt Lake City, Utah.

Crowell, N. A., & Burgess, A. W. (Eds.) (1996). *Understanding violence against women.* Washington, DC: National Academy Press.

Davidson, J. O. (1998). *Prostitution, power, and freedom.* Ann Arbor: University of Michigan Press.

Dean-Patterson, S. (1999, March 3). Remarks at United Nations Commission on Status of Women. New York.

Dehne, K. L., Khodakevich, L., Hamers, F., & Schwartlander, B. (1999). The HIV/AIDS epidemic in eastern Europe: Recent patterns and trends and their implications for policy-makers. *AIDS*, *13*, 741-749.

Deren, S., Sanchez, J., Sheldon, M., Davis, W. R., Be Ardsley, M., Des-Parlays, D., & Miller, K. (1996). HIV Risk Behaviors among Dominican brothel and street prostitutes in New York City. *AIDS Education and Prevention*, 8, 444-456.

de Sanjose, S., Palace, V., Tofu, L., Vasquez, S., Espitia, V., Vazquez, F., Roman, G., Munoz, N., & Bosch, F. (1993). Prostitution, HIV, and cervical neoplasia: A survey in Spain and Colombia. *Cancer Epidemiology, Biomarkers and Prevention*, *2*, 531-535.

Dworkin, A. (1981). *Pornography: Men possessing women.* New York: Putnam.

Dworkin, A. (1997). *Prostitution and male supremacy in life and death.* New York: Free Press.

Dworkin, A. (2000). *Scapegoat: The Jews, Israel, and Women's liberation.* New York: Free Press.

Farley, M., Cotton, A., Zumbeck, S., Lynne, J., Spiwak, U., & Gonzales, K. (in press). Prostitution in nine countries: Violence and posttraumatic stress disorder. In M. Farley (Ed.) *Prostitution and Traumatic Stress,* Binghamton, NY: The Haworth Press, Inc.

Farley, M., Baral, I., Gonzales, K., Kiremire, M., Sezgin, U., Spiwak, F., & Taylor, T. (2000, January 28). *Prostitution: Health Consequences of Physical Violence and Psychological Trauma.* Paper presented at 11th International Congress on Women's Health Issues, University of California College of Nursing, San Francisco, CA.

Farley, M., Baral, I., Kiremire, M., & Sezgin, U. (1998). Prostitution in five countries: Violence and posttraumatic stress disorder. *Feminism & Psychology, 8,* 415-426.

Farley, M., & Barkan, H. (1998). Prostitution, violence and posttraumatic stress disorder. *Women & Health, 27,* 37-49.

Farley, M., & Kelly, V. (2000). Prostitution: A critical review of the medical and social science literature. *Women & Criminal Justice, 11,* 29-64.

Farley, M., & Lynne, J. (2000). *Pilot study of 40 prostituted women and girls in Vancouver, Canada.* Unpublished manuscript.

Farley, M., Lynne, J., & Cotton, A. (2001). *The pimping of nations: Prostitution, colonialism and gender inequality in Canada.* [paper submitted for publication]

Farr, F., Castro, L., DiSantostefano, R., Claassen, E., & Olguin, F. (1996). Use of spermicide and impact of prophylactic condom use among sex workers in Santa Fe de Bogota, Colombia. *Sexually Transmitted Diseases, 23,* 206-212.

Ford, N., & Koetsawang, S. (1991). The socio-cultural context of the transmission of HIV in Thailand. *Social Science and Medicine, 33,* 405-414.

Friedman, J., & Yehuda, R. (1995). Post-traumatic stress disorder and comorbidity: Psychobiological approaches to differential diagnosis. In Friedman, J., Charney, D., & Dutch, A. (Eds.) *Neurobiological and Clinical Consequences of Stress: From Normal Adaptation to Posttraumatic Stress Disorder* (pp. 429-445). Philadelphia: Lippincott-Raven.

Funari, V. (1997). Naked, naughty, nasty: Peepshow reflections. In J. Nagle (Ed.) *Whores and Other Feminists.* New York: Routledge.

Giobbe, E. (1991). Prostitution: Buying the right to rape. In A. W. Burgess (Ed.), *Rape and sexual assault III: A research handbook.* New York: Garland Press.

Giobbe, E. (1992). Juvenile prostitution: Profile of recruitment. In A. W. Burgess (Ed.), *Child trauma: Issues & research.* New York. Garland Publishing.

Giobbe, E. (1993). An analysis of individual, institutional & cultural pimping. *Michigan Journal of Gender & Law, 1,* 33-57.

Giobbe, E., Harrigan, M., Ryan, J., & Gamache, D. (1990). *Prostitution: A matter of violence against women.* Minneapolis: WHISPER.

Golding, J. (1994). Sexual assault history and physical health in randomly selected Los Angeles women. *Health Promotion*, 13, 130-138.

Goodman, L. & Fallot, R. (1998). HIV risk-behavior in poor urban women with serious mental disorders: Association with childhood physical and sexual abuse. *American Journal of Orthopsychiatry*, 68, 73-83.

Graham, D. L. R., with Rawlings, E., & Rigsby, R. (1994). *Loving to survive: Sexual terror, men's violence and women's lives*. New York: New York University Press.

Green, S. T., Goldberg, D. J., Christie, P. R., Frischer, M., Thomson, A., Carr, S. V., & Taylor, A. (1993). Female streetworker-prostitutes in Glasgow: A descriptive study of their lifestyle. *AIDS Care*, 5, 321-335.

Hamers, F., Downs, A., Infuso, A., & Brunet, J. (1998). Diversity of the HIV/AIDS epidemic in Europe. *AIDS*, 12 (suppl. A), S63-S70.

Herman, J. L. (1992). *Trauma and recovery*. New York, Basic Books.

Hernandez, T. K. (2001). Sexual harassment and racial disparity: The mutual construction of gender and race, *University of Iowa Journal of Gender, Race & Justice*, 4, 183-224.

Hoigard, C., & Finstad, L. (1986). *Backstreets: Prostitution, money and love*. University Park: Pennsylvania State University Press.

Holsopple, K. (1998). *Stripclubs according to strippers: Exposing workplace violence*. Unpublished Paper.

Houskamp, B. M., & Foy, D. W. (1991). The assessment of post-traumatic stress disorder in battered women. *Journal of Interpersonal Violence*, 6, 367-75.

Hughes, D. M. (1999). *Pimps and predators on the internet–globalizing the sexual exploitation of women and children*. Kingston, Rhode Island: The Coalition Against Trafficking in Women.

Hughes, D. M. (2000). The 'Natasha' trade: The transnational shadow market of trafficking in women. *Journal of International Affairs*, 53, 625-651.

Hunter, S. K. (1994). Prostitution is cruelty and abuse to women and children. *Michigan Journal of Gender and Law*, 1, 1-14.

Jaget, C. (1980). *Prostitutes–Our life*. Bristol: Falling Wall Press.

Jeffreys, S. (1997). *The idea of prostitution*. North Melbourne, Spinifex Press.

Kalichman, S. C., Kelly, J. A., Shaboltas, A., & Granskaya, J. (2000). Violence against women and the impending AIDS crisis in Russia. *American Psychologist*, 55, 279-280.

Kalichman, S. C., Williams, E. A., Cheery, C., Belcher, L., & Nachimson, D. (1998). Sexual coercion, domestic violence, and negotiating condom use among low-income African American women. *Journal of Women's Health*, 7, 371-378.

Karim, Q. A., Karim, S. S., Soldan, K., & Zondi, M. (1995). Reducing the risk of HIV infection among South African sex workers: Socioeconomic and gender barriers. *American Journal of Public Health*, 85, 1521-1525.

Kinsey, A. C., Pomeroy, W. B., & Martin, C. E. (1949). *Sexual behavior in the human male*. Philadelphia, W. B. Saunders.

Koss, M., Goodman, A., Browne, L., Fitzgerald, G., Keita, G., & Russo, N. (1994). *No safe haven*. Washington, DC: American Psychological Association.

Koss, M., & Heslet, L. (1992). Somatic consequences of violence against women. *Archives of Family Medicine*, 1, 53-59.

Leidholdt, D. (1993). Prostitution: A violation of women's human rights. *Cardozo Women's Law Journal*, 1, 133-147.

Lewis, J. (1998). Lap dancing: Personal and legal implications for exotic dancers. In J. A. Elias, V. L. Bullough, V. Elias, & G. Brewer (Eds.), *Prostitution: On whores, hustlers, and johns*. Amherst, NY: Prometheus Books.

Lim, L. L. (ed.). (1998). *The sex sector: The economic and social bases of prostitution in southeast Asia*. Geneva: International Labor Organization.

Lombroso, C., & Ferraro, W. (1898). *The female offender*. New York: Appleton and Company.

Louie, L., Luu, M., & Tong, B. (1991). *Chinese American adolescent runaways*. Paper presented at Annual Convention of the Asian American Psychological Association. San Francisco, August.

Lucas, B., & Hackett, L. (1995). *Street youth: On their own in Indianapolis*. Indianapolis: Health Foundation of Greater Indianapolis.

MacKinnon, C. A. (1993). Prostitution and civil rights. *Michigan Journal of Gender and Law*, 1, 13-31.

MacKinnon, C. A. & Dworkin, A. (1997). *In harm's way: The pornography civil rights hearings*. Cambridge: Harvard University Press.

MacVicar, K., & Dillon, M. (1980). Childhood and adolescent development of ten female prostitutes. *Journal of the American Academy of Child Psychiatry*, 19, 145-159.

Masters, W., & Johnson, V. (1973). Ten sex myths exploded. *The Sensuous Society*. Chicago: Playboy Press.

McKeganey, N., & Barnard, M. (1996). *Sex work on the streets: Prostitutes and their clients*. Buckingham, Scotland: Milton Keynes Open University Press.

Miller, E. M. (1986). *Street woman*. Philadelphia: Temple University Press.

Miller, J. (1995). Gender and power on the streets: Street prostitution in the era of crack cocaine. *Journal of Contemporary Ethnography*, 23, 427-452.

Miller, J., & Schwartz, M. D. (1995). Rape myths against street prostitutes. *Deviant Behavior*, 16, 1-23.

Monto, M. (1999, August). *Prostitution and human commodification: Study of arrested clients of female street prostitutes*. Paper presented at the annual convention of American Sociological Association, Chicago, Illinois.

Morrison, C. L., McGee, A., & Ruben, S. M. (1995). Alcohol and drug misuse in prostitutes. *Addiction*, 90, 292-293.

Nadon, S. M., Koverola, C., & Schludermann, E. H. (1998). Antecedents to prostitution: Childhood victimization. *Journal of Interpersonal Violence*, 13, 206-221.

Nakashima, K., Kashiwagi, S., Hayashi, J., Urabe, K., Minami, K., & Maeda, Y. (1996). Prevalence of hepatitis C virus infection among female prostitutes in Fukuoka, Japan. *Journal of Gastroenterology*, 31, 664-448.

Nelson, V. (1993). Prostitution: Where racism and sexism intersect. *Michigan Journal of Gender & Law*, 1, 81-89.

Parriott, R. (1994). *Health experiences of Twin Cities women used in prostitution*. Unpublished survey initiated by WHISPER, Minneapolis.

Pelzer, A., Duncan, M., Tibaux, G., & Mehari, L. (1992). A study of cervical cancer in Ethiopian women. *Cytopathology, 3* (3), 139-148.

Perkins, R., & Bennett, G. (1985). *Being a prostitute: Prostitute women and prostitute men*. Sydney: George Allen and Unwin.

Pheterson, G. (1996). *The prostitution prism*. Amsterdam: Amsterdam University Press.

Phoenix, J. (1999). *Making sense of prostitution*. London: MacMillan Press.

Piot, P. (1999, March 3). *Remarks at United Nations Commission on the Status of Women*. New York: United Nations Press Release.

Plumridge, E. W., Chetwynd, J. W., Reed, A., & Gifford, S. J. (1997). Discourses of emotionality in commercial sex: The missing client voice. *Feminism & Psychology, 7*, 165-181.

Putnam, F. (1990). Disturbances of 'self' in victims of childhood sexual abuse. In R. Kluft (Ed.) *Incest-related syndromes of adult psychopathology* (p. 113-131).Washington, DC: American Psychiatric Press.

Radomsky, N. A. (1995). *Lost voices: Women, chronic pain, and abuse*. New York: Harrington Park Press.

Ramsay, R., Gorst-Unsworth, C., & Turner, S. (1993). Psychiatric morbidity in survivors of organised state violence including torture: A retrospective series. *British Journal of Psychiatry, 162*, 55-59.

Raymond, J. (1998). Prostitution as violence against women: NGO stonewalling in Beijing and elsewhere. *Women's Studies International Forum*, 21, 1-9.

Reitman, B. (1931). *The second oldest profession: A study of the prostitute's business manager*. New York: Vanguard Press.

Root, M. P. P. (1996). Women of Color and traumatic stress in 'domestic captivity': Gender and race as disempowering statuses. In A. J. Marsella, M. J. Friedman, E. T. Gerrity, & R. M. Scurfield (Eds.), *Ethnocultural aspects of posttraumatic stress disorder: Issues, research, and clinical applications*. Washington, DC: American Psychological Association.

Rosiello, F. (1993). The interplay of masochism and narcissism in the treatment of two prostitutes. *Contemporary Psychotherapy Review, 8*, 28-43.

Ross, C. A., Anderson, G., Heber, S., & Norton, G. R. (1990). Dissociation and abuse among multiple personality patients, prostitutes and exotic dancers. *Hospital and Community Psychiatry*, 41, 328-330.

Scambler, G., & Scambler, A. (1995). Social change and health promotion among women sex workers in London. *Health Promotion International*, 10, 17-24.

Schmidt, M., Cotton, A., & Farley, M. (2000). *Attitudes toward prostitution and self-reported sexual violence in college students*. Presentation at the 16th Annual Meeting of the International Society for Traumatic Stress Studies, San Antonio, Texas, November 18.

Schoenbaum, E., & Webber, M. (1993). The underrecognition of HIV infection in an inner-city emergency room. *American Journal of Public Health, 83*, 363-368.

Schwartz, H. L. (2000). *Dialogues with forgotten voices: Relational perspective on child abuse trauma and treatment of dissociative disorders.* New York: Basic Books.

Seabrook, J. (1996). *Travels in the skin trade: Tourism and the sex industry.* London: Pluto Press.

Silbert, M. H., & Pines, A. M. (1981). Sexual child abuse as an antecedent to prostitution. *Child Abuse & Neglect, 5,* 407-411.

Silbert, M. H. & Pines, A. M. (1982a). Entrance into prostitution. *Youth & Society, 13,* 471-500.

Silbert, M. H. & Pines, A. M. (1982b). Victimization of street prostitutes. *Victimology, 7,* 122-133.

Silbert, M. H. & Pines, A. M. (1983). Early sexual exploitation as an influence in prostitution. *Social Work, 28,* 285-289.

Silbert, M. H., Pines, A. M., & Lynch, T. (1982). *Sexual assault of prostitutes.* San Francisco: National Center for the Prevention and Control of Rape, National Institute of Mental Health, Delancey Street Foundation.

Smolskaya, T., Momot, O. F., Tahkinova, I. P., & Kotova, S. V. (1998). *Behavioral studies and HIV/AIDS prevention policy in Russia.* Paper presented at the 12th World Aids Conference, Geneva. July.

Southwick, S., Yehuda, R., & Morgan, C. (1995). Clinical studies of neurotransmitter alterations in post-traumatic stress disorder. In J. Friedman, D. Charney, & A. Dutch (Eds.), *Neurobiological and clinical consequences of stress: From normal adaptation to posttraumatic stress disorder.* Philadelphia: Lippincott-Raven.

Special Committee on Pornography and Prostitution (1985). *Pornography and prostitution in Canada,* 350.

Spiwak, F. (1999). *Prostitution of women and children in Bogota.* Unpublished Manuscript.

Sturdevant, S., & Stolzfus, B. (1992). *Let the good times roll: Prostitution and the US military in Asia.* New York: The New Press.

Szasz, T. (1980). *Sex by prescription.* New York: Doubleday.

Valera, R. (1999). *Street prostitution, violence, and post-traumatic stress disorder in Washington, D.C.* Master of Arts Thesis submitted to Graduate School of Department of Health Education of University of Maryland. University of Maryland, College Park.

Vanwesenbeeck, I. (1994). *Prostitutes' well-being and risk.* Amsterdam: VU University Press.

Vanwesenbeeck, I., de Graaf, R., van Zessen, G., Straver, C. J. & Visser, J. H. (1995). Professional HIV risk taking, levels of victimization, and well-being in female prostitutes in the Netherlands. *Archives of Sexual Behavior, 24,* 503-515.

Weisberg, D. K. (1985). *Children of the night: A study of adolescent prostitution.* Lexington: Lexington Books.

White, J. W., & Koss, M. P. (1993). Adolescent sexual aggression within heterosexual relationships: Prevalence, characteristics, and causes. In H. E. Barbarize, W. L.

Marshall, & D. R. Laws (Eds.), *The Juvenile Sex Offender*. New York: Guilford Press.

Williams, J. L. (1991). *Sold out: A recovery guide for Prostitutes Anonymous*. 11225 Magnolia Blvd, #181 N. Hollywood Blvd, CA.

Wood, M. (1995). *Just a prostitute*. Queensland: University of Queensland Press.

World Health Organization (1998). *Report on the global HIV/AIDS epidemic*.

EMPOWERMENT: USING CULTURE AND CONTEXT TO ENHANCE AND FACILITATE FEMINIST THERAPY

INTEGRATING SPIRITUALITY, HISTORY, AND WOMEN'S WAYS OF KNOWING INTO THERAPY

Prayer as Interpersonal Coping in the Lives of Mothers with HIV

E. James Baesler
Valerian J. Derlega
Barbara A. Winstead
Anita Barbee

E. James Baesler (PhD, University of Arizona) is Associate Professor of Communication in the Department of Communication and Theatre Arts, Old Dominion University. Valerian J. Derlega (PhD, University of Maryland) is Professor of Social Psychology in the Department of Psychology at Old Dominion University. Barbara A. Winstead (PhD, Harvard University) is Department Chair and Professor of Clinical Psychology in the Department of Psychology at Old Dominion University. Anita Barbee (PhD, University of Georgia) is Associate Professor of Social Work in the School of Social Work at University of Louisville.

Address correspondence to: E. James Baesler, Department of Communication and Theatre Arts, Old Dominion University, Norfolk, VA 23539 (E-mail: jbaesler@odu.edu)

The authors gratefully acknowledge Mary Elizabeth Baesler for assistance in coding the spiritual activities and beliefs of mothers in the sample.

This research is partly supported by research grant # R01DA13145-01A1 from the National Institute on Drug Abuse of the National Institutes of Health.

[Haworth co-indexing entry note]: "Prayer as Interpersonal Coping in the Lives of Mothers with HIV." Baesler, E. James et al. Co-published simultaneously in *Women & Therapy* (The Haworth Press, Inc.) Vol. 26, No. 3/4, 2003, pp. 283-295; and: *Women with Visible and Invisible Disabilities: Multiple Intersections, Multiple Issues, Multiple Therapies* (ed: Martha E. Banks, and Ellyn Kaschak) The Haworth Press, Inc., 2003, pp. 283-295. Single or multiple copies of this article are available for a fee from The Haworth Document Delivery Service [1-800-HAWORTH, 9:00 a.m. - 5:00 p.m. (EST). E-mail address: getinfo@haworthpressinc.com].

283

SUMMARY. The spirituality of 22 mothers diagnosed with HIV was explored through face-to-face interviews and revealed that 95% of the mothers pray. Active prayers (e.g., talking to God by adoring, thanking, confessing, and supplicating) were more frequently reported than receptive prayers (e.g., quietly listening to God, being open, surrendering). Supplicatory or petitionary prayers for help and health were the most frequent type of prayer, and adoration was the least frequent. The majority of mothers in the sample perceived prayer as a positive coping mechanism associated with outcomes such as: support, positive attitude/affect, and peace. Overall, results supported expanding the boundary conditions of the interpersonal coping component of the Social Interaction Model (Derlega & Barbee, 1998) to include the spiritual dimension of prayer. *[Article copies available for a fee from The Haworth Document Delivery Service: 1-800-HAWORTH. E-mail address: <getinfo@haworthpressinc.com> Website: <http://www.HaworthPress.com> © 2003 by The Haworth Press, Inc. All rights reserved.]*

KEYWORDS. Mothers, women, HIV, prayer, religion, spirituality

Many people with HIV live with a kind of invisible disability, an illness that remains unknown to others unless purposely or unintentionally disclosed. With the passage of time HIV, the infection that causes AIDS, becomes increasingly disabling and visible to others in the form of rashes, unintentional weight loss, fatigue, and other health problems (Hoffmann, 1996; Kalichman, 1995). Thus, those living with HIV/AIDS carry a double burden, that of an initially invisible disease which eventually manifests itself through visibly disabling symptoms. In recent years, with the development of antiretroviral combination therapies (Joyce, 1997), many individuals with HIV can live for years without developing any AIDS-defined clinical symptoms. However, there is the stark reality that HIV eventually becomes a disabling and life-threatening disease.

Statistics on HIV in the U.S. population revealed that women comprised about 32% of the reported cases of HIV last year (10,469 cases) according to the Center for Disease Control and Prevention's (CDCP) *HIV/AIDS Surveillance Report* (2000).[1] This trend has remained consistent over the last several years (women made up 32.4% of the HIV cases in 2000, 31.9% in 1999, and 31.9% in 1998 according to CDCP data). As with any serious illness, women living with HIV deal with a number of critical issues: physiological (e.g., health complications), psychological (e.g., anxiety and worry about health, work, and child care), and social (e.g., conflict and disruption in relationships). For physiological issues there is medical treatment, and for psychological and social issues there is individual counseling, group therapy, and a variety of other types of social support including close interpersonal relationships.

The social support coping mechanisms relevant to women living with HIV has been described in the Social Interaction Model of Coping with HIV infection (Derlega & Barbee, 1998). The model described several factors relevant to women coping with HIV: reactions to the diagnosis, self-identity issues, personal coping, interpersonal coping, and outcome issues. The "interpersonal coping" component of the model includes three variables that influence relationship disclosure and seeking social support: (a) characteristics of the HIV-infected person, (b) characteristics of the relationship, and (c) characteristics of partner. The present inquiry proposes to expand the boundary conditions for the "interpersonal coping" component of the model by adding a spiritual/religious dimension. The addition of a spiritual dimension is justifiable for at least two reasons. First, more of the social science disciplines, such as psychology and communication, are arguing for the study of spirituality as a legitimate area of social inquiry in the academy and for the importance of investigating religion/spirituality as a variable in health studies. For instance, a recent issue of *Journal of Community Psychology* presented several articles that proposed the integration of spirituality into community psychology (Hill, 2000), and a recent meta-analysis of 41 research studies found that religious involvement was significantly related to lower mortality (McCullough, Hoyt, Larson, Koenig, & Thoresen, 2000). A second reason for the study of spirituality is that 60% of Americans consider "religion" to be highly important in their lives (Newport & Sand, 1997), and as many as 93% identify themselves as "spiritual" (Zinnbauer et al., 1997). Thus, religion and spirituality are important facets in the lives of most Americans. To further understand the spiritual dimension of interpersonal coping within the context of the Social Interaction Model, the literature relevant to spiritual relationships and prayer was examined.

Spiritual beliefs and experiences, for many individuals in the west, presuppose a relationship between the believer and, for example, Allah (Islam), Yahweh (Judaism), or the Trinity (Christianity). This "relationship with God" is usually created and sustained through some type of communication called prayer. Heiler's (1932) classic work in religion described several characteristics of prayer, including conversation, fellowship, mutual intercourse, and communication. These terms highlight the essential relational quality of prayer, namely that prayer is a social phenomenon reflected by an understanding of close personal relationships such as the relationships between child and mother (Heiler, 1932), bride and bridegroom (Talbot, 1985), and friend to friend (Kempis, 1955). Thus, prayer is a specialized type of communication that occurs in the context of a spiritual relationship.[2] Approximately 90% of Americans report that they pray, according to Gallup poll research, and this percentage has not changed more than plus or minus 2% in the last 40 years (Gallup Organization, 2001). There are a number of examples of prayer occurring in a variety of contexts: (a) personal prayer between an individual believer and God, (b) prayer with a small group of believers and God, and (c) corporate, liturgical, and other types of public prayer. Among these contexts, we chose to limit the scope of this initial inquiry to the personal prayer between a believer and God since this is the fundamental building block for all other types of prayer. In sum, we are interested in exploring the impact of personal prayer in the lives of women living with HIV as one spiritual facet of interpersonal coping in the context of the Social Interaction Model.

The empirical landscape describing the relationship between prayer and HIV is quite sparse with the exception of one study which found that, while HIV-infected women pray more than non HIV-infected women, HIV-infected women reported that prayer is less effective in coping with a "chronic illness" than non HIV-infected women (Biggar et al., 1999). This latter finding deserves some explanation. The mean scores for both HIV and non-HIV women were well above the mid-point of the 1-4 point scale (Ms = 3.65 and 3.88, respectively), meaning that both samples of women believed that prayer *was effective* in coping with chronic illness. In addition to this single study on prayer and HIV, there are a number of empirical studies that examined the relationship between prayer and non-HIV health issues such as chronic pain, life stressors, the death of a spouse, and other medical problems (see review by McCullough, 1995). In general, this line of research on prayer and health has demonstrated the positive impact of frequency of prayer on physiological (e.g., cardiovascular, brain electrical activity, muscle relaxation) and psychological health outcomes (e.g., structure meaning, provide hope, appraisals of stress). One limitation of these research studies on prayer and health is that prayer was operationalized as a single global estimate which does not address the different types of prayer. Perhaps some types of prayers provide more physiological or psychological comfort/relief than others. There is also the possibility that particular types of prayer during an illness can facilitate a closer relationship with God just as one can experience a closer relationship through the pain of working through conflict in human relationships. No research was found that examined the relationship between types of prayer and relationship with God for individuals living with HIV, but some research has examined the relationship between types of prayer and closeness to God.

The only programmatic empirical research on different types of prayer using large samples is the work of Poloma and her associates (Poloma, 1993; Poloma & Gallup, 1991; Poloma & Pendleton, 1991). Poloma et al. asked individuals if they pray in particular ways and found, across all three studies, that meditative prayer was the best predictor of a single item measure for "closeness to God." Among other efforts to categorize various types of prayer, Baesler (1999) described a Model of Interpersonal Prayer[3] that outlines the developmental process of prayer, beginning with active and culminating with receptive prayer. Active prayer emphasizes the "activity" of the believer during prayer such as presenting God with a litany of needs/wants, and trying to resolve some problem by talking it over with God. One way to categorize types of active prayer is to employ a functional typology, describing the purposes of prayer as ACTS: Adoration (worship and praise), Confession (also called reconciliation), Thanksgiving (such as counting one's blessings), and Supplication (petitions for self and others). Other writers on prayer have developed categories of active prayer similar to the ACTS typology (Ai, Dunkle, Peterson, and Bolling, 1998; Kreeft, 1991). In contrast to active prayer, receptive prayer places less emphasis on outward activity and more emphasis on a contemplative attitude of openness, cooperation, and receptivity. The contemplative attitude is generally the fruit of a mature prayer life and predisposes the believer to receive the infusion of God's grace, described in the Interpersonal Prayer Model as a range of experiences from gentle/peaceful to rapture/ecstasy.

In summary, prayer as a spiritual dimension of interpersonal coping in the lives of women living with HIV will be tested and explored through the following hypotheses and research questions:

H1:   The majority of women living with HIV will engage in more active than receptive types of prayer.

RQ1: What is the rank order frequency for active prayers as denoted by the ACTS prayer typology (adoration, confession, thanksgiving, and supplication), and what is the rank order frequency of particular types of receptive prayers?

H2:   The majority of women living with HIV will report that prayer functions as a positive interpersonal coping mechanism.

RQ2: How do women living with HIV describe their relationship with God?

RQ3: In addition to prayer, are there other spiritual activities reported by women living with HIV that assist them in coping with their illness?

METHOD

Participants

Twenty-five mothers[4] (64% African American and 36% European American) ranging in age from 18-54 years (average age 35 years) were recruited from HIV/AIDS service organizations in Virginia during 1997-1998. The participants had known their diagnoses for 1-12 years (average 5 years).

Interviews

Semi-structured interviews lasting from 60-90 minutes were conducted by the second author as part of a larger study (Winstead et al., 2001). One of the questions asked participants about their "spiritual beliefs." This open ended question was designed to determine if prayer emerges with sufficient frequency to be considered an important dimension of mothers' spiritual life. Participants were also asked how having HIV had affected their close relationships, including their relationship with God. If the premise that prayer is the spiritual communication link in an interpersonal relationship between the believer and God, then participants will not only reveal that they pray, but also how prayer functions (positively or negatively) in coping with HIV. This question was also designed to explore the quality of mothers' relationship with God. After collecting the data, all of the interviews were transcribed and a coding scheme was inductively developed to identify all of the issues that emerged in the data. Two trained coders independently rated the issues in terms of frequency with coder percentage agreement ranging from 80-100%. The spiritual issues in the coding scheme were categorized by the first author into various spiritual subcategories such as types of prayer, types of coping, and so on. Samples of the subcategories were independently coded by one other individual and compared to authors' coding, resulting in inter-coder reliability (Phi coefficient; Scott, 1955) ranging from .73-.95. The results section includes excerpts from the original narratives to illustrate the content of the spiritual subcategories based on the coding scheme.

RESULTS

Of the 22 participants who were asked about their spirituality, 95% of them reported engaging in one or more activities that could be classified as personal prayer. Prayer was described by 18 of the 22 mothers using the term prayer or a derivative thereof (e.g., prayed, praying), three respondents used other terms to describe prayer as "talking to God," "feeling God's presence," and "worship," and one participant did not describe any activity related to prayer, maintaining that, ". . . it [religion] wasn't a big issue." Fifteen participants disclosed information regarding the frequency of their prayer with 93% praying at least once a day (e.g., "once a day," "every single day," "on a daily basis"). Several participants reported praying more than once a day (e.g., "every morning and every evening," "constantly," "all the time"). Based on a total of 65 responses related to prayer, 83% were categorized as active prayer and 9% receptive prayer (8% unclassifiable) (see Table 1). These frequency estimates support H1, indicating that the majority of mothers living with HIV engaged in more active than receptive prayers.

RQ1 was addressed by performing frequency counts for the subcategories of active and receptive types of prayer. The rank order frequency (low to high) for active prayers accounted for by the ACTS typology was as follows: adoration, confession, thanksgiving, and supplication (see Table 1 for percentages). The rank order frequency (low to high) for receptive prayers was: silence, feeling God's presence, and surrender to God (e.g., "put in God's hands," "turn it over to God," "give it to Him"). Of the 31 supplicatory prayers, the most common content themes were prayers for the health of self and others (23% of all prayers), and help of various kinds not related to health (e.g., guidance, safe travel, financial, worries) (25% of all prayers). There were 21 additional responses that could not be classified by the ACTS functional typology since the content of the prayer was not specified, but given the information regarding the prayer "form," all but one of these prayers could be categorized as active types of prayer (see Table 1).

TABLE 1. Prayer Types by Percentage and Frequency

Active Prayers	Percent		Receptive Prayers	Percent	
Supplication	47.7	(31)	Surrender	4.6	(3)
Talking to God	18.5	(12)	Feeling God's Presence	3.1	(2)
Thanksgiving	6.2	(4)	Silence	1.5	(1)
Crying	4.6	(3)	Subtotal	9.2	(6)
Confession	3.1	(2)			
Adoration	1.5	(1)			
Singing	1.5	(1)			
Subtotal	83.1	(54)			

Note. Percentages were based on a total of 65 prayer responses from 21 mothers living with HIV. Numbers in parentheses represented frequency counts. One type of prayer was unclassifiable (praying on one's knees, 7.7% (5)).

H2, predicting that prayer functions to help women living with HIV cope with their illness and life in a variety of positive ways, was supported. Mothers with HIV turned to God via supplicatory prayers for help and health in 48% of the prayer responses. In addition, participants attributed particular positive outcomes in their life to the action of God as facilitated by prayer. Positive outcomes that represented a theme of general spiritual support (frequency = 17) included: "God is helping me," "God takes the burden off me," "God keeps me going," "Prayer is helping me cope," "After prayer things just work out." Along with spiritual support, other common themes suggesting that prayer functions as a positive coping mechanism were: positive attitude (e.g., "feel good," "life is more positive," "feel happy," "enjoy life," "feeling blessed") (frequency = 18), sense of peace ("peace of mind," "peace in my heart," "load off my heart," "more peaceful") (frequency = 9), and improved health ("health got better," "not as sick," "feel healthy") (frequency = 7). We noted two cases of mothers who reported praying but did not perceive prayer as a positive coping mechanism, describing their experiences of prayer as: frustrating ("I can't finish [my prayer]," "My mind wanders"), confusing ("It's just so confusing with Him [God]"), and uncertain ("I don't know [re: help from God]").

Beyond the observations that a majority of the participants affirmed a belief in God, and that they were in relationships with God, there was not much specific information on the quality of participants' relationships with God to answer RQ2. Several participants reported positive images associated with God, such as Creator, Healer, Father, and All

Loving, which suggested that their relationship with God was a positive one. But, beyond indirect support for the idea of a benevolent God that helps them cope with HIV and life, the data are not explicit enough to describe any details of mothers' relationships with God.

RQ3 asked if there were any other spiritual activities in addition to prayer that might help mothers cope with HIV. The spiritual activity of church attendance[5] was the only theme that emerged with sufficient frequency to answer RQ3. Frequency of church attendance was reported by 14 of the 22 participants. Twelve of the 14 mothers reported attending church, and two participants did not attend church. Representative responses for the 55% of mothers that attended church were phrased as follows: "I started going to church," "I go to church more often," or simply "I go to church." Among these responses three participants reported feelings of "love," "specialness," and "support" by the church members or congregation. We also noted two reports where social support was *not* evident in the church, possibly due to the stigma associated with HIV that resulted in negative consequences for two of the mothers (reaction of "fear" by a pastor, and refusal to baptize by immersion).

DISCUSSION

Women living with HIV were asked a series of questions related to types of social support and, in response to an open ended query regarding their spiritual beliefs and practices, many women reported that their *relationship with God* was an important type of interpersonal support that helped them cope with their illness. What is noteworthy about this finding is that the majority of women discussed their personal *prayer lives* vis-à-vis their relationships with God. Specifically, 95% of the mothers living with HIV engaged in one or more activities that could be described as prayer, the spiritual communication between a believer and God. While the 95% figure from this study appeared somewhat higher than Poloma and Gallup's (1991) national survey finding that 91% of women pray, the qualitative data from the specialized sample in this study is not statistically comparable to the quantitative polling data from Poloma and Gallup's sample. However, at least one study (Biggar et al., 1999) has shown that women with HIV pray more ($M = 4.43$ on a 1-5 scale, 5 = pray several times a day, $n = 99$) than a comparable sample of women without HIV ($M = 4.08$), $t(203) = 2.39$, $p < .05$.

We expected in H1, and the data supported, that active prayers (especially supplication) were more typical than receptive prayers in this sample of mothers living with HIV. Given the myriad of life changing issues that HIV creates, turning to God for support via supplicatory prayer seemed logical, but why were receptive prayers in comparison so infrequently reported (only 9% of the total prayers)? According to the Interpersonal Prayer Model, receptive prayer is the fruit of a mature prayer life. Spiritual growth generally progresses over the course of time from "active only" prayers to "receptive and active" prayers. For at least one-third of the sample, participants reported recently beginning a relationship with God or renewing their relationship with God. Thus, these relationships have not developed the growth needed to sustain a receptive life of prayer. For others in the sample, perhaps the receptive prayers of quiet, simplicity, and openness were not modeled or taught to them. Future research could test the model's hypothesis that women with mature relationships with God engage in more receptive types of prayer than those with less mature relationships.

Not all types of active prayer were reported with equal frequency. For instance, the active prayer of adoration was reported only once in the sample of 65 reports of various types and forms of prayer. This is unfortunate since the prayer of adoration has been shown to predict closeness/intimacy with God better than any other type of active prayer in Poloma and Gallup's national study (1991)[6] and in a study of two samples of college students (ns = 84 and 107, Baesler, 2001). There were several instances in the present investigation of mothers' reporting a desire for a closer relationship with God. To address this need, future research might explore different models for teaching/learning various types of prayer and then evaluate their effectiveness in facilitating a closer relationship with God.

Consistent with McCollough's (1995) finding that prayer generally functioned as a positive psychological coping mechanism for non-HIV illnesses, this investigation found that prayer functioned as a positive interpersonal coping mechanism for mothers living with HIV. One explanation for this finding is that, in cases of serious illness such as HIV, individuals experience a shift of priorities. Material things become less important and relationships become vitally important. As individuals turn to others for social support during their illness, so too, for people of faith, there is a turning to God in prayer for spiritual support. Several findings from the present data supported this line of reasoning. All but one participant in the sample reported that they engaged in one or more forms of active prayer. When the content of these prayers were analyzed, many participants asked God for guidance, help, and good health in addition to thanking God for blessings. There was a sense of optimism in the attitudes of the majority of women as they described the specific outcomes of prayer and their attribution to God's work in their life: feeling supported by God, a positive attitude, a sense of peace, and physical health. These results are also consistent with the finding by Biggar et al. (1999) that women living with HIV rated prayer as an effective method of coping with HIV. Related to these positive outcomes were descriptions of positive images of God as: creator, healer, father, and all loving. Within the overall positive portrait of the effects of prayer, we noted two cases in which mothers reported that prayer was *not* a helpful coping mechanism, producing feelings of frustration, confusion, and uncertainty.

In summary, the frequency, type, content, and outcomes associated with the personal prayer lives of women living with HIV in this sample supported the claim that prayer generally functions as a positive interpersonal coping mechanism. Thus, we recommend the expansion of the Social Interaction Model to include prayer as a spiritual dimension of interpersonal coping. In addition to prayer, attendance at church services was another type of spiritual support reported by 12 of the 22 mothers. Curiously, the two participants that reported *not* attending church both indicated that they still pray, and that their reason for not attending church was: "You don't have to go to Church to praise God" and "I don't need Church because God's already in the [my] house." Future research could examine church attendance by religion/denomination to uncover the dynamics of prayer during church services that might impact coping with HIV.

The present investigation of the prayer lives of mothers living with HIV represents the recognition and renewed interest of spirituality as a legitimate area of inquiry in the social sciences. The benefits of exploring spirituality as an important variable in the field of women's health in this study had theoretical and practical implications. Theoretically, the finding that women with HIV pray in the context of a personal relationship with God provided evidence for the inclusion of a spiritual dimension in the Social Interaction Model of coping with HIV, and the active and receptive prayer categories posited by the Interpersonal Prayer Model were able to account for the majority of prayers. Pragmatically, the findings showed that prayer generally functioned in a positive manner, assisting mothers in coping with their illness and life. Perhaps future research can investigate how specific types of prayer function to help mothers cope with HIV.

NOTES

1. CDC data for women included U. S. states reporting adolescent and adult cases of HIV which had *not* developed into AIDS.

2. The human-Divine relationship has similarities with human interpersonal relationships, including: (a) dyadic relationship between entities developing over time, (b) initial intent to communicate, and (c) specific types of communication. There are also points of contrast, including: (a) the nature of the relational beings, (b) locus of initial intent, and (c) empirical verifiability of communication (see Baesler, 1999).

3. The original model was entitled, "Interpersonal Christian Prayer Model" (Baesler, 1999). The current version of the model reads, "Relational Prayer Model" (Baesler, 2001).

4. Of the 25 participants, 22 were asked about their spiritual beliefs; thus, results were based on 22 of the original participants.

5. All of the mothers who disclosed information relating to religious/spiritual activities with others used the term "church" or "congregation." None reported other places of religious worship (e.g., synagogue, mosque, or temple).

6. Poloma and Gallup's term "meditative prayer" represented a cluster of prayers: thinking about God, feeling God's presence, worshiping and adoring God, and listening to God speak. "Worshiping and adoring God" in meditative prayer directly corresponded with the active prayer of adoration in the present study.

REFERENCES

Ai, A. L., Dunkle, R. E., Peterson, C., & Bolling, S. F. (1998). The role of private prayer in psychological recovery among mid-life and aged patients following cardiac surgery. *Gerontologist, 38,* 591-601.

Baesler, E. J. (1999). A model of interpersonal Christian prayer. *Journal of Communication and Religion, 22,* 40-64.

Baesler, E. J. (2001). *Prayer and relationship with God: Two tests of the Relational Prayer Model.* Manuscript submitted for publication, Old Dominion University.

Biggar, H., Forehand, R., Devine, D., Brody, G., Armistead, L., Morse, E., & Simon, P. (1999). Women who are HIV infected: The role of religious activity in psychosocial adjustment. *AIDS Care, 11,* 195-199.

Center for Disease Control and Prevention. (2000). *HIV/AIDS Surveillance Report, 12.* [On-line]. Available: http://www.cdc.gov/hiv/stats/hasr1201/table6.htm.

Derlega, V., & Barbee, A. (1998). What is the impact of the HIV infection on individuals' social interactions and relationships? In V. Derlega & A. Barbee (Eds.), *HIV and social interaction* (pp. 1-11). Thousand Oaks, CA: Sage.

Gallup Organization (2001). *Poll releases: As nation observes National Day of Prayer, 9 in 10 pray–3 in 4 daily* [On-line]. Available: http://www.gallup.com/poll/releases/pr990506.asp.

Heiler, R. (1932). *Prayer: A study in the history and psychology of religion.* London: Oxford University Press.

Hill, J. (2000). A rationale for the integration of spirituality into community psychology. *Journal of Community Psychology, 28,* 139-149.

Hoffman, M. A. (1996). *Counseling clients with HIV disease: Assessment, intervention, and prevention.* New York: Guilford.

Joyce, M. (1997, July 15). AIDS deaths drop by 19 percent. *Virginian-Pilot,* pp. A1, A12.

Kalichman, S. C. (1995). *Understanding AIDS: A guide for mental health professionals.* Washington, DC: American Psychological Association.

Kempis, T. (1955). *The imitation of Christ.* (Richard Witford, Trans.). NY: Image Books. (Original work published 1530).

Kreeft, P. (1991). *Prayer: Conversing with God.* Grand Rapids, MI: Zondervan.

McCullough, M. E. (1995). Prayer and health: Conceptual issues, research review, and research agenda. *Journal of Psychology and Theology, 23,* 15-29.

McCullough, M., Hoyt, W., Larson, D., Koenig, H., & Thoresen, C. (2000). Religious involvement and mortality: A meta-analytic review. *Health Psychology, 19,* 211-222.

Newport, F., & Sand, L. (1997). *Religious faith is widespread but many skip church: Little change in recent years.* The Gallup Organization [On-line]. Available: http://www.198.175.140.8/POLL_ARCHIVES/970329.htm.

Poloma, M. (1993). The effects of prayer on mental well-being. *Second Opinion: Health, Faith, and Ethics, 18,* 37-51.

Poloma, M., & Gallup, G., Jr. (1991). *Varieties of prayer: A survey report.* Philadelphia: Trinity Press.

Poloma, M., & Pendleton, B. F. (1991). The effects of prayer and prayer experiences on measures of general well-being. *Journal of Psychology and Theology, 19,* 71-83.

Scott, W. A. (1955). Reliability of content analysis: The case of nominal scale coding. *Public Opinion Quarterly, 19,* 321-325.

Talbot, M. (1985). *The lover and the beloved: A way of Franciscan prayer.* NY: Crossroad Publishing.

Winstead, B. A., Derlega, V., Barbee, A., Sachdedev, M., Antle, B., & Greene, K. (2001). *Impact of HIV on the close relationships of mothers living with HIV.* Manuscript submitted for publication, Old Dominion University, Virginia Consortium Program in Clinical Psychology, University of Louisville, & East Carolina University.

Zinnbauer, B., Pargament, K., Cole, B., Rye, M., Butter, E., Belavich, T., Hipp, K., Scott, A., & Kadar, J. (1997). Religion and spirituality: Unfuzzying the fuzzy. *Journal for the Scientific Study of Religion, 36,* 549-564.

The Call of the Wild Woman:
Models of Healing

Marie A. DiCowden

SUMMARY. Women have a longstanding and unique connection to healing and health care. The feminine perspective, however, has been discounted and decimated through the last 600 years. Now general social and political changes, as well as increasing numbers of women practitioners in health and mental health, are leading to a re-emergence of the feminine perspective in addressing women's needs and in providing health care. This paper traces some of the elements in the history of women and their influences on present day models of health care. It emphasizes women's roles as healers, as patients and as crafters of a new synthesis of health care delivery in the 21st century. *[Article copies available for a fee from The Haworth Document Delivery Service: 1-800-HAWORTH. E-mail address: <getinfo@haworthpressinc.com> Website: <http://www.HaworthPress.com> © 2003 by The Haworth Press, Inc. All rights reserved.]*

KEYWORDS. Healing, healthcare community, mind/body, patriarchy, matriarchy, wild/wise woman

---

Marie A. DiCowden, PhD, is Founder and Executive Director of The Biscayne Institutes of Health & Living, Inc. She holds Adjunct Professorships at the University of Miami School of Medicine and Saybrook Graduate School.

Address correspondence to: Dr. DiCowden, The Biscayne Institutes of Health & Living, Inc., 2785 N.E. 183rd Street, Miami, FL 33160.

Thanks to Dr. Marc Pilisuk for his comments on this article.

[Haworth co-indexing entry note]: "The Call of the Wild Woman: Models of Healing." DiCowden, Marie A. Co-published simultaneously in *Women & Therapy* (The Haworth Press, Inc.) Vol. 26, No. 3/4, 2003, pp. 297-310; and: *Women with Visible and Invisible Disabilities: Multiple Intersections, Multiple Issues, Multiple Therapies* (ed: Martha E. Banks, and Ellyn Kaschak) The Haworth Press, Inc., 2003, pp. 297-310. Single or multiple copies of this article are available for a fee from The Haworth Document Delivery Service [1-800-HAWORTH, 9:00 a.m. - 5:00 p.m. (EST). E-mail address: getinfo@haworthpressinc.com].

297

MODELS OF HEALING

Illness and injury are universal experiences. Depending upon the culture and the times in which people live, the understanding of why illness and injury occur differs. Krippner and Welch (1992) provide an excellent analysis of early and varied models of healing. It is clear from their review that earlier models of healing included a major component embracing a spiritual dimension. Shamanic work from all cultures, e.g., Chicano curanderos, Pima Indians, and native healers from Fiji, was enhanced by a concept of spirituality. The energy of that belief system was seen as an integral part in both cause and cure of illness.

Traditional Chinese medicine (Beinfield & Korngold, 1991) has also embraced a concept of energy related to spirituality in its healing model. Spiritual flow of life energy known as Chi is a critical element in applying appropriate herbal remedies and acupuncture. In addition, the Chinese model of healing also included a concept of balance among the five elements that make up the individual: fire, water, wood, metal, and air. These elements, imbued with Chi, were seen as integral to the individual's health. The natural environment, including the energy flow of inanimate as well as animate objects, was considered to affect the balance of the elements, and was also part of the Chinese healing model.

Only in the last several hundred years have we developed a model of illness and healing which has focused on a mind/body dualism. The evolution of modern history and science has led to an understanding of the etiology of illness, and the appropriate treatment to apply, as dissected from the whole. Modern allopathic models have embraced the approach to treating trauma and disease of the body as separate and distinct from treating issues of the mind. In the last twenty years, research and development in modern chemistry have emphasized issues of the mind as more subject to applications of chemical cures that effect the bodily structure of the brain, rather than addressing the process of the mind itself in combination with the electrochemical system.

THE WILD WOMAN AS HEALER

Until modern times, women have historically taken a lead role in healing practices. Women's natural link to the mysteries of childbirth inextricably intertwined women with the mysteries of life and death and all aspects in-between. Women from earliest times took part in the rituals that combined religious aspects of those mysteries with healing ceremonies. During the Middle Ages, the primary focus in the Western world was on healing traditions as practiced by women.

Historical accounts from Europe and the British Isles indicate that, from A.D. 500 through A.D. 1300, women were the primary healers, using combinations of herbal remedies and colorful and imaginative rituals to cure and to maintain health (Achterberg, 1985). Women used both non-rational personal rituals and herbal extracts for healing, as ways of combining both their imagination and their reason, to reach all aspects of the individual. The archetype of the Wild Woman/Wise Woman as healer was not only known in Europe and the British Isles. In *Women Who Run with the Wolves*, Pinkola Estes (1992) has chronicled stories from many societies and countries that give flesh and form to the concept of the Wild Woman/Wise Woman and her medicine–a medicine that embraces a holistic approach. The powerful, passionate, healing Force captured in these stories indeed underscores that it is both the non-rational intuitive combined with specific earthly aspects of knowledge which unleash the powerful mysteries of life and death. And, as the patient hangs in the balance, it is this same Force that facilitates healing.

Achterberg (1985) stated that women characteristically have a unique perspective as health providers. In the Middle Ages, women healers often focused on three unique factors that distinguished the feminine approach to healing: intuition, an underlying concept of unity, and communication. Women's regard for the natural intuitive forces of healing residing within each individual, as well as the specific herbal remedies that developed throughout the years, underscored a holistic connection that unified all forms of life. Communication through personal instruction in herbs passed from one generation to the next, as well as the stories and incantations that communicated the more soulful expressions of healing, which were also revered and valued. Truly the Wild Woman/Wise Woman was a notable holistic practitioner of both an intuitive and empirically based type of health care.

When the political power structure of the patriarchy began to emerge through the Church, and in governments in Europe, England and the Americas, these native healing women and their approach to health and healing began to be discounted. In 1518, The College of Physicians was established and clearly defined those who could not practice medicine–this included women. Medicine became the purview of a male elite and was available only to the more exclusive members of society. Great masses of the poor, who could only have access to non-licensed healers, were also prohibited from seeking folk medicine as practiced by women as women's approach to healing was determined "magic"–which was expressly forbidden during that time (Achterberg, 1985).

In the midst of outlawing women's approach to healing, one of the most horrific events in the history of women occurred. That was the Great Witch Hunt. It has been estimated that as many as nine million women were condemned and slaughtered between 1500 and 1650. Women were an easy focus because of their tendency to affiliate, which often occurred in the market place, around wells, and in carrying out basic tasks of village life, e.g., baking, sewing and birthing. This affiliation was seen as a threat which could lead to the organization of women and create a potential for women's economic and political influence. This influence and control, along with women's effect on the masses and their power to heal, made them threats to and clear targets of the shifting political and economic forces moving from matriarchy to patriarchy.

Women were also prejudicially cited for insatiable sexual energies. This energy was linked to the innate power perceived in women, who by biological virtue of being women, had the ability for childbirth. This ability was often equated to power over life. Early cultures worshipped women for this ability by revering goddesses and consorts of the Horned One. However, as society developed in complexity, with the evolving division of labor between men and women, and as epidemics such as The Great Plague ravaged England and Europe, women's connection to life-giving power, their attendant sexual demands, and the connection to life and death came under scrutiny and suspicion.

In her dramatic discussion of the fate of Wild Women/Wise Women at the hands of the growing patriarchy during this time, Achterberg (1985) recounts some chilling facts. In Wurzburg, Germany, 900 women were killed in one year alone. Near Como, Italy, one hundred were killed in one year. In Toulouse, France, 400 were murdered in one day. And, in 1585, in the Bishopric of Trier, only one woman was left in each of two villages. By virtue of slaughter, women's influence was decimated in home life and village life. Women who were put to death often had their goods and holdings divided among their accusers–thus, further eroding women's political and economic influence.

By thoroughly unseating women's power and influence professionally and economically, the patriarchy severely altered the value system that revered and embraced the intuitive and non-rational by taking the non-rational to paranoid, fanatic proportions and turning it against women themselves. The beliefs underlying the Great Witch Hunt are an ironic testimony to the power of the non-rational to influence life and death. This routing of women's influence further impacted women's approach and contribution to healing. And that loss has continued to haunt medicine's legacy over the last five hundred years.

The paradigm of science was shifting along with political and economic paradigms. Women were caught between the shifting planes of these moving paradigms. Wholesale purging of the non-rational and intuitive approaches to life eliminated women's threat and their purported ignorance to make way for a new world based on Newtonian science.

THE WHEEL TURNS

The Age of Reason and the scientific method have ushered in 500 years in which attempts to dissect elements of the intuitive and dispose of the non-rational have prevailed. Originally, women were outlawed from these scientific and medical pursuits. However, women, eventually learned to package elements of the Wild Woman/Wise Woman's knowledge in strictly rational terms. Despite this sojourn into purely reasoned logic professionally, the slow process of restoring the Wild Woman/Wise Woman's fuller awareness and influence began to evolve.

However, to exist at all the Wild Woman/Wise Woman has had to allow herself to be seduced by approaches that delegitimized the intuitive altogether and embraced only the empirical. Now, after centuries of seduction by the rational, the energy to re-establish the equivalent importance of the non-rational is resurfacing. Despite the banishment of the Wild Woman/Wise Woman, and her holistic view of unity that joined the intuitive and the empirical, the pendulum is swinging and the paradigm is shifting again.

Quantum physics has evolved as a counterpoint to Newtonian science. More recently joining both views with superstring theory, we are moving into a new era of understanding the connection between what, at first, appeared to be mutually exclusive concepts (Greene, 2000). Evidence for these shifting paradigms in thinking can be found in many areas. The holographic/holomovement model lends credence to the scientific method of the ancient Wild Woman/Wise Woman's understanding of an inner order for all properties. This inner or implicate order runs through and unifies all aspects of the universe (Bell, 1988; Bohm, 1987; Pribram, 1977) echoing the old feminine belief in an underlying concept of unity.

The understanding of this model is moving into multiple aspects of psychology, medicine, and health care. It is now allowing us to begin to understand how consciousness and matter are intertwined in the body. The growing body of literature in psychoneuroimmunology and psychophysiology has clearly documented the differential impact of social stressors and supports in individual health and illness (Pelletier, 1977; Wickramasekera, 1994, 1998; Wickramasekera, Davies, & Davies, 1996). Extensive work is also available not only connecting the mind with consciousness and matter within the individual, but to society in a larger context. Healing, as a part of a larger social context, has always been known by the ancient practitioners, particularly the Wild Women/Wise Women. The enunciation of this understanding in modern research terminology has been appearing in peer-reviewed journals and general literature since the 1970s (Cobb, 1976; Pilisuk & Froland, 1978; Tolsdorf, 1976). As early as 1976, Cassell examined populations for a wide-range of diseases and found that those individuals with the greatest incident of pathology were persons who had either been low on social support or recently lost their customary supports. In the early 1980s the need and establishment of supportive networks, particularly for the mentally ill and for the elderly, came more clearly into focus (Pilisuk & Minkler, 1980; Pilisuk, Parks, Kelley, & Turner, 1982). By the mid-1980s, professional literature reflected a need for social connectedness and caring relationships as a means to directly affect health and disease resistance. Infrastructure related to family and friendship, as well as assistance at school and work, were all seen as mediators of the immune system (Broadhead, Kaplan, & James, 1983; Pilisuk, Boyland, & Aciedolo, 1987; Pilisuk & Parks, 1986).

Evidence of the general public acknowledgement of the role of the non-rational combined with the empirically based and rational is seen in the Eisenberg et al. (1993) study indicating that 13.7 billion dollars a year is spent on alternative health care as opposed to strictly allopathic care. An updated study by Eisenberg et al. (1998) showed that figure has increased to over 21 billion dollars. Recent research by the American Psychological Association (1995) also indicated that 85% of the general public recognizes the connection between emotional issues and physical health. The development of the American Holistic Medical Association over the last ten years, spearheaded by the surgeon Norman Shealy, MD, as well as the founding of the Integrative Medicine Program at the University of Arizona by Andrew Weil, MD, underscores the current movement within the health professions that validates the

Wild Woman/Wise Woman's ancient approach of combining the non-rational and empirical.

Women as healers, and our holistic, intuitive approach to healing, have been discounted for centuries. It is no wonder that women as patients then, in acute care or in rehabilitation settings, have had so little of their specific needs addressed. Now that the wheel is turning once again, it is important that women, in voicing needs as patients and in making contributions as healers, step forward as Wild Women/Wise Women (Gilligan, 1983). We must seek to integrate story and the non-rational as equally important medicine as the medicine that derives from the advance of the rational, scientific method. We must not commit in reverse the error of past history by discounting or purging rational empiricism. Our job is much more challenging. Our job is one of synthesis as well as analysis. We must again weave the power of the numinous into the fabric of rational healing. The substance of health care and the way in which health care is delivered could well benefit from a review of the Wild Woman/Wise Woman's legacy of the past, where unity, family, community, touch, story, music and prayers were equally as attended to as medicines, herbs and physical interventions.

THE LADY OF THE LAKE RE-EMERGES

In the late 19th Century and over the course of the 20th Century, feminine perspective and influence have continued to re-emerge and impact the general culture. Beginning with early writers, such as George Eliot, who had to disguise her own gender under a masculine pen name, and Virginia Woolf to more recent writers, such as Alice Walker and Joanna Macy, women's issues in relationship to health and mental health have become more defined. In addition to her magnificent fiction, Walker (1998) has clearly documented the importance of women in preserving the health of community and culture. She has also been a vociferous advocate for women's rights and contributions to healing, speaking strongly against the practice of genital mutilation of women that continues even in certain present day cultures. Such mutilation is a direct assault on women's health, the ability to promote health for others and the basic biological attributes of the mystery of women's sexuality and life/death connection. Joanna Macy (1991), women's advocate and social activist, has also written eloquently about the contribution of the Wild Woman/ Wise Woman to issues of personal health as connected to the larger concept of health of humankind and the health of our planet, Mother Earth.

The Wild Woman/Wise Woman's message has also begun to be heard in our political system. Appointments in the last twenty years of the first female Surgeon General and female Secretary of Health in the United States are clearly history making. In the last decade, Hillary Clinton, as First Lady and now as Senator, has championed the health needs of women and children as well as the community-at-large. In a very visible way, she has helped to bring the Wild Woman/Wise Woman's message closer to the emerging political consciousness of women and men in our country.

Concurrently, within the health professions, we have begun to see a growth in the number of women who pursue professional training and who practice in health professions. The American Psychological Association (2001) reports a 12% increase in the number of women receiving doctorates in psychology over the last ten years. In 1998, 47.7% of APA members were women. Although only 34% of the members of Division 22, Rehabilitation Psychology, are women, this division has also shown an increase in the number of women pursuing the healing profession in an area of psychology that closely combines mind and body.

Literature published by the American Medical Women's Association (2001) indicates an increase in the number of women physicians in this country. In 1998, 23% of practicing physicians were women and the growth rate of women physicians is estimated at 7% over the next ten years. It is of note that while the number of female health care providers has increased in both the mental health and health fields, the rate of increase of women physicians has been considerably slower than the rate of increase of doctoral level women psychologists. Vestiges of the Wild Woman/Wise Woman's disenfranchisement, as a healer of the body as well as the mind, still echo the sentiments of The College of Physicians over 580 years later.

THE HEALTHCARE COMMUNITY©

There is evidence, however, of change. Evidence exists in the growth of numbers of women in the health care professions overall. Change is being acknowledged by both women and men in general, in social and political life. And change is also evident in the development and growth of expanded models of health care delivery that reflect a more feminine perspective.

The HealthCare Community© structure, which has emerged over the last decade, is one such model that heralds this change. It has been informed by a feminine approach to health care delivery. The prototype of the HealthCare Community©, developed at the Biscayne Institutes of Health and Living, Inc., is located in Miami, Florida. This model of health care (Figure 1) provides a full continuum of integrative health care under one roof. By the creation of a community, within the community-at-large, that combines health in all respects, both adults and children are treated by many disciplines working in a team context. Preventive health and wellness programs are provided in this model, along with general integrative family care and daily rehabilitation for more serious problems, such as brain injury, spinal cord injury and chronic disease.

FIGURE 1. The HealthCare Community© Structure

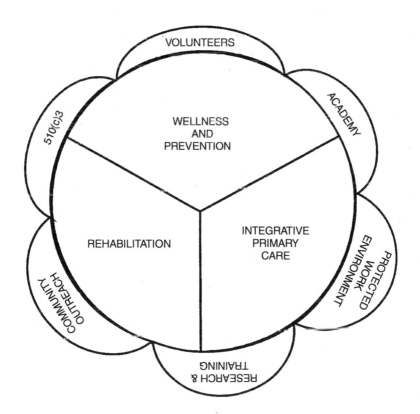

Although the Biscayne rehabilitation program is provided in an expanded concept of health care delivery, it maintains all standards and accreditations for the highest recognition offered to rehabilitation facilities. It is a federally designated Comprehensive Outpatient Rehabilitation Facility (CORF). It holds accreditation by the Commission on Accreditation of Rehabilitation Facilities (CARF) as both an Adult and Pediatric Brain Injury Program and an Adult and Pediatric Outpatient Medical Rehabilitation program. In Florida, where Medicaid services are administered through the State, Biscayne Institutes' HealthCare Community© model holds a Medicaid waiver as a private facility to provide needed health care to an underprivileged population. Biscayne Institutes is also a State designated provider by Florida's Brain and Spinal Cord Injury Council, meeting the accreditation standards for both adults and children.

However, in addition to meeting stringent standards of care in the current medical system, numerous aspects evidence the Wild Woman/ Wise Woman's influence on this model of health care delivery. Beginning with demographics alone, a preponderance of feminine influence can be noted. Overall, 80% of the personnel at Biscayne Institutes are women. In clinical services, 85% are female health care providers. In administration, 75% are female. Biscayne students trained in many disciplines, e.g., psychology, neuropsychology, physical and occupational therapy, speech therapy, social work, etc., average 66% female.

Within the rehabilitation program, specifically, there is an underlying feminine emphasis on unity and community. There is an equal focus on the broader aspects of the individual's rehabilitation within the context of their community role as there is on increasing the individual's function. Indeed, the mission statement for rehabilitation at Biscayne provides a mandate to "rehabilitate for life, not merely rehabilitate for function." Psychology heads the teams within this HealthCare Community© rehabilitation model. The medical personnel, as well as other disciplines that more directly intervene physiologically, work within the context of treating the person who has the disability as opposed to treating the disability that a person has. In the Brain Injury Program, incorporation of the arts, including art therapy and music as part of cognitive retraining, are core to re-establishing the person's capacities. Specialized groups, that emphasize the "story" of the individual's life and trauma, are highly emphasized.

In Florida, where traditional Chinese medicine practitioners are licensed as general physicians, T.C.M. (Traditional Chinese Medicine) is also part of the team along with orthopedics, neurology and other allopathic specialties. Discussions of herbal remedies as well as acupuncture occurs at rounds, along with discussions of range of motion, need for surgical intervention, prescription drugs, the patient's marital issues, sexual functioning, schooling, work life, self-image, depression, and other aspects of physical/emotional/social well-being.

Figure 1 also denotes the continuum of care in the context of other components of the HealthCare Community©. Because health care and rehabilitation are embedded in a larger community context, additional programs on the physical premises are integrated with rehabilitation services. These programs include: an Academy for children from kindergarten through the 12th grade; a protected work environment; a volunteer program for rehabilitation graduates as well as volunteers from the community-at-large. Patients in the HealthCare Community© milieu also are always interacting with representatives of the community-at-large in wellness and prevention programs as part of their ongoing rehabilitation. A particular emphasis of the Community Outreach Programs, as part of this HealthCare Community© structure, provides a direct interface with the larger community and interweaving patient rehabilitation with outside schools, work settings, elderly living facilities and other community structures, e.g., The Kiwanis Club, which meets on-site, and other non-profit organizations.

Another highly important aspect of this model is that its focus is on health and quality of daily living–which includes an emphasis on beauty. The physical structure in which the HealthCare Community© is housed emphasizes wellness and attractive surroundings. It provides a marked departure from traditional hospital, rehabilitation and clinic settings. There is an emphasis on soft colors, beautiful furniture and lighting. Natural light, through floor to ceiling windows, clerestory windows and skylights are used throughout. Incandescent and halogen lighting are also used whenever possible. Carefully selected music, which can be individually controlled at local targeted treatment areas, is also integral to healing within the HealthCare Community© space.

Outside landscaping, that provides blooming plants at alternating times of the year, a meditation garden, and fountains, with the calming sound of running water, is also used. As part of their rehabilitation, the children in the special school located on the HealthCare Community© premises have constructed a Butterfly Garden as part of a cognitive retraining and science project. The addition of an ongoing habitat for numerous butterflies, as well as a resting place for migrating butterflies, has had a magical, transforming effect not only on the children but on adult patients and staff as well. It provides a daily physical and scientifically-based reminder of hope and the possibilities inherent in transformation.

A most important element for staff and patients in this particular model for health care delivery is a large, round Meditation Room. This room is one and one-half stories high and 120 feet in circumference. While tables and chairs are brought in as needed for various programs and activities, the room is normally left vacant. It is a place of community gatherings for the patients, for staff meetings and for community outreach programs. It is used for yoga, tai chi, and body work in wellness and prevention programs. Most importantly, however, this room serves as the circle for meditation which is held daily at noon, free of charge, for patients, staff, and the community-at-large. It is in this space that people gather in wheelchairs, regular chairs, and on the floor cross-legged, to join in silence and to honor the interweaving of the numinous with the material of everyday life. It is in this space that unity of mind, body, and spirit occurs. It is in this space that unity of the individual, able bodied or disabled, with the community-at-large is underscored. It is a setting and a time where the applications of the rational and empirical are joined with the intuitive and spiritual of the Wild Woman/Wise Woman.

HEALTH CARE IN THE 21ST CENTURY–
ANSWERING THE CALL OF THE WILD WOMAN

The vision of what health care can be in the twenty-first century is only limited by our ability to see clearly into the past and connect that with the future. If we listen to the call of the Wild Woman/Wise Woman as well as see clearly the history we have left behind, we might be able to cross the threshold of transformation of health care and a threshold of transformation for ourselves. If we are flexible enough, as individuals and as a society, to shift our paradigms once again, the tools are available for this transformation. To use these tools, however, means embracing a more holographic definition of health and health care as did the Wild Women/Wise Women before us. It means an integration of mind, body, and spirit from the most basic and fundamental level of our individual existence to the higher level of delivery of health care services. It means embracing and marrying the non-rational and the empirical.

We now stand challenged by the definition of health and ourselves as healthy human beings. We also stand challenged by our connectedness to one another to form a healthy society living on a healthy planet. To meet this challenge, the Wild Woman/Wise Woman calls again for us to embrace an integrated paradigm. This paradigm must be founded on co-operation, regard for the dignity of life and the elimination of fear. All of life must be seen as a central element in this system. We must not abandon the lessons developed in Newtonian science and through the patriarchal applications of that model. However, the Wild Woman/ Wise Woman must rise to a greater challenge to incorporate these lessons into a larger Whole. This Whole must combine and be supported by the best of empiricism guided by intuitive understanding and intentionality.

If we intend to change our health system and truly meet the needs of ourselves, our families and our friends; if we intend to honor the integration of body, mind and spirit in a quality and cost effective way, we can. In *The Life We Are Given* (1995), Leonard and Murphy write, "Ultimately human intentionality is the most powerful evolutionary force on this planet" (p. 61). Where we choose to place our conscious intention has the potential to make major changes in the national policies that affect health care in this country. It has the potential to change how we meet the needs of those who seek and those who provide health care. It ultimately has the potential to make major changes in the lives of our patients, our students, our friends, our families and ourselves. The Wild Woman/Wise Woman knows this already.

REFERENCES

Achterberg, J. (1985). *Imagery in healing: Shamanism and modern medicine.* Boston: Shambala Publications, Inc.

American Medical Women's Association. (2001). *History of AMWA.* Available: http://www.amwa-doc.org/about/history.htm.

American Psychological Association. (1995). *Public perceptions of the value of psychological services.* Washington, DC.

American Psychological Association. (2001). *Women in the American Psychological Association.* Available: http//www.apa.org/pi/wpo/wapa/final.html.

Beinfield, H., & Korngold, E. (1991). *Between Heaven and earth.* New York: Ballantine Books.

Bell, J. S. (1988, Fall-Winter). Nonlocality in physics and psychology: An interview. *Psychological Perspectives,* 306.

Bohm, D. (1987). Hidden variables and the implicate order. In J. M. Basil & F. D. Peat (Eds.), *Quantum implications.* London: Routledge & Kegan Paul.

Broadhead, W. E., Kaplan, B. M., & James, S. A. (1983). The epidemiological evidence for a relationship between social support and health. *American Journal of Epidemiology, 117,* 521-537.

Cassell, J. (1976). The contribution of the social environment to host resistance. *American Journal of Epidemiology, 104,* 107-123.

Cobb, S. (1976). Social support as a moderator of life stress. *Psychosomatic Medicine, 38,* 300-313.

Eisenberg, D., Kessler, R. C., Foster, C., Norlock, F., Collins, D., & Delbanco, T. (1993). Unconventional medicine in the United States. *The New England Journal of Medicine, 328,* 246-252.

Eisenberg, D., Davis, R. B., Ettner, S. L., Appel, S., Wilkey, S., Van Rompay, M., & Kessler, R. C. (1998). Trends in alternative medicine use in the United States, 1990-1997. *Journal of American Medical Association, 280,* 1569-1575.

Gilligan, C. (1983). *In a different voice.* Harvard: Harvard University Press.

Greene, B. (2000). *The elegant universe.* New York: Vintage Books/Random House.

Krippner, S., & Welch, P. (1992). *Spiritual dimensions of healing.* New York: Irvington Publishers, Inc.

Leonard, G., & Murphy, M. (1995). *The life we are given.* New York: Jeremy P. Archer/Putnam.

Macy, J. (1991). *World as lover, world as self.* Berkeley, CA: Parallax Press.

Pelletier, K. (1977). *Mind as Healer, Mind as Slayer: A holistic approach to preventing stress disorders.* New York: Delta.

Pilisuk, M., Boyland, R., & Acieodolo, C. (1987). Social support, life stress and subsequent medical care utilization. *Health Psychology, 6,* 273-288.

Pilisuk, M., & Froland, C. (1978). Kinship, social networks, health. *Social Science and Medicine, 12B,* 273-280.

Pilisuk, M., & Minkler, M. (1980). Supportive networks: Life ties for the elderly. *Journal of Social Issues, 16,* 93-116.

Pilisuk, M., & Parks, S. M. (1986). *The healing web.* Hanover and London: University Press of New England.

Pilisuk, M., Parks, S. M., Kelly, J., & Turner, E. (1982). The helping network approach: Community promotion of mental health. *Journal of Primary Prevention, 3,* 116-132.

Pinkola Estes, C. 1992. *Women who run with the wolves.* New York: Ballantine Books.

Pribram, K. (1977). *Languages of the brain.* Monterey, CA: Wadsworth Publishing.

Tolsdorf, C. (1976). Social networks, support and coping: An exploratory study. *Family Relations, 5,* 407-418.

Walker, A. (1998). *Anything we love can be saved.* New York: Ballantine Publishing Group.

Wickramasekera, I. (1994). Somatic to psychological symptoms and information transfer from implicit to explicit memory: A controlled case study with predictions from the high risk model of threat perception. *Dissociation, VII,* 153-166.

Wickramasekera, I. (1998). Secrets kept from the mind but not the body or behavior: The unsolved problems of identifying and treating somaticization and psychophysiological disease, *Advances in Mind-Body Medicine, 14,* 81-132.

Wickramasekera, I., Davies, T. E., & Davies, S. M. (1996). Applied psychophysiology: A bridge between the biomedical model in family medicine, *Professional Psychology: Research and Practice, 27,* 221-233.

ONE SIZE DOES NOT FIT ALL: INTEGRATING MULTIPLE ISSUES INTO FEMINIST THERAPY FOR WOMEN WITH DISABILITIES

Special Issues in Psychotherapy with Minority Deaf Women

Carolyn A. Corbett

Carolyn A. Corbett, PhD, is Associate Professor in the Department of Psychology at Gallaudet University.

Address correspondence to: Dr. Carolyn A. Corbett, Gallaudet University, Department of Psychology, Room W312 Hall Memorial Building, 800 Florida Avenue NE, Washington, District of Columbia, 20002 (E-mail: Carolyn.Corbett@gallaudet.edu).

Client examples used in the current manuscript were constructed according to the Ethical Principles and Code of Conduct of the American Psychological Association. The names used are fictitious, and identifying information was altered or removed to protect client confidentiality. The examples provided do not reflect individual clients, rather, a consolidation of characteristics found in the author's work with minority Deaf women. These characteristics were combined to illustrate salient issues that impact the community.

[Haworth co-indexing entry note]: "Special Issues in Psychotherapy with Minority Deaf Women." Corbett, Carolyn A. Co-published simultaneously in *Women & Therapy* (The Haworth Press, Inc.) Vol. 26, No. 3/4, 2003, pp. 311-329; and: *Women with Visible and Invisible Disabilities: Multiple Intersections, Multiple Issues, Multiple Therapies* (ed: Martha E. Banks, and Ellyn Kaschak) The Haworth Press, Inc., 2003, pp. 311-329. Single or multiple copies of this article are available for a fee from The Haworth Document Delivery Service [1-800-HAWORTH, 9:00 a.m. - 5:00 p.m. (EST). E-mail address: getinfo@haworthpressinc.com].

SUMMARY. Minority Deaf women have been traditionally underserved by mental health professionals, and specifically, therapists are unaware of issues unique to this population. It would be highly unlikely for a minority Deaf woman to have a therapist who matches her in racial background, hearing status, and communication mode. Therefore, the therapy process will be completely cross-cultural. Therapists who provide psychotherapy services to minority Deaf women need to be aware that their clients are members of a community where deafness is a culture and not a disability. Minority Deaf women are also likely to report feeling forced to choose between competing identities in order to get important needs met. In the following article, case examples are provided which illustrate some of the major issues that are likely to arise in therapy with minority Deaf women. These issues include: access to important information; communication, support and level of involvement with biological families; competing cultural demands; health concerns; and coping with chronic mental illness. *[Article copies available for a fee from The Haworth Document Delivery Service: 1-800-HAWORTH. E-mail address: <getinfo@haworthpressinc.com> Website: <http://www.HaworthPress.com> © 2003 by The Haworth Press, Inc. All rights reserved.]*

KEYWORDS. Minority, deaf, psychotherapy, sign language

The current article will focus on some of the unique aspects of providing psychotherapy services to minority Deaf women. The author of this article is a hearing, African American psychologist who has worked for twenty years as a psychotherapist in the Deaf community. Until quite recently, published information about psychotherapy with Deaf individuals has been minimal, most often published by agencies or organizations serving the Deaf community (Brauer, 1980; Glickman & Harvey, 1996; Gough, 1990; Harvey, 1989; Leigh, 1991; Myers, 1995; Sussman & Stewart, 1971). There is only one major publication that highlights the special issues of culturally diverse Deaf persons in treatment (Leigh, 1999). In the current article, the author will provide examples of how issues of culture vs. disability, racism, sexism, and communication preference simultaneously impact the lives of minority Deaf women. Client examples will highlight how these concerns might manifest themselves during the therapy process.

Before embarking on this journey, it will be important to provide some operational definitions. For the purposes of this article, the term minority refers to women of color. Although the term "women of color" is commonly used in the psychological literature (Comas-Díaz & Greene, 1994), it is not a phrase that is used within the Deaf community. Therefore, the author has chosen to use the term minority in order to be consistent with what is used by the clients. The word Deaf is capitalized because it is used to describe a specific population of individuals with hearing loss, who consider their deafness as a culture and not a disability (Glickman, 1993; Lane, Hoffmeister & Bahan, 1996; Maxwell & Zea, 1998; Padden, 1980; Sussman & Brauer, 1999). The women presented in this chapter are also members of the Deaf community. Members of the Deaf community most often have the following characteristics: hearing loss prior to age 17; education in a school or educational program for the deaf; self-identification as Deaf, not "hard of hearing" or "hearing-impaired"; and, fluency in American Sign Language (ASL; Higgins, 1987; Padden, 1980). As members of the minority Deaf community, these women also have variations in American Sign Language which reflect their cultural experiences (Aramburo, 1992).

Therapists who provide culturally competent psychotherapy services to minority Deaf women must make a serious commitment to learning about how competing forces impact their client's lives. As Deaf individuals, the clients have to contend with living in a world dominated by hearing people who use speech as their primary mode of communication. Within hearing culture, major decisions are made based on the calibre of an individual's speaking skills. Deaf people who do not use speech and/or do not understand speech face many prejudices and oppression. These issues are compounded when the Deaf person is also a member of a racial minority group. The individual is likely to encounter racism in both the hearing and Deaf communities (Anderson, 1992; Anderson & Grace, 1991; Corbett, 1999; Hairston & Smith, 1983). When the Deaf person is a woman, she is likely to experience sexism as well.

Minority Deaf women often report feeling forced to choose between identities in order to get important needs met (Younkin, 1990). Very often, the Deaf community asks the women to focus only on their Deaf identities and to deny their minority status. The minority hearing community often sees the women as belonging to the Deaf community because of their hearing loss. Both communities ask the women not to focus on gender issues, because this might take away from the focus on the "real struggles" of the larger group. As a result, many minority Deaf women who seek psychotherapy services experience isolation and marginalization from their peer reference groups.

When considering which examples to include in the current article, the author selected some client examples which highlight themes that are often raised by minority Deaf women in psychotherapy. The issues to be presented include the importance of access to information, family issues, cultural collisions, physical health, and chronic mental illness. While writing the chapter, the author realized that the headings in the following sections are not mutually exclusive. Each example could possibly fit in another category as well, due to the complexity of issues presented. However, the author chose the particular section for each example based on the client's identification of salience of the problem in her life.

THE IMPORTANCE OF ACCESS TO INFORMATION

Access to information is of critical importance to minority Deaf women and being "left out" is an issue that is often expressed in psychotherapy. As a beginning therapist working with this community, the author did not realize how intensely minority Deaf women felt about "not knowing about something." When a client would say "Oh, really? I didn't know about that" or "Nobody ever told me that before," the therapist responded as if she would a hearing person by thinking or saying "OK, well now you know that information." However, time after time, the client expressed a need to process this lack of knowledge and discuss the pain associated with it.

Minority deaf women have wanted to discuss, in therapy, issues like proper procedures for cashing checks, or filling out applications for employment. One client knew that having sex would make you pregnant, but did not know that having a baby hurt. When she began having contractions, she called stating that she was in pain. Fortunately, she was able to reach someone who could tell her that she was in labor. Lack of access to information can have devastating consequences that severely impact the individual's mental health. The following client example illustrates this problem:

> Vanessa, a 23-year-old Deaf Cuban woman, came to the United States with her family, through a relief organization sponsored by the church. She was 8 years old at the time of her arrival in the United States. Spanish was spoken as the primary language in the home and Vanessa's parents communicated with her through gestures. Shortly after her arrival in the United States, Vanessa's par-

ents enrolled her in a residential school for the deaf. At this school, Vanessa learned American Sign Language. On weekends home, she taught her mother to sign and her mother took the initiative to enroll in sign language courses at the local community center. Vanessa's father continued to communicate primarily in Spanish. After many years in the residential school, Vanessa's ability to understand Spanish deteriorated and her mother began to interpret Vanessa's conversations with her father into ASL. After completing high school, Vanessa enrolled in a residential vocational training program in another state, but continued to visit her family one weekend per month.

When Vanessa was 22 years old, her mother was diagnosed with terminal cancer. Vanessa was committed to visiting with her mother on weekends and spent many hours with her. As her mother's condition worsened, she and Vanessa began to discuss her funeral. It was decided that there would be a short memorial service, with a closed casket, with a reception held at a neighbor's home after the services. Several weeks later, Vanessa receives a TTY call from her father saying, "Come home. Funeral in two days." Vanessa is grief stricken over her mother's death. She rushes home and arrives on the morning of the funeral. They rush her to the church. She sits on the front row. People come by to shake her hand and tell her that they are sorry for her loss. Everyone is speaking in Spanish. There is no sign language interpreter for the funeral. Vanessa does not know what is going on, and feels very depressed and disappointed that she does not know what people are saying about her mother. Her father is overcome by grief. The reception is held at the neighbor's house as planned. Vanessa is encouraged by her father to go back to her program, so she leaves the next day. Upon her arrival at her program, Vanessa receives a lot of support from her classmates and teachers.

Two weeks later, Vanessa gets another TTY call from her father. He says "Mother died yesterday. Come home funeral." Vanessa is shocked because she thought she already attended her mother's funeral. She asked her father whose funeral she had attended. She found out that it had been the neighbor's funeral. Vanessa is devastated. She attempts to tell her friends what happened. They think she is lying and do not want to associate with her. Vanessa is isolated and alone, and grief stricken over missing the last two weeks of her mother's life. She is seen for individual psychotherapy with the diagnosis of depression.

What is important about the above case is not whether Vanessa is telling the truth or lying. It is the fact that serious communication gaps often exist between Deaf individuals and people who provide significant support in their lives. This can include immediate family members primarily responsible for their care, extended family members, ministers, employers, and romantic partners. Lack of access to even simple information intensified the experience of loss for the client, which she experienced twice, unnecessarily. Within minority Deaf communities, sign language interpreters of color often donate their services to minority families during funeral services. In this way, it can be assured that the Deaf person is able to fully participate in the mourning process for her family member.

FAMILY ISSUES: COMMUNICATION, SUPPORT, AND LEVEL OF INVOLVEMENT

Within the Deaf community, parental hearing status plays a major role. Leadership in the community, social popularity or inclusion on the "A list" for events, and even choice of romantic partnerships often use the criterion of parental hearing status for decision-making. Parental hearing status is important because Deaf children of Deaf parents are considered keepers of the culture; they have access to the purest forms of American Sign Language and knowledge about traditions in the Deaf community. Within minority communities, deafness is a low-incidence condition that most often does not involve genetic factors (Holt & Hotto, 1994). Rubella, high fever, chronic ear infections, and meningitis are all frequent causes of deafness in minority individuals (Corbett, 1999). Therefore, minority Deaf women are more likely to come from families that have hearing parents. Deaf women who have hearing parents often struggle with issues involving communication, social support, and degree of involvement they will have with their biological families as adults.

Deaf individuals who have severe to profound hearing loss are often educated at residential schools, which takes them out of the day-to-day interaction with their families of origin. As they become more proficient in sign language use, the communication gap between child and parent widens, especially as the child matures. For minority Deaf individuals, who most often do not have Deaf parents, this places them in an odd situation where they are torn between their biological families and their "family" that they develop with deaf peers. The author has seen several minority Deaf women in therapy who struggled with issues of being both an "insider" and an "outsider" in their own families. The following client examples will illustrate this issue. Two major issues to be highlighted are over-involvement and isolation from one's family of origin.

Jamillah, an African American Deaf college student, always returned home to her family during school breaks. The student was from a large extended family and the home of the maternal grandfather was the central meeting place of the family. Two of the Jamillah's adult cousins, whom she described as "irresponsible," resided with the grandfather. Although they both worked full time, the cousins did not contribute financially to the household and did not help with the grandfather's care. On one spring break at home, Jamillah began to notice that her grandfather was beginning to deteriorate both physically and mentally. Jamillah became concerned that her grandfather would no longer be able to take care of himself. Since his retirement, her grandfather had attended a day program for senior citizens in their community, but recently began stating that he didn't want to go any more. He also had "Meals on Wheels" delivered to his home, but was not eating. Jamillah contacted the local adult protective services to request help.

While at home, Jamillah used her own money to pay some of her grandfather's bills and to buy groceries for the entire household. However, upon her return to school, she often did not eat because she had spent the money on family bills. Jamillah expressed her concerns to one of her uncles, who was considered the "head" of the family, due to his financial standing. The uncle called a meeting of the family while Jamillah was at school. She received a letter from her uncle outlining the expenses related to her grandfather's care and it contained a "bill" for her share of the expenses each month. The bill did not take into account all of the money she had already contributed to the family. Jamillah supported herself on Supplemental Security Income (SSI) in the amount of $175/month. The bill presented exceeded this amount. The student was not allowed to work because she would lose her SSI benefits and possibly her vocational rehabilitation support for school.

As therapy progressed, Jamillah became anxious because she thought that if she refused to pay the bill, she would no longer have a family. Jamillah continued to struggle in therapy about how much involvement she should have with her family, especially when they were expecting her to take on responsibilities they were not willing to do themselves.

Marta, a 35-year-old Puerto Rican returning adult student, came into the mental health clinic at her college. She was brought in by her partner because she was experiencing severe depression. For the previous two months, she had been unable to contact any of her family of origin. She was the oldest of five siblings and the only Deaf member of her family. The family was extremely poor and her father had died approximately 16 years previously. The family agreed that they would all work together to make sure that each person got to attend college. So, Marta worked and provided major financial support for each of her siblings to go to school. The siblings were supposed to return the privilege when it was Marta's turn.

Marta knew that the family was discussing returning to Puerto Rico because their mother wanted to retire there. However, when Marta departed for college the family was still in discussion about these plans. Marta completed her first year of college, with sporadic contact with family members, which she did not find unusual. However, when it was time for her to go home for the summer, all of the family telephone numbers were disconnected. The client's siblings were supposed to be providing financial assistance during the summer months. After two months, and an actual visit to Chicago, she was unable to find any of her family members. The client had never been to Puerto Rico and did not know the names of extended family that lived there.

In therapy, the client discussed feelings of abandonment, rage, and helplessness. After six months of silence from the family and untold emotional agony to the client, one of her brothers called, nonchalantly, as if nothing was wrong to say that the family was still in Chicago, just in a different part of town.

Families where there are both Deaf and hearing members often struggle with how much involvement they will have with each other, what types of communication they will use, and who will be responsible for organizing things. When psychopathology already exists in the family, the deaf person is often blamed or given inappropriate amounts of responsibility for remedying the situation. Or, as presented in the second client example, the person is completely ignored for long periods of time and then blamed for protesting about being excluded.

THE STRESS OF COMPETING CULTURAL DEMANDS

Women who are Deaf and members of ethnic minority groups often report feeling pressured to choose between identities in order to get important needs met. Within the Deaf community, deafness is considered of primary importance. As stated previously, other identities (e.g., minority, religious, or sexual orientation) are given less consideration, with the idea that these issues take away from the focus of "empowering" the Deaf community first (Valentine, 1996; Younkin, 1990). In contrast, ethnic minority communities often view their deaf members as belonging to the Deaf community (Corbett, 1999). Thus, they do not have to be responsible for learning to communicate with minority Deaf people or make other accommodations. Given this exclusion from two larger groups, many minority Deaf individuals establish their own communities, separate from the white Deaf and minority hearing cultures. These minority deaf communities may range from informal social groups or sports clubs (Hairston & Smith, 1983), to formal political organizations (e.g., Intertribal Council of the Deaf), and households consisting of multi-generational minority Deaf members.

The author has provided psychotherapy services to minority Deaf women where the major concern was that expectations from Deaf culture, hearing culture, and their minority culture of origin were competing in such a way that their emotional functioning was compromised. Two examples are presented below:

> Kenya, an African American Deaf woman with a major in computer information systems, sought therapy at a university counseling center due to feelings of anxiety over returning to her family home during summer break. Kenya's parents were executives in a large technology firm, and were encouraging her to submit her resume to their company for summer employment. In an effort to "help," Kenya's mother requested that she be able to review her daughter's resume before it was submitted to the personnel office. Kenya's resume clearly stated that she was a student at the college for D/deaf students and that she used American Sign Language. After reading the resume, Kenya's mother suggested that *"just in case" the employers might think she was really deaf,* she should put down on her resume that she spoke Spanish as well. This made Kenya feel extremely anxious because she knew that she had only one Spanish course in high school, and that it consisted of reading, not speaking.

> In therapy, Kenya reported feeling upset that again her mother had not truly accepted her deafness. She also felt that this was just the beginning of several unrealistic expectations that would be placed on her during her summer, such as behaving like a hearing person. This was especially defeating because while at college, Kenya was just beginning to feel proud of her signing and Deaf identity.

In the example, the client comes from an African American middle class family, which places a high value on education and achievement for all of its members. At the same time, this family is illustrative of a common situation that many Deaf people face: *The parents have not accepted that their adult child truly cannot hear.* There are several circumstances that perpetuate this type of problem for minority Deaf women. Minority hearing parents are less likely to find themselves in circumstances in which they can actively participate in activities with the Deaf community or see their child interacting with Deaf peers (Kluwin & Corbett, 1998). The outcome is that sign language is something that is used at school, and "lipreading"/gestures are used at home. As a result, parents often maintain the illusion that their child can hear more than is the case, or that the child is able to comprehend during their spoken interactions. Thus, for many minority Deaf women, a common theme in therapy is loss regarding relationships with their parents. There are also feelings of sadness over lost opportunities to know more about their minority culture of origin, participate in family traditions, and/or learn family history that is generally passed down orally. For many minority Deaf women, trips home are sometimes traumatic because they begin to realize just how much interaction with family they have missed. Therapists who treat minority Deaf women can help them to become more empowered by addressing family communication issues more assertively. For example, one former client brought a sign language interpreter to a Thanksgiving dinner with her extended family network. Although at first the family was shocked, they began to realize that they learned more about their family member during this one dinner than they had during her entire life.

The second example involves a psychotherapy experience with an Asian Deaf woman, who was part of an extended network of Asian Deaf persons in the San Francisco Bay Area.

> Lily, a 22-year-old Deaf woman from Japan resided in a large private home with other Asian Deaf women. There were 12 women

in the household, ranging in age from 18 to 54 years. Several blocks away, there was a similar household consisting of Asian Deaf men. Both households were very actively involved in the Asian American Union of the Deaf, and several members participated in sports teams. The client was dating a young man named Daniel from the other household for several years. Daniel, who was also Japanese, was from a family that lived in Hawaii. They both tried out for and made the team going to the World Games For the Deaf which was to be held in Japan. Both households were actively and successfully involved in fundraising activities to finance the couple's trip to Japan for the competition. This was considered an honor, and they were to represent their organization.

Approximately six weeks prior to the trip, Daniel informed Lily that he no longer wanted to be in a relationship with her, and that he was interested in dating another member of her household. Lily became very depressed and suicidal. The couple also became physically combative with each other. The elders of the households called a meeting with the couple, and demanded that they seek counseling. The elders then proceeded to bring the couple for therapy at a local mental health center that provided mental health treatment to deaf people. The elders explained to the therapist their culture and living arrangements. Of primary concern to both households were the suicidal gestures, the domestic violence, and the financial burden of the trips. After several meetings and negotiations with the therapist, the couple, and the elders, the couple decided that they would still go to Japan in order to compete because it was expected of them in their culture. Couples counseling and individual therapy were extended to facilitate the trip and the termination of the relationship.

In individual therapy with Lily, in addition to crisis resolution and reduction of suicidal ideation, the focus was on how she would successfully negotiate the culture in order to bring this relationship to a close. Lily reported to the therapist that propriety required that she and the "ex" boyfriend stop at his parents' home in Hawaii on their way to Japan. This stay would be one week minimum. Then during the World Games, she and Daniel would stay at her parents' home in Japan for two weeks. Each was also required to bring "gifts" to the other's family. The client anticipated that she would have to bring approximately $700 worth of gifts for Daniel's family. Although she didn't really want to have anything more to do with Daniel, she wanted to fulfill her obligation to her household which sponsored her competition, and she wanted to be able to live in the same community upon her return. Lily also wanted to be known within her community as a person who understood the honor associated with her selection for the team and who fulfilled her commitments.

This example is interesting because it illustrates the importance of understanding the culture of the client in order to provide quality mental health services. In this case, the leaders of the community, namely the elders, initiated contact with the service providing agency. When working with the minority Deaf community, service providers must be flexible in how they engage clients, because this population is severely underserved. If the agency had rejected the call by stating that the couple needed to initiate their own services, it is possible that no treatment would have been provided and the potential danger of the situation could have escalated. The second major issue in this example is that the client provided education to the therapist about what was required in order for her to maintain standing within her community and to maintain her own self-respect. There were places where the client's cultural expectations did not match those of the therapist's culture. However, the goal of treatment was not for the therapist to agree with what the client was doing, but to facilitate healthy resolution of the problems.

MINORITY DEAF WOMEN AND HEALTH CONCERNS

National health statistics indicate that women of color are more likely to have severe health problems than are white American women. Cancer, heart disease, hypertension, diabetes, and AIDS are all diseases that have had a major impact on minority communities (National Center for Health Statistics, 2001). Minority Deaf women share with their hearing sisters of color similar health concerns. However, communication access and literacy issues decrease the likelihood that they will receive quality health care (Corbett, 1999; Leigh, 1999; Myers, 1995).

A large number of minority Deaf women receive SSI as their primary means of income and Medicaid as their health insurance. Although sign language interpreters are supposed to be covered as part of their health insurance benefits, in practice this tends to be the exception rather than the rule. Very often, minority Deaf women seek health care at a time of a health crisis, when interpreters might not be immediately available. As a result, they often receive medical treatment in circumstances in which they are not able to communicate their concerns effectively with their doctors, and are not able to understand what the doctor is recommending for them in terms of treatment. Literacy issues also have a major impact in the health arena. Nationally, the average reading level for Deaf adults is approximately third grade; minority Deaf individuals read at even lower levels (Traxler, 2000). Poor reading comprehension reduces the likelihood that a minority Deaf woman would be able to accurately complete her written medical history without assistance, understand the doctor's written instructions, or actively investigate her own health issues through independent reading. When the woman is facing long-term health intervention, the potential for gaps in treatment increases exponentially. These issues are illustrated in the following client example.

The client, Ms. Wynn, is a 35 year old, single, African American woman, originally from South Carolina. Ms. Wynn became deaf at age 3, due to spinal meningitis. Although Ms. Wynn is able to use her voice for communication, she prefers American Sign Language and she is unable to understand any sounds in the speech range. Ms. Wynn has renal failure due to a long history of severe obesity and severe hypertension. Ms. Wynn received a special education diploma from a residential school for the deaf. Ms. Wynn is the mother of one daughter, Roslyn, who is currently six years old.

Ms. Wynn was referred for psychotherapeutic intervention because she was having significant difficulty following her renal dialysis program. She is scheduled for three dialysis sessions per week, which last for three hours each. She has been receiving dialysis for approximately three years. However, over the past four months, Ms. Wynn has missed at least one appointment per week. In the opinion of her physician, Ms. Wynn's physical condition is deteriorating unnecessarily because of her failure to keep her appointments. According to the report of multidisciplinary team at the hospital she receives treatment, Ms. Wynn seemed to be pushing the limits recently, skipping appointments, rescheduling days, almost to the point where her life is in jeopardy.

The multidisciplinary team decided to refer Ms. Wynn for immediate intervention after an event which occurred the previous afternoon. Ms. Wynn came in for her dialysis appointment with her daughter, Roslyn. It is strictly against policy of the Unit for a parent to leave a child unattended when he/she is receiving dialysis. Ms. Wynn had already rescheduled her appointment, meaning she was one day late, and when confronted by the social worker, she stated "I didn't have a babysitter . . . I told you people I didn't have a babysitter . . . You people keep expecting me to come in for these appointments and I don't have anyone to take care of my child. You all just don't understand what I've been going through." According to the social worker's report, "Ms. Wynn then turned to the child and informed her 'Because of you, I am missing my appointments, which means I am going to die soon. It's your fault. I will be dead before the month is over.' At this point, Roslyn began to cry hysterically and had to be seen by an emergency child therapist."

During the first session of therapy, as part of the history, Ms. Wynn was asked if she planned to have a have a kidney transplant. She states "Oh, my name isn't even on the list for that." When the therapist explores further, Ms. Wynn says "Oh, I never even finished the evaluation for that. They had all these papers that I couldn't even read and no one would help me. I started it, but then my shunt collapsed and I had to go into the hospital. So that means I have to start all over again, and I just haven't had the time to do it . . . (When was this? "A year ago"). But, really, think about it, I am a poor, black, Deaf woman on Medicaid. Who the hell is going to give me a kidney, anyway? What's the point? Those medical people aren't even thinking about me. Black people are the last people to get transplants anyway. I'll be dead before the list ever comes to my name." The therapist asks Ms. Wynn about her relationship with Roslyn. She says "Oh, Roslyn's a good kid. She can take care of herself, most of the time. She can make herself a sandwich, or make Oodles of Noodles. *She doesn't need me for much.* We get along OK." When asked if she thought Roslyn had any feelings about her illness, she said, "Roslyn doesn't need to talk about anything like that. "

Home-based individual therapy services were provided to Ms. Wynn and home-based family therapy was provided for Ms. Wynn and Roslyn. The therapist was hearing and had expertise in providing therapy to clients with chronic medical concerns. The therapist did not sign herself, but was accompanied each week by a registered interpreter for the deaf. Even though the services were brought to the client's door, Ms. Wynn continued to be resistant. In therapy, Ms. Wynn struggled over whether she was going to actively live or plan her death (intentionally or unintentionally). Ms. Wynn was encouraged to become more actively involved in the Deaf community in her area as a means of social support. Literacy support services and interpreting services were provided in order to assist Ms. Wynn in completing the evaluation for the kidney transplant program. The focus of family therapy was on improving parenting and communication skills, and reuniting Ms. Wynn and Roslyn with their extended family network.

MINORITY DEAF WOMEN
WITH CHRONIC MENTAL ILLNESS

Anderson (1992) discussed the "triple threat" of being a member of a minority group, Deaf, and mentally ill. In the current article, the issue of gender is entered into the equation. Deaf women of color who are mentally ill face racism, sexism, discrimination because of their mental illness, and oppression by hearing individuals, at a minimum. However, they face the additional issue of being excluded from participation within the Deaf and minority Deaf communities as well. The stigma of mental illness that is common in hearing communities also filters to the Deaf community. In addition, mental illness affects thought processes and thus interrupts the flow of communication. This has a significant impact on American Sign Language production and comprehension, both of which are critical for full participation in the Deaf community.

Minority families with members who are Deaf and mentally ill face many challenges. First, mental illness interrupts the sometimes tenuous connection that the family already has to a member who cannot hear and communicates using sign language. Minority families have difficulty finding the appropriate resources to assist them in providing treatment to their Deaf mentally ill relative. Thus, they are often isolated and overwhelmed by the level of stressors involved. Families also struggle with caretaking responsibilities and the financial considerations. Rejection of the mentally ill Deaf person from the Deaf community intensifies the confusion that hearing extended families already have about the best place for their relative. The following client example provides some perspective on this problem.

The client, Ms. Pagan, is a 33-year-old Deaf single female, whose family is from the Dominican Republic. The client was born in the Dominican Republic but states she was raised by her "adoptive" parents in New Jersey. She claims that she was left on the doorstep of the Pagan family and that they knew her "real" mother. The therapist has the occasion to meet Ms. Pagan's father; she looks exactly like him. The therapist learned from Mr. Pagan that he and his wife raised her and that she is their biological daughter.

Ms. Pagan has enrolled as a returning adult student in college and presents herself for therapy at the Counseling Service. She is required to attend counseling in order to have the Bureau of Vocational Rehabilitation (VR) pay for her school. When asked why counseling was *ordered* by VR, Ms. Pagan stated, "I have a bad temper. It gets me in trouble sometimes." When asked if she had been in counseling before, she stated that she saw a psychiatrist, Dr. M. at University Hospital. When asked if she was on any medications she stated that she was. In her purse she had Haldol, an antipsychotic, and several other psychotropic meds. When asked if she was taking her medications, Ms. Pagan stated "the doctor told me only to take it if I get in a bad mood." The therapist asked Ms. Pagan to sign a release of information so that she could talk with Dr. M. She was more than happy to comply.

The therapist talked with Dr. M. He stated that Ms. Pagan was well known to him, having been an institutionalized patient at Forest Haven for 13 years. He described Ms. Pagan as "a tough lady who likes to have her own way." She was known to have an explosive temper with frequent outbursts against family members. Ms. Pagan is quite bright and it was suggested to VR by University Hospital that she might be allowed to attend college. Two weeks before she was to begin college, Ms. Pagan became explosively angry and physically assaulted her mother. She was hospitalized for approximately twelve days at that time. *She was released from the inpatient unit at University Hospital two days before arriving at the college.*

In therapy Ms. Pagan was always on time, if not early, for every appointment. She was lively and energetic. She told many horrific stories, such as "In high school, I was chased home from school every day by boys. They called me names, beat me up, and broke my glasses. I wished someone would have helped me." She hinted at being raped/sexually abused by several uncles during her childhood period. She stated these things matter-of-factly, often with a smile.

Ms. Pagan's adjustment in college began to deteriorate because she stopped taking her medication. She spent hours in chat-rooms on-line; she interrupted many courses on campus that had on-line activities/discussion groups. Her computer activities caused a significant stir on campus when she used it to "preach the gospel." The therapist was able to read some of the postings on-line, which were open to the campus community. The therapist found Ms. Pagan's writings to be frequently incoherent and twisted interpretations of biblical passages, with bizarre word usage. Ms. Pagan stopped attending classes and spent most of her time in the computer lab. She was in the process of failing all of her courses. Her on-line activities became even more incoherent, and she was being threatened with physical harm by other students of the campus. Ms. Pagan's on-line privileges were revoked when she send a string of emails containing long paragraphs of profanity to the entire campus community. After a hearing with the Campus Disciplinary Board, Ms. Pagan was told that she would not be allowed to return to school the following semester.

Upon news of her dismissal and revocation of her computer privileges, Ms. Pagan became more difficult to manage. She was unable to manage on her own, requiring daily (sometimes hourly) therapy sessions. She became loud and unruly. Ms. Pagan began to believe some of the threats she had received. She called her father to ask him to pick her up.

The therapist had a chance to meet with the father, at the client's insistence. Mr. Pagan stated that he and his wife had been attempting to manage their daughter's mental illness for several years. However, now they were getting older and on the verge of retirement. He said that although they knew it was a long-shot, they decided to send their daughter to college so that she could get some experiences away from home. They also used her time away as a respite from the long-term treatment that they had provided.

In the current client example, the family attempted to exercise an option that was unlikely to succeed in the long run, but useful for their immediate goal of getting some respite from an emotionally intense situation. The family would benefit from receiving ongoing support services, and assistance in helping their daughter to make the transition to a community residential facility.

CONCLUSION

In the current article, the author has presented several issues that are likely to arise when providing psychotherapy services to minority Deaf women. In psychotherapy, it is highly unlikely that the minority Deaf woman will have a therapist who matches her in racial background, gender, hearing status, and communication choice. At a minimum, therapy with minority Deaf women should include clear interaction/communication with the therapist, based on the client's communication preference. If the therapist is not fluent in sign language, it is appropriate to hire a *professional* sign language interpreter to ensure communication effectiveness. The therapist is also responsible to do her own self-work on how her hearing status, racial background, and communication style impact the therapeutic relationship. The therapist should also educate herself about the local Deaf community, its activities, and leadership.

REFERENCES

Anderson, G. B., & Grace, C. B. (1991). Black deaf adolescents: A diverse and underserved population. *Volta Review, 93*, 73-86.

Anderson, R. P. (1992). Black, deaf and mentally ill: Triple jeopardy. In College for Continuing Education (Eds.), *Proceedings of the empowerment and Black Deaf persons conference* (pp. 89-103). Washington, DC: Gallaudet University.

Aramburo, A. J. (1992). Sociolinguistic aspects of the Black deaf community. In College for Continuing Education (Eds.), *Proceedings of the empowerment and Black Deaf persons conference* (pp. 67-88). Washington, DC: Gallaudet University.

Brauer, B. A. (1980). Perspectives on psychotherapy with deaf persons. *Mental Health in Deafness, Experimental Issue, NIMH, 4*, 4-8.

Comas-Díaz, L., & Greene, B. (1994). *Women of color: Integrating ethnic and racial identities in psychotherapy.* New York: Guilford Press.

Corbett, C. A. (1999). Mental health issues for African American Deaf persons. In I. W. Leigh (Ed.) *Psychotherapy with deaf clients from diverse groups.* (pp. 151-176). Washington, DC: Gallaudet University Press.

Glickman, N. S. (1993). Deaf identity development: Construction and validation of theoretical model. Unpublished doctoral dissertation, University of Massachusetts, Amherst.

Glickman, N. S., & Harvey, M. A. (Eds.) (1996). *Culturally affirmative psychotherapy with Deaf persons.* Mahwah, NJ: Lawrence Erlbaum.

Gough, D. L. (1990). Rational-emotive therapy: A cognitive-behavioral approach to working with hearing impaired clients. *Journal of Rehabilitation of the Deaf, 23* (3), 96-104.

Hairston, E., & Smith, L. (1983). *Black and Deaf in America: Are we that different?* Silver Spring, MD: T. J. Publishers.

Harvey, M. A. (1989). *Psychotherapy with deaf and hard of hearing persons: A systemic model.* Hillsdale, NJ: Lawrence Erlbaum.

Higgins, P. C. (1987). The deaf community. In P. C. Higgins and J. E. Nash (Eds.), *Understanding deafness socially* (pp. 151-170). Springfield, IL: Charles C. Thomas.

Holt, J. A., & Hotto, S. A. (1994). *Demographic aspects of hearing impairment: Questions and answers* (3rd ed.). Washington, DC: Gallaudet University Center for Assessment and Demographic Studies.

Kluwin, T. N., & Corbett, C. A. (1998). Parent characteristics and educational program involvement. *American Annals of the Deaf, 143* (5), 425-432.

Lane, H., Hoffmeister, R., & Bahan, B. (1996). *A journey into the Deaf-world.* San Diego: Dawn Sign Press.

Leigh, I. W. (1991). Deaf therapists: Impact on treatment. In Proceedings of the eleventh world congress of the World Federation of the Deaf: Equality and self-reliance (pp. 290-297). Tokyo: World Federation of the Deaf.

Leigh, I. W. (1999). *Psychotherapy with deaf clients from diverse groups.* Washington, DC: Gallaudet University Press.

Maxwell, D., & Zea, M. C. (1998, August). *The Deaf Acculturation Scale (DAS): Development, reliability, and validity.* Poster session presented at the annual convention of the American Psychological Association, San Francisco, CA.

Myers, R. R. (1995). Standards of care for service delivery to individuals who are deaf or hard of hearing. Silver Spring, MD: National Association of the Deaf.

National Center for Health Statistics (2001). *Fast statistics A to Z.* [On-line}. Available at www.cdc.gov/nchs/default.htm.

Padden, C. (1980). The deaf community and the culture of deaf people. In C. Baker & R. Battison (Eds.). *Sign language and the deaf community* (pp. 89-103). Silver Spring, MD: National Association of the Deaf.

Sussman, A. E., & Brauer, B. A. (1999). On being a psychotherapist with Deaf clients. In I. W. Leigh (Ed.) *Psychotherapy with deaf clients from diverse groups.* (pp. 3-22). Washington, DC: Gallaudet University Press.

Sussman, A. E., & Stewart, L. G. (Eds.) (1971). *Counseling with Deaf people.* New York: New York Deafness Research and Training Center, New York University School of Education.

Traxler, C. B. (2000). The Stanford Achievement Test 9th Edition: National norming and performance standards for deaf and hard-of-hearing students. *Journal of Deaf Studies and Deaf Education, 5*(4), 337-348.

Valentine, V. (1996, December/January). Being Black and Deaf. *Emerge, 7*(3), 56-69.

Younkin, L. (1990, January/February). Between two worlds: Black and deaf in America. *Disability Rag,* pp. 30-33.

Womanist Therapy
with African American Women
with Disabilities

Nina A. Nabors
Melanie F. Pettee

SUMMARY. African American women are at increased risk for disabilities. There is very little information available, however, regarding psychological interventions with African American women with disabilities. The purpose of this article is to discuss psychological intervention in working with African American women with acquired disabilities from a womanist perspective. Themes and interventions will be discussed. Recommendations for working with African American women with disabilities in a therapeutic context will be offered. *[Article copies available for a fee from The Haworth Document Delivery Service: 1-800-HAWORTH. E-mail address: <getinfo@haworthpressinc.com> Website: <http://www.HaworthPress.com> © 2003 by The Haworth Press, Inc. All rights reserved.]*

KEYWORDS. African American, womanist therapy, disability, women

Nina A. Nabors, PhD, is Assistant Professor in Clinical Psychology at Eastern Michigan University. This manuscript is based on her ongoing work with African American women with disabilities in her clinical practice in Detroit, Michigan. Melanie F. Pettee was, at the time of this writing, an outstanding undergraduate psychology student (graduation date 4/01) at Eastern Michigan University.

Address correspondence to: Nina A. Nabors, PhD, Psychology Department, Eastern Michigan University, Ypsilanti, MI 48197.

[Haworth co-indexing entry note]: "Womanist Therapy with African American Women with Disabilities." Nabors, Nina A., and Melanie F. Pettee. Co-published simultaneously in *Women & Therapy* (The Haworth Press, Inc.) Vol. 26, No. 3/4, 2003, pp. 331-341; and: *Women with Visible and Invisible Disabilities: Multiple Intersections, Multiple Issues, Multiple Therapies* (ed: Martha E. Banks, and Ellyn Kaschak) The Haworth Press, Inc., 2003, pp. 331-341. Single or multiple copies of this article are available for a fee from The Haworth Document Delivery Service [1-800-HAWORTH, 9:00 a.m. - 5:00 p.m. (EST). E-mail address: getinfo@haworthpressinc.com].

Feminist therapy, an expansion of psychotherapy, is a theoretical orientation that contributes to the well-being of women as well as social change and deconstruction of women's symptoms as pathological. Feminist therapists utilize a broad conceptual framework that allows for appropriate views of women's problems in therapy. This includes ideas such as "the personal is political," which addresses the idea that personal problems are not separate from the social and political constructs in which women are socialized but rather inextricably interwoven, and the symptoms that women experience are not pathological, rather are mechanisms to survive oppressive conditions.

Considering that values are influential in all therapies, feminist therapy recognizes the importance of the values of the therapist and the client that are brought into a therapeutic dyad and recommends that values be discussed when a therapeutic relationship is formed. Feminist therapy is client-centered. Inasmuch as the client is the most knowledgeable person of her own experiences, she can provide a critical evaluation of the therapists' interpretation. Egalitarian relationships are also a vital component. The identification of commonalties through self-disclosure can decrease the client's sense of isolation and empower her to act on her own behalf (Enns, 1997).

Goals of feminist therapy are oriented towards change, which contrasts with traditional psychotherapies, which promote adjustment. Breaking down traditional gender roles helps clients create a sense of equality. For example, feminist therapists encourage employment to achieve financial power, but also emphasize that it is crucial to not invalidate the experiences of women who do choose to engage in unpaid work because they often belittle their own experiences (Enns, 1997).

An important goal of feminist therapy is empowerment. Women who are empowered have an understanding of the power structures that permeate our society, the way women are socialized, how to effectively obtain power in every facet of their lives, and the ability to empower other women and other oppressed individuals. The notion that women are expected to always be the caregivers and never the "care-receivers" is also addressed. An emphasis on taking care of oneself before others is not valued, rather considered self-absorbed, and creates a difficult conflict for women to work through. Feminist therapy encourages self-nurturance, avoidance of detachment from emotion and development of a sense of autonomy.

The structure of feminist therapy was originally formulated by white women for white women. Today the experiences of Women of Color are explored, appreciated, and for the most part included. The feminist therapist must take on the role of discovering her client's cultural differences and educating herself on the culture. Historically, respecting diversity has been equated with the inclusion of Women of Color. Feminist therapy should also include the experience of women with other marginalized identities such as women with disabilities. There is a deficiency of research and literature on the experience of women with disabilities and effective methods of therapy. Women with disabilities endure a dual marked status of being female and disabled that delivers hefty amounts of oppression.

Wendell (1997) states that women with disabilities struggle with both the oppressions of being a woman in male-dominated societies and the oppressions of being disabled in societies dominated by the able-bodied. Wendell and others (e.g., Prilleltensky, 1996) acknowledge the exclusion of women with disabilities within feminist theory and therapy. Wendell highlights the fundamental idea that to build a feminist theory of disability that takes adequate account of our differences, we will need to know how experiences of disability and the social oppression of people with disabilities interact with sexism, racism, and class oppression.

Another component of the woman with disability's experience is the inability to control one's own body within society's norm. Wendell (1997) addresses this point when she states, "in a culture, which loves the idea that the body can be controlled, those who cannot control their bodies are seen (as many might see themselves) as failures." The need in our culture of control, especially of the body, is manifested in the prevalence of eating disorders among women and obsessive exercise. When women who are able-bodied find it difficult to achieve the ideal body set forth by society, what does this do to women with disabilities? Its sets them further into the realm of undesirables. This generates another tribulation for the woman with a disability.

"If our culture views being female and disabled as 'redundant,' whereas male and disabled is a contradiction, we must ponder the effects of such role definitions and social options on the self-concept of the woman with a disability" (Asch & Fine, 1997). The desire of a woman with a disability to be "normal" and "like other women" [sic] might actually foster women with disability's tolerance of sexism. Women with disabilities can never fight such sexism until they are enabled to discover the commonalties with women who are able-bodied (Asch & Fine, 1997). Lisi (1993) explains this concept, for example, as, "not all of us take being a sex object for granted" (p. 197). For someone who does not expect to be viewed as attractive, a wolf whistle from a passing truck can be a great experience.

Integrating feminist theory and theory to provide effective client-centered therapy for women with disabilities can be a difficult task. Feminist therapy, as a client-centered therapy, must allow the client to comfortably communicate her needs and expectations of the therapeutic experience, so that no assumptions are made that could potentially lead to ineffective therapy and client dissatisfaction. Solomon (1993) discusses the importance of the therapist as not assuming that a woman that has a disability is seeking treatment because of her disability and that a silence about her disability means that it is not an issue for her. A woman with a disability entering therapy might very well be seeking treatment to come to terms with her disability, but it might not be the only concern she would like to address, if at all. Cole (1988) emphasizes this point in her article in a recommendation to therapists to conduct a thorough assessment of the true and underlying issues which women with disabilities might have before launching into a therapeutic pattern which is already familiar to a therapist.

Esten and Willmott (1993) address a few last important points that feminist therapists must keep in mind when dealing with a client with a disability. Avoid trying to assist the client in getting over or curing her disability; rather, assist the client to learn how to live a content and full life with her disability. Although client satisfaction is generally higher when the therapist-client dyad is mirrored, it is not imperative for the therapist to experience a similar disability for therapy to be effective.

African American women are at an increased risk for disability. It is estimated that 13.4 million working age adults have disabilities and, of that number, 2.4 million (18%) are African American (Belgrave & Jarama, 2000). African American women comprise over 54% of African Americans with disabilities (Alston & Mngadi, 1992) and two-thirds of African Americans with physical disabilities (Asbury, Walker, Maholmes, Rackley, & White, 1991). Research regarding African American women with disabilities is scarce (Solomon, 1993), but studies that have focused on African American women suggest that African American women with disabilities experience significant hardship. They are less likely to be employed, have a lower average level of education, and less likely to receive appropriate health care compared to African American men with disabilities and European American men and women with disabilities (Belgrave & Jarama, 2000; Hanna & Rogovsky, 1992). While this information is vital to addressing the inequities in their lives based on oppression, information is needed that addresses how these women adjust to their circumstances. What specific issues arise for African American women with disabilities that therapists need to be aware of in order to help them improve their lives?

This article will focus on working with African American women with acquired disabilities in a therapeutic context. Specifically, a womanist approach to therapy was used to address particular issues that arose in therapy for these women. A womanist is "a [B]lack feminist or feminist of color who appreciates women's culture, strength and emotional flexibility. A womanist is committed to the survival and wholeness of an entire people, male and female" (Walker, 1983). Therapy from a womanist perspective focuses on incorporating the Africentric values related to family, religion, and community life combined with feminist perspectives related to the impact of oppression (i.e., sexism, racism, heterosexism, and classism) on personal adjustment. It incorporates the ideas of feminist therapy including valuing the female perspective and the focus on issues of power between therapist and client.

This perspective will be presented in the first author's therapeutic work with African American women with acquired disabilities. Themes from the therapy with three different women and how a womanist approach was used to facilitate the understanding and working through of these issues will be addressed. It is hoped that these examples will further the knowledge about working with this unique group of women. First, a little background on the three women: The first woman, "Ms. Brown," is approximately 60 years of age and was severely injured in an automobile accident 10 years prior to my seeing her. While she is completely rehabilitated physically (except for some ongoing pulmonary concerns), she continues to experience difficulties with concentration and memory loss. She came to therapy with complaints of anxiety and depression related to working and driving. The second woman, "Ms. Howard," is in her early 50s and was injured in an automobile accident one year prior to my seeing her. She suffered a mild head injury and significant orthopedic trauma. She came to therapy with complaints of depression and feeling disconnected. The third woman, "Mrs. Smith," is in her late 40s and was diagnosed with multiple sclerosis 5 years prior to seeing me. She also came to therapy with complaints of depression. These women presented with different circumstances, but similar themes emerged in therapy. In this paper, two of the major themes will be identified, discussing how these themes relate to the experiences of African American women and to women with disabilities. Then the interventions used to conceptualize these issues from a womanist perspective and how these themes manifested themselves in the therapeutic process will be addressed. Finally, recommendations for working with African American women with disabilities in therapy will be presented.

THEME ONE: FAMILY ROLES

One of the most common and important issues for these women related to their relationships with their families. In each case the women were caretakers of other family members including spouses, older parents, adult children and adult siblings. The women expressed the idea that even though they were experiencing difficulties related to their disabilities, their families had the same expectations of them as prior to the acquiring of the disabilities. "Ms. Howard," for example, was expected to take care of her younger brother following his stroke. The stroke occurred one month following her own release from the rehabilitation hospital. Thus the client's adjustment to her own disabilities was put on hold, while she managed the family crisis and eventually moved her brother into her living space to take care of his needs. According to "Ms. Howard," her family was supportive while she was hospitalized, but once she was released they expected her to resume her role as matriarch and all that entailed. "Mrs. Smith" worked in an extremely stressful occupation (advertising), but was responsible for all of the household responsibilities as well. She reported that even though she was having difficulty with her vision, balance and fatigue, there was still the expectation that she would take care of her household responsibilities (cooking, cleaning, grocery shopping, paying the bills, and laundry).

In this society, the stereotyped expectation of women as caretakers/nurturers is well documented. The nurturer or caretaker role is the primary gender role for women. This is also true in part for African American women, although the worker role is also central for African American women. In contrast, traditionally women with disabilities are seen as less capable of nurturing and in fact are in need of nurturing themselves (Hanna & Rogovsky, 1992).The experience of these African American women with regard to the continued expectations of nurturing and caretaker regardless of the disability relates to the perception of African American women as "superwomen" (Sparks, 1996). According to this stereotype, African American women are strong and able to overcome any adversity. Thus the families expected the African American woman to "overcome" the disabilities and resume their expected roles in their families (Hanna & Rogovsky, 1992).

THEME TWO: PATIENT ROLES

Each woman described the perception that she was invisible to the medical community. "Ms. Howard," for example, discussed the idea that in her outpatient rehabilitation she felt as if the therapists didn't hear her or understand her needs. She reported that they had an agenda for her rehabilitation, told her what was important to work on in therapy and didn't listen when she stated what *she* felt was important in her rehabilitation care. "Ms. Howard" described the situation of "feeling like she was jumping up and down waving her hands in the air for them to see her," but being invisible. "Ms. Brown," who was placed in a day treatment program following inpatient rehabilitation, reported feeling as if she were seen as just another "hysterical woman." She reported that when she would voice her issues surrounding her fears of driving and crossing high volume traffic streets, they were ignored or minimized. On the other hand, the idea that she was horribly impaired and would always be impaired were emphasized.

Women experiencing patronizing treatment within the health system has also been well documented (Matlin, 2000). Women have reported feeling as if their needs are unimportant and as if they are not supposed to ask questions or have input into their treatment. While the perception is that African American women are stereotypically more assertive than European American women (Niemann, Jennings, Rozelle, Baxter & Sullivan, 1994), they are perceived as less visible within the predominantly European American health care system. This is also the case for women with disabilities (Prilleltensky, 1996).

INTERVENTIONS

In addressing the first theme, it was important to discuss with the client, societal and cultural expectations for African American women with regard to the nurturing role. We discussed the superwoman image and how this myth relates to the expectations by their families. We then addressed how their own expectations of their roles influenced the expectations by their families. For example, "Mrs. Smith" acknowledged that she carried out the expectations of her family without question. In fact, when her family attempted to help out with the household tasks, she would criticize their help thus leading to their being less likely to help in the future. We discussed this issue, focusing on what messages she was giving her family about her ability to handle the household tasks. "Mrs. Smith" figured out that she felt needed by taking on the household tasks, and believed that giving up these tasks to her family somehow lessened her usefulness to the family. We discussed the idea that she is only acceptable to herself if she is in the superwoman role. It was also pointed out that maintaining these rigorous personal expectations allowed her to remain in denial about the disability and its eventual effects on her ability to perform these tasks. With "Ms. Howard," we discussed ways of letting the family know how her own needs were being ignored. We outlined ways to elicit more assistance from the family and when that didn't change her family's participation, discussed ways to decrease her burden (such as finding an assisted living placement for her brother), in order to give her the time needed to heal.

In discussing the theme of feeling invisible to the medical community, intervention included discussing the patriarchal nature of health care and how people who have felt confident in their lives, suddenly lose this assertiveness after putting on a hospital gown. For all three clients, it was important to specifically focus on the patriarchal nature of the rehabilitation system. For example, in working with "Ms. Howard," we discussed the idea that both inpatient and outpatient rehabilitation treatment teams are used to patients who are more severely cognitively impaired than she was. So in addition to the general patriarchal attitude of "treatment team knows best," rehabilitation treatment teams typically do not expect their patients with cognitive impairment to express dissatisfaction with their treatment. Consequently, the treatment team was not used to accommodating the expressed needs of a patient with brain injury and might have experienced her expressed wishes as an anomaly rather than due to more intact cognitive functioning.

It was very important to have the clients believe that their experiences of invisibility were not being repeated in therapy. It was important to empower the clients to express their needs in therapy and to identify which issues they wanted to address. Occasionally, even with the best intentions, this didn't work as planned. For example, one of the difficult issues that surfaced with "Ms. Howard" was having that invisibility repeated in the therapeutic context. We had spent several sessions early in treatment discussing her continued feelings of being overburdened and strategizing ways to decrease these feelings of burden. Several sessions later in the therapy, "Ms. Howard" reported that she felt as if I were implying that she wasn't following through on the discussed recommendations. She indicated that she had tried several options to decrease the burden and they hadn't worked. She expressed feeling the same frustration with me that she felt with the other rehabilitation professionals with regard to not feeling heard. We discussed this concern and "Ms. Howard" was encouraged to explore her role in not being heard. It was also important to address the ways that I was recreating the feeling of invisibility in the session.

Other important therapeutic issues that were addressed related to the interplay of African American cultural norms and the issue of egalitarian power in the therapeutic relationship. As mentioned earlier, it was important to emphasize to the clients that they were the experts on their own lives. Yet it was also important for both the clients and the therapist to maintain the respect accorded to clients and to African American professionals. For the therapist, this respect was shown through addressing the clients by their last names at all times unless otherwise directed by the clients. This was due in part to the fact that the clients tended to address the therapist by her title out of respect for her accomplishments. Rather than the egalitarian relationship being emphasized through being on a first name basis, it was shown through mutual respect accorded individuals in the African American community. This was also important as the therapist was younger than all of these clients. My addressing them formally expressed respect for their knowledge about themselves, while their addressing me formally expressed respect for my education and experience.

An additional important therapeutic issue related to ethnic matching between clients and therapist. In all three cases, the clients were seeking African American female therapists. They all expressed the belief that they would feel more understood than they perceived they were when dealing with European American health care professionals. The clients were correct in assuming, in my case, that being of the same ethnic background meant that I was educated with regard to general expectations within the African American community. It was important, however, for me to maintain vigilance against presuming too much about my clients based on ethnicity. For example, it was important not to deny the clients' disabilities by focusing on the superwoman expectations that were a significant part of my upbringing as well. In addition, being influenced by the stereotype that all African American women are naturally assertive, I had to monitor this attitude in assisting the clients in dealing with their families.

CONCLUSIONS AND RECOMMENDATIONS

The purpose of this article is to highlight some of the issues that can arise in therapy for African American women with disabilities. With the increasing incidence of disability among African American women, it is vital to increase research about useful interventions. While studies have shown that African Americans tend to report higher client satisfaction and lower therapy drop-out rates when ethnically matched (Sue & Sue, 1999), it is clear that there are many fewer African American therapists than African American women with disabilities needing services. Thus more often than not, African American women with disabilities in need of support will be receiving therapeutic services from mental health providers from ethnic backgrounds that are different from their own.

To that end the following recommendations are suggested for people interested in therapeutic work with African American women with disabilities. Some of the readers are very familiar with these suggestions, but they bear repeating:

1. Educate yourselves regarding the African American culture, including perceptions of mental health services, perceptions of disabilities, and the roles of women in the African American community.
2. Give clients permission to talk about racism, sexism, ableism, and other types of oppression by educating them about the general role of oppression in the maintenance of these stereotypes and forms of discrimination.
3. Do not assume that each client will have the same issues regarding these areas of oppression or the same acculturation within the African American community. Explore with each client her own perceptions of her culture.
4. When possible involve family members in treatment. Involving "Mrs. Howard's" husband in treatment helped to get at the ways that her presentation about the family's expectations were in some cases encouraged by her own behavior. This was very important information for treatment.
5. Spend time educating the rehabilitation professionals in your area regarding the influence of ethnicity and gender on treatment. Unfortunately, there is very little of this occurring in our academic and clinical settings.

REFERENCES

Alston, R. J., & Mngadi, S. (1992). The interaction between disability status and the African American Experience: Implications for Rehabilitation Counseling. *Journal of Applied Rehabilitation Counseling, 23* (2), 12-15.

Asbury, C. A., Walker, S., Maholmes, V., Rackley, C., & White, S. (1991). *Disability prevalence and demographic association among race/ethnicity minority popula-*

tions in the United States: Implications for the 21st century. Washington DC: Howard University, Research and Training Center for Access to Rehabilitation and Economic Opportunity.

Asch, A., & Fine, M. (1997). Nurturance, sexuality, and women with disabilities. In L. J. Davis (Ed.), *The disability studies reader.* (pp. 241-259). New York: Routledge.

Belgrave, F. Z., & Jarama, S. L. (2000). Culture and the disability and rehabilitation experience: An African American example. In R. G. Frank, & T. R. Elliot (Eds.), *Handbook of Rehabilitation Psychology* (pp. 585-600). Washington, DC: American Psychological Association.

Cole, S. (1988). Women, sexuality, and disabilities. *Women & Therapy, 7,* 277-294.

Enns, C. (1997). *Feminist theories and feminist psychotherapies: Origins, themes, and variations.* Binghamton, NY: The Harrington Park Press.

Esten, G., & Willmott, L. (1993). Double bind messages: The effect of attitude towards disability on therapy. *Women & Therapy, 14,* 29-41.

Hanna, W. J., & Rogovsky, E. (1992). On the situation of African-American women with physical disabilities. *Journal of Applied Rehabilitation Counseling, 23,* 39-45.

Lisi, D. (1993). Found voices: Women, disability and cultural transformation. *Women & Therapy, 14* (3/4), 195-209.

Matlin, M. (2000). *The Psychology of Women* (4th Ed). Orlando, FL: Harcourt Brace.

Niemann, Y. F., Jennings, L., Rozelle, R. M., Baxter, J. C., & Sullivan, E. (1994). Use of free responses and cluster analysis to determine stereotypes of eight groups. *Personality and Social Psychology Bulletin, 20,* 379-390.

Prilleltensky, O. (1996). Women with disabilities and feminist therapy. *Women & Therapy, 18,* 87-91.

Solomon, S. E. (1993). Women and physical distinction: A review of the literature and suggestions for intervention. *Women & Therapy, 14,* 91-103.

Sparks, E. E. (1996). Overcoming stereotypes of mothers in the African American context. In K. F. Wyche & F. J. Crosby (Eds.), *Women's ethnicities: Journeys through psychology* (pp. 67-86). Boulder, CO: Westview Press.

Sue, D. W., & Sue, D. (1999). *Counseling the culturally different.* (3rd Ed). New York: John Wiley & Sons.

Walker, A. (1983). *In search of our mother's gardens: Womanist prose.* New York: Harcourt, Brace, Jovanich.

Wendell, S. (1997). Toward a feminist theory of disability. In L. J. Davis (Ed.), *The disability studies reader.* (pp. 260-278). New York: Routledge.

Assessment, Treatment, and Rehabilitation for Interpersonal Violence Victims: Women Sustaining Head Injuries

Rosalie J. Ackerman
Martha E. Banks

SUMMARY. Psychotherapists who have received minimal training in neuropsychology do not consider cognitive rehabilitation among the treatment options for their clients who have mild traumatic brain injury (mTBI). Historical perspectives on mTBI did not acknowledge brain plasticity and/or rehabilitation, yet rehabilitation might provide a necessary foundation for a client to be able to benefit from traditional feminist psychotherapy. This article provides an overview of two treatment modalities, biofeedback and neuropsychologically-informed feminist psychotherapy, for women with mTBI who sought relief from interstitial cystitis and headaches. Assessment for neuropsychological treatment planning and monitoring is illustrated with employment of the *Ackerman-Banks Neuropsychological Rehabilitation Battery*. Clinical examples are provided to demonstrate a variety of manifestations of mTBI and responses to treatment. *[Article copies available for a fee from The Haworth Document Delivery Service: 1-800-HAWORTH. E-mail address: <getinfo@haworthpressinc.com>*

Rosalie J. Ackerman, PhD, is a clinical neuropsychologist and Martha E. Banks, PhD, is a research neuropsychologist in the Research & Development Division of ABackans Diversified Computer Processing, Inc.

Address correspondence to: Rosalie J. Ackerman, PhD, ABackans DCP, Inc., 566 White Pond Drive, Suite C #178, Akron, OH 44320-1116 (E-mail: Ackerman@abackans.com).

[Haworth co-indexing entry note]: "Assessment, Treatment, and Rehabilitation for Interpersonal Violence Victims: Women Sustaining Head Injuries." Ackerman, Rosalie J., and Martha E. Banks. Co-published simultaneously in *Women & Therapy* (The Haworth Press, Inc.) Vol. 26, No. 3/4, 2003, pp. 343-363; and: *Women with Visible and Invisible Disabilities: Multiple Intersections, Multiple Issues, Multiple Therapies* (ed: Martha E. Banks, and Ellyn Kaschak) The Haworth Press, Inc., 2003, pp. 343-363. Single or multiple copies of this article are available for a fee from The Haworth Document Delivery Service [1-800-HAWORTH, 9:00 a.m. - 5:00 p.m. (EST). E-mail address: getinfo@haworthpressinc.com].

343

KEYWORDS. mTBI, *Ackerman-Banks Neuropsychological Rehabilitation Battery*, rehabilitation, neuropsychology, women, biofeedback, feminist psychotherapy, pelvic disorders, interstitial cystitis, pain, cardiovascular

Mild traumatic brain injury (mTBI) is a life-altering experience and can be a source of chronic, sometimes hidden, disability in the absence of appropriate rehabilitation. Often, diagnosis of mTBI is not made, even though a woman had an obvious head injury (e.g., broken teeth, ruptured eyeball, sudden hearing loss) or had been unconscious after interpersonal violence (IV), a moving vehicle accident, or other physical trauma. There is no positive neuroimaging technique that supports a diagnosis of mTBI. Misdiagnoses and omission of diagnoses are significant for women with mTBI. "Victims of violence experience both psychological and physical trauma. Most treating professionals focus exclusively on either psychological or physical concerns. It is critical to consider both aspects when treating clients" (Banks & Ackerman, 1997, p. 2). Psychotherapists who have received minimal training in neuropsychology do not consider cognitive rehabilitation among the treatment options for their clients who have mTBI. Historical perspectives on mTBI did not acknowledge brain plasticity and/or rehabilitation (Rosenzweig, Leiman, & Breedlove, 2002); yet, rehabilitation might provide a necessary foundation for a client to be able to benefit from traditional feminist psychotherapy. PTSD and Borderline Personality Disorder are diagnoses frequently given to women who have experienced mTBI.

People in the social circles of women with mTBI often complain that those women have "changed" or seem to have different "personalities." Repercussions and maladaptive behavioral reactions within family systems often trigger requests for professionals to help stabilize family functioning. The chronic nature of IV, and in particular intimate partner violence (IPV), leads to multiple physical injuries with an accumulation of residual scar tissue in the brain which results in changed immune systems and other dysfunction of the nervous system. Such injuries have been studied in (mostly young and male) athletes and generated specific strategies for quick assessment of mTBI, treatment, and preventative measures. Similar injuries in victims of IV, however, are not assessed and treated, nor are preventions implemented (Abbott, 1997; Ackerman & Banks, 2001; Ackerman, Banks, & Corbett, 1998; Ayers & Flitcraft, 1996; Manetta, 1999; Monahan & O'Leary, 1999; Tjaden & Thoennes, 1998, 2000). For athletes, second impact prior to healing after initial brain trauma has been demonstrated to result in dementia and, in some cases, death (Collins et al., 1999). IPV victims (mostly female) in the absence of assessment and treatment are at extremely high risk for second impact syndrome (Greenfeld et al., 1998; Wadman & Muelleman, 1999).

Women and girls who have sustained mTBI suffer long-term difficulties with cognition, emotions, and somatic complaints. Often, these symptoms are ignored or not recognized in emergency rooms or other treatment settings. Typical symptoms include frequent headaches, ease of fatigue, blurred vision, hearing problems, distractibility, difficulty focusing (mentally and physically), and dizziness. In a sample of battered[1] women, Monahan and O'Leary (1999) reported cognitive problems such as retaining information, following directions, concentration issues, poor self-initiation, poor abstract reasoning, rapid mental fatigue, memory loss, poor processing of complex information, and poor planning and execution of goals. Emotional complaints included depressed mood, irritability, agitation, low frustration tolerance, and apathy. Somatic complaints included poor sleep, vision, and hearing; seizures; and headaches (see also Raskin, 1997).

This article focuses on assessment and treatment for the neuropsychological consequences of head injury sustained through intimate partner violence. Issues discussed include differential diagnoses, general medical care considerations, including rehabilitation, and clinical practice models for assessment and treatment.

COMPREHENSIVE ASSESSMENT
FOR VICTIMS OF INTERPERSONAL VIOLENCE

The client, family[2], and treatment team members need to have valid, accurate, descriptions of behaviors, strengths or appropriately functioning behaviors, and situational triggers for strengths and poor function, in order to provide culturally relevant rehabilitation for the client (Belgrave & Jarama, 2000; Bell & Mattis, 2000). Screening and assessment for mTBI, alcoholism and other substance abuse, sexual abuse, and family violence have been urgently encouraged (Campbell, Campbell, King, Parker, & Ryan, 1994; Campbell, Raja, & Grining, 1999; Cohall,

Cohall, Bannister, & Northridge, 1999; Coker & Smith, 2001; Covington, Dalton, Diehl, Wright, & Piner, 1997; Dearwater et al., 1998; Koss, Ingram, & Pepper, 1997; Raskin, 1997; Wolkenstein & Sterman, 1998). Many times clients have not been diagnosed with mTBI, yet assessment, at least broad screening, should be conducted (Banks & Ackerman, 1997; Monahan & O'Leary, 1999).

As noted above, many women who are victims of IV are not assessed for mTBI. Without specific treatment for the mTBI, a constellation of symptoms can interfere with psychotherapy. Wolkenstein and Sterman (1998) noted, "What have traditionally been diagnosed as serious and persistent mental disorders in old women may turn out, for many, to be some type of post-abuse syndrome" (p. 347). Psychotherapists are advised to consider a possible diagnosis of mTBI when clients manifest those symptoms. It is important to realize that women who have mTBI do not have similar psychological profiles. Each person has a unique residual brain-behavior pattern due to accumulated physical trauma of brain tissue. Interviews to document timelines of injury, assaults, and psychological threats are essential for appropriate therapy. Additional information should be obtained from significant others, coworkers, and those in the clients' social support networks. The questions and descriptions below are adapted from the symptom domains of the authors' *Post-Assault Traumatic Brain Injury Interview & Checklist,* developed as a screen for all psychotherapists (Banks & Ackerman, 1997), and the *Ackerman-Banks Neuropsychological Rehabilitation Battery,* developed specifically for psychologists (Ackerman & Banks, 1994a, 2001).

Alertness

One of the first questions is "Why isn't the client getting better?" If a client has made progress and then suddenly stops progressing or regresses to an earlier stage of therapy, it is critical to assess changes in physical status as well as to explore resistance. One of the reactions that psychotherapists have when working with a client with undiagnosed mTBI is "Why do I feel so burned out after our psychotherapeutic session?" It is important to monitor if the client initiates discussion or only responds to questions and comments from the therapist.

Emotional Processing

Emotional behaviors are very subdued relative to the level of arousal the client espouses. Typical symptoms include minimal changes in facial expression, flat voice intonation, and few words for the expression of emotion. In addition, the client is unable to accurately interpret the emotions of other people. This is described as dysprosody by neuro-psychologists (Ross, 1988) and as alexithymia by PTSD specialists (Zeitlin, McNally, & Cassiday, 1993).

Memory

"There is so much repetition in the therapy sessions; doesn't the client learn from mistakes?" The client should be assessed for memory problems. If material from psychotherapy sessions is not remembered, the client will not be able to progress.

Sensorimotor Functions

If the client has visible bruises, it is incumbent upon the therapist to ask about the source of those bruises and to determine if the client's response is congruent with the general nature of the bruises. The congruence should involve not only the cause of the bruises, but also the client's description of pain associated with the bruises. For clients with dark skin, the therapist should check for variations in coloring that might appear different from bruises on clients with light skin.

Muscular tremors are occasionally observed by the therapist, but the client does not notice or seem to be bothered by them. If such tremors are accompanied or followed by slight confusion, consideration should be given to assessment for possible seizure activity. Other sensorimotor symptoms include blurred vision, difficulty hearing, and clumsiness.

Speech

Is the client's speech difficult to understand because of slurring, hesitations, or frequent use of wrong words? If the client has previously demonstrated the ability to speak clearly and fluently, the disrupted speech might be a symptom which needs further evaluation, possibly through referral to a speech therapist.

Academic Abilities

Is the client currently unable to handle finances or read and fill out consent and other forms in the therapist's office, despite previously being able to manage such tasks? The client's background should be checked closely for both amount *and quality* of education (Manly & Jacobs, 2001). If the educational background and past function are better than the current level of function, further evaluation of intellectual processing might be needed.

Cognitive Problem Solving

One difficulty for clients with mTBI is the inability to move beyond rote learning and to generalize experiences. The client does not have "ah-ha" experiences in therapy. Cognitive confusion can lead to dangerous physical activities because of poor judgment. It can also result in an inability to resume past levels of community interactions, such as employment.

Does the client have an insecure attachment style that prevents her from individuating from the psychotherapist? If the client relates to the therapist in an immature manner, it is useful to determine if this is a change in behavior or if it is consistent with past *adulthood* behavior.

Organic Emotions

Depression is severe, often with suicidal ideation and, perhaps, a history of serious attempts. For many people with acquired brain injury, there is a tendency to miscalculate their personal limitations. As a result, generally learned helplessness is not a feature; instead, there is a tendency to try to do more than is possible. The depression arises from repeated frustration with being unable to do as much as the person could do prior to the injury.

With increased anxiety, there are often many somatic symptoms and complaints of diffuse pain; it is important to refer the client for medical evaluation. Is the client impulsive, rushing to move ahead prematurely or jumping to illogical conclusions? Impulsivity is noted in many clients with mTBI.

Laterality

Does the client get lost easily and repeatedly? Inability to read maps and confusion of left and right are common with mTBI.

Treatment Problems

Typical treatment problems for clients with mTBI include lack of awareness of mistakes, low frustration tolerance, and loss of inhibition, manifested by socially inappropriate behavior. This can include substance abuse. Clients with these treatment problems are often given Axis II diagnoses.

If the above symptoms are familiar, it would be helpful to consider that the client has hidden disabilities due to mTBI. Referral for a thorough *and culturally relevant* neuropsychological evaluation is essential. Getting the client into appropriate rehabilitation treatment can be critical for survival (Gordon et al., 1998; Wadman & Muelleman, 1999).

TWO APPROACHES TO FEMINIST PSYCHOTHERAPY FOR CLIENTS WITH mTBI

For clients in abusive relationships, the questions "How can I get her to avoid physical violence and move out of the relationship?" and "What obstacles keep her in a battering intimate partner relationship?" are critical. The risk of intimate partner violence escalates at the point of separation; leaving is extremely dangerous for abused women (Heise, Ellsberg, & Gottemoeller, 1999; Kyriacou et al., 1999). Women are most likely to be murdered when attempting to report abuse or to leave abusive relationships (Wuest & Merritt-Gray, 1999). Campbell and Soeken (1999) observed that "women with dangerous batterers may stay with them out of fear" (p. 35). Brice-Baker (1994) described cultural issues that trap immigrant women into staying in violent relationships–fear of deportation, cultural belief systems about why abuse occurs, economic limitations, and language barriers. In addition, Fleury, Sullivan, Bybee, and Davidson (1998) noted that victims prevented from calling police or who had no telephone available, suffered more physical injuries than victims who had access to help. It is important that professionals not fall prey to myths that victims are unlikely to leave abusive relationships, that victims are passive and self-defeating, and that physical violence is more devastating than psychological abuse.

In order to benefit from therapy, the client must be able to implement suggestions for safety. If there are serious problems in any of the aforementioned symptom domains, the psychotherapy might need to involve concrete directives. The challenge, for example, of a client's not being able to learn or initiate new behaviors requires that the therapist rely on a different set of theories to direct treatment. *The impetus for the therapeutic work would be in the hands of the therapist rather than the client.*

Behavioral approaches to psychotherapy are strongly recommended. It is often useful to have the client keep a pocket notebook for recording designated tasks to be accomplished between therapy sessions. Two treatment approaches will be provided with suggestions for work with women with mTBI[3], interstitial cystitis, urinary and bowel dysregulation, and overwhelming generalized pain.

Biofeedback as an Adjunct to Feminist Psychotherapy[4]

Biofeedback involves helping the client control muscles, body temperature, and heart rate. Treatment starts with measurements of blood pressure, heart rate, surface body temperature, and muscle tension of relaxed and unrelaxed muscles. The goal of treatment is for the client to learn how to make deliberate changes in the above functions. Biofeedback for clients who have neurological damage has been used for them to achieve higher quality of living through improved bodily control. With the use of biofeedback equipment, the client receives immediate feedback about gaining control of her[5] body (Ackerman & Banks, 1994b; Basmajian, 1989). In neuropsychological rehabilitation biofeedback, the treatment involves several considerations:

1. The client brings her own baseline of behaviors into therapy. During the course of therapy, the client is encouraged to try different thoughts, movements, and coping strategies to get a sense of her personal and culturally relevant range of behaviors. This flexible therapeutic approach encourages self-experimentation, while providing material for treatment planning and measurable outcome behaviors.

2. The multiple baseline technique (i.e., measuring blood pressure, heart rate, body temperature, and muscle tension in more than one part of the body) permits the client to have more control in the learning process. The client can act as her own "clinical scientist"; automated documentation helps to demonstrate treatment progress.

3. The training process usually begins with deep diaphragmatic breathing. This is a critical skill that is strongly recommended, and the therapist must be able to coach the client to attain this level of muscle relaxation. When the client achieves deep muscle relaxation, blood pressure, heart rate, and muscle tension decrease, and body temperature rises; the biofeedback equipment provides information on the progress from baseline to relaxation. The client must be able to demonstrate that she "feels" relaxed when the biofeedback indicates that her muscles are relaxed. In the state of deep relaxation, clients usually report feeling

"better." For clients with impaired emotional processing, this initial process takes longer than it does for other clients.

4. Motivation to continue therapeutic work between sessions is increased as the client perceives improvement in her ability to control part of her life. Transference and countertransference issues abound with biofeedback monitoring because of physical touching involved in electrode placement and removal from the body of the client by the therapist. For treatment of specific work on strengthening and/or relaxation of pelvic muscles, biofeedback training equipment is placed in the client's rectum by a gastroenterologist or a trained nurse (Schuster procedure; Schuster, 1977). The physician and the nurse do not remain in the psychotherapy office during the actual treatment sessions. The psychotherapist places blood pressure, heart rate, and surface temperature sensors on the client's arm and finger.

5. A part of treatment is identifying the triggers of psychological and physical distress. While the client is discussing trauma in psychotherapy, the biofeedback equipment monitors changes in bodily functions. This assists the therapist and client in determining which areas of the client's life create the most stress and the nature of circumstances in which the client is able to relax. Without biofeedback, the process is hidden and remains unavailable to both the client and the therapist. The addition of biofeedback to traditional feminist psychotherapy helps to shorten the treatment course.

6. The usual duration of therapy ranges from 12 to 25 weeks. Each session begins with deep muscle relaxation. Initially, sessions are scheduled twice weekly. When the client masters deep muscle relaxation within 5 minutes, therapy is reduced to once a week. The client is encouraged to implement relaxation procedures in community settings. Psychotherapy is terminated two weeks after the client and therapist agree that goals have been met. The final two sessions are devoted to termination issues; this is critical because some clients perceive a loss of control without the feedback from the instruments and the loss of the therapist to guide lifestyle changes and new opportunities. Clients are invited to monitor their status three, six, or nine months after therapy termination. Because this process is time-limited and addresses specific symptoms for individual clients, it facilitates compliance with managed care demands.

Neuropsychologically-Informed Feminist Psychotherapy

Rehabilitation neuropsychology has a positive focus on diagnosis and treatment, using the philosophy that patients with neuropsychological impairments (a) can benefit from treatment, (b) have strengths and weaknesses, and (c) have varying levels of impairment in several areas. This is a paradigmatic shift from the psychiatric and medical deficit models that have strongly influenced the development of most psychological and neuropsychological tests. Most patients referred for neuropsychological and/or cognitive rehabilitation have already undergone in-depth neurological and other medical evaluations; such patients need to be referred to specific therapists so that treatment can begin with minimal delay. The neuropsychological rehabilitation psychologist can provide information on patients' strengths and weaknesses in order to facilitate the rehabilitation process.

Ideal neuropsychologically-informed treatment involves a multidisciplinary model of which psychotherapy is only one modality (Malec & Basford, 1996; Malec & Ponsford, 2000). For many women with mTBI, there is either no treatment or treatment for obvious physical problems and/or psychological treatment for PTSD without regard to community reintegration (see Figure 1). In recent years, managed care has been reluctant to fund multidisciplinary treatment for mTBI; this has been successfully challenged in a federal court by DiCowden at the Biscayne Institutes of Health and Living (DiCowden, 2003; Foxhall, 2001).

TREATMENT EXAMPLES

Client examples include two women who were victims of sexual assault by intimate partners and one woman who sustained a head injury as the result of an automobile accident. The treatment of all three clients involved feminist psychotherapy with adjunctive biofeedback; this is an innovative approach to treatment, specifically tailored to the clients' symptoms and therapy goals. The third client was treated with both biofeedback and neuropsychologically-informed feminist psychotherapy as part of multidisciplinary rehabilitation.

Client 1

The first client was a 48-year-old divorced European American woman who had urinary incontinence and a 10-year history of constipation which required 2-3 daily enemas. The incontinence was caused by interstitial cystitis (inflammation of soft tissues in the abdomen; Ritter, 1994).[6] She also experienced anxiety and depression. On a stress checklist (Miller & Smith, 1987), the client indicated multiple stressors related to unemployment and difficult transitions in her family.

At the onset of psychotherapy, the client was unable to relax. She was unwilling to work on development of deep muscle relaxation, seeking instead immediate relief from her physical pain. During the three months of therapy, the client described physical abuse that she had received from her ex-husband and worked on safety issues. At the suggestion of the therapist, she moved into a relative's home during the first week of therapy. She was highly anxious, in part, because she still feared that her ex-husband would injure her when she took her children to him for visitation. At times, he appeared without warning at her job site; his behavior was threatening and her employers responded by laying her off (Browne, Salomon, & Bassuk, 1999).

FIGURE 1. Multidisciplinary Model of Rehabilitation for mTBI

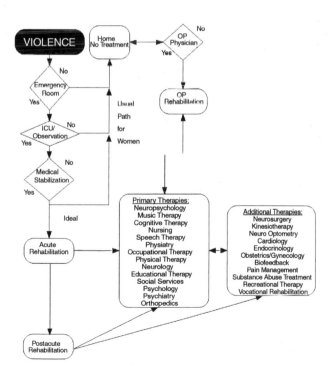

She acknowledged that the physical violence involved his hitting her in the head. Some of the symptoms of mTBI for this client included inability to concentrate or focus on anything but her physical symptoms, flat voice intonation, inability to respond to emotions accurately, difficulty remembering telephone messages, denial of facial pain despite obvious bruising, telegraphic speech, somatic symptoms consistent with organic anxiety and depression, and very low frustration tolerance. Her poor cognitive function was manifested, in part, by her dogmatic refusal to participate in psychological evaluation despite explanations of the potential benefits. As a result, the only formal testing involved her partial completion of a stress checklist.

During therapy, her eyes were observed to have been blackened several times, reflecting multiple injuries (Díaz-Olavarrieta, Campbell, Garcia de la Cadena, Paz, & Villa, 1999). The therapist recommended that the client pursue medical treatment for the obvious head injuries, but the client refused, because she did not want her ex-husband to find out how seriously he had injured her. Similarly, she paid cash for her treatment in order to avoid a record with her insurance company; she believed that her ex-husband had access to her insurance records.

The focus of treatment was on relief of physical pain, urinary incontinence, and constipation. The goals of biofeedback included strengthening of the urinary sphincter and relaxation of the rectal sphincter. At onset of therapy, the client's blood pressure, heart rate, and her body surface temperature were all elevated (Table 1). In the first week, the client regained control of urination and no longer experienced incontinence. By the end of the second week of therapy, the level of constipation had decreased significantly so that only one small enema was used daily. The focus of psychotherapy continued to be on safety issues, including not revealing the location of new employment to the client's ex-husband.

At the end of therapy, the client was still anxious as she was struggling with finances. However, her constipation was considerably relieved. The client described herself as less depressed due to her increased control over her body. She was actively pursuing positive activities with her children. Termination issues included dealing with her insurance company while trying to maintain her privacy. Although the client benefited from treatment, additional psychotherapy was strongly recommended. Similar to other clients with mTBI, who remain unaware of their deficits, she refused follow-up treatment to address loss, anxiety, and depression. She was no longer in acute pain, had urinary control, and had achieved safety from her abusive husband.

Client 2

The second client was a 44-year-old divorced European American woman who had been injured in an automobile accident. Her injuries included closed head injury, a broken pelvis, and torn muscles around her bladder. She had subsequent infections and the patient was diagnosed with interstitial cystitis. Her physical symptoms included painful urination and urinary incontinence. Similar to Client 1, she was treated with biofeedback using the Schuster procedure. The client mastered deep muscle relaxation within two weeks (Table 1) and maintained similar physical function throughout therapy. She was very cooperative with all phases of treatment. The client gained control of her urinary function by the end of twelve weeks of treatment.

Similar to Client 1, Client 2 had some difficulty with concentration, memory problems which impeded time management (she missed several appointments), her speech was simplistic, and her cognitive function was limited to concrete processing. She exhibited muscle tremors

TABLE 1. Physical Status in Biofeedback

	Blood pressure	Heart rate	Body surface temperature
Client 1			
Initial	132/89	89	97.0
End of Second Week	120/68	72	97.0
Final	118/84	78	94.7
Client 2			
Initial	158/98	90	96.0
End of Second Week	112/78	88	99.2
Client 3*			
Initial	138/–	106	90.3
End of First Session	82/–	126	93.9
One Month Before Termination	>160/–	94	97.5
Final	116/–	91	91.6

Blood pressure is presented as systolic/diastolic in millimeters of mercury (mmHg), heart rate is the number of heartbeats per minute (bpm), and body surface temperature is in degrees Fahrenheit (°F). Based on regional (Pennsylvania and Ohio) normative data (Guyll, Matthews, & Bromberger, 2001), for European American women, the baseline blood pressure is 109/70 mmHg and for African American women, the baseline blood pressure is 115/73 mmHg. Baseline heart rate for women in both ethnic groups is 70 bpm. Guyll et al. (2001) also noted that, when stressed by discrimination, average blood pressure for European American women rose to 140/81 mmHg and with an average heart rate of 82 bpm. African Americans, when similarly stressed by discrimination, had blood pressures averaging 141/80 mmHg and heart rates of 80 bpm. Ideal relaxed body surface temperature is 97.5°F (Basmajian, 1989).
* Client 3 had blood pressure monitored by a surface finger sensor. The numbers reported are estimated systolic pressures.

in her hands and arms. Due to her broken pelvis, physical pain, and memory problems, the client was dependent on other people to manage her schedule and provide transportation for therapy. Psychotherapy included work on loss issues. The client had initially lost her ability to walk, although she later regained function of her hips and legs. She was unable to resume secretarial work. The client verbalized concern about her dependence on family members, yet her emotional expression was incongruent with her verbalizations. For example, she laughed inappropriately when describing her pain. Due to her concrete thinking, the client was unable to process deeper psychological concerns.

Termination occurred when the therapist moved out of the area. Telephone contact was made with the client's family to ensure follow-up and referral for continued psychotherapy. Ideally, work with this client would have moved toward neuropsychologically-informed feminist psychotherapy to improve memory and assist her adjustment from total independence to reliance on family members for personal assistance.

Client 3

The third client is a 46-year-old separated African American woman who entered psychotherapy with complaints of headache, insomnia, tremors, constipation, and occasional urinary incontinence. Twelve years before the onset of therapy, she had been a victim of sexual and physical abuse across twenty years. Six years prior to entering therapy, she had motor seizures and was diagnosed with multiple sclerosis. Three years later, she experienced auditory and visual hallucinations; at that time, she was diagnosed with paranoid schizophrenia. Psychotherapy began shortly after the client had a mild stroke. The client underwent behavioral feminist psychotherapy, with a focus on cognitive rehabilitation, following childhood incest and intimate partner violence.

The client was treated with neuropsychologically informed feminist psychotherapy for eighteen months as a part of mTBI rehabilitation. She was evaluated with the *Ackerman-Banks Neuropsychological Rehabilitation Battery* (Ackerman & Banks, 1994a). The client had difficulty paying attention and concentrating on tasks. Her performance during testing was very slow. She was able, however, to formulate correct responses. She had a great deal of trouble reading printed materials, despite the large print size of the stimulus items; this was due to difficulties with visual perception and discrimination. Her short-term memory was slightly impaired. One residual effect of the multiple sclerosis and/or the stroke was poor hand coordination which affected her ability to write and draw. She had trouble finding words to express herself. Despite holding an advanced degree, the client had trouble with simple and complex mathematical problems, reading, and writing. The client exhibited symptoms of organic depression, anxiety, and impulsivity. She had difficulty with directions, confusing her left and right sides. For tasks to which she responded impulsively, she was not aware that she made mistakes. This client had relatively strong function in perceiving and expressing emotions, understanding aural information, motor function, handling of abstractions, integrating information for problem solving, good judgment, and high frustration tolerance. She was referred to physical, occupational, and speech therapies. The client received three months of inpatient therapy, followed by fifteen months of outpatient treatment; speech therapy was discontinued when the client was discharged from the inpatient unit. She was evaluated and followed by a physiatrist and a neurologist.

The goal of neuropsychologically informed feminist psychotherapy was to decrease headaches and to work on unresolved issues arising from her history of abuse. As a result of the client's memory difficulties, psychotherapy involved the therapist's providing explanations to the client and having the client repeat the explanations. If she had not understood, the explanations were simplified and the client was again asked to repeat. This process was repeated until it was clear that the client understood. Verbal information was supplemented with written material. Due to the client's difficulty with reading, a review was necessary to ensure that she understood. Among the written materials were schedules to assist the client in handling treatment appointments. The client valued the therapist-client relationship and benefited from verbal positive reinforcement. Negative reinforcement was used to minimize tangential comments.

At the onset of therapy, the client focused on the sexual and physical abuse she had received. It was the first time that she had revealed her victimization to anyone. Biofeedback involved monitoring of blood pressure, heart rate, and body surface temperature with the goal of decreasing headaches and improving relaxation so that she could improve the quality of her sleep. The client was not willing to receive training for pelvic muscle control. She had a difficult time learning to relax; this was reflected in her very high heart rate and low body temperature (see Table 1). One month before termination, she had relaxed considerably; her heart rate was significantly lower and her body temperature was considerably higher than when she began therapy. She was, however, highly anxious at the time of termination; her blood pressure increased as she discussed the impact of "losing [her] therapist."

After one year of treatment, the client's neuropsychological function improved in several areas. Her attention and concentration improved, although she was slightly more distractible. She showed improvement in visual processing, including reading. Her speech, although still slightly slurred, was easier to understand and she was better able to find words. The client's depression had lifted; she was still anxious and impulsive.

DISCUSSION

The focus of psychotherapy for all three of the clients described was on difficult interpersonal relationships within their families. Two of the women dealt with interpersonal violence and the third struggled with dependence as the result of injury. All three clients had memory problems as a result of acquired mTBI. As a result, cognitive behavioral techniques were used to assist them in benefiting from psychotherapy. The psychotherapist was active in directing the therapy with the goal of empowering the women to gain greater control of their lives.

All three of the clients entered therapy with complaints of chronic pain. Each experienced decrease in pain over the course of therapy through learning application of deep muscle relaxation. In addition, all three clients had interstitial cystitis with symptoms of incontinence. Use of muscle control training provided considerable relief from those symptoms. This involved a multidisciplinary approach to treatment that goes beyond traditional feminist psychotherapy.

Successful neuropsychologically-informed feminist psychotherapy with those clients involved:

1. Selecting culturally relevant, comprehensive assessment instruments to determine client strengths and weaknesses for the development of realistic treatment plans,
2. Identifying an appropriate culturally relevant normative database to develop therapeutic goals,
3. Selecting treatment goals that were mutually agreeable to the client and the therapist,
4. Using therapeutic protocols that had demonstrated success,

5. Monitoring progress in psychotherapy and determining areas of particular difficulty,
6. Referring to professionals in other disciplines when the client was unable to progress appropriately in psychotherapy (see Figure 1), and
7. Making certain that the client and therapist had developed sound safety plans in the event that the client was in the process of leaving an abusive relationship.

CONCLUSION

It is critical for psychotherapists to determine if clients have sustained head injuries. If so, it is incumbent upon the therapists to either assess the clients' neuropsychological status or refer for neuropsychological evaluation. Clients with closed head injuries should be evaluated for mTBI and psychotherapy should be modified to address the clients' needs. If the neuropsychological problems are not adequately addressed, the clients will not be able to progress appropriately in psychotherapy nor will they be able to regain control of their lives.

Mild traumatic brain injury is a frequent result of interpersonal violence and other physical trauma experienced by women. Typical symptoms have been reviewed to assist psychotherapists in making referral decisions for clients with mTBI. Two treatment modalities have been described and illustrated with client descriptions. For women who are victims of intimate partner violence, treatment for mTBI can provide a necessary foundation for them to benefit from education about safety in order to prevent them from further injury, and in the worst situations, to save their lives.

NOTES

1. Battered is the term used by Monahan and O'Leary (1999). The current preferred terminology is victim of intimate partner violence.
2. The term family is used to include significant others who are involved in the well-being of the client. Family in this context can include blood relatives, fictive kin, and friends.
3. The clients described were assessed and treated by the first author. Every effort has been made to protect the confidentiality of the women.
4. Clients who have medical and neurological diagnoses, including mTBI, must have medical examinations before biofeedback and other similar techniques are initiated.

Risks for strokes in the brain and potential for heart or other vascular dysfunction must be identified before engaging in a therapy regimen.

5. Biofeedback is a treatment available for women and men. For this article, the pronouns "she" and "her" will be used, as the client examples provided involve women.

6. Dr. Justine Ritter (1994) and the first author designed a biofeedback model for treating interstitial cystitis in women who had painful bladder, bowel, vaginal, and intercourse symptoms with biofeedback. For example, inflammation of the bladder leading to increased frequency and excruciatingly painful urination is common.

REFERENCES

Abbott, J. (1997). Injuries and illnesses of domestic violence. *Annals of Emergency Medicine, 29*, 781-785.

Ackerman, R. J., & Banks, M. E. (1994a). *Ackerman-Banks Neuropsychological Rehabilitation Battery*© *Professional Manual*, Third Edition. Uniontown, OH: ABackans Diversified Computer Processing, Inc.

Ackerman, R. J., & Banks, M. E. (1994b). New treatment: Biofeedback and Neurological Injuries. Paper presented at Psychosocial and Behavioral Factors in Women's Health: Creating an Agenda for the 21st Century, Washington, DC. Abstract available: http://abackans.com/BF-NPWom.htm.

Ackerman, R. J., & Banks, M. E. (2001). Epilogue: Looking for the threads: Commonalities and differences. In F. R. Ferraro (Ed.) *Minority and Cross-Cultural Aspects of Neuropsychological Assessment*. Heereweg, Lisse, The Netherlands: Swets & Zeitlinger Publishers.

Ackerman, R. J., Banks, M. E., & Corbett, C. A. (1998). When women deal with head injuries. In O. Nnaemeka (Ed.), *Women in Africa and the African Diaspora: Building Bridges of Knowledge and Power. Volume II: Health, Human Rights, and the Environment* (pp. 5-22). Indianapolis: Association of African Women Scholars.

Ayers, R. T., & Flitcraft, A. (1996, November). The many faces of domestic violence. *Violence Against Women Act News* [On-line serial], *5*. Available at: http://www.usdoj.gov/vawo/newsletter/nov.htm.

Banks, M. E., & Ackerman, R. J. (1997). *Post-Assault Traumatic Brain Injury Interview & Checklist Manual*. Uniontown, OH: ABackans Diversified Computer Processing, Inc.

Basmajian, J. V. (Ed.). (1989). *Biofeedback: Principles and Practice for Clinicians*. Williams and Wilkins, Baltimore.

Belgrave, F. Z., & Jarama, S. L. (2000). Culture and the disability and rehabilitation experience: An African American example. In R. G. Frank & T. R. Elliott (Eds.), *Handbook of rehabilitation psychology* (pp. 585-600). Washington, DC: American Psychological Association.

Bell, C. C., & Mattis, J. (2000). The importance of cultural competence in ministering to African American victims of domestic violence. *Violence Against Women, 6*, 515-532.

Brice-Baker, J. R. (1994). Domestic violence in African-American and African-Caribbean families. *Journal of Social Distress and the Homeless, 3,* 23-38.

Browne, A., Salomon, A., & Bassuk, S. S. (1999). The impact of recent partner violence on poor women's capacity to maintain work. *Violence Against Women, 5,* 393-462.

Campbell, D. W., Campbell, J., King, C., Parker, B., & Ryan, J. (1994). The reliability and factor structure of the Index of Spouse Abuse with African-American women. *Violence and Victims, 9,* 259-274.

Campbell, J. C., & Soeken, K. L. (1999). Women's responses to battering over time: An analysis of change. *Journal of Interpersonal Violence, 14,* 21-40.

Campbell, R., Raja, S., & Grining, P. L. (1999). Training mental health professionals on violence against women. *Journal of Interpersonal Violence, 14,* 1003-1013.

Cohall, A., Cohall, R., Bannister, H., & Northridge, M. (1999). Love shouldn't hurt: Strategies for health care providers to address adolescent dating violence. *Journal of the American Medical Women's Association, 54,* 144-148.

Coker, A. L., & Smith, P. H. (2001). New screening tool identifies intimate partner violence. *Journal of the American Medical Women's Association, 56,* 19-23.

Collins, M. W., Grindel, S. H., Lovell, M. R., Dede, D. E., Moser, D. J., Phalin, B. R., Nogle, S., Waist, M., Cordry, D., Daugherty, M. K., Sears, S. F., Nicolette, G., Indelicato, P., & McKeag, D. B. (1999). Relationship between concussion and neuropsychological performance in college football players. *Journal of the American Medical Association, 282,* 964-970.

Covington, D. L., Dalton, V. K., Diehl, S. J., Wright, B. D., & Piner, M. H. (1997). Improving detection of violence among pregnant adolescents. *Journal of Adolescent Health, 21,* 18-24.

Dearwater, S. R., Coben, J. H., Campbell, J. C., Nah, G., Glass, N., McLoughlin, E., & Bekemeir, B. (1998). Prevalence of intimate partner abuse in women treated at community hospital emergency departments. *Journal of the American Medical Association, 280,* 433-438.

Díaz-Olavarrieta, C., Campbell, J., Garcia de la Cadena, C., Paz, F., & Villa, A. R. (1999). Domestic violence against patients with chronic neurologic disorders. *Archives of Neurology, 56,* 681-685.

DiCowden, M. A. (2003). The call of the wild woman: Models of healing. *Women & Therapy, 26* (3/4), 297-310.

Fleury, R. E., Sullivan, C. M., Bybee, D. I., & Davidson II, W. S. (1998). "Why don't they just call the cops?": Reasons for differential police contact among women with abusive partners. *Violence and Victims, 13,* 333-346.

Foxhall, K. (2001, September). Winning one with Medicare. *Monitor on Psychology, 32* (8), 64-65.

Gordon, W. A., Brown, M., Sliwinski, M., Hibbard, M. R., Patti, N., Weiss, M. J., Kalinsky, R., & Sheerer, M. (1998). The enigma of "hidden" traumatic brain injury. *Journal of Head Trauma Rehabilitation, 13,* 39-56.

Greenfeld, L. A., Rand, M. R., Craven, D., Klaus, P. A., Perkins, C. A., Ringel, C., Warchol, G., Maston, C., & Fox, J. A. (1998). *Violence by intimates: Analysis of data on crimes by current or former spouses, boyfriends, and girlfriends.* (Bureau of Justice Statistics Factbook; NCJ-167237). Washington, DC: National Institute of Justice.

Guyll, M., Matthews, K. A., & Bromberger, J. T. (2001). Discrimination and unfair treatment: Relationship to cardiovascular reactivity among African American and European American women. *Health Psychology, 20,* 315-325.

Heise, L., Ellsberg, M., & Gottemoeller, M. (1999, December). Ending violence against women. *Population Reports, Series L,* Number 11. Baltimore: Johns Hopkins University School of Public Health, Population Information Program. Available at: http://www.jhuccp.org/pr/l11edsum.stm.

Koss, M. P., Ingram, M., & Pepper, S. (1997). Psychotherapists' role in the medical response to male-partner violence. *Psychotherapy: Theory, Research and Practice, 34,* 386-396.

Kyriacou, D. N., Angelin, D., Taliaferro, E., Stone, S., Tubb, T., Linden, J. A., Muelleman, R., Barton, E., & Kraus, J. F. (1999). Risk factors for injury to women from domestic violence. *New England Journal of Medicine, 341,* 1892-1898.

Malec, J. F., & Basford, J. S. (1996). Postacute brain injury rehabilitation. *Archives of Physical Medicine & Rehabilitation, 77,* 198-207.

Malec, J. F., & Ponsford, J. L. (2000). Postacute brain injury. In R. G. Frank & T. R. Elliott (Eds.), *Handbook of rehabilitation psychology* (pp. 417-439). Washington, DC: American Psychological Association.

Manetta, A. A. (1999). Interpersonal violence and suicidal behavior in midlife African American women. *Journal of Black Studies, 29,* 510-522.

Manly, J. J., & Jacobs, D. M. (2001). Future directions in neuropsychological assessment with African Americans. In F. R. Ferraro (Ed.) *Minority and Cross-Cultural Aspects of Neuropsychological Assessment.* Heereweg, Lisse, The Netherlands: Swets & Zeitlinger Publishers.

Miller, L. H., & Smith, A. D. (1987). *Vulnerability to stress scale.* Brookline, MA: Biobehavioral Associates.

Monahan, K., & O'Leary, K. D. (1999). Head injury and battered women: An initial inquiry. *Health & Social Work, 24,* 269-278.

Raskin, S. A. (1997). The relationship between sexual abuse and mild traumatic brain injury. *Brain Injury, 11,* 587-603.

Ritter, J. C. (1994). A self-regulatory treatment of interstitial cystitis using biofeedback and therapies. *Dissertation Abstracts International: Section B: The Sciences and Engineering. 54*(9-B). 4932.

Rosenzweig, M. R., Leiman, A. L., & Breedlove, S. M. (2002). *Biological Psychology: An Introduction to Behavioral, Cognitive, and Clinical Neuroscience* (3rd ed.). Sinauer Associates, Inc., Sunderland, MA.

Ross, E. D. (1988). Prosody and brain lateralization: Fact vs. fancy or is all just semantics? *Archives of Neurology, 45,* 338-339.

Schuster, M. M. (1977). Biofeedback treatment of gastrointestinal disorders. *Medical Clinics of North America, 61,* 907-912.

Tjaden, P., & Thoennes, N. (1998). *Prevalence, incidence, and consequences of violence against women: Findings from the National Violence Against Women survey* (NCJ-172837). Washington, DC: U. S. Department of Justice, Bureau of Justice Statistics.

Tjaden, P., & Thoennes, N. (2000). *Extent, nature, and consequences of intimate partner violence: Findings from the National Violence Against Women survey* (NCJ-181867). Washington, DC: U. S. Department of Justice, Bureau of Justice Statistics.

Wadman, M. C., & Muelleman, R. L. (1999). Domestic violence homicides: ED use before victimization. *American Journal of Emergency Medicine, 17*, 689-691.

Wolkenstein, B. H., & Sterman, L. (1998). Unmet needs of older women in a clinic population: The discovery of possible long-term sequelae of domestic violence. *Professional Psychology: Research and Practice, 29*, 341-348.

Wuest, J., & Merritt-Gray, M. (1999). Not going back: Sustaining the separation in the process of leaving abusive relationships. *Violence Against Women, 5*, 110-133.

Zeitlin, S. B., McNally, R. J., & Cassiday, K. L. (1993). Alexithymia in victims of sexual assault: An effect of repeated traumatization? *American Journal of Psychiatry, 150*, 661-663.

Professional Training for Feminist Therapists: Personal Memoirs, edited by Esther D. Rothblum, PhD, and Ellen Cole, PhD (Vol. 11, No. 1, 1991). *"Exciting, interesting, and filled with the angst and the energies that directed these women to develop an entirely different approach to counseling." (Science Books & Films)*

Jewish Women in Therapy: Seen But Not Heard, edited by Rachel Josefowitz Siegel, MSW, and Ellen Cole, PhD (Vol. 10, No. 4, 1991). *"A varied collection of prose and poetry, first-person stories, and accessible theoretical pieces that can help Jews and non-Jews, women and men, therapists and patients, and general readers to grapple with questions of Jewish women's identities and diversity." (Canadian Psychology)*

Women's Mental Health in Africa, edited by Esther D. Rothblum, PhD, and Ellen Cole, PhD (Vol. 10, No. 3, 1990). *"A valuable contribution and will be of particular interest to scholars in women's studies, mental health, and cross-cultural psychology." (Contemporary Psychology)*

Motherhood: A Feminist Perspective, edited by Jane Price Knowles, MD, and Ellen Cole, PhD (Vol. 10, No. 1/2, 1990). *"Provides some enlightening perspectives. . . . It is worth the time of both male and female readers." (Contemporary Psychology)*

Diversity and Complexity in Feminist Therapy, edited by Laura Brown, PhD, ABPP, and Maria P. P. Root, PhD (Vol. 9, No. 1/2, 1990). *"A most convincing discussion and illustration of the importance of adopting a multicultural perspective for theory building in feminist therapy. . . . This book is a must for therapists and should be included on psychology of women syllabi." (Association for Women in Psychology Newsletter)*

Fat Oppression and Psychotherapy, edited by Laura S. Brown, PhD, and Esther D. Rothblum, PhD (Vol. 8, No. 3, 1990). *"Challenges many traditional beliefs about being fat . . . A refreshing new perspective for approaching and thinking about issues related to weight." (Association for Women in Psychology Newsletter)*

Lesbianism: Affirming Nontraditional Roles, edited by Esther D. Rothblum, PhD, and Ellen Cole, PhD (Vol. 8, No. 1/2, 1989). *"Touches on many of the most significant issues brought before therapists today." (Newsletter of the Association of Gay & Lesbian Psychiatrists)*

Women and Sex Therapy: Closing the Circle of Sexual Knowledge, edited by Ellen Cole, PhD, and Esther D. Rothblum, PhD (Vol. 7, No. 2/3, 1989). *"Adds immeasureably to the feminist therapy literature that dispels male paradigms of pathology with regard to women." (Journal of Sex Education & Therapy)*

The Politics of Race and Gender in Therapy, edited by Lenora Fulani, PhD (Vol. 6, No. 4, 1988). *Women of color examine newer therapies that encourage them to develop their historical identity.*

Treating Women's Fear of Failure, edited by Esther D. Rothblum, PhD, and Ellen Cole, PhD (Vol. 6, No. 3, 1988). *"Should be recommended reading for all mental health professionals, social workers, educators, and vocational counselors who work with women." (The Journal of Clinical Psychiatry)*

Women, Power, and Therapy: Issues for Women, edited by Marjorie Braude, MD (Vol. 6, No. 1/2, 1987). *"Raise[s] therapists' consciousness about the importance of considering gender-based power in therapy . . . welcome contribution." (Australian Journal of Psychology)*

Dynamics of Feminist Therapy, edited by Doris Howard (Vol. 5, No. 2/3, 1987). *"A comprehensive treatment of an important and vexing subject." (Australian Journal of Sex, Marriage and Family)*

A Woman's Recovery from the Trauma of War: Twelve Responses from Feminist Therapists and Activists, edited by Esther D. Rothblum, PhD, and Ellen Cole, PhD (Vol. 5, No. 1, 1986). *"A milestone. In it, twelve women pay very close attention to a woman who has been deeply wounded by war." (The World)*

Women and Mental Health: New Directions for Change, edited by Carol T. Mowbray, PhD, Susan Lanir, MA, and Marilyn Hulce, MSW, ACSW (Vol. 3, No. 3/4, 1985). *"The overview of sex differences in disorders is clear and sensitive, as is the review of sexual exploitation of clients by therapists. . . . Mandatory reading for all therapists who work with women." (British Journal of Medical Psychology and The British Psychological Society)*

Women Changing Therapy: New Assessments, Values, and Strategies in Feminist Therapy, edited by Joan Hamerman Robbins and Rachel Josefowitz Siegel, MSW (Vol. 2, No. 2/3, 1983). *"An excellent collection to use in teaching therapists that reflection and resolution in treatment do not simply lead to adaptation, but to an active inner process of judging." (News for Women in Psychiatry)*

Current Feminist Issues in Psychotherapy, edited by The New England Association for Women in Psychology (Vol. 1, No. 3, 1983). *Addresses depression, displaced homemakers, sibling incest, and body image from a feminist perspective.*

Index

Abuse
  child, sexual, as risk factor for
    prostitution, 255-259
  emotional, of disabled women,
    xxx-xxxi
  physical, of disabled women,
    xxx-xxxi
  substance, xxvi. *See* Substance abuse
Academic abilities, of victims of
  interpersonal violence, 347-348
Achterberg, J., 299,300
Ackerman, R.J., xxxii,343
Ackerman-Banks Neuropsychological
  Rehabilitation Battery, 346,
  356
Acquired immunodeficiency syndrome
  (AIDS), xxv
  African-American women with,
    27-44,225-226. *See also*
    African-American women,
    with HIV/AIDS prevalence
    of, 28
ACTS: Adoration (worship and practice),
  Confession (also called
  reconciliation), Thanksgiving
  (such as counting one's
  blessings), and Supplication,
  287
ADA. *See* Americans with Disabilities
  Act (ADA)
ADD. *See* Attention deficit disorder
  (ADD)
Adjustment, to HIV/AIDS, by African-
  American women, 31-37,32t
Advertising, politics of, 102-103
Affirmation of life, of African-American
  women with HIV/AIDS, 35
African-American women
  conceptions of illness and disability
  of, 138-139

disabled, 233-236. *See also*
  Disability(ies), in African-
  American women
  womanist therapy for, 331-341
  family roles in, 336
  goals of, 332
  interventions in, 337-339
  patients' roles in, 337
  recommendations related to,
    339-340
  structure of, 332-333
eating disorders among, 57-79. *See*
  also Eating disorders, among
  urban and rural African-
  American and European-
  American women
with HIV/AIDS, 27-44
  adjustment of, stages of,
    31-37,32t
  age as factor in, 28
  life affirmation of, 35
  literature related to, 28-29
  meaning of life for, 35-36
  mental health effects of, 30-31
  mental health issues related to,
    31-37,32t
  mental health of, impact on
    significant others, 37-40
  multiple illnesses in, 30
  overview of, 29-31
  reckoning with death by, 32-35
  redefining relationships by,
    36-37
  self-affirmation of, 36-37
  service efforts for, 40-41
  severe illness in, 30
HIV/AIDS in, 225-226
middle-aged, with arthritis,
  conceptions of illness and
  disability of, 127-143. *See*

also Arthritis, middle-aged
   Africsan-American women
   with, conceptions of illness
   and disability of
substance abuse in, 223-226. *See
   also* Substance abuse, in
   African-American women
Age, as factor in African American
   women with HIV/AIDS, 28
Age of Reason, 301
AIDS. *See* Acquired immunodeficiency
   syndrome (AIDS)
Alertness, of victims of interpersonal
   violence, 346
Allen, D., 260
American Holistic Medical Association,
   302
American Medical Women's Association,
   304
American Psychological Association
   (APA), 302,304
   CDIP of, xxxiii
American Sign Language, xxviii
American Sign Language (ASL), 313,
   325
Americans with Disabilities Act (ADA),
   xviii,169,170,171-172,173,174
   accommodation for therapists with
      disabilities in clinical training,
      155-168
   classroom accommodations,
      162-163
   clinic accommodations, 163-166
   requests for, 157-158
   at training sites, 161-162
Anderson, G.B., 325
Anorexia. *See also* Eating disorders
Anorexia, symptoms of, 62-63
Anosognosia
   defined, 7
   traumatic brain injury and, 7
Anxiety
   disability and, xxvi
   social, xxvi
Anxiety diorders, xxvi

APA. *See* American Psychological
   Association (APA)
APPIC. *See* Association of Psychology
   & Postdoctoral Internship
   Centers (APPIC)
Aral, S.O., 260
Arthritis, xxiv
   middle-aged African-American women
   with
   conceptions of illness and disability
      of, 127-143
   communal model of health of,
      135-137
   discussion of, 134-139
   peer group experience with,
      130-134
   health promotion efforts for,
      concerns related to, 137-138
Asbury, C., 243
ASL. *See* American Sign Language (ASL)
Association of Psychology &
   Postdoctoral Internship
   Centers (APPIC), 159,160
Asthana, S., 271
Attention deficit disorder (ADD), 173
Attention disorders, xxv-xxvi

Back pain, violence against women and,
   47
Baesler, E.J., xxv,283,287
Bagley, C.A., 57
Balcazar, F.E., 243
Baldwin, M.A., 251
Banks, M.E., xxi,xxxii,343
Baral, L., 251
Barbee, A., 283
Barlow, J.H., 137
Barnard, M., 251
Barron, B., 184
Barry, K., 251,253,272
BDI. *See Beck Depression Inventory*
   (BDI)
Beatty, L.A., xxvi,223
Beck Depression Inventory (BDI), 63

Bedimo, A.L., 33
Behavior(s), emotional, of victims of
    interpersonal violence, 346-347
Belcher, L., 260
Belgrave, F.Z., 243
Belton, R., 253
Bethea, L., 158
Biggar, H., 293
Biofeedback, as adjunct to feminist
    psychotherapy, for victims of
    interpersonal violence,
    350-351
Biscayne Institutes' HealthCare
    Community Model, 306
Biscayne Institutes of Health and
    Living, Inc., 305
Bishop, R., 255
Bonuck, K.A., 38-39
Book of Leviticus, 99
Bourg, E., 161,162
Boyd-Franklin, N., 136
Boyer, D., 251
Brain injury, traumatic. *See* Traumatic
    brain injury (TBI)
Brain Injury Association, 23
Breast exams, of disabled women, 197
Brice-Baker, J.R., 349
BSE class. *See* "Special Touch" Breast
    Self-Exam (BSE) Class
Bulimia nervosa. *See also* Eating
    disorders
  symptoms of, 62-63
Butterfly Garden, 307
Bybee, D.I., 349

Cain, V.A., 29
Campbell, J.C., 349
Cancer, disabilities related to, xxv
Caoile, J.D., 161
Cardiac disease, xxiv
CARF. *See* Commission on Accreditation
    of Rehabilitation Facilities
    (CARF)
Cassell, J., 302

CDCP. *See* Center for Disease Control
    and Prevention (CDCP)
CDIP. *See* Committee on Disabilities
    in Psychology (CDIP)
CDRSQ. *See Chronic Disease Risk &*
    Symptom Questionnaire
    (CDRSQ)
Center for Research on Women with
    Disabilities (CROWD), 243
Center on Emergent Disability, 227
Centers for Disease Control and
    Prevention (CDCP),
    114,129,260,284
CFSEI. *See Culture Free Self-Esteem*
    Inventory (CFSEI)
Chan, F., 243
Chapman, L., 251
Character, C.D., 57
Chartbook on Women and Disability in
    the United States, xxiii
Cheery, C., 260
Chen, J.S., 155
Chesler, P., 251
Chetwynd, J.W., 271-272
Chi, 298
Child sexual abuse, as risk factor for
    prostitution, 255-259
Chin, J.L., xix
Choi, K., 243
Christian, L., 195
Chronic Disease Risk & Symptom
    Questionnaire (CDRSQ),
    116-117,121
Chronic fatigue syndrome, xxiv
Chronic pain, health care costs of, 46
Chronic pain syndromes, violence
    against women and, 45-56
  chronic pain due to, 46-47
  depression, 52-53
  fibromyalgia syndrome, 47-48
  health care costs of, 46
  hypersensitivity and, 47
  pain, 52-53
  research questions related to, 49
  study of
    depression in, 51

discussion of, 51-53
limitations of, 53
method in, 49-50
pain symptoms in, 50,51t
participants in, 49-50
questionnaire in, 50
results of, 50-51,51t
Clinton, H., 304
CMSA. *See* Houston-Galveston-
Brazoria TX Consolidated
Metropolitan Statistical Area
(CMSA)
Coble, A.C., xxx,162
Cognitive problem solving, of victims
of interpersonal violence, 348
Cognitive problems, xxv-xxvi
Cohen, D., 103
Cohen, M.A.A., 38
Cole, S., 334
College of Physicians, 299
Colonialism, in prostitution, invisibility
of, 254-255
Commission on Accreditation of
Rehabilitation Facilities (CARF),
306
Committee on Disability Issues in
Psychology (CDIP), 160
ADA's, xxxiii
Communication
emotional, expression and
understanding of, loss of,
xxv-xxvi
of minority deaf women, 316-318
Communication breakdown, xxv
Community Outreach Programs, 307
Comprehensive Outpatient
Rehabilitation Facility
(CORF), 306
Compulsion(s), in OCD, 171
Consent, in prostitution, 249
Context, in feminist therapy
enhancement, xxxi-xxxii
Coping mechanisms, of urban and
rural African-American and
European-American women

with eating disorders,
68-69,69t
Corbett, C.A., xxxii,311
CORF. *See* Comprehensive Outpatient
Rehabilitation Facility
(CORF)
Cottler, L.B., 228
Cotton, A., 268,272
Council for Prostitution Alternatives,
252,256
Cowley, G., 101
Crawford, D.E., 29,179
Crewe, N.M., 162
CROWD. *See* Center for Research on
Women with Disabilities
(CROWD)
Cultural demands, on minority deaf
women, stress of, 319-322
Culture, in feminist therapy
enhancement, xxxi-xxxii
Culture Free Self-Esteem Inventory
(CFSEI), 63
Cystitis, interstitial, xxv

D'Alonzo, B.J., 243
Dalton, K., 100
Davidson, W.S., II, 349
Deaf women, minority
chronic mental illness in, 325-327
cultural demands on, stress of, 319-322
health concerns of, 322-325
psychotherapy issues related to,
311-329
access to information,
314-316,317-318,319-322,
323-324,325-327
case examples of,
314-316,317-318,319-322,
323-324,325-327
family issues, 316-318
Deafness, xxiv
Death, of African-American women
with HIV/AIDS, reckoning
with, 32-35

Deering, M.J., 31
Demographics, effect on urban and
rural African-American and
European-American women
with eating disorders, 72-73
Denial, psychological, after traumatic
brain injury, 7
DeNoon, D.J., 38
Depression
among urban and rural African-
American and European-
American women with eating
disorders, 69-70,69t,73
disability and, xxvi
Prozac for, 101,102
violence against women and,
51,52-53
Zoloft for, 101
Derlega, V.J., 283
Diabetes, xxiv
*Diagnostic and Statistical Manual of
Mental Disorders (DSM-IV)*,
104
DiCowden, M.A., xxviii,xxxii,297
Dillon, M., 270
Dimensions of Control Scale (DOCS),
118
Disability(ies). *See also specific types,
e.g.,* Diabetes
in African-American women,
233-236
described, 226-228
substance abuse and, 229-231
womanist therapy for, 331-341.
See also African-American
women, disabled, womanist
therapy for
African-American women's voices
in discourse related to, 138-139
clinical trainees with
ADA's accommodations for,
155-168. *See also* Americans
with Disabilities Act (ADA),
accommodation for therapists
with disabilities in clinical
training

dilemma facing, 159-160
cultural stereotypes of, 180
defined, xxii,96,171-172
dormant, xxvi
education for women with, xxviii
employment for women with, xxviii
empowerment over, xxxi-xxxii
identity effects of, xxvii-xxviii
invisibility of, 156-158
invisible, xxiv-xxvi,158
types of, xxiv-xxv
learning, author's experience with,
145-154,146f. *See also*
Learning disabilities
legislation related to, types of,
156-157
OCD as, 171-174
parenting by women with, xxix
part-time, xxvi
personal concerns related to,
xxvii-xxxi
physical. *See* Physical
disability(ies)
psychologists with, 159
safety concerns related to, xxx-xxxi
sexuality issues related to, xxviii-xxix
situational, xxvi
social construction of, xxii-xxiv,
xxvii-xxviii
societal isolation imposed by,
180-181
spectrum of, 156-158
technology effects on, xix-xx
visible, xxiv-xxvi
types of, xxiv
women with
breast exams for, 197
gynecological health care of, 197
involuntary sterilization of, 198
lesbians, 198
masturbation by, 198
obstacles facing, 183-184
perspectives on health care,
sexuality, and reproductive
rights, 195-209

study of
    case examples of, 201-207
    discussion of, 201-207
    instrumentation in, 199-200
    method in, 199-201
    participants in, 199
    procedures in, 200-201
    results of, 201-207
representations of disability on
    interpersonal relationships of,
    179-194
sexual acts of, 198
sexual exploitation of, 182-183
sexual options for, 211-221. *See
    also* Personal Assistance
    Services (PASs), for sexual
    expression by disabled
    women
sexuality of, cultural discourse
    regarding, 182
STDs in, PASs for, 219
study of
    discussion of, 190-192
    method in, 185-186
    participants in, 185
    procedure in, 185
    results of, 186-190
"Disabled hero," 181
Divison 22, Rehabilitation Psychology,
    304
DOCS. *See* Dimensions of Control Scale
    (DOCS)
Dotson, L.A., xxxii,195
DSM-IV. *See* 97
du Plessis, 256
Dunbar, H.T., 30,31,32,33,35,36
Dworkin, A., 256
Dworkin, S.K., 251

Earle, S., 217
Eating Disorder Inventory (EDI), 58
Eating disorders, xxvi
    among urban and rural African-
        American and European-
        American women, 57-79

depression associated with, 73
education level and, 72
geographic influence on, 72-73
self-esteem of, 73
study of
    coping mechanisms in, 68-69,
        69t
    data analysis in, 64
    data collection in, 64
    demographics of, 64-65,65t
    depression in, 69-70,69t
    described, 66-68,67t
    discussion of, 70-77
    instrumentation in, 62-63
    method in, 61-64
    participants in, 61-62
    procedures for, 64
    resources for, 70
    results of, 64-70,65t,67t,69t
    self-esteem in, 69-70,69t
symptoms of
    elimination of, 73-77
    prevention of, 73-77
ethnicity in, role of, 59-61
Eating Disorders Inventory-2 (EDI-2),
    62-63
Eating patterns, healthy vs. unhealthy,
    71
EDI. *See* Eating Disorder Inventory
    (EDI)
EDI-2. *See Eating Disorders
    Inventory-2* (EDI-2)
Education
    for disabled women, xxviii
    of urban and rural
        African-American and
        European-American women
        with eating disorders, 72
EEOC. *See* Equal Employment Opportunity
    Commission (EEOC)
Ehrhardt, A.A., 35
Eisenberg, D., 302
Eliot, G., 303
Elks, M.L., 104
Emotion(s), organic, of victims of
    interpersonal violence, 348

Emotional abuse, of disabled women, xxx-xxxi
Emotional behaviors, of victims of interpersonal violence, 346-347
Emotional communication, expression and understanding of, loss of, xxv-xxvi
Emotional distress, after traumatic brain injury, 16-20
Emotional functioning, after traumatic brain injury, 8,16-20
Employment, for disabled women, xxviii
Empowerment, over disabilities, xxxi-xxxii
Engelson, E.S., 34
Equal Employment Opportunity Commission (EEOC), 164
Erickson, G.N., 155
Esten, G., 334
Ethnicity, in eating disorders, role of, 59-61
Eugenics Movements, 198
European-American women, eating disorders among, 57-79. *See also* Eating disorders, among urban and rural African-American and European-American women

Fallot, R., 253
Family(ies), role in womanist therapy for disabled African-American women, 336
Family issues, of minority deaf women, 316-318
Fang, X.S., 243
Farley, M., 247,251,252,256-257,272
Fatigue, in HIV infection, 30
Fatness, xxvi
Feist-Price, S., xxv,27
Feldman, S.I., 127
Felitti, V., 46
"Female hysteria," xxiv
Feminist psychotherapy

neuropsychologically-informed, for victims of interpersonal violence, 351-352,353f
for victims of interpersonal violence
approaches to, 349-352
biofeedback as adjunct to, 350-351
Feminist therapy
for disabled African-American women, 331-341. *See also* African-American women, disabled, womanist therapy for
for disabled women
culture and context in, xxxi-xxxii
multiple issues in, xxxii
Ferguson, S., 135
Ferraro, W., 269
Fibromyalgia syndrome (FMS), xxiv
violence against women and, 47-48
Finstad, L., 251,263
Fleury, R.E., 349
Flitcraft, A., xxx
Florida's Brain and Spinal Cord Injury Council, 306
FMS. *See* Fibromyalgia syndrome (FMS)
Forster, C., 268
Fraguli, J., 162
Frame, M.W., 165
Frazier, W., xxx
Friesen, N.L., 155
Frustration, disability and, xxvi
Fullilove, M.T., 229
Fullilove, R.E., 229
Funari, V., 263-264

Gainey, M.H., 161
Gallup, G., Jr., 291,292
Gastrointestinal problems, xxiv
Gender, as factor in traumatic brain injury, 5
Ghiselli, N.A., 162
Gifford, S.J., 271-272

Giobbe, E., 251,253
Giordano, G., 243
Goggin, K., 34
Goodman, L., 253
Gorey, E., 31
Gouliquer, L., xxxii, 95
Granskaya, J., 260
Great Witch Hunt, 300-301
Green, L., 243
Gutman, V.A., 162
Gynecological health care, of disabled
        women, 197

Ha, M., 111
Hahn, R.A., 114
Hantula, D.A., 165
Harlan, S.L., 157,158
Hauser, P.C., 162
Havens, J.F., 28,30,31,35,37,38
Head injuries, women sustaining,
        343-363. See also Violence,
        interpersonal victims of
Headache(s), violence against women
        and, 47
Healer(s), wild woman as, 298-301
Healing, models of, 297-310,305f
Health and Sexuality Interview, 199
Health care
    in 21st century, 308-309
    of disabled women, disabled women's
        perspectives on, 195-209
Health concerns, of minority deaf
        women, 322-325
Health Resource Center for Women with
        Disabilities, at Rehabilitation
        Institute of Chicago, 5,23
HealthCare Community model, 304-308,
        305f
Heart disease, xxiv
Heiler, R., 285-286
Heller, W., 3,5,10,13-14,18-19
Hines, P., 135-136
Hinton, K., 172

Hinton, S., 172
Hippocrates, 99
HIV infection. See Human
        immunodeficiency virus (HIV)
        infection
HIV/AIDS Surveillance Report, 284
HIV/STDs. See Human
        immunodeficiency virus
        (HIV)/sexually transmitted
        diseases (STDs)
Hoffschmidt, S.J., 81
Hoigard, C., 251,263
Holsopple, K., 251-252
Holzapfel, K.M., 29
Honolulu Heart Program, 114
Horned One, 300
Houston-Galveston-Brazoria TX
        Consolidated Metropolitan
        Statistical Area (CMSA), 115
Hoyert, D.L., 113
Hughes, D.M., 251
Human immunodeficiency virus (HIV)
        infection, xxv
    African-American women with,
        27-44,225-226. See also
        African-American women,
        with HIV/AIDS
    prevalence of, 28
    diagnosis of, 29
    fatigue in, 30
    mothers with, prayer as interpersonal
        coping in lives of, 282-295
    study of
        discussion of, 291-293
        interviews in, 288-289
        method in, 288-289
        participants in, 288
        results of, 289-291,290t
Human immunodeficiency virus
        (HIV)/sexually transmitted
        diseases (STDs), prostitution
        and, 259-261
Humphrey, C., 170,172-174
Hunter, S.K., 251

Hurt, S., 104
Hypersensitivity, violence against women and, 47
Hypoactive Sexual Desire Disorder, 34
Hysteria, female, xxiv

IBS. *See* Irritable bowel syndrome (IBS)
ILO. *See* International Labor Organization (ILO)
International Labor Organization (ILO), 248
Interpersonal Prayer Model, 287,292
Interpersonal relationships, of disabled women, 179-194
Interstitial cystitis, xxv
Irritable bowel syndrome (IBS), violence against women and, 48
Isolation, social, traumatic brain injury and, 7-8,12-15

Jans, L., 227
Japan Hawaii Cancer study, 114
Jeffreys, S., 251
Job Action Network, 243
Johnson, V., 269
Johnstone, D., 229
Journal of Community Psychology, 285

Kalichman, S.C., 260
Kalyanpur, M., 243
Karim, Q.A., 251,259
Karim, S.S., 251
Kaschak, E., xxxi
Kato-Palmer, S., 114
Kelly, J.A., 260
Kemp, H.V., 155
Kendall-Tackett, K., xxxii, 45
Key, K., 38
Keys, 243

King, T., 135
Kinsey, A.C., 269
Kinzie Depression scale, 118
Kiremire, M., 251
Kiwanis Club, 307
Koss, M.P., 272
Kotler, D.P., 34
Koverola, C., 256
Krippner, S., 298
Krupka, L., 102,103
Kumanyika, S., 60
Kung, H.C., 113

Lam, C., 243
Land, H., 38,39,41
Lang, J., 243
Langer, K.G., 8
LaPlante, M.P., 227
Laterality, of victims of interpersonal violence, 348
Law, rape, 248
Learning disabilities, xxv
author's experience with, 145-154, 146f
Learning disorders, silent, effect on women's lives, 81-94. *See also* Silent learning disorders, effect on women's lives
Legal issues, PASs and, 219-220
Leidholdt, D., 251
Leigh, I.W., 162
Leonard, G., 309
Lesbian(s), disabled, part-time, 95-108
study of, introduction to, 98
Leserman, J., 52
Leung, P., 243
Levy, J., 10
Life affirmation, of African-American women with HIV/AIDS, 35
Linn, J.G., 29
Lipson, L.G., 114
Lisi, D., 333-334
Listening to Prozac, 102
Locust, C., 243

Lombroso, C., 269
Lown, E.A., 229
Lynch, T., 251
Lynne, J., 256-257

MacArthur Foundation Study, 112
MacKinnon, C.A., 251
MacLean's, 102
MacVicar, K., 270
Macy, J., 303
Maholmes, V., 243
Mann, J.M., 260
MANOVA. *See* Multivariate Analysis
       of Variance (MANOVA)
Marshall, B.K., 251
Marshall, R., 45
Martin, C.E., 269
Masters, W., 269
Masturbation, by disabled women, 198
Maxwell-McCaw, D.L., 162
McCarthy, M., 196
McCollough, M.E., 292
McKeganey, N., 251
Medicaid, 306,322
Mellins, C.A., 28,30,31,35,37,38
Memory, of victims of interpersonal
       violence, 347
Mendelson, L.L., 169
Mental health, of African-American
       women with HIV/AIDS, 27-44.
       See also African-American
       women, with HIV/AIDS
Mental health issues, of African-American
       women with HIV/AIDS, 31-37,
       32t
   impact on significant others, 37-40
Mental illness, chronic, in minority deaf
       women, 325-327
Merck Manual of Diagnosis and Therapy,
       100-101
Merck Research Laboratories, 101
Mild traumatic brain injury (mTBI),
       344-345
Miller, J., 251,262

Model of Interpersonal Prayer, 287
Mona, L.R., 211
Monahan, K., 345
Monto, M., 272
Morning sickness, pregnancy-related,
       xxvi
Motion sickness, xxvi
MS. *See* Multiple sclerosis (MS)
mTBI. *See* Mild traumatic brain injury
       (mTBI)
Mueller, C.W., 30,31,32,33,35,36
Mukherjee, D., xxix,xxxii,3,5,10-12,
       14-15,19-20
Multiple sclerosis (MS), xxiv
Multivariate Analysis of Variance
       (MANOVA), 119,120t
Murphy, M., 309

Nabors, N.A., xxxii,331
Nachimson, D., 260
Nadon, S.M., 256
National Household Survey on Drug
       Abuse (NHSDA), 224-225
National Institute on Disability and
       Rehabilitation Research
       (NIDRR), xxiii,227
National Institute on Drug Abuse
       (NIDA), 231-232
National Institutes of Health (NIH)
       Consensus Statement on
       Rehabilitation of Persons
       with Traumatic Brain Injury, 6
National Research Council (NRC), 113
Neal-Barnett, A., 169
Ness, K., 45
Neuropsychology, rehabilitation, for
       victims of interpersonal
       violence, 351-352,353f
Neuropsychology Symptom Checklist,
       93
Newsweek, 102
Nguyen, H.T., 111
NHSDA. *See* National Household Survey
       on Drug Abuse (NHSDA)

Nichols, S.E., 30-31,36
NIDA. *See* National Institute on Drug
　　Abuse (NIDA)
NIDRR. *See* National Institute on
　　Disability and Rehabilitation
　　Research (NIDRR)
NRC. *See* National Research Council
　　(NRC)

Obsession(s), in OCD, 170-171
Obsessive compulsive disorder (OCD)
　　compulsions in, 171
　　described, 170-171
　　as disability, 171-174
　　obsessions in, 170-171
　　in workplace, 169-178
　　　　case examples of, 176-177
　　　　education and awareness
　　　　　　programs on, 175
OCD. *See* Obsessive compulsive disorder
　　(OCD)
O'Leary, K.D., 345
Olkin, R., xxiii-xxiv,136,161,162,237
Oostvogels, R., 271
Oprah Winfrey Show, 173
Organic emotions, of victims of
　　interpersonal violence, 348
Ostrove, J.M., 179
Osvold, L.L., 58
Oxford Dictionary, 96
Oyenque, W., 243

Pain. *See also specific site., e.g.,* Back
　　pain
　　back, violence against women and,
　　　　47
　　chronic, health care costs of, 46
　　disorders related to, xxv
　　pelvic, violence against women
　　　　and, 47
　　violence against women and, 52-53
Parenting
　　by disabled women, xxix
　　traumatic brain injury effects on, 20-22

Parriott, R., 252,267
PASs. *See* Personal Assistance Services
　　(PASs)
Pelvic pain, violence against women and,
　　47
Personal Assistance Services (PASs)
　　activity examples of, 213t
　　defined, 213-214
　　described, 213-214,213t,214t
　　service domains of, 213t
　　for sexual expression by disabled
　　　　women, 211-221
　　　　legal issues related to, 219-220
　　　　provider selection in, 216
　　　　provider's comfort in,
　　　　　　217-218,218t
　　　　safety issues related to, 219
　　　　sexual-related activities requiring,
　　　　　　214t
　　statistics related to, 215-216
Pettee, M.F., xxxii, 331
Physical abuse, of disabled women,
　　xxx-xxxi
Physical disability(ies), women with,
　　　　who want to leave their
　　　　partners, 237-246
　　custody concerns of, 241
　　financial needs of, 240
　　physical needs of, 239-240
　　relationship issues of, 241-242
　　suggestions for therapists regarding,
　　　　242-243
Pimping, 250
Pines, A.M., 251,258
Pinkola Estes, C., 299
Piot, P., 259-260
Playboy, 269
Plumridge, E.W., 271-272
PMDD. *See* Premenstrual dysphoric
　　disorder (PMDD)
PMS. *See* Premenstrual syndrome (PMS)
Poku, K.A., 29
Poloma, M., 291,292
Pomeroy, W.B., 269

Post-Assault Traumatic Brain Injury Interview & Checklist, 346
Positive Reappraisal scale, 76
Posttraumatic stress disorder (PTSD), disability and, xxvi
Poulin, C., xxxii,95
Prayer, as interpersonal coping in lives of mothers with HIV infection, 282-295. *See also* Human immunodeficiency virus (HIV) infection, mothers with, prayer as interpersonal coping in lives of
Pregnancy
    after traumatic brain injury, 20-22
    morning sickness in, xxvi
Premenstrual dysphoric disorder (PMDD), 101,103-104
Premenstrual syndrome (PMS), xxvi, 95-108
    conceptualization of, 98
    creation of, 99-100
    defined, 98,103
    Prozac for, 101-102
    study of, introduction to, 98
    treatment of, 100-102
    Valium for, 102
Premenstrual tension, 100
Prigatano, G.P., 7
Problem solving, cognitive, of victims of interpersonal violence, 348
Prostitution, xxvi
    child abuse and, 255-259
    colonialism in, invisibility of, 254-255
    consent in, 249
    defined, 247,268
    disabled women and, xxxi
    harm of
        introduction to, 247-249
        invisibility of, 247-280
            pervasiveness of, 251-253
        health consequences of, 259-270
        HIV/STD due to, 259-261

psychological symptoms among women in, invisibility of, 262-268
    racism in, invisibility of, 254-255
    synonyms for, 250
Prostitution Research & Education website, 272
Prozac
    for depression, 101,102
    described, 103
    for PMS, 101-102
Psychiatric disabilities, xxvi
Psychological denial, after traumatic brain injury, 7
Psychologist(s), with disabilities, 159
Psychotherapy
    feminist
        neuropsychologically-informed, for victims of interpersonal violence, 351-352,353f
    for victims of interpersonal violence
        approaches to, 349-352
        biofeedback as adjunct to, 350-351
    for minority deaf women, issues related to, 311-329. *See also* Deaf women, minority, psychotherapy issues related to
    for traumatic brain injury, 4,12-22
PTSD. *See* Posttraumatic stress disorder (PTSD)

Rabkin, J.G., 34
Racism, in prostitution, invisibility of, 254-255
Ralston, P.A., 136
Rao, S.S., 243
Rape law, 248
Rapoport, J., 171
Ravels, V.H., 31
Raymond, J., 251
Reed, A., 271-272

Rehabilitation Act of 1973, Section 504 of, 158

Rehabilitation Institute of Chicago, Health Resource Center for Women with Disabilities at, 5,23

Rehabilitation neuropsychology, for victims of interpersonal violence, 351-352,353f

Rehabilitation Psychology News, xxxiii

Reilly, N.A., 165

Reis, J.P., 3,5,8,9,12-13,16-18,20-22, 22-23

Reitman, B., 269

Relationship(s)
of African-American women with HIV/AIDS, redefining of, 36-37
interpersonal, of disabled women, 179-194

Reproduction, disability effects on, xxviii-xxix

Reproductive rights, of disabled women, disabled women's perspectives on, 195-209

Resourceful Woman, 23

Rey Osterrieth Complex Figure, 87,88f

Riger, S., 136-137

Robert, P.M., 157,158

Robinson, L.S., 255

Roessler, R.T., 157

Rosiello, F., 270

Russell, J.M., 34

Sabatino, C., 220

Safety concerns, for disabled women, xxx-xxxi

Safety issues, PASs and, 219

Scarinci, I.C., 49

Schludermann, E.H., 256

Schmidt, M., 272

Schnurr, P., 104

Sebesta, D.S., 227

Self-affirmation, of African-American women with HIV/AIDS, 36-37

Self-esteem, of urban and rural African-American and European-American women with eating disorders, 69-70,69t,73

Sensorimotor functions, of victims of interpersonal violence, 347

Sexality issues, disability and, xxviii-xxix

Sexual abuse, in children, as risk factor for prostitution, 255-259

Sexual acts, of disabled women, 198

Sexual exploitation, of disabled women, 182-183

Sexual expression, of disabled women, 211-221. *See also* Personal Assistance Services (PASs), for sexual expression by disabled women

Sexuality
disability effects on, xxviii-xxix
of disabled women
cultural discourse regarding, 182
disabled women's perspectives on, 195-209

Sexually transmitted diseases (STDs), in disabled women, 219

Sezgin, U., 251

Shaboltas, L., 260

Shelton, L., 57

Siegal, K., 31

Significant others, of African-American women with HIV/AIDS, mental health effects on, 37-40

Silbert, M.H., 251,252,258

Silent learning disorders, effect on women's lives, 81-94
case examples of, 84-89,88f,90f,91
characteristics of, 83
detection of, 91-93,92t
implications of, 83-84
introduction to, 82-84

model for, 89-90,90f
treatment of, 91-93,92t
from vulnerability to deficit in, 89-90,
   90f
Site Visitor Training Manual, 160,161,
   163,164,165
Situational disabilities, xxvi
Smart, D.W., 243
Smart, J.F., 243
Smedley, B.D., 112
Smith, K., 34
Social anxiety, xxvi
Social constructionism, disability-
   related, 180-181
Social Interaction Model, 293
Social Interaction Model of Coping
   with HIV infection, 285
Social isolation, traumatic brain injury
   and, 7-8,12-15
Social Security Disability Income
   (SSDI), xxiii
Social Security Disability Insurance
   (SSDI) program, 156,228
Sodowsky, G.R., 58
Soeken, J.K., 349
Soldan, K., 251
Solomon, S.E., 334
"Special Touch" Breast Self-Exam
   (BSE) Class, 207
Speech, of victims of interpersonal
   violence, 347
SSDI. *See* Social Security Disability
   Income (SSDI); Social
   Security Disability Insurance
   (SSDI) program
SSI. *See* Supplemental Security
   Income (SSI)
Stark, E., xxx
Startle reactions, xxv
State of Iowa, Department of
   Education, Special Education
   Parent Consultant, 185
Statistical Analysis Package, 64
STDs. *See* Sexually transmitted
   diseases (STDs)

Sterilization, involuntary, of disabled
   women, 198
Sterman, L., 346
Stevens-Smith, P., 165
Stinson, J., 195
Stoddard, S., 227
Stout, A., 104
Stress, of cultural demands on minority
   deaf women, 319-322
Suarez-Balcazar, J., 243
Substance abuse, xxvi
   in African-American women, 223-226
   causes of, 228-229
   described, 224-226
   disabilities resulting from, 229-231
   research on, 231-232
   treatment of, 231-232
Sullivan, C.M., 349
Sumner, G., 157
Supplemental Security Income (SSI),
   for minority deaf women,
   317-318
Support, for minority deaf women,
   316-318
Survey of Income and Program
   Participation, 226
Syme, S.L., 112
Szasz, T., 269

TBI. *See* Traumatic brain injury (TBI)
T.C.M. (Traditional Chinese
   Medicine), 306-307
Technology, effect on disabilities,
   xix-xx
Tegart, G., 127
"Ten Sex Myths Exploded," 269
Tension, premenstrual, 100
The Great Plague, 300
The Life We Are Given, 309
The Playboy Press, 269
The Process of Transcendence, 30,32
Thomas, V.G., 60
Thompson, A.R., 158
Thompson, B.W., 61,74

Thyroid dysfunction, xxv
Traditional Chinese Medicine (T.C.M.),
        306-307
Traumatic brain injury (TBI), xxv-xxvi,
        3-26
    anosognosia due to, 7
    brain structures involved in, 5
    case examples of, 9-12
    context of, importance of, 24
    emotional distress after, 16-20
    emotional functioning after, 8,16-20
    gender predilection for, 5
    organic vs. nonorganic sequelae of, 7
    parenting after, 20-22
    pregnancy after, 20-22
    prevalence of, 4
    psychological denial after, 7
    psychotherapy for, 4
    psychotherapy issues related to, 12-22
    recommendations related to, 22-24
    social isolation after, 7-8
    social isolation due to, 12-15
    treatment of, types of, 6
        goals of, 7
Treatment, of victims of interpersonal
        violence, problems associated
        with, 348-349
Turner, J., 158

United Air Lines, 172
United Nations, 112
United States Department of Justice,
        157
United States Supreme Court, 172
University of Arizona, 302-303
University of Chicago, 5,10,17
University of Illinois, Urbana-
        Champaign, 5
Upadhyay, W.S., xxxii,145
U.S. 9th Circuit Court of Appeals, 174
U.S. Public Health Service, 117-118

Valera, R., 251
Valium, for PMS, 102

Van Servellen, G., 29,30
Vanwesenbeeck, I., 251,252,265,267
Vener, M., 102,103
Vietnamese, chronic disease health
        beliefs and lifestyle practices
        among, 111-125
    study of
        discussion of, 121-123
        method in, 115-118
        participant recruitment for, 115-116
        procedure in, 116
        results of, 119-121,120t,119t
        sample characteristics of, 119-121,
            120t,119t
        sampling strategy in, 115-116
        survey instruments and
            questionnaire in, 116-118
Villarosa, L., 74
Violence
    interpersonal victims of, 343-363
        academic abilities of, 347-348
        alertness in, 346
        cognitive problem solving in, 348
        comprehensive assessment for,
            345-349
        emotional processing of, 346-347
        feminist psychotherapy for
            approaches to, 349-352
            biofeedback as adjunct to,
                350-351
            neuropsychologically-informed,
                351-352,353f
        laterality in, 348
        memory of, 347
        organic emotions in, 348
        sensorimotor functions in, 347
        speech of, 347
        treatment for, case examples of,
            352-358,355t
        treatment of, problems
            associated with, 348-349
    in prostitution, invisibility of,
        247-280. *See also*
        Prostitution

against women, chronic pain
    syndromes due to, 45-56. *See
    also* Chronic pain syndromes,
    violence against women and
Vision, limited, xxiv
von Feuchtersleben, E., 99
Vulnerability, of silent learning disorders
    on women's lives, 89-90, 90f

Walker, A.E., 100,303
Walker, S., 243
Wallerstein, N., 137
Waxman, B., 184
Ways of Coping Scale (WCS), 63
WCS. *See Ways of Coping Scale* (WCS)
Webster's Seventh Collegiate Dictionary,
    xxii
Weight, disorders related to, xxv
Weil, A., 302-303
Weinstein, C.S., 81
Weisberg, D.K., 251,263
Welch, P., 298
Wendell, S., 333
Wender Utah Scale, 93
*What Psychotherapists Should Know
    About Disability,* 242-243
White, J.W., 272
WHO. *See* World Health Organization
    (WHO)
Wild woman
    call of, 297-310,305f
    as healer, 298-301
Williams, B., 137
Williams, E.A., 260

Williams, M., xxxii,145,162
Williamson, R., 161
Willmott, L., 334
Winfrey, O., 173
Winstead, B.A., 283
Wolkenstein, B.H., 346
Womanist therapy, for disabled
    African-American women,
    331-341. *See also* African-
    American women, disabled,
    womanist therapy for
Women, "men's" illness overlooked
    in, xxiv-xxvi
Women Who Run with the Wolves, 299
"Women's" illness
    dismissal of, xxiv-xxvi
    misdiagnosis of, xxiv-xxvi
Wong, D., 243
Woolf, V., 303
Workplace, OCD in, 169-178. *See also*
    Obsessive compulsive disorder
    (OCD), in workplace
World Health Organization (WHO),
    260, 268
Wright, L.B., 27
Wright, L.W., xxv
Wynne, M., 243

Yamada, M., 146f
Yee, B.W.K., 111

Zoloft, for depression, 101
Zondi, M., 251